The True History
of the
Black Adder

J. F. ROBERTS

preface
publishing

Published by Preface 2012

10 9 8 7 6 5 4 3 2 1

First published in Great Britain in 2012 by Preface Publishing
20 Vauxhall Bridge Road
London, SW1V 2SA
An imprint of The Random House Group Limited
www.randomhouse.co.uk

www.prefacepublishing.co.uk

Addresses for companies within The Random House Group Limited
can be found at www.randomhouse.co.uk
The Random House Group Limited Reg. No. 954009

A CIP catalogue record for this book is available from the British Library

ISBN 978 1 84809 346 1

The Random House Group Limited supports The Forest Stewardship Council (FSC®),
the leading international forest certification organisation. Our books carrying the FSC
label are printed on FSC® certified paper. FSC is the only forest certification scheme
endorsed by the leading environmental organisations, including Greenpeace. Our paper
procurement policy can be found at www.randomhouse.co.uk/environment

Mixed Sources
Product group from well-managed
forests and other controlled sources
www.fsc.org Cert no. TT-COC-2139
© 1996 Forest Stewardship Council
FSC

Text design and typesetting by Carrdesignstudio.com

Printed and bound in Great Britain by Clays, St Ives PLC

For My Own Dark Dynasty

✣

This True History would remain villainously repressed if it weren't for the kindness and support of many, many people who gave me their time. Most particularly Rowan Atkinson, Brian Blessed, Richard Curtis CBE, Ben Elton, Stephen Fry, Tony Robinson and especially John Lloyd CBE.

BLACKADDER

Veni Vidi Castratavi Illegitimos

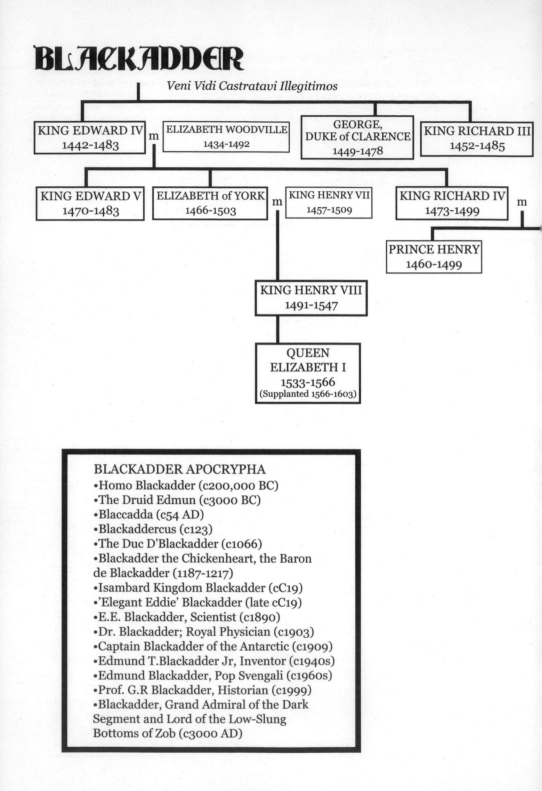

KING EDWARD IV
1442-1483

m

ELIZABETH WOODVILLE
1434-1492

GEORGE,
DUKE of CLARENCE
1449-1478

KING RICHARD III
1452-1485

KING EDWARD V
1470-1483

ELIZABETH of YORK
1466-1503

m

KING HENRY VII
1457-1509

KING RICHARD IV
1473-1499

m

PRINCE HENRY
1460-1499

KING HENRY VIII
1491-1547

QUEEN
ELIZABETH I
1533-1566
(Supplanted 1566-1603)

BLACKADDER APOCRYPHA
- Homo Blackadder (c200,000 BC)
- The Druid Edmun (c3000 BC)
- Blaccadda (c54 AD)
- Blackaddercus (c123)
- The Duc D'Blackadder (c1066)
- Blackadder the Chickenheart, the Baron de Blackadder (1187-1217)
- Isambard Kingdom Blackadder (cC19)
- 'Elegant Eddie' Blackadder (late cC19)
- E.E. Blackadder, Scientist (c1890)
- Dr. Blackadder; Royal Physician (c1903)
- Captain Blackadder of the Antarctic (c1909)
- Edmund T.Blackadder Jr, Inventor (c1940s)
- Edmund Blackadder, Pop Svengali (c1960s)
- Prof. G.R Blackadder, Historian (c1999)
- Blackadder, Grand Admiral of the Dark Segment and Lord of the Low-Slung Bottoms of Zob (c3000 AD)

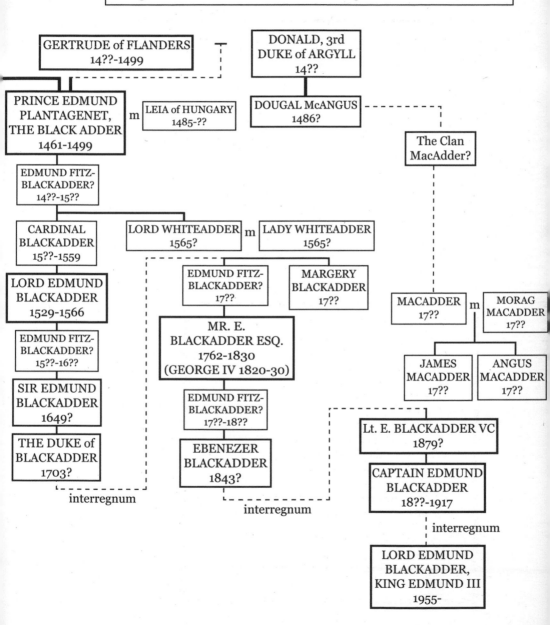

CONTENTS

Parte the First:

OUR BASTARD HISTORY

Enter EDMUND.

Thou, nature, art my goddess; to thy law
My services are bound. Wherefore should I
Stand in the plague of custom, and permit
The curiosity of nations to deprive me
For that I am some twelve or fourteen moonshines
Lag of a brother? Why bastard? Wherefore base?
When my dimensions are as well compact,
My mind as generous, and my shape as true,
As honest madam's issue? . . . I grow; I prosper:
Now, gods, stand up for bastards!

King Lear, Act 1, Scene 2

istory has known many great bastards, but it has been chronicled by almost as many. For the majority of the history of History, the ever-so-humble scribe who picked up the quill and positioned the vellum for any form of 'factual' chronicle generally sat down to begin work with a cry of 'Payback time!' ringing in their ears. Terry Jones – noted medieval historian, author of *Who Murdered Chaucer* and Python – puts it best: 'Propaganda's nothing new, it's always been there, and historians just use whatever they've got at the time.'

The story of our governance is by its very nature one of the gaining and retaining of power, and power is fuelled by propaganda, the facts be damned. Once power was obtained (certainly in antiquity), the ruler's word tended to become law anyway, and it was difficult for any medieval conspiracy theorist to offer so much as a 'Hang on . . .' without it being taken as a request for voluntary physical dissection.

It's only when there's an unexpected transfer of power that the mechanism behind the forging of History becomes apparent. One scribe's gospel truth becomes pernicious tittle-tattle, while the heresy of a traitor can become state-approved fact, if it suits the tenant of the throne and his or her friends. This doesn't just involve textual gainsaying like a sundered celebrity couple in competing tabloids, either. For new histories to be written, old ones were necessarily burned, ripped, expunged from existence, and the keepers of the closest thing to 'the facts' silenced.

This political vandalism would be bad enough, if priceless archives and precious artefacts hadn't also fallen victim to the more freakish forces of nature: fire, flood and Vikings with no appreciation of the value of a good monastic library. The Roman Catholic Church may not have been the most moral of organisations (and the Romans themselves had hardly been that bothered about preserving the culture and history of the ancient Britons they crushed under foot – not to mention that nasty business in the library at Alexandria), but when the executives of Henry VIII's Reformation watched the scriptoriums of Britain's monasteries crumble into ash, did they spare a thought for the knowledge being theoretically scattered to the winds?

One of the few early historians whose particular jumble of events has survived, Geoffrey of Monmouth, wrote in his *Historia Regum Britanniae* of figures like Arthur, Lear, and many other possible flesh-and-blood Britons since consigned to the world of myth, and insisted that his evidence came from an 'ancient book in the British language that told in orderly fashion the deeds of all the Kings of Britain' – a source which has never been identified, presumed destroyed. Some modern historians even happily claim that Geoffrey's story of working from existing sources is a fantasy in itself, but in the realm of hearsay why deny the more interesting version of events? The party line that tends to begin the History of Britain with the Roman Invasion, many millennia after the country was first settled, is the result of centuries of academic party-pooping and cowardly clinging to the state-approved propaganda machine. If a new version of our history could be found, one not told by the Powers That Have Been, but by the little man, the underachiever with perhaps an eye but barely a buttock on the throne, then its retelling of our country's story should be taken in and digested fully, for the healthiest record of our evolution as a nation to be regurgitated.

This is why the Blackadder Chronicles are such a precious primary source for anybody with even the vaguest interest in British History. Although it's now three decades since word first emerged of the Chronicles' discovery, they have remained unexamined in any scholarly depth. Yet they tell us of an entirely forgotten epoch, an undocumented reign in which the Wars of the Roses became but a memory. The propaganda commissioned by Henry VII successfully silenced the sworn statements of the Blackadder family for five hundred years, but now is the time for the Truth to be heard. Or *a* truth, at least – an unlikely truth perhaps, and a *bastard's* truth, but a more entertaining story than the official rubbish invented by King Henry's hired hacks, anyway.

Primary sources backing up the Blackadder family's claims have remained impossible to identify since the Chronicles' discovery – and it is true that only one academic has ever been allowed direct access to the documents themselves, J. H. W. Lloyd (putative Professor of Loafing at the University of Camelot) gaining the exclusive honour thirty years ago, since when the priceless volumes have remained behind locked doors. But in this history, with the help of one of Britain's foremost historical experts, Professor Justin Pollard, we will be revisiting Lloyd's research, and holding his findings up to the light of established history, to see just how much water the Blackadder version of our nation's narrative can hold – or, indeed, how far existing British History has been perverted in order to keep the noble family out of the limelight, and promote the version of events approved by each successive royal winner.

When a new king is crowned, what he says is the True History, becomes the True History. This is the True History of the Blackadder Chronicles.

Chapter One

THE FORETELLING

'I want to be remembered when I'm dead. I want books written about me, I want songs sung about me. And then hundreds of years from now I want episodes from my life to be played out weekly at half past nine by some great heroic actor of the age . . .'

Three Great Universities – Oxford, Cambridge and, not Hull, but Manchester – provided the breeding grounds for the work of comedy excellence we are preparing to celebrate. This is the story of several highly driven men, and supremely talented women. In fact, there are very few people featured within this book who are not very, very talented – if a series of brilliant artists pointing out each other's brilliance is the kind of thing likely to inspire uncontrollable spurts of fluids from your body, read no further. Without that mutual respect, without the arrogance of youth allied to that Oxbridge expectation of greatness, the 1980s would have been a dramatically less amusing period in our nation's history. Oxford and Cambridge of course have a great tradition of collaborating to hilarious effect, but in the eighties, as the stranglehold of Oxbridge began to slacken, it was the cream of the alumni of this *trinity* of institutions who would discover each other and merge to forge the finest comic half-hours of the decade – a television programme which would have its own distinct, lasting and devastating effect on the nation's funny bone for generations to come.

In terms of sheer logical chronology, however, it must be Cambridge that gets the first word in edgeways – sometime in the early seventies in fact, with the relative flop of that year's Footlights outing, *Every Packet Carries a Government Health Warning*.

Row, Row, Row Your Punt . . .

Peter Cook and his chums burst the dam of vociferously amusing jokers waiting to explode out of the university's Footlights club at the end of the fifties, triggering a relay of comic brilliance which flowed from year to year, through Frost, Cleese, Brooke-Taylor, Garden, Idle, Greer et al. But by the year 1973, when a tall, handsome yet frazzled-looking undergraduate with piercing blue eyes called John Lloyd found himself in his last year studying Law at Trinity College, that exciting comedic flow had long since given up any pretence of being even a trickle. Despite this, ten years on from the Footlights' biggest international revue success, *Cambridge Circus*, 1973's wacky funsters were certain that they'd found the right formula to recapture the greatness of Cook, Miller and the Cambridge Pythons. 'The worst thing about *Every Packet*', Lloyd says, 'was the title.'

The cast included his friend, the limelight-stealing budding director Griffith Rhys Jones, but, oddly, also Lloyd himself. Not that John Lloyd performing comedy should be odd, but for him to be a Footlighter was never part of his plan when signing up for further education. Like his even taller friend Douglas Adams (who only scraped into the club with the aid of Simon Jones), John enjoyed getting laughs, but wasn't really accepted by Footlights.

Forty years on, Lloyd laughs, 'Footlights was a joke. None of us worth our salt would have gone near the place. People who ran the stall at the freshers' fair we thought were a bunch of wankers.' Nevertheless, he auditioned simply to please his girlfriend of the time, and was begrudgingly welcomed into the club. 'The first thing I did was the Footlights panto. If you got in the panto, then you'd try and get in the spring revue, and if you got in that then you'd probably get into the May Week revue, which was the big one. It had to have good jokes in it, but it didn't have to have anything particularly radical or satirical to say, so it was a good testing ground for people who just wanted to be funny, which suited me down to the ground, really.'

JOHN HARDRESS WILFRED LLOYD
BORN: 30 September 1951, Dover, Kent

It's fitting, in this history of a great British dynasty, that many of the central team have a singularly detailed knowledge of their own ancestry that comes from generations of meticulous marriage and breeding. Lloyd is descended from an illustrious Anglo-Irish family, and says, 'John and Hardress are family names that have attached themselves to firstborn male Lloyds since at least the beginning of the seventeenth century. My father's genealogical research goes right back to the town of Ardres in northern France and (or so he claimed) a bloke called D'Ardres, who came over with William the Conqueror. Or possibly,' he adds with all humility, 'it's from the ancient Welsh "hardd", which means handsome.' When John was born, the family already had one celebrated member, his namesake great-uncle being a brigadier general rewarded with the DSO and the Légion d'honneur for his bravery in the First World War, as well as an Olympian polo player.

Lloyd was a late starter in formal education, his father's career in the navy making any kind of stability impossible during his early years (on retirement, Lloyd senior was offered the post of Admiral of the Ethiopian Navy). His formative years were a blur of troop ships and exotic locales, particularly Malta, where the young John grew up speaking English and Maltese, before he faced the shock of being sent to prep school at West Hill Park in Hampshire, and then the King's School, Canterbury. While attending the latter, it was school policy for every pupil to undergo an IQ test – John was the only child in his class who was not allowed to know his own results, for fear of complacency.

Lloyd paints his school years as being all but inspired by the Lindsay Anderson film *If*, a grey existence after his globe-trotting infancy, and he grew up seemingly cut off from popular culture – while his contemporaries were glued to TV programmes like *Not Only But Also*, Lloyd remained blisslessly ignorant of the great developments in British comedy, until his arrival at Trinity College, Cambridge, to study Law coincided with the first wave of Python-mania, and Comedy began to suck him in.

✤

'I literally went up to Cambridge not knowing what the Footlights was, I'd never heard of it – I was that ignorant!' John admits today, 'And although I loved jokes, I never thought of joining the club until I was in my last year in '73, because I did college revues. Douglas Adams and I both had a slightly strange relationship with Footlights, because they never put Douglas in a revue, they always thought he was too arcane, even though he was a big star of the St John's revue. But at that time, Footlights was seen as kind of superannuated and hopeless. There hadn't been a really, really funny show since *Cambridge Circus*. And so our revue, in '73, was considered not in any way the most innovative offering, but a return to that old tradition of great jokes, lots of fun and larks and all that kind of thing.' The result of their labours was a very silly brew, consciously harking back to the pun-slinging of the sixties, kicking off with the cast singing a reggae song while dressed as fag packets and ending with a jungle-based panto.

The show did not prove to be the Access All Areas pass to media greatness that critics of Oxbridge would assume. Just as the revue was set for the Edinburgh Festival, there was bad news for John. 'I was sacked from Footlights for fear that I would ruin the serious play they were taking up, but in a way I was allowed to go and do the Footlights radio show as a consolation prize. At first I was completely horrified and heartbroken because it looked like the other lot were all going to go into television, but then I remembered that the comedy I really loved were those Sunday lunchtime radio shows like *The Navy Lark* and *I'm Sorry I'll Read That Again*.' When told that Edinburgh was out of bounds for him because he 'couldn't act', Lloyd burst into tears. Despite this being a deliberate spot of thespianism, it made no difference.

Lloyd's saviour had been a champion of great comedy since joining the BBC ten years previously: 'David Hatch came to see the Footlights show in '73 along with Simon Brett, and recruited me. We got on really well, so when I got offered the radio show, I already knew these guys and liked them.' Hatch had been one of the original *Cambridge Circus* cast, celebrated as 'Boring Old Kipperfeet Announcer Hatch' in Humphrey Barclay's radio spin-off *ISIRTA* until the start of the seventies, as well as being an inspirational producer, launching indestructible radio institutions like *Just a Minute* and *I'm Sorry I Haven't a Clue*. Now Hatch was the boss, and continued to search for talented types at his alma mater just as he himself had been headhunted a decade previously, and he struck gold when he tapped on John's shoulder. The new boy began his first day at BBC Radio on 2 January 1974, sleeping on the floor of a council flat rented by two banker friends.

Did Lloyd feel honoured to be snapped up by Auntie? 'One forgets – well, I don't forget – the appalling arrogance of people who come out of Oxbridge. Most people think at that age, because they've done a revue or whatever, that they're stars, that they're *going to be* stars. Cocky, and not very experienced. All I wanted to do was something that I enjoyed. I got a terrible law degree, I couldn't get on with the law at all. I had a fierce sense of justice, and wanted to be a kind of John

Mortimer defence barrister, an advocate. And they beat that stuff out of you at Cambridge, they laugh at you if you think the law is anything to do with justice. It's just a lot of facts and case law and so on, so I sort of clocked off very early on, and started doing other things – university journalism, politics, all sorts. Then I discovered in my last year that writing jokes was what I liked doing more than anything else. I said I'd give myself a year to see whether I could make a living at comedy, and if I didn't make it in a year I'd go and take my Bar exams and settle down to a tedious life. But it can't have been much more than six months later that I got the job.'

Besides, it could have been worse. While Lloyd was in the early stages of his tutelage under Hatch, that year's Footlights show (still with Rhys Jones, but this time also featuring Clive Anderson and Geoffrey McGivern) was taking a spectacular dive. Lloyd had a writing credit, and was there to witness the nightmare. 'The next year, *Chox*, looked like it was going to be huge, and that had a London premiere, plus they did a pilot for a television show. They had this gala opening, all the Pythons went, and it was a complete disaster. It closed within days, I think. Oddly enough I was stranded on the safe beach of radio, because it was going very well. I was doing a lot of writing with Jon Canter and a guy called Gerry Brown, which led to a commission for a Footlights radio series called *Oh No It Isn't!* We dubbed it that because we were fearful of getting bad reviews – nobody could say anything more negative than that!' Produced by Simon Brett as Lloyd learned the ropes, the radio show could have taken off, but a perfectionist even at this stage, John decided it was time to move on after one short run.

Lloyd was still performing at this time, but despite many offers to be on the microphone (or indeed in front of the camera, if he'd taken the job of being one of Esther Rantzen's smug boys on *That's Life*), he soon found that producing was not just his niche, but a passion. He did once admit: 'I became a producer because Douglas was my best friend, he was obviously a better writer than me, and Griff was the comedy star, obviously forty times as good an actor, so I got the sort of comedy cleaning-lady job, the sort of job that nobody else particularly wanted, but which had to be done.' But on reflection, musing on the chance given to him by the late David Hatch, Lloyd adds, 'He was such a supportive, energetic guy, he gave me my life's motivation in a way, because he showed that it *was* a great thing to be the person behind the scenes. That it wasn't a lesser thing to be the producer, but it was a noble and brave and difficult job, and that somebody has to do it, and you may as well do it well. And that's sort of gone, really, to a large extent. Unless you're a celeb, you don't count these days – they don't give a shit who the producer is.'

Given this chance, the now ex-comedy performer went at it with far more than aplomb. 'I was only twenty-two, so I had lots of energy and got a lot of work done. By the mid-seventies I'd done *Just a Minute* and *Week Ending* and started *Quote Unquote* and *The News Huddlines* and *The News Quiz*. Around that time Douglas was offered a job, and suddenly everyone at the BBC was young! When I first went there everybody was wearing tweed suits and seemed to be about eighty, very sort of serious and lined.' John had already made a name for himself head and shoulders above all the new interns, especially for his innovative eye for editing. 'One thing that annoyed some of the producers in the department,' he remembers, 'I was the third of the producers of *Just a Minute*, and because David was always in a hurry, he used to give the show to an editor called Butcher Bert. Bert Fisher was known as the fastest editor in the BBC, famous for getting so annoyed with one young producer that he literally tied the quarter-inch tape together like a bootlace and put it through, and it was a perfect edit! When David edited he would just take out a round or something like that, so he could process more shows. And I thought I could do it another way, because I'm far more pedantic, and I used to edit it very tightly, take out coughs and "um"s and "er"s, and it used to drive this bloke Bert absolutely nuts. But it made the programme extremely tight. That's a lesson I learned very young and I've always done it since.'

11

'I got a review in *The Times*, I think, which began: "John Lloyd's *Just a Minute* goes from strength to strength!" Giving a radio producer who would have been twenty-three, twenty-four, the credit in a national newspaper? Everyone was saying, "What the fuck's he done to get all this credit? That doesn't seem on." But I ratcheted it up, and it started to get noticed a bit more.'

Besides the trailblazing production work, John continued to write like a machine, working with his struggling flatmate and others. *Week Ending* had amassed an army of writers who would go on to script some of the best comedy of the next few decades, from Cambridge graduates like Andy Hamilton and Guy Jenkin to grammar-school jokesmiths David Renwick and Andrew Marshall – creators, alongside John Mason, of cult radio sketch show *The Burkiss Way*, which was produced for one series by 'John Lloyd of Europe'. Marshall and Renwick had first come across Lloyd and Adams when they were in the audience for the Adams–Smith–Adams undergraduate revue *The Patter of Tiny Minds*, which had briefly played in London, with Lloyd and his girlfriend, Mary Allen, fleshing out the cast.

Of all these early connections, John's close and complicated comradeship with Douglas has been the most widely examined and discussed over the years. Adams entered a postgraduation malaise in the late seventies, which was barely helped by his ambitious fraternising with the *Python* team, stepping in to be one of Chapman's collaborators after Cleese left the TV show, co-creating the aborted Chapman sketch show *Out of the Trees* and an unmade TV special for a real Beatle, *The Ringo Starr Show*. But these exciting inroads to showbiz all seemed to lead to a dead end.

During this early stage of their careers John and Douglas shared a flat owned by another of Chapman's script facilitators, Bernard McKenna, and a hard day's slog at BBC Radio's Light Entertainment HQ at Aeolian House for John would often culminate with attempts to gee up his morose giant of a friend, working together on pitches for

TV shows such as *Sno 7 and the White Dwarfs*. This sci-fi sitcom pilot concerned a couple of astrophysicists in an observatory on the top of Mount Everest who discover that an intergalactic advertising agency aim to write a slogan across the galaxy in supernovae – 'Things Go Better With Bulp!' – with Earth selected as the full stop. The space slogan was an idea which would eventually be used by Rob Grant and Doug Naylor in their *Red Dwarf* novels, but back in the late seventies the BBC considered science fiction to be 'too fifties', and the idea was canned. As Lloyd told Neil Gaiman in 2002, 'The idea was minimum casting, minimum number of sets, and we'd just try to sell the series on cheapness. That failed to come to anything.' The same fate awaited a movie treatment the duo wrote for Robert Stigwood, in which a hostile alien race challenges our planet in a series of feats taken from *The Guinness Book of Records* – but at least they got a holiday in Corfu out of sketching that one out (which was only slightly marred by the dashing Lloyd ending up with his friend's hoped-for love interest).

You couldn't blame Lloyd for needing a holiday – even a working one. Few people in BBC history had established themselves quite so rapidly and impressively – and it all came down to his ferocious work ethic at this time. Perhaps the most telling capsule of this stage of Lloyd's career was mockingly quoted in Nick Webb's official Adams biography, *Wish You Were Here* – while his contemporaries blundered into post-grad life, Lloyd's usual patter was along the lines of 'I'm so, so jealous that you have time to offer me a beer. If only I could. Such an enviable quality of life – a moment to oneself to think. Oh God. I have at least a hundred programmes to produce, and three attractive women to juggle.'

Yet despite having graduated from campus to corporation, this comedic whirling dervish still set aside time to be up in Edinburgh every August. Lloyd's name was usually somewhere in smallish print on Footlights Fringe shows for a good while after he'd graduated, including being director of 1975's *Paradise Mislaid* (starring Rhys Jones of course, whose sister was now Lloyd's girlfriend). In the following year he and Adams formed a team with the creators of *The Burkiss Way*, to put on a show called *The Unpleasantness at Brodie's Close*. Crammed into a tiny room in a Masonic hall, the team (minus Marshall, who was teaching) fitted a bizarre array of sketches around the framework of a *Brief Encounter*-esque meeting in a train station between two lovers who keep getting interrupted. The cast were responsible for everything, even making the props, and had a reasonable smash with it, packing audiences in beyond fire safety regulations. They even left Edinburgh with £10 profit each.

However, the following year, while at the Fringe as part of his duties producing Radio 2 arts programme *Late Night Extra*, John was witness to the red-hot response given to a show put on by a small team from Oxford just round the corner from Brodie's Close, and had to concede that there were performers out there who came from a completely different universe. Having exhausted himself laughing at this student revue, he was determined to meet its star, convinced he could well have found the equal of Chaplin.

RICHARD WHALLEY ANTHONY CURTIS
BORN: 8 November 1956, Wellington, New Zealand

Richard Curtis's father was a self-made man, an Italian resident in Czechoslovakia who anglicised his name from 'Anton Cecutte' to the respectable-sounding 'Tony Curtis' – a year or so before the Hollywood star became a household name. As an executive at Unilever, Tony and his wife Glyness travelled the world, and Richard, the first of two sons, happened to be born during a sojourn in New Zealand.

The Curtis family's next home was Manila, where young

Richard developed an American accent, and first became aware that his relatively cosseted existence was not shared by everyone. 'Every day as my driver took me back to my house with a swimming pool I could see huge slums with people living under corrugated-iron roofs.' More importantly, he was shown how to try and do something about such inequality. 'My mum cancelled Christmas in 1968. No presents. No special food. We gave all the money to the Biafra appeal. I was thrilled because it meant I could watch *Top of the Pops*, which was normally spoiled by Christmas lunch lasting forever.'

After Manila came Stockholm, and then only at the age of eleven did Curtis permanently take up residence in the UK, moving with the family to Folkestone, then Warrington, before being sent to Papplewick School in Ascot. Shortly after, he won a scholarship to the exalted establishment of Harrow, where the bright pupil was made head boy: 'I think I was put there as a sort of antidote to every other head of school, because I was known to be very left wing, if there is such a thing at Harrow.' Certainly, during Curtis's tenure the ancient practice of fagging was finally abolished – and swiftly reinstated after he left for Oxford.

Although theatre became his passion, young Richard's main preoccupation during his schooldays was, he admits, a desire to be a Beatle. 'From the age of about six, music was my life. . . In about 1963, bad babysitters started bringing pop records into the house – the Supremes, the Beatles and, since we were living in Sweden, the Hepstars and, my particular favourite, Ola & the Janglers – and my life changed forever.' When his own rock group, Versus, flunked the only gig they ever had by chickening out of introducing rock to the staid Harrow Concert, Curtis decided his future pointed towards the stage. He was only half right . . .

⚜

15

Puck Will Make Amends. . .

In the autumn of 1975 Richard Curtis, a softly-spoken bespectacled English scholar with a riot of fair curly hair like two rhododendron bushes very close together, arrived in Oxford, burning to act. 'I started off working hard in the first term,' he says, 'but then realised that didn't seem to be strictly necessary. I had a very good time, just enjoying myself with friends. I made most of my best friends for life.'

His experiences onstage at Harrow may not have been the most convincing presages of thespian greatness, but he did have the balls to go beyond the traditional school Shakespeare production (in which he tended to play women, in badly fitting wigs) to stage *The Erpingham Camp* – surely the first time that any Joe Orton play was performed at Harrow, let alone the playwright's most pointed work, attacking organised religion and authority in general. When he enrolled to study English at Christ Church college, Curtis was convinced that the extracurricular theatrical opportunities offered by the celebrated Oxford University Dramatic Society would finally allow him to make his mark. 'All the greats lay before me,' he recalled. 'I was ready for Pinter, I was ready for Beckett, my Macbeth was bursting to come out in all its bloody horror . . .'

His first experience with OUDS was not encouraging – while the actor Hugh Quarshie earned plaudits playing the title role in *Othello*, Curtis was initially cast as 'Clown'. A stroke of luck came when that part was cut and he was given a few lines as 'Third Gentleman' in the storm scene, but sadly the storm was so loud it drowned out all the dialogue. 'The director said our inaudibility was a brilliant metaphor for something,' Curtis said. 'I have forgotten what.' Undeterred, the young thesp spent his first few terms diligently turning up to every audition he saw advertised. 'In *Twelfth Night*, I was cast as Fabian, a character who makes Clown look important. I got a good part in *French Without Tears* but the production was cancelled. Everything else, I came away empty-handed, while handsome boys with chiselled jaws and hints of dark sexuality got every part.'

This called for drastic measures, and a switch from Drama to Comedy. 'Finally, I had to take a pre-emptive strike. I decided, if no one else would give me decent parts, I would write them for myself. I wrote and staged a little revue and did get three or four laughs.' At last, Curtis had found his calling. There was a fine tradition of comedy at the university stretching back at least as far as the setting up of the Oxford Theatre Group in the early fifties, with alumni including Alan Bennett, Dudley Moore, Michael Palin and Terry Jones – and Richard Curtis felt he could become the comic performer to top them all.* But Perkins had left Oxford before Curtis's arrival, and now was a time for a new generation. When Richard spied an advert for auditions for that year's revue in the student newspaper, it must have seemed like fate – the cocky Harrovian knew that it was 'my moment to shine, my moment to step forward, the best, the funniest, the actor's actor'.

He threw himself into the early script meetings with unmistakable vim, standing out among the several faceless fellow students who gathered in a tutor's study every Thursday evening to haggle over sketch material. He was discovering his voice as a humorist, with a knack for precise wordplay and an eye for characterisation that exemplified the frustrated actor, and he showed that he could easily run the whole show on his own. For two meetings he enthused about his ideas and became confident that the 1976 Oxford Revue would be his first big break.

At the third meeting, just as a running order was beginning to take shape, one curiously coy student arose to finally share his own ideas with the gang. Curtis had sized this fellow up in the first meeting, where he was to be found skulking silently in the corner, and had long ago dismissed him as part of the furniture – a cushion or, at best, some form of stuffed toy. He had a curious appearance certainly, bespectacled and

---

* The Oxford Revue had been in good hands with Geoffrey Perkins in the early seventies and, if nothing else, his surname provided them with a multitude of sketch characters – 'Come in, Perkins!' becoming a meme shared by a whole generation of sketch writers.

17

with black curls in such abundance that the two of them could have been negative reflections of each other. But nobody had paid him very much attention at all – until now.

The human cushion quietly explained that he had a couple of sketch ideas of his own, and proceeded to drop every jaw in the room with a transformation into a living cartoon, or some kind of creature from another dimension, in two astonishing comic turns. 'He did a monologue about driving followed by the thing where he mimed and talked at the same time,' Curtis recalls. 'It was unlike anything else I had ever seen.' There was no doubt who the star of the 1976 revue would be.

ROWAN SEBASTIAN ATKINSON
BORN: 6 January 1955, Consett, County Durham

As the youngest of three sons – Rupert, Rodney (subsequently a UKIP candidate) and Rowan – born to farmers Eric and Ella, Atkinson grew up in the shade of Consett Steelworks, among the rusting tractors of the family farm, midway between Durham and Newcastle upon Tyne (the home, Hole Row Farm, is now the Royal Derwent Hotel). Despite this agricultural upbringing, Rowan was aware that show business was in his family, thanks to his grandfather Edward Atkinson, proprietor of a whole chain of picture houses across the North-East – one of which had been run by Stan Laurel's father, Arthur Jefferson – and as a boy Rowan would visit the Consett Empire for free movie shows, in lieu of TV.

Like his brothers, Atkinson was sent to board at the Durham Cathedral Choristers' School (where he was a year behind Tony Blair), and then to St Bees School on the Cumbrian coast, within dashing distance of the Windscale nuclear power plant, latterly Sellafield. It was at St Bees that Atkinson had his first real comic awakening, getting laughs from his friends, who dubbed him 'Dopey', 'Zoonie', 'Green Man' and 'Moon Man', as his distinctively animated features began to develop.

Atkinson was an upstanding student, joining the cadets and the school choir, and yet he still had plenty to rebel against at St Bees, where misdemeanours were punished with compulsory horse-dung-shovelling, for which, he recalled, 'Only the privileged few were given shovels.' Young Rowan soon developed a talent for facetiousness, once being punished for responding to one master's assertion that he should pull his socks up by laboriously and pointedly following the order literally, and also reportedly teaching another master's small child to parrot the phrase 'fuck off' at will. 'I never meant any harm or offence to anyone,' he was to insist, 'I was just trying to enjoy myself. Because, make no mistake, life is short.'

Although Rowan showed a flair for science, having an obsession with engines (at home, he drove around the farm in his mother's old Morris Minor, which he had saved from the scrapheap and rebuilt from scratch), the schoolboy's most notable achievements were in the arts. As one of two pupils given the job of running the St Bees Film Society 'with no democracy whatsoever', Atkinson was thrilled to receive a print of Jacques Tati's wordless classic M. Hulot's Holiday, and besides the official showing on Saturday night, he and his friends gleefully sat through the entire film seven times in one weekend.

He had been in plays before St Bees, including an early triumph as the Dauphin in Saint Joan, but Atkinson's initial involvement with the school's theatrical side was predictably technical. However, as part of the lighting team for one school production, he remembers 'looking down from the lighting gantry on to the stage during the performance and thinking, "I've made the wrong decision – I'd prefer to be down there."'

19

His subsequent performances, including a notable Mephistophilis in *Doctor Faustus*, earned him the stunned applause of his peers, astonished that the odd-looking stammering lad had such a range of extraordinary characters brewing within him.

Atkinson's headmaster Geoffrey Lees took a particular interest in his charge's future, spurring Rowan on to pass his English O level by betting against him. Two years later, with Atkinson receiving top-grade science A levels and considering a Technical Drama course in Portsmouth or a BSc in Electrical and Electronic Engineering at Newcastle University, Lees broke the habit of a lifetime when he took the budding engineer aside and confided, 'I have never recommended to anyone that they should take up a career in the entertainment industry, but it would seem silly for you, Atkinson, not at least to try.' 'I didn't know quite what I wanted to do when I left,' he admits, 'but I certainly didn't have very high expectations of the future . . .'

✤

'It was instantly clear that he was a real genius,' Curtis recalls with mock chagrin. 'He got every single laugh in the summer show. I did have one quite funny monologue, but just before opening we decided to give it to Rowan because he would be funnier . . . And it was downhill from there.' The story of Atkinson's apparent transformation from meek cuddly toy to comic master has always been somewhat disingenuous, though – by the time he knocked Curtis's socks off, he was already more than familiar with the Edinburgh Fringe scene, and had even attempted a small revue there in 1975, before enrolling at Oxford for his MSc in Engineering Science.

Prophetically, his first Edinburgh experience had been as part of a group of ex-pupils and budding actors a year after leaving St Bees, playing the role of Captain Starkey in Joseph Heller's anti-war play *They Bombed at Newhaven*, directed by English master Richard Elgood. Heller had based the action on the Vietnam War, but its message about the madness of conflict was equally applicable to any hostility in history, and would set the young actor in good stead for future comedic clashes with the military. Rowan's main experience of army life had been a period of guard duty with the cadets – forced to remain vigilant out on the Cumbrian moors from 8 p.m. to 2 a.m., in a foot of water, with nothing to comfort him but a soaking wet cigarette. Whether this informed his performance is debatable, but his portrayal of Captain Starkey – a quiet man who during the course of the play goes through a complete breakdown – singled Atkinson out for praise from the *Scotsman* when he was barely past adolescence.

It would be two years before he returned to the Fringe, during which time he was at Newcastle University. He was always drawn to the 'sparks' side of show business, harbouring thoughts of maybe making it as a BBC cameraman, or a sound engineer, but still the lure of being in the spotlight kept getting in the way. By his own admission, 'There was something inside me crying to get out.'

Atkinson's second Fringe experience was, via tenuous connections, with the Dundee University Theatre Group, who cast him in the central role of the sexually frustrated city official Angelo in *Measure for Measure* – a play with the dubious reputation of being by far the least amusing of all Shakespeare's 'comedies'. This one foray into interpreting Shakespeare was not a pleasant experience for young Rowan, who says, 'It takes a hell of a lot of time and a lot of effort to get even the most willing audience to smile at someone like Touchstone (and I speak from bitter experience).' So while in Edinburgh doing his best by the Bard, he took his chance to try something different with one of his friends, hiring the Roxburgh Reading Rooms for a lunchtime comedy revue. 'No more than thirteen people came – probably because the show was absolutely diabolical. It was me doing impersonations of Denis Healey and things like that, so you can imagine how grim it was.'

Having got a 2:1 from Newcastle, you would be forgiven for thinking that it was the tug of stardom which took Atkinson to

Oxford for his Master's, but on arrival at the historic university, his first time living in the south, away from home, it took a long time for this garlanded student performer to return to the stage, and he spent much of his first term 'just relishing the whole slightly olde worlde privileged nature of the place, and going to endless organ recitals, I was a great lover of the organ' – indeed, he was even compiling a book on the history of Oxford's organs, and trying to design a synthesiser of his own.

So the explosion of comic invention Richard Curtis witnessed that Thursday evening had been bottled up for quite a long time. 'I saw this little advert in the university newspaper saying, you know, "We're thinking of getting a comedy revue together,"' Atkinson recalls, 'so I thought I'd beetle along, because I felt as though I had an interest. And Richard was there . . . So that was our first meeting – I said very little, and I'm sure Richard said a great deal.'

It's in My Blood and in My Soul

There was, of course, a whole pantheon of future stars and media darlings at Oxford alongside Curtis and Atkinson in the mid-seventies. Older boy Mel Smith had just progressed from the Oxford Revue and OUDS to a budding career in theatre, and the new blood included Tim McInnerny and Helen Atkinson-Wood, with most of the rest of the *Radio Active* team, Angus Deayton, Michael Fenton Stevens and Philip Pope, arriving a year or two afterwards. McInnerny was one of the brightest stars of OUDS, but couldn't shake off a natural comic flair, and became one of Curtis's favoured performers – at least, for any sketch that wouldn't have suited Atkinson.

Atkinson-Wood similarly filled her time with comedy performing when she wasn't studying Fine Art at the Ruskin School, and came from the same part of the world as McInnerny, being from a well-to-do family in Cheadle Hulme, head girl of her school and crazy about ponies, despite a near-fatal riding accident at the age of sixteen.*

Helen recalls: 'I arrived a year after them. I was doing a show called *The Female Person's Show* in my very first term – written by Marcy Kahan – which Richard saw, and asked if I would like to come and audition for the revue. It's fair to say that even at that point, Rowan was becoming a legendary comedy figure, because there was nobody else like him . . . Tim and I also did serious drama – we were in a production of *Measure for Measure* at the Oxford Playhouse – so, very illustrious productions, alongside horsing around with our pals.'

TIMOTHY MCINNERNY
BORN: 18 September 1956, Cheadle Hulme, Cheshire

Born to William and Mary McInnerny in a corner of what is now part of Greater Manchester, Tim McInnerny's background may be a degree less highfalutin than his Harrovian and Etonian colleagues, but a desire to perform was clearly in the blood – Lizzie, his younger sister, is also a successful star of stage and screen. While others in this history went through the public-school system, Tim graduated from grammar school, the Marling School in Stroud, before earning his place at Wadham College, Oxford. He paused for a year's backpacking around the world (and being held up at gunpoint by a gang of drunken Italian policemen, for a laugh) before launching himself into the Oxonian theatre scene in 1975.

⚜

Rowan couldn't hog all the limelight at the Oxford Revue shows, and Curtis had plenty of sketches which wouldn't have suited him anyway –

---

* She was also a close friend of Ian Curtis, who was morbidly drawn to the girl who had cheated death – though by the time Helen arrived at Oxford he was back in Manchester, performing with his new band Joy Division.

many of them, perhaps unsurprisingly, involving love and relationships, including the clever 'Prompt', originally penned for Tim and Helen.

TIM:	We thought we'd just slip back on and have a private word . . . First perhaps we should get introduced. Her name's Helen.
HELEN:	And his name's Tim.
TIM:	And together we make Tim and Helen. (*Smiles.*) We thought we might, I don't know why, just, you know, talk about how we first met, how we fell in love . . . Right, well, Helen, you start away.
HELEN:	OK. Um . . . Prompt.
PROMPT:	(*Off*) I don't know what to say really.
HELEN:	I don't know what to say really, I'm not very good at . . . Prompt.
PROMPT:	Improvisation.
HELEN:	Improvisation. Prompt.
TIM:	Come on, Helen. Think!
HELEN:	What do you mean, 'Come on'? . . . You just don't seem to care at all any longer, Tim.
TIM:	Oh I do care, Helen, for heaven's sake, I . . . Prompt?

All the young sketch performers knew that Atkinson was a different breed of performer, and even if they never shared a stage, friendships soon budded. Atkinson-Wood recalls, 'When I first met him he was nervous, and he was odd. I mean, there was a lot of sort of nervousness about being around women generally, which of course was fantastically endearing.' To add to this great herd of thespians, Bridget Jones creator Helen Fielding dated Curtis during her time at Oxford, and elsewhere in their year you could find two future TV executives, Kevin Lygo and

Jon Plowman, and comedy writer Tony Sarchet. But Atkinson, once his comedic cat was out of the bag, immediately stood apart from all of his contemporaries.

He prepared himself to unleash his stage persona for the first time by returning to his halls, his bedroom littered with coils of insulated wire and electrical tinkerings for the synthesiser that would never be completed, and gazed at himself in the mirror. 'I don't think it was a time when people who pulled faces were admired,' he once admitted to the *Telegraph*, but amid the undergraduate linguists, all trying to outdo each other with their witticisms, he knew there was something in his features which gave him an edge. 'I remember when I discovered how extreme my facial expressions could be for comic effect, and practising them, and thinking, "Gosh, that looks pretty funny to me, I think I'll try that tomorrow night in front of a paying audience, and see how they react."' He was sure the malleable chops and elastic facial muscles that had entertained his school chums at St Bees could be just as funny to his sophisticated college colleagues, and he set to, creating an act that used his abilities to the full, without requiring a single word to be written down.

When he emerged onstage at the first show, hair sculpted into *Eraserhead* topiary, clad in crumpled pyjamas (later, a shockingly clinging leotard), the spectators weren't sure whether to laugh or call the authorities – but they settled for the former. This fledgling act consisted of Rowan appearing from the shadows with a mysterious crumpled envelope, proffering it to the audience, and then jealously snatching it back with a wash of emotions – suspicion, pride, anger, confusion – playing over his striking features, 'like Peter Lorre in a panic'. Despite the simplicity of the act, he could make it last for twice the length of most sketches, keeping the laughter rolling, abating and returning for far longer than would seem plausible. Although a lifelong cynic when it came to mime (an art form he described as 'so worthy of draughty community halls'), Rowan was clearly a natural – or, rather, he

25

was a pedantic technician, with every single tic and nuance perfected and primed well in advance.

By the time that year's revue was ready for the Playhouse, the bevy of ambitious comics who had first met to discuss the show had been whittled right down – there were few who could keep up with Atkinson, but Curtis had immediately recognised his new friend's comic powers, and the two began working closely together almost immediately, experimenting with Rowan's comic machinery in much the same way that he himself tinkered with anything that required a plug. 'I was doing a tremendous amount of visual stuff at the time, and it was that side of me that I think Richard particularly latched on to,' he recalls; although Curtis puts it more humbly: 'Rowan was clearly so much better than all the rest of us put together that I hung on to his coat-tails for a decade.'

Overly humble or not, the critics of the *Oxford Mail* would have agreed. After the first night of the Easter revue, Atkinson was paid a gushing tribute which made it clear that his former headmaster had been right about his performing potential, and there was to be no more talk of life as an engineer – or indeed as a student. Atkinson himself estimated that in his first term, his time at Oxford had been 90 per cent study to 10 per cent performing (and that included his stint as drummer in a hard-rock band). But after this first revue, the ratio was switched.

Remembering his earliest acclaim in 1988, he outlined the original formation of a plan that was to have immediate success: 'I'd got a very good notice in the *Oxford Mail*, that redoubtable publication of the Midlands. It really was an extremely good crit. It was very much one of these, you know, "the next John Cleese" sort of things. I remember asking this other man, who was doing Zoology or something, what you did if you wanted to be in show business and he said, "Try and find out who the agents of the people you admire are and write to them." So I did, and I wrote to nine agents that summer before I went to Edinburgh, saying, "Now look, I'm going to do the Edinburgh Fringe," and I enclosed a photocopy of the review. Nobody replied, except Richard Armitage. He flew up especially to see me and we worked together from the day that he came.'

The son of the composer Noel Gay, Armitage was a theatrical legend who had played with the Grades when they were children, taken over Noel Gay artist management in 1950, and had showbiz running through every major artery. He was also John Cleese's agent, which made Atkinson all the more overjoyed to be scooped up. Armitage claimed that he was first drawn to Atkinson by his letter, which humbly began 'Dear Sir or Madam', but one sight of the 1976 revue was enough for Armitage to add the 21-year-old to his personal stable. This was also good news for Mrs Atkinson, who was terrified for her youngest son, making his way in the seamy world of showbiz. 'She thought it was full of bouncing cheques and homosexuals and nasty men in velvet bow ties, so I got a really well-dressed middle-class agent who looked like a bank manager and that reassured her a lot. She found that not everyone wears bow ties, so her view was modified to an extent.'

The 1976 Edinburgh show, staged at St Mary's Street Hall (just round the corner from where Lloyd was performing in *The Unpleasantness at Brodie's Close*) was a semi-refined hotchpotch of the best of the Oxford Revue, but the production basically amounted to Curtis and Atkinson travelling up in Rowan's VW camper van – this 'Oxford Theatre Group' only had one star, already tooled up to take the comedy scene by storm.

However, there was the matter of actual study. Returning for their second year at Oxford, Rowan and Richard moved into a house together on Woodstock Road, and began to revel in being the driving force of the university's comedy scene. Rowan naturally found himself on the revue stall at that year's freshers' fair – just in time to meet a musical master, and make a friend for life.

Howard Goodall was born in Bromley, but the family moved to Rutland, and then Oxford, when he was still small – and music was the younger son's obsession from the very start. He became a chorister aged eight while attending New College prep school, then began to master the organ at Stowe school in Buckinghamshire, before forming a band (featuring his older brother Ashley) at Lord William's school in Thame. When he landed a place studying Music at Christ Church college in 1976, it would have been little surprise to anyone to learn that he was headed for a first.

'In my first week at university I went to the freshers' fair and I had decided that I wanted to be involved, as a musician, with the revue. So I went to the desk, and I said to the guy, "Look, I'd really like to be involved musically, I don't know how." We talked for a little bit, and he said, "Well, someone will come and see you." It turned out the guy behind the desk was Rowan Atkinson, and then when I went back to my room that afternoon, Richard Curtis came to see me, and he said, "Me and Rowan are doing a show, like a student revue, in three weeks' time at the Oxford Playhouse. Would you like to do the music?" So I said, "Yeah!"' Goodall expected nothing more at first than a bit of scene-shifting, but he was instantly put to work at the keyboard crafting material with Oxford's brightest duo. Seeing his new chum in the spotlight, he was as stunned as anyone. 'When they saw him for the first time, people were just really helpless. For whole periods of the show, they would be just out of control laughing so much, because it was so different.'

With Atkinson, Curtis and Goodall working on the faces, words and music, the Oxford Playhouse shows went from strength to strength – one early audience member who was impressed enough to pop round backstage for a private chat about TV opportunities was the celebrated LWT producer Humphrey Barclay, beating the BBC's Bill Cotton by a whole year. Barclay recalled his first impressions of the new talent whom everyone was whispering about: 'While clearly still an undergraduate performer, he displayed the rare talent of physical comedy: not knockabout, but visually creative, in the style of Jacques Tati or Robert Hirsch of the Comédie Française, instantly conjuring hilarious characters by contortions of his flexibly angular body and his odd deadpan face. I didn't laugh at everything, but hugely at most of the show, and when the odd sketch didn't appeal to me, I took in the fact that the house around me was falling about. Here was a talent to amuse, big time.' By coincidence the show's rave reviews had already caught the attention of those higher up the LWT echelons, and John Birt and Michael Grade detailed Barclay to bring Atkinson into the fold.

Amid all this success, however, Atkinson's 1977 Fringe experience began as an absolute disaster. The friend from the Dundee University Theatre Group whom Atkinson had been working with on and off for years convinced him to do away with anything else which had been going on in the revue. 'We kind of took it over. I think we were completely cruel and selfish in setting up virtually a one-man show, but I can't remember. You forget these things,' Atkinson didn't quite recall in 1988. 'The first night was awful. It was his fault really and I think he would accept the blame. It was full of long parodies of Brecht and the like, which if you're going to get away with it anywhere then Edinburgh will let you get away with it, but it wasn't really the stuff of popular entertainment. I'm someone who's always preferred to entertain *for* people rather than *to* people. I thought it wasn't working, so I cancelled it for three nights and we rustled up a new revue.' Eager punters were ushered across the road to the pub for a few days as Atkinson marshalled his trusted friends around him to come up with a plan B. The resultant one-man revue – featuring more than one man, plus Helen, who was at the Fringe performing in Goodall's musical, *The Loved One* – was to become the basis of Atkinson's breakthrough show the following year.

If it seems odd that Atkinson was in cahoots with anyone other than Curtis at this time, then the latter has the definitive excuse for his absence. 'I fell in love, and that dominated my second year; and then I got heartbroken and that dominated the next year, entirely. I did a lot of work in the end, simply so I could hide from my heartbreak.' Though remaining Rowan's right-hand man for several more years as Atkinson took centre stage, Curtis was also busy organising the traditional Oxford

Revues, giving first chances to Deayton and the future *KYTV* team.

Besides this lovelorn industriousness, one other notable positive came out of young Curtis's romantic desolation in 1977 – a lifelong comedic war against Bernards in all forms. As if being dumped in your teens isn't bad enough, it is on record that Curtis's girlfriend Anne left him for – and married – Bernard Jenkin, a future Tory MP and vice chairman of the Conservative Party. From that day forward, Curtis resolved to mock Bernards however he could in every fiction he created.* Curtis's youthful heartbreak would ultimately be the making of him. 'Maybe if I hadn't gone out with that particular girl then I would have been happier but, on the other hand, I don't think I would have written all the films that I then wrote to, as it were, "put life right" . . . I had at least fifteen years of making love affairs turn out right, to try and make up for what happened outside Magdalen College.'

While Atkinson was stitching together his replacement show at St Mary's Street Hall, Griff Rhys Jones was directing that year's Footlights offering, *Tag*, and was to record a fateful first clash between the two Oxbridge factions who would go on to all but run British comedy for the following decades. If a gas explosion had levelled St Mary's in the summer of '77, cutting off all those students in their prime – Atkinson, Curtis, Rhys Jones, Deayton, Peter Fincham, Rory McGrath, Jimmy Mulville, to name just several – then British comedy today would be unrecognisable.†

On the first day at St Mary's Street Hall, both the Oxford Theatre Group and Footlights, each with their own spots in the venue's schedule, dropped off their gear and decamped to different pubs. When

---

* The campaign has to date included the sex-mad gawd-help-us played by David Haig in *Four Weddings and a Funeral*, Alan Cumming's naive loser in *Bernard & the Genie*, another no-hoper played by Hugh Bonneville in *Notting Hill*, and of course, a bear-baiter and a celebrated Tudor nurse.

† One of the few major comedy bosses to have escaped would have been Peter Bennett-Jones, who was present with the Footlights the year before just in time to wonder at Atkinson's first show, but by 1977 had moved into theatre production.

Curtis, Deayton and co. finally returned to find that their tinfoil set had been unwittingly cut into ribbons by Rhys Jones's mob for their carnival float, righteous indignation rapidly melted into retreat as they saw that their far more drunken counterparts – Griff, Rory and Jimmy (a fiery scouse Classics student, already married at twenty-two and largely at Cambridge because his dad had put a bet on him) – were not to be messed with. Mulville went on the offensive, grabbing the enemy by the lapels and spitting, 'See that wall over there? If you come any closer I'll paint it red with your blood!' 'Although the two sets which had first met or mingled at this grubby church hall were to go on holiday together, intermarry, send their children to the same schools and meet frequently over the next thirty years,' Griff recalls, 'I never felt that the first sharp thwack of that initial meeting was ever forgotten.'

AINSLEY AND PLECTRUM AND ZOB

Ultimately, the squabbles between the Oxbridge kids were made irrelevant by the re-emergence of Rowan Atkinson into the spotlight, in the hastily cobbled-together *Beyond a Joke*. 'A rather pretentious and inaccurate title.' This was the tour de force that saw Rowan being compared favourably with the earlier wobbly-limbed graduate clown, Jonathan Miller; the performance which didn't just catch John Lloyd's talent-scout eye, but yanked it out of its socket and sent him pelting off to have a word with the star. John sat and watched Rowan play invisible drums and piano, portray beings from other universes, and create the first in an incredibly long line of fruity clergymen, from the pen of Richard Curtis.

VICAR: You know, a lot of prospective brides ask me these days, 'Father, what is the Church's attitude towards fellatio?' And I tend to reply by telling

31

them a little story . . . A couple of years ago, a
young attractive bride-to-be came up to me after
the service and asked me just that question.
'Father, what is the Church's attitude towards
fellatio?' And I replied, 'Well, you know, Joanne,
I'd *like* to tell you, but unfortunately, I don't
know what fellatio is!' And so, she showed me.
And ever since, whenever anyone has asked
me the question 'Father, what is the Church's
attitude towards fellatio?' I always reply, 'Well,
you know, I'd *like* to tell you . . .'

'Undoubtedly,' Rowan says, 'the Edinburgh Fringe was a sort of
melting pot, in terms of people seeing me and what I was doing, or what
Richard Curtis and I, more accurately, were doing.' John Lloyd recalls
his first experience of the show itself: 'It was unlike any revue that
I had ever seen. Partly because of Richard's genius, the lateral jumps
it made in terms of subject matter – it didn't obey any of the rules of
student sketch writing, it wasn't like what we were all doing at the time
. . . Very beguiling and odd, and then suddenly this fantastically rude
vicar talking about blow jobs, you know?' But the young producer's first
impressions of his future collaborator offstage weren't promising. 'He
was a very closed down, eccentric person, really, quite lonely-looking
and shy. He was very offhand with us – quite frightening, actually.
He had no idea who I was, and in those days I looked like a fifteen-
year-old who'd been up all night. He obviously thought, "Who's this
git?" But Rowan is a perfectionist, and he didn't think he did well
in that performance, so we hovered for a while, but as he was very
unforthcoming, we went to the pub.'

Back down at Oxford, *Beyond a Joke* was to reach greater heights of
success, with Atkinson-Wood alternating with Julia Hills as Rowan's
one co-star; and soon there were plans to move the show to London

– in fact, to move to London full stop, with finals out of the way, as Atkinson got his Master's degree and decamped to west London (Curtis would get a first the following year, alongside Goodall). Conveniently, another Oxford graduate, Michael Rudman, had already approached Rowan with the idea of mounting a new iteration of his latest revue at the tiny Hampstead Theatre in Swiss Cottage.

This evolution of *Beyond a Joke* was supplemented by brand-new material, with one notable highlight being the 'Schoolmaster' sketch written by Richard Sparks – a graduate a few years ahead of Curtis and Atkinson, whose then comedy partner Peter Wilson joined Rowan in the cast, alongside actress Elspeth Walker. The new line-up required a few fresh items, such as a trio of Barclays Bank staff who stage a Christmas musical – but everybody knew that it would be the star's solo spots, like the 'Schoolmaster' sketch, that people would remember. Sparks's opening roll-call of ridiculously named pupils was the perfect vehicle for Atkinson's other wild card as a performer – his unique delivery, born of the stammer which had afflicted him since he was small. 'I do have a problem with the letter B, quite often when B is followed by a vowel . . . I remember at school my schoolmates getting a lot of amusement out of getting me to say the word "Bubble" and me stammering a bit.'

Having had his natural Tyneside vowels 'thrashed out' of him at school, Rowan had developed a pretty good ability as a mimic (as well as a mime), but he could never be a true chameleon – his diction was as unique as his facial apparatus. 'I do have a natural stammer,' he says, 'which I usually manage to contain, particularly when I'm acting, and saying lines that I have rehearsed well, it means that I've got very familiar and very confident with them. I mean, stammering is in the end a thing about confidence.' It was the gaining of this confidence, syllable by syllable, which gave the Oxford star the ability to get laughs out of shopping lists. Tony Robinson rightly notes, 'Rowan has this unique gift of being able to wring every single nuance out of every syllable of every single word. The over-articulation becomes funny in itself. That's how he learned to overcome his stutter, and it's become this great comic gift.'

The 'Schoolmaster' sketch was a supreme example of this gift. Rowan froze in the spotlight, glaring at the audience and daring them to titter as name after name was called out from the attendance register, each less likely than the former – from 'Ainsley' and 'Bland' to 'Nibble' and the ever-absent 'Zob', via 'Haemoglobin' and 'Nancyboy-Possum':

MASTER: All right, your essays. 'Discuss the contention that Cleopatra had the body of a roll-top desk and the mind of a duck.' Oxford and Cambridge Board all over paper 1976. Don't fidget, Bland. The answer: Yes. Jones M., Orifice, Sediment and Undermanager, see me afterwards . . . Put it away, Plectrum! If I see it once more this period, Plectrum, I shall have to tweak you . . . You're a moron, Undermanager. A carbuncle on the backside of humanity. Don't snigger, Babcock! It's not funny. *Antony and Cleopatra* is not a funny play. If Shakespeare had meant it to be funny, he would have put a joke in it.

In these sketches, *Beyond a Joke* didn't really reflect the politically flammable, punk-spattered late seventies one iota, but harked back to the previous generation of Oxbridge comedy. Like Cleese, the striking twenty-something sketch actor excelled in patrician roles of beleaguered authority, and it's little wonder that his Python idol was encouraged to pop along the road to Swiss Cottage to see what it was that had caught the eye of their mutual agent. Being immersed in the creation of both *Life of Brian* and *Fawlty Towers*, this was the zenith of

Cleese's career, but he had time to scope out the competition. 'I was very intrigued,' he admitted to the press. 'He's very, very good, he was making people laugh with some material I'd have paid money to avoid.' With this final caveat, Cleese reflected some of the show's less gushing write-ups, but even the generally scathing *Time Out* concluded that 'with the right material, Atkinson could be very funny indeed'.

Atkinson's venue was well placed: Hampstead is a vast faux-rural comic's retreat, and if the approval and patronage of Cleese wasn't high praise enough, another famous Hampstead resident made it down the hill to check out the young pretender. But Peter Cook, having seen the show and struck up a rapport with its star, was more holistically charmed, insisting, 'It is impossible not to be funny when you are around the man. He's positively inspiring.' Twenty years on from his own game-changing theatrical breakthrough *Beyond the Fringe*, it was likely – particularly during this dramatic period in his own career, with Dudley Moore having finally decamped to LA – that Cook was alert to the torch-passing element of his approval of *Beyond a Joke*, unwitting though the revue title's similarity was. One of the undeniable high spots in the show was Curtis's Tory MP, Sir Marcus Browning, a senile loon directly descended from Cook's infamous Macmillan impersonation.

MARCUS: There comes a time when we must all stand
up and be counted. I am standing up now, and
can be counted. One. To each of you, I say:
you are a One. And Ones are about to become
singularly important – because Britain is facing
the gravest economic crisis since 1380. And
you know, many of us still remember those
days: the eternal torment, worry, exasperation
and all manner of strife . . .

After his graduation, there was some hope in Atkinson's family that he would consider a move back to take over duties at the farm in Consett, as both his older brothers had fled the nest and were forging their own careers. But show business had already got him, 100 per cent. Rowan Atkinson in 1978 was standing centre stage – lauded by his heroes, under the wing of a hotshot agent, best friends with a hilarious writer, and with a whole raft of exciting job offers from the biggest movers in light entertainment: Bill Cotton, Humphrey Barclay and the ambitious radio producer John Lloyd.

Don't Panic

Any comedy producer who had achieved what John Lloyd had by 1978 could unquestionably have parked themselves comfortably on their laurels and been confident that their contribution would be celebrated for years to come. Revitalising *Just a Minute* and launching quick hits *The News Quiz*, *Quote Unquote* and *The News Huddlines* provided a CV any producer would maim for, but it couldn't be enough for a man as restless as Lloyd. There's a natural suspicion in Radio 4 circles that any talented young producer is just killing time until their big TV break comes along, but Lloyd insists it wasn't quite like that for him. 'I had five years in radio. I was happy there, felt privileged to be there. Nowadays people are in radio for a year and they want to get straight into telly and then make their first film.' But having achieved so much in just a few years, with an estimated five hundred programmes to his credit, the odd niggle soon turned into a nudge. His mentor Hatch telling him 'Lloyd, play your cards right, in seven years you could be deputy head of this department!' when he was only twenty-five and seven years sounded like a life sentence, for instance. The main spur in Lloyd's side, however, was *The Hitchhiker's Guide to the Galaxy*. After years of anguished inaction, Douglas Adams's perseverance with the comedy sci-fi serial idea, which had first occurred to him while hitchhiking round Europe before attending Cambridge, had finally paid off, partly due to the huge success of *Star Wars*. Simon Brett backed him up, producing a pilot for the series in the summer of 1977, complete with a Footlighter-packed cast headed by Simon Jones. Brett's own move to television then saw the drafting in of Lloyd's one contender for golden boy of BBC Radio LE, Geoffrey Perkins, to carry out the Herculean task of producing a complete run of six episodes of Adams's outrageously sonically ambitious saga.

The problem was that Adams's pilot script had so impressed the *Doctor Who* bosses at TV Centre that by the time the full series needed to be ready to air by spring 1978, he had been commissioned to write a four-part serial of the programme, *The Pirate Planet*, and would go on to be Script Editor, albeit briefly, in 1979. This was all too much for a deadline-phobe like Adams to bear, and in desperation he turned to his most regular collaborator for support. 'I was living in Knightsbridge at the time, in the flat of a rather well-off friend,' Lloyd told Nick Webb for *Wish You Were Here*. 'There was a kind of garage that had been converted into a rough-and-ready office where we worked. And although it had taken Douglas almost ten months to write the first four episodes, the last two we wrote in three weeks . . . We laughed a lot.' They had only recently received a handy £500 for writing a couple of quite interesting episodes of bizarre Dutch cartoon series *Dr Snuggles*, so they usually had something brewing on the typewriter together anyway.

One of Lloyd's numerous irons in the fire was his science-fiction comedy novel, *GiGax* – which may well mean 'the greatest area which could be encompassed by the human imagination', but was also named in honour of the creator of Dungeons & Dragons, Gary Gygax. Lloyd had filled the story with ideas both complex and incredibly silly, but was way off reaching any kind of conclusion, working away at every thread in his tale with characteristic logical precision. He generously showered Douglas with pages, and invited him to cherry-pick the ideas which best suited Arthur Dent's odyssey of oddities. 'Mine was a rather pretentious book I suppose, but there were quite a lot of crucial ideas in it and Douglas had this wonderful way of taking a kernel of an idea and turning it round to make it funnier. He always had a way of putting a gag on the end, whereas my natural inclination was to go forward with the basic idea to try to find a solution rather than a gag. It was in that garage that we jointly came up with the number 42 and the Scrabble set, which even at the time seemed the most wonderful, striking, simple and hilarious idea.'

John Lloyd's equal input into the last two episodes of the first series of H2G2 was to be only the start, with a co-written Christmas special and a second series on the cards, plus a novelisation under joint contract. This had been happily agreed between them face to face, but when Lloyd later received a letter from his friend explaining his decision to take back control of his characters and write the book on his own, Lloyd was utterly crushed. Losing his chance to finally be part of a successful sci-fi franchise was one thing, but being informed by mail when he was just in the next room seemed to make the rejection far worse. It was also true that John was in the red, and greatly needed his half of the handsome advance paid by Pan Books. The furious Lloyd found himself an agent as quickly as possible and – despite being advised to accept 15 per cent of the H2G2 profits in perpetuity – he negotiated half of the existing advance, and nipped the issue in the bud. It wasn't quite so easy to shake off his indignation at Adams's use of him as an 'emotional football', however – even Douglas's mother had to step in to placate John and try to put an end to the feud.

Mrs Adams's intervention may have been the clincher – certainly, by the end of the year the two friends were not just talking again, but working together. The instant popularity of H2G2 led to Adams himself joining Lloyd as a radio producer, doing the odd shift on Week Ending and producing that year's panto, celebrating ninety-five years of the Footlights, Black Cinderella II Goes East. Douglas began his first big production with great confidence, hiring pals Clive Anderson and

Rory McGrath to pen a corny script inspired by *ISIRTA*,* and sending word out to vintage Footlights stars including Cleese (although he insisted on pre-recording his role of 'Fairy Godperson' at home), Richard 'Stinker' Murdoch, and, in the spectacularly nasty plum role of Prince Disgusting, Peter Cook. However, with the Christmas recording getting closer and closer, Douglas had to admit that he had bitten off more than he could chew, and called on his old friend in the next room to act as co-producer. 'I was called in to help at the very last minute – if not days before the recording, then not much more than that. I came along because at least I knew about, you know, warm-ups and how to do read-throughs and all that.'

As with so many other green striplings in this story, the elder statesman Cook was to welcome Lloyd into his intimate circle of ribaldry without a qualm – even though, due to his lack of exposure to British TV in his schooldays, John wasn't an avid fan. 'I came to know Peter pretty well as a person,' he says, 'but I never got round to catching up on the fine detail of his career. Most famous people, I think, would have found this either offensive or incompetent. Peter couldn't have cared less. He had the gift of being able to treat everyone absolutely equally, and he made no exception of himself.'

Another reason that Lloyd was clearly happy to help with the panto was that he had already put a new plan of his own into action. He had taken the book debacle with Douglas to heart, and at the same time as his old housemate's mammoth success was beginning, all around him his colleagues seemed to be getting ahead, leaving for TV, finding their niche, while he was headed for thirty, working round the clock on radio shows with only a vague promise of promotion years ahead. When his radio hit *To the Manor Born* transferred to TV without him it all became too much for the young Lloyd, and on the most decisive

---

* A script which, ironically, he had to personally wrench out of the tardy writers to meet their deadline.

working day of his life he left his office, marched over to TV Centre, and as good as banged on comedy boss Jimmy Gilbert's desk demanding a chance at producing a TV show. 'To my huge surprise, they said, "Of course. What took you so long to ask? Would six programmes be enough?" They could do that sort of thing then.'

Lloyd's commission was to create a brand-new satirical comedy show for the eighties – on the understanding that he share duties with Current Affairs producer and fellow Cantabrigian Sean Hardie, who had a habit of sneaking jokes into *Panorama*. The two put their heads together and began plotting a pilot for the spring of 1979. 'It started off being called *Sacred Cows*, that was the BBC's title for it, and it was designed to be a dissing of all the things that you weren't supposed to diss.' Hardie's participation was always going to give the programme a more topical feel, but for Lloyd, this was in a way the creation of another in a long line of revues – and he knew which performer he wanted to head the cast.

A Plan Most Cunning

Atkinson and Lloyd had a near miss immediately prior to the launch of this new TV show, as Curtis and the comedy world's greatest new visual performer readied their one and only foray into radio. Like *The Burkiss Way* team before them, Curtis and Atkinson started their audio experiment in the sober atmosphere of Radio 3, which perfectly suited their mockumentary style. Originally piloted as *Rowan Atkinson's Profiles* in 1978, *The Atkinson People*, which debuted on 24 April 1979, was planned as a series of biographical studies of fictional men of achievement – Shakespearean actor Sir Corin Basin, politician and Renaissance man Sir Benjamin Fletcher, French philosopher George Dupont and the 'Pope of Pop' Barry Good. 'I was script editor for the department,' John confirms, 'so I suppose I must have read the scripts, but I don't remember it. I was the censor – in that strange way institutions have of making the naughtiest boy in the school the head prefect.' It was an understated, cerebral series, recorded without an audience and with the help of *Beyond a Joke* player Peter Wilson and actor Hugh Thomas*, and can be most closely compared to painstakingly crafted spoofs such as *On the Hour*. The roles were quite equally shared out, although Atkinson played all but one of the subjects – an old bore (which allowed him to repeat his Marcus Browning speech), an outrageous Frenchman and a burned-out rocker, in depictions that seemed innocuously genuine to the casual ear, but were packed with verbal idiocy when you actually paid attention.

Although Rowan didn't play Sir Corin, he did appear as a Jacobean villain in the first episode, in a faux-archive recording of the actor's performance in *The Tragedy of Terence, or The Recalcitrant Lunatic*, which allowed Curtis and he to continue their assault on Shakespeare – revenge for all those dud roles given to Curtis at Oxford. Spot the first arrangement of a most famous phrase.

TERENCE: Ah, now I am alone. Oh woe, they do think
                    that I am mad, but no, I do but counterfeit,
                    and have a plan most cunning, and yet . . .
                    most cunning. But wait! Here comes my
                    brother the usurper. See him smile; he feels he
                    is on a winning wicket. Little does he know
                    that in a trice he'll kick it.
USURPER: Hail, Terence, how goes it?
TERENCE: Most porky, m'lud! Most porky! . . . Aye,
                    m'lud! Mad I am! Woo!
USURPER: Away, away, thou ravest.
TERENCE: Nooo! 'Tis thou that ravest, foul usurper,

---

* Who would crop up in other Curtis/Atkinson projects, most notably as the barking doctor in *The Tall Guy*.

> prepare to meet thy doom! See, I cast aside my
> madman's guise and stand before thee the man
> I was: thy wronged brother, fair Antonio . . .

USURPER: Loon, I begin to tire of thee. I have no brother,
nor is Antonio's name a name beknown to me.

TERENCE: No?

USURPER: No.

TERENCE: . . . Then I must be none other than Mad
Terence, the foetid stirp?

USURPER: True, loon! Away, I am full of business . . .

It may have seemed ironic to Lloyd that Atkinson was making his radio debut just as he was moving on from the medium, but as the series was produced by his old friend and pseudo-brother-in-law Griff Rhys Jones (one of his few productions in his short time as a radio producer), John was hardly that far out of the loop, and he listened in to the shows keenly, wondering how Rowan's astounding live performances would translate to radio and, indeed, his own TV show.

Lloyd and Hardie's programme would not be Atkinson's first appearance on TV, though. Besides a fleeting appearance on a Richard Stilgoe special, *And Now the Good News*, Rowan had also been interviewed to publicise the Hampstead show, and in these early days, Afro'ed and bespectacled, he seemed happy to open up about his inner fears admitting, 'I have a lot of fits of depression and lack of satisfaction, but they're nearly all associated with the entertainment industry, and actually my other interests in life – I mean, silly things, but things I happen to enjoy doing a fantastic amount, like electronics, like driving trucks – are very simple. And the trouble with show business is that what you're doing is exposing yourself entirely, and your heart and soul is being torn out and shown to millions of people.'

Richard Armitage had given Atkinson his first performing break on the small screen, in a way that it can only be presumed the two of them agreed never to discuss again: the 'Children's Revue' *A Bundle of Bungles*. This attempt at preschool comedy (which would result in the popular show *Jigsaw*) was broadcast only once, in early '79, and featured the young comedy star in the role of 'Mr Ree', performing his more child-friendly mime skits surrounded by sad-faced clowns and mime artists, with Howard Goodall accompanying him on the organ, in between airings of bizarre Eastern European cartoons. Over the years Atkinson's work would have huge appeal to children, and even before the *Mr Bean* cartoon launched in 2002, younger viewers would flock to his post-watershed programmes, but *A Bundle of Bungles* was his one foray into performing specifically for an infant audience. It was a most unexpected debut for a comic already in the sights of some of the biggest names in TV comedy.

Humphrey Barclay remained fascinated by the possibility of putting Atkinson on screen, but went about it in an unorthodox way. Rowan remembers, despite having just completed his final exams, 'He asked me to write an essay on what kind of comedy programme I would like to be involved with. And it was all tremendously pretentious stuff – that there shouldn't be a studio audience and it should all be shot on location on film, desperately trying to get away from the traditional sitcom or sketch-show format that was popular then, as now. In the end it was largely ambitious but pretentious waffle. Trying to be original merely because you've learned to be different rarely works. You should try and learn from the past, rather than rejecting it outright.'

Despite the naivety of young Rowan's argument against laughter tracks, the issue would seem to have inspired him in the creation of his first real TV comedy showcase, *Rowan Atkinson Presents . . . Canned Laughter*, broadcast on ITV on 8 April 1979. Without Curtis's aid, the young comic pieced together the best showcase for his characterisations he could, in a sitcom format to be recorded with a live audience. 'It was basically a chance for Rowan to use a few of his existing characters, woven into a story of sorts,' Barclay confirms. 'I turned to the director of Marshall & Renwick's *End of Part One*, Geoffrey Sax. Geoffrey had blagged his way into the director's chair for that very funny series, and brought to it a striking visual element which was a cut above the normal for TV comedy.' This try-out episode was mostly fresh material – with a few well-tested turns.

The hero of the piece, Robert Box, is certainly the closest forerunner of Bean on Atkinson's CV – an awkward, selfish, unpopular and childish disaster magnet. Rowan himself always claimed, 'I'm best at playing lonely and vulnerable people in small-scale comedies of tiny situations.' Box is in love with a cute work colleague played by Sue Holderness*, and *Canned Laughter* follows him on the day that he finally plucks up the courage to ask her out – from his hectic morning routine to inevitable late-night rejection. Box's bizarrely florid gesticulations, elastic expressions and slapstick reflexes gave Atkinson the perfect excuse to revisit some business he had been performing since the earliest Oxford Revues, as Box's morning rush required him to ingest coffee on the fly, putting granules, milk and water straight from the kettle into his mouth and mixing them on the go, plus shaving his entire face – bar eyebrows – with an electric razor. Repressing young Robert is his cold-hearted boss Mr Marshall, also played by Atkinson, with a third character coming from left field, in the form of Dave Perry – a struggling (and hopeless) Geordie comedian who is over the moon to get a booking at the restaurant where Robert takes his date. This seems like a transparent display of unusual openness from Atkinson, in a sense splitting his personality and laying it bare for all to see. On the other hand, Perry's chirpiness in the face of a complete lack of prospects or talent was simply very amusing:

DAVE:	Good morning, Mrs Nolan!
MRS N:	Morning, Mr Perry, you're up with the lark.

---

* The future Marlene Boyce in *Only Fools and Horses* and *The Green Green Grass*, at that time starring in the aforementioned *End of Part One*, the TV incarnation of *The Burkiss Way*.

DAVE:	Oh yes. I've got to see my agent about a booking. He wants to try me in a swish restaurant in Camden Town. Could be the big break, Mrs Nolan!
MRS N:	Oh, I've never been in a Swiss restaurant.
DAVE:	No, swish! Posh.
MRS N:	Oh, well, I hope you're funny.
DAVE:	Oh, so do I, Mrs Nolan. That's what I'll be paid for, after all!

There's a lot to raise one's eyebrows at in *Canned Laughter* – besides Atkinson's set-piece routines of social awkwardness, an odd melancholia hangs over the whole half-hour, the episode concluding with the broken Box and Perry slumped in despair together in the seedy restaurant as a looped, distorted sample of canned laughter plays, the lights dim and the viewer is left not just nonplussed, but disconcerted. Still, it would have been interesting to see how the idea could have been stretched to a series – if such a course wasn't made null and void by the acceptance of Lloyd's offer of a sketch show on the BBC. Barclay now admits, 'I was elated at the quality of the piece, and having had the power to take someone right at the beginning of his career and give him his own TV show. My plan was immediately to proceed to a series, probably called *Rowan Atkinson Presents*, which would be a collection of individual half-hours. When I put this plan over the telephone to Richard Armitage, I was absolutely flabbergasted to learn that, undivulged to me, Rowan had simultaneously been working with another team on a sketch show . . . I went ballistic.'

Atkinson's agreement to join the BBC camp was not obtained without some difficulty. John recalls his first tremulous dealings with the mighty Armitage: 'He was a very classic old-fashioned agent; he looked the part, he was sort of squat and enormously upper class, smoked cigars – the most powerful agent in light entertainment in the country at that time.' Lloyd had to make it clear that his brief was to create a team for a topical show, and although Atkinson was much sought after, this was not a solo vehicle. 'He brought his boy in, Rowan, the young star, and they clearly thought this was going to be "The Rowan Atkinson Show". BBC management in those days was very powerful in its own right, and they were very sure of themselves, and although in the politest way, they said, "We want to get some other talented people, and put them around Rowan, so that if he's good he'll shine by comparison, and they'll support him. He won't have to carry the whole weight, and also it won't use up the material nearly so fast." And to do Richard and Rowan credit, they saw the point of that, and bought into it, and the rest is history.' Atkinson confirmed years later, 'My instincts undoubtedly were to protect myself really, to sort of be part of a group of people as I explored the wonders of television.'

The first episode of *Not the Nine O'Clock News** appeared in the *Radio Times* listings with little fanfare, set for broadcast on 2 April 1979 – a week before *Canned Laughter* was shown on the other side. Keeping as up to the minute as possible, Atkinson was in the studio to record the programme just three days earlier, although he had to wait a full fifteen minutes to get his face in edgeways – performing the Marcus Browning speech again. The *Not* 'pilot that wasn't' is a cold affair in general, with Atkinson's original cohorts being Chris Langham, ex-Scaffold and then-*Tiswas* joker John Gorman, Jonathan Hyde and Christopher Godwin, with gags supplied by some of *Week Ending*'s finest, including Andy Hamilton and Laurie Rowley – but John and Sean had a nightmare getting it in the can and it shows. Some crucial touchstones of the future show were there from the start – edited news footage was always central to the humour, despite the BBC having

---

* Named in honour of *Not the New York Times,* a parody printed during US print strikes in 1978.

always bridled at the idea of mocking politicians by showing them out of context (apparently the public were ready for this by 1979). Quick-fire topical gags were also dominant, albeit mainly relayed via electronic billboard, slowly, as the audience cough.

There was even a sign of Lloyd's future plans, with rudimentary *Spitting Image*-style skits featuring Denis Healey and Bob Hope. Lloyd was convinced that a satirical TV show with puppet caricatures inspired by the modelling work of Peter Fluck and Roger Law, and utilising the voice and script talents he knew well from *Week Ending*, would be a hit. However, on approaching Fluck & Law, he was told something along the lines of, quote, 'We don't know how to make puppets, fuck off!' so he gave it a go anyway with limited BBC resources, and Chris Emmett providing the voices for crudely animated masks. The end result is interesting, but probably no more biting or funny than Rowan's Healey impressions in 1975.

Another item very much at odds with *Not* as we know it was a tiny historical joke, with a picture of a castle and the caption 'Worcester 1641'. Roundhead forces cry out: 'All right, Your Majesty, you're surrounded! Now come out with your head under your arm.' The fact that Charles I would not face arrest until seven years after that date provides a tantalising early example of complete anachronism, in favour of a decent joke.*

Only at the end of the first pilot does the crucial *Not* idea of having the cast – including Atkinson – sitting at news desks churning out topical gags come into play. But one bonus this try-out did have was the ultimate endorsement from the funniest show on TV. With industrial action delaying the final episode of *Fawlty Towers*, 'Basil the Rat', the director Bob Spiers (who also helmed the *Not* pilot) and star Cleese took a moment to record a special introduction for a 'cheap tatty revue',

---

* Generally *Not* avoided period sketches, unless they were sending up BBC costume dramas – perhaps the only exception being a Stone Age quickie featuring Rowan as a caveman who gets to clobber Griff with his club.

seeing as he refused to 'do' Basil that week – there was even a short epilogue featuring Manuel. Cleese would eventually put in a 'celebrity' appearance in series three (non-speaking), so he clearly never regretted this largesse.

The *Fawlty* endorsement was such a crucial fillip for the team that it was certain to be recycled for the eventual series, but the same could not be said of the rest of the rudimentary revue – with Labour PM Jim Callaghan calling an election just a couple of days before the recording, at the eleventh hour the BBC confirmed that their new experiment in biting satire would have to obediently wait its turn for broadcast, at a less politically sensitive date, and was halted.

Lloyd could not have been more relieved – he knew his TV debut was not at all up to scratch. 'I prayed every night of that week, it was the most stressful thing, I thought that was the end of my career, because I had no idea, I was a radio producer! I had no idea of all the things you need, car parking, food, lights, that kind of thing.' The last-minute reprieve – the allotted Thursday-evening slot being given to US sitcom *Rhoda* – was the best thing that could have happened for the project. John had asked Mel Smith to join the team from the start, and despite having formed a double act with Bob Goody at the time, Mel would have been at the recording but for a stint directing at the Liverpool Everyman Theatre. When shown what was now deemed the 'pilot', he agreed that it was 'sort of awful', but was in. Forming a new team with him and retaining Atkinson and Langham, Lloyd and Hardie now had an eventful summer in which to rethink their show. Recalling the back-to-basics process Hardie says: 'We found we disliked the same things. That's where the whole *Not* idea came from really – we ran through all the shows we hated. And we wanted to be slightly more out in the street than comedy had been for a long time. And who better qualified to find out what the working class were up to than two Oxbridge graduates with public-school backgrounds?'

Will This Wind Be So Mighty . . .?

The following month gave a perfect opportunity to see what was going on in comedy in Thatcher's brand-spanking-new Britain, as a club called the Comedy Store opened its doors, in a venue hidden away above a Soho strip club, and Lloyd made sure to be there on the first night – as was agonisingly pointed out by terrified Footlighter turned barrister Clive Anderson in his debut stand-up set, alerting the crowd to the presence of the big-shot comedy producer. All around Lloyd harrumphed the stirrings of a revolution in British comedy that could form part of the manifesto of the rejigged *Not*. 'There were two things really,' Lloyd recalls of the programme's ambitions. 'One was to create something that was huge fun – like going to see your favourite rock band or going to a party, that kind of thing. And the other was to kind of reinvent what you could be funny about. Seventies comedy was all sort of very right wing, all the comedy was about cripples and fat women and gays – you wouldn't even call them gays, you'd call them poofs in those days. There was a guy called Gus Macdonald who made a speech at the Edinburgh Television Festival in the seventies which I for some reason dropped in on, and he talked about stereotyping in comedy, how dreadful it was that we'd all got stuck in these habits. And at the same time the Comedy Store was starting . . . It was a complete coincidence that they were doing on the stage what we were trying to do on telly.' But sadly once Anderson had pointed out one of the Oxbridge lot to the assembled crowds and acts, Lloyd was lucky to escape intact – and was in fact wedged in the lift by Keith Allen jamming a radiator into the door. In truth, the number of genuinely working-class acts who emerged to fame from the club which helped kick-start the 'Alternative Comedy' boom was very small indeed. For every Keith Allen, Tony Allen or Malcolm Hardee there were a dozen middle-class lads like Lloyd hoping to make punters laugh – and some of them had plenty to say, too. Ultimately, *Not* wouldn't be identifiably 'Alternative'. It would have its smattering of Irish jokes and a big helping of 'busty substances', and where the radical comics would have fought the power, *Not* stood on the sidelines, laughing at everybody.

One month after Lloyd's lift calamity, very near geographically but in the smarter environs of Her Majesty's Theatre, Rowan Atkinson was honouring the invitation of a lifetime. Once again, his fairy godperson John Cleese had conferred a great honour upon him by asking him to feature in the third of the Amnesty benefit concerts, to be called *The Secret Policeman's Ball*. Clydeside Humblebum Billy Connolly would also be making his Amnesty debut, amid returning Oxbridge greats like Cook, Palin, Jones and Bron, and musicians like Pete Townshend and Tom Robinson, but Atkinson was clearly the stand-out act on the first night. 'No one really knew who I was or what I did, they were sort of educated in those three or four spots throughout the evening; and the Schoolmaster was I think the first thing that I did, which kind of said, "Well, here I am, and this is what I do."' The Schoolmaster and Pianist skits wowed the crowd enough, but to be actually invited to make up the quartet for the 'Four Yorkshiremen' sketch* was an unexpected welcome into the highest echelons of the comedy mafia. 'For me, I was living a fantasy,' Atkinson recalled for the thirtieth anniversary, 'of actually being onstage with the *Monty Python* team doing a *Monty Python* sketch. Generally speaking, I think I felt as though I kept my end up as best I could. But it was a great privilege.'

If Rowan merely 'kept his end up' with the comedy gods of the decade, however, he almost inadvertently upstaged the true comedy Godfather, Peter Cook, in the climactic *Beyond the Fringe* sketch 'The End of the World', as the whole cast gathered with pullovers pulled over their heads in anticipation of the apocalypse.

---

* Originally written by Cleese & Chapman with Marty Feldman and Tim Brooke-Taylor for *At Last the 1948 Show*, but since sucked into *Python* lore.

COOK: It will be, as 'twere, a mighty rending in the sky, and the mountains shall sink and the valleys shall rise and great shall be the tumult thereof, I should think . . . Certainly there will be a mighty wind, if the word of God is anything to go by.

ATKINSON: *Will this wind be so mighty as to lay low the mountains of the Earth?*

COOK: Can't hear a blind word you're saying. You're speaking too softly for the human ear, which is what I'm equipped with. You'll have to speak a little more loudly, please.

ATKINSON: *About this wind . . .*

COOK: No better, is it? I ask you to speak more loudly and you speak more softly. A strange reaction from a follower, or perhaps I'm very old-fashioned, expecting you to speak louder . . .

ATKINSON: Yes, you are.

Atkinson has claimed that his bizarre strangulated squeaks (perhaps best described as his 'funny little croaky one who isn't anyone in particular, but is *such* a scream') were an attempt to pay tribute to Dudley Moore's original performance, but his unique cartoonishness, a melancholy alien among the tableau of comic masters, was the final cherry on top of his triumph as star of the show.

Or rather, that may have been the case were it not for Cook's infamously sharp, rapid and devastating reaction to one of the first show's reviews, a *Telegraph* article which denounced the evening for having no satirical bite. 'Entirely a Matter For You' was a lampoon of the biased summing-up of the infamous trial of Liberal politician Jeremy Thorpe on grounds of conspiracy to murder, as made by Mr Justice Cantley. This blistering destruction of Cantley's calumny was pieced together on the fly by Cook

51

with input from the whole cast, and utterly slayed the audience for the remaining three nights, becoming, in some people's view, the last great creative flourish from Cook for at least a decade.

So popular – and indeed, satirically urgent – was the monologue that Cook decided to record it and release it as a single as quickly as possible, and there was no one better equipped to help him achieve his goal than John Lloyd, who was lurking in the shadows, as at any moment of comedic urgency. Brought in by the show's producer Martin Lewis, his role on the EP *Here Comes the Judge* was to capture Cook's timely masterpiece on vinyl, but for the B-side he found himself having to perform opposite the great man himself, delivering a fine Dagenham twang in a *Derek & Clive*-style sketch about the 'Well Hung Jury', and a desperate toff looking to get his wife wiped out in 'Rad Job'. This was to be his final spot of comedy acting, and he remembers not feeling equal to the challenge. 'I briefly became Peter Cook's straight man. It was The Worst Job I Ever Had: the straight man who couldn't stop laughing – a sort of dud Dud.'

Six Shall He Gather

These last performances quite closely presaged Lloyd's last credit as a scriptwriter, certainly for a fiction of his own invention. Having seen the giddying heights of *H2G2*'s success, Adams's old muckers Lloyd and Andrew Marshall already had their own idea for an epic radio comedy saga, tying into their own branch of geekiness: *Hordes of the Things*. In the wake of Peter Jackson's blockbuster movie franchise, Tolkien spoofs seem trite and opportunistic, but when A. P. R. Marshall and J. H. W. Lloyd brought their swords 'n' sorcery yarn to Radio 4 in 1980, they were not only treading on virgin snow (perhaps excepting Terry Gilliam's *Jabberwocky* from 1977), but the programme's broadcast even pre-empted the famed BBC Radio adaptation of *The Lord of the Rings* – which any Tolkien fan would assume they were aping – by a whole year.

Produced with his signature ear for ambitious atmosphere by Geoffrey Perkins, fresh off the back of *H2G2*, *Hordes of the Things* tells the incredibly sorry tale of the pre-Time world of Middle-Sea – or more specifically the land of Albion, ruled by the inaccurately named King Yulfric the Wise III. Even more specifically, it is the cliché-ridden heroic quest of the wood-poacher Agar, son of Athar, and his minotaur friend Stephen.

As the weak ruler is played by Paul Eddington, it's all too tempting to draw parallels with his greatest portrayal of all, Jim Hacker in *Yes Minister*, which had debuted on BBC2 at the start of the year – and coincidentally, the sitcom's co-creator Jonathan Lynn also featured in the radio saga as the greedy dwarf Golin Longshanks. But these weren't the only well-known voices in the cast – Irish actor Patrick Magee spat out the lunatic narration with rumbling rapidity, Maggie Steed played Queen Elfreda, Prince Veganin was Simon Callow in full Shakespearean bombast, the great Ballard Berkeley popped up briefly, and the crucial role of ineffective wizard Radox the Green was filled by Frank Middlemass. Perkins was also very lucky to retain the services of the extraordinarily versatile voice artist Miriam Margolyes, in the role of Agar's gorgon mother, Dyandetes the Three-Faced Sybil, and sundry harpies. Despite being an Oxford native, of Jewish Belarusian descent, Margolyes had first shown her comedic flair in the Footlights, back in the days when girls were barely tolerated, let alone allowed into the club. She filled the allotted non-masculine roles in *Double Take* (with Cleese, Chapman, Barclay, Brooke-Taylor and Tony Hendra) in 1961, but sadly that was no breakthrough year, and neither were the first two subsequent decades of her career. But as her vocal expertise was always hugely in demand, she crammed in a dizzying array of jobs over the years, from *Jackanory* to the Cadbury's Caramel bunny, the female roles in the TV series *Monkey*, and even recording audio porn. But her abilities stretched far beyond the microphone, as time would eventually prove.

The dry and linguistically pedantic humour of *Hordes of the Things* naturally bears some resemblance to *H2G2*, but in its epic nature the one comedy programme it feels closest to is undoubtedly *The Black Adder*. The sound aesthetic of the two programmes – mocking melodrama, setting up impressively epic scenarios from a time of kings and castles, battles and fresh horses, and then instantly undercutting them with silly pathos – makes them non-identical twins, but twins nonetheless.

RADOX: Harpies have never dared approach the hidden glade before – it's restricted, you see. You must have something very precious for them to seek you out like this. A magic coat of mail? A shield? A ring, perhaps?

AGAR: A ring? What use to anyone is a ring? (*STEPHEN groans.*) Oh, yes! There's my sword. Observe the scabbard of jewelled copper.

RADOX: It's magic, there is no doubt! I mean, look at the ivory inlay, the ebony motifs, and here on the blade, in fiery runes for all to see! The words of the elder tongue! (*Reads*) '*Tra-gu-dan-borith, tra-corna-pagadarith . . .*'

AGAR: Could it . . . Does it mean, 'One man shall save the realm, six shall he gather'?

RADOX: I've no idea, I failed Runes.

Callow's foghorn soliloquising as Veganin so blatantly foreshadows Brian Blessed's terrifying Richard IV that it's easy to imagine him being second on the list for the latter role, and the way that Lloyd & Marshall presented their four-part saga, with a meticulously constructed alternative reality in which their alter egos smoked pipes with the rest of Oxford's Inklings in the 1930s (as outlined in the *Radio Times*), also gave Lloyd his first experience of rewriting history, creating an entire false reality to surround a single comedy programme.

Unfortunately (and perhaps due to a deliberately disappointing and far from epic conclusion), *Hordes of the Things* was swiftly forgotten by all but the most retentive fantasy fans, until BBC7 repeats finally paved the way for a CD release in 2009. With Tolkien still titanic box office, if we enjoyed a British film industry, it could form the basis for the best British spoof film since the Pythons were in their pomp.

NOT NOW NATIONWIDE

There's a whole book to be written about the enormous success and lasting influence of *Not the Nine O'Clock News* – but this is not it. The struggling growth and heyday of the show will have to be glimpsed only in fleeting detail, as the seventies give way to the eighties and a whole new comedy landscape opens up in British culture.

Prior to starting on the series, Atkinson had enjoyed another sell-out Edinburgh Fringe show alongside Curtis and Goodall at the Wireworks, a huge, bare venue which required him to help design and build his own stage – a dream come true for such a passionate engineer, but one which proved an almost impossible task. Rowan remembers, 'It was a tremendous engineering and technical exercise and you couldn't see the stage from the gallery, except from the front row . . . It was a huge and horrible exercise really, the whole thing. In the end you look back and say, "It was all worth it," but I'm not absolutely convinced that it was.' These technical niggles didn't stop the show from having a Fringe First to take back to London as work started on the new programme.

Having amassed his final team for a full series in October 1979, John Lloyd immediately had pause for thought. 'We had this famous lunch, and I'm sitting there thinking, "I can't imagine what I've done here, I've made the most horrible mistake . . . apart from a skip out of the back of Madame Tussaud's, I can't think of a more weird collection of people." It was the most uncomfortable lunch, we had absolutely nothing to say to each other, and rehearsals started a couple of days later.' The stunning and chameleonic Pamela Stephenson had entered the fray after Lloyd had scoured the comedy world to find the right female quarter for his cast, with both Victoria Wood and Alison Steadman turning him down, until (in true *H2G2* fashion) Pamela's dazzling personality called to him at a party, and his chat-up line soon developed into an invite to join the hottest comedy team in the country. 'The first time people saw Pamela,' Lloyd complains, 'she turned up in a microskirt, very tottery high heels, and loads of make-up and lots of nail varnish, and I remember seeing Mel and Rowan – who always did, and still do, have a very similar sense of humour – standing behind a pillar laughing themselves stupid thinking, "This is John's shag!" And it was so unfair, because it wasn't true, I never slept with Pamela!'

The show's viewing figures were not encouraging at first, which was good news for everyone in a way as much tinkering with the format was required throughout the first series. Lloyd says, 'In the theatre, you've basically got one shot to do it, and if it's crap on the first night, that's your lot. With telly or radio, you can do the first series and make an awful mess of it, and in the second series – if you get one – you can improve it. And that is basically what I have done all my life – every first series I've done, virtually, has been a disaster . . . The only show I did that was good to start with was *The News Quiz*.'

But the first series, although a rough try-out by any standards, did contain several sketches now considered classics, including a stand-off between trade union leaders and management which called for a guest spot from Jim Broadbent. Acting was a calling that seemed fated for Jim since he was born to artist parents, conscientious objectors in World War II who were sent to the village of Holton-cum-Beckering to work the land, and founded a theatrical company there. By the age of thirty, eight years into his acting career, Broadbent had barely had a glimpse of a TV studio when he landed the *Not* job, and Lloyd knew he would be a handy name to remember for future comic roles.

A further quickly established memorable feature of the programme was Atkinson's turn as a hectoring, reactionary member of the public (ultimately monikered 'Eric Swannage of Liverpool'), who was liable to interrupt the proceedings with a litany of outrageous complaints at any moment. For the general public, who had not seen the young comic's live shows, this persona was surely their first opportunity to pigeonhole him – a bizarre, anoraked figure ranting as he struggled through the audience, very much not part of the crowd.

One final sketch in the last episode has gone down in history, Lloyd himself claiming it as the moment when the series really gelled. As a timely reaction to the outcry attending the release of *Life of Brian* (and, more specifically, the famed clash between Cleese and Palin and Malcolm Muggeridge and the Bishop of Southwark on the TV discussion programme *Friday Night, Saturday Morning*), regular contributor Colin Bostock-Smith penned 'The Life of Christ', twisting the issue round by presenting Atkinson as the director of a movie accused of blaspheming against the hallowed name of Python. Langham, who had been a support player in the real film, was uneasy with what he saw as self-indulgence and comedic incest, but that alone was not the reason he wasn't invited back for the second series in 1980. His own problems relating to addiction to sundry narcotics at this time had helped to warrant a call from Head of Comedy John Howard Davies for his removal from the team – a task which Lloyd was dismayed to have to carry out, and finally left to his boss, despite Atkinson putting pressure on him to give Langham a reprieve.

Nevertheless, with the trusty Rhys Jones elevated from bit-part player to full member of the team, it was the second series in the spring of 1980 which saw *Not* take off as a real cogent comedic voice for the new decade, famed for its edgy piss-takes of every public figure in the news, its gross extended spoofs of TV hits, its talking daffodils and, of course, hedgehog abuse. The show became a haven not just for the cast, but for a whole host of great writers spilling out from the BBC Radio contacts book. The first among equals, however, was Richard Curtis. His father had suggested that a career in personnel at Unilever might be a more suitable career, as Curtis recalled on *Desert Island Discs* in 1991. 'He was very keen I should do a proper job, and he wasn't sure that writing was a proper job. So after I left Oxford he said, "I'll give you a year, and at the end of it we can see how much money you've earned." And I think I'd earned about £367 or something like that, but just before the year was up, Rowan got asked to do *Not the Nine O'Clock News*, and all was well.'

Looking back at the stress required to get the show made every week, Lloyd says, 'It was a nightmare of overwork, I mean, everything was stressful, we used to be green with exhaustion. We were within an ace of disaster more or less every week. It was amazing what we did, and we were only able to do it by basically going without sleep for a week. But for the actors it was a very nice job.' He estimates that Curtis contributed 'about half' of the scripts, becoming a major part of the show's voice, though this is only partly confirmed by Curtis himself. 'My major memory of the show is sitting in a basement in Camden Town, writing lots and lots and lots. Sometimes of course you'd watch a show and there was nothing by you.' With Rowan as his muse, Curtis came up with reams of material for every series. 'We tried to work out things which were odd, and which Rowan and I would sort of do more onstage, rather than writing satirical things about trade unions, or train timetables, stuff like that.'

The weekly production process was more like going to a youth club than a BBC rehearsal – the team even had their own pinball table. 'It was amazing,' Curtis recalls. 'The energy and the fire and creative enthusiasm in the room when they were playing pinball was devastating. And then they'd say "we'd better get back to the sketches", and everybody would go "ugh . . ." just waiting for something funny to be said.' For Rowan, with his natural abilities never allowing anyone to forget who the star of the show was, this period seemed idyllic. 'My job on *Not*, I always felt, was quite straightforward – I just learned the scripts, and turned up on Sunday and recorded them! It seemed like a very simple job.' But what was simple for Atkinson was a revelation to everybody else – his gobbledegook rendition of the poem 'Abou Ben Adhem', for instance, left his colleagues aghast at where it was all coming from.

Led by Mel Smith, a naturalistic style of performance was established which marked *Not* out from everything before it, and everything around it, Curtis attests. 'It was definitely negatively influenced by *Monty Python*. So the thing we took particular joy in was naturalistic performances, because the *Python* style had been so high.' Atkinson agrees. 'It was something that I'd never done, because even then I tended to do characters that were rather extreme, either extremely old or extremely silly, or facially very active.' Figures of authority were still a speciality, of course – the senior policeman in 'Constable Savage', numerous politicians, judges, vicars of all descriptions and even a gorilla called Gerald, who managed to maintain an air of ineffable superiority despite having a mouth patently incapable of accommodating bananas.

Not's line in inspired musical pastiche – be it punk, ska, heavy metal, country or Olivia Newton John – also gave a helping hand for the third member of Atkinson's regular team: as well as being Rowan's housemate, Howard Goodall became the show's musical director and formed a house band for the show, often including himself on the organ.*

While Goodall shared composition duties with future TV music greats like Peter Brewis and Philip Pope, who became Curtis's musical collaborator on *Radio Active*, the Oxford Review show which transferred to radio in 1980 at the behest of budding producer Jimmy Mulville, showing that his original violent reaction to the gang had long since dissolved. In the same year, Pope and Curtis's Bee Gees hatchet job, 'Meaningless Songs in Very High Voices' (as performed by Phil, Angus and Michael as the Hee Bee Gee Bees), may not have troubled the

---

* The rest of the cast mimed along as best they could but besides Atkinson's passion for percussion, the quartet's ability as a band may have been one thing which inspired Douglas Adams to opine: '*Not the Nine O'Clock News* is to *Monty Python* what the Monkees were to the Beatles.'

UK charts, but it did get to number 2 in Australia, where the team had enjoyed a successful tour.

Not's success was really brought home to everyone by the massive sales of the first tie-in book (a magazine spoof simply entitled *Not!*), and indeed the first album, both released hot on the heels of the second series and snapped up in unexpectedly astronomical amounts. When the team agreed to do a signing session in Oxford, the queue stretched the length of the high street and lorry loads of extra books had to be sent for to meet with demand. The first album went double platinum, knocking Queen off the top of the charts, and the following year the show won the *Smash Hits* TV award – even *Monty Python* hadn't reached such heights of youth appeal, certainly not so quickly.

Lloyd had always wanted his own hit comedy franchise, and here it was – TV, books, albums, all hits, not just artistically, but commercially. Rowan Atkinson and his retinue were the biggest thing in UK comedy, and the decade had only just begun. There was also the financial reward to be considered, Atkinson recalls. 'Suddenly the royalties started to come in, because the record sales were quite bizarrely large. And my predominant thought was probably "Which model of Aston Martin will this buy me?" I suspect that was my priority – when looking at a large cheque it was always immediately cars that would sort of flash in my head.'

Having turned away from his technical ambitions, and completed one of the most impressive rises to greatness in British Comedy history, he remained, at heart, a petrolhead, only happy when behind the wheel or under the bonnet. It had taken him a few attempts to pass his driving test, but despite all his achievements, the greatest moment of his life came in the same decade as all these glorious comic successes, on the day that he received his HGV licence. 'The thrill of making two thousand people in a theatre laugh is but a light breeze compared to the tornado of excitement that I felt at that moment,' he admits. 'I've always been a bit of a loner and lorry driving is a loner's dream. I love the sense of power and responsibility. I suppose it reveals a suppressed megalomania . . .'

Parte the Second:

THE TUDOR
BASTARD

enry Tudor was a very clever bastard – albeit one who was, strictly speaking, born in wedlock. John Lennon claimed that 'You have to be a bastard to make it, and that's a fact,' and if 'making it' comprises ending the aristocratic civil war that would come to be known as the War of the Roses and establishing a new royal dynasty in the back-stabbing environment of medieval England, then Henry, Earl of Richmond, more than deserves the bastard crown.

When the Black Prince, eldest son of Edward III, succumbed to illness in 1376, leaving his infant son Richard on the verge of inheriting the kingdom, a course was set which would lead to the end of centuries of solid hereditary rule, in favour of the worst culture of crown-grabbing among the big nobs since King Stephen took on the Empress Matilda. Henry Bolingbroke, son of the Black Prince's powerful kid brother John of Gaunt, felt compelled to flex his muscles and usurp the rightful but inept monarch Richard II, and in the process opened up a whole new world of opportunity for blue bloods – not just in warfare, but propaganda. Terry Jones has made it his business to try and see through the lies, and reveals, 'There's a couple of Northern Chronicles where at some point somebody takes over and says, "There's a lot of stuff written here that shouldn't have been written! Henry's a jolly good man!" I'm sure it's ex-Archbishop Thomas Arundel who creates this propaganda, to make out that Richard was a tyrant, and Henry was welcomed by the majority of English people. And he rewrites history! He puts out this spin, he wants the chroniclers to fall over backwards to write propaganda for Henry.'

By the time Henry's soppy namesake grandson was barely balancing the British crown on his head in the mid-fifteenth century, the extended British royal family were embroiled in a vicious loop of ambition, treachery, bloodshed, exile, invasion and murder, with each move awaiting a write-up from some chronicler or other, for some faction or other. Grabbing the crown was one thing, but keeping it safe from an uppity third cousin with a chip on his shoulder and an army on his payroll was quite another. Convincing all posterity that you are the one and only true King of England required a hugely impressive flair for lies and obfuscation.

As has become apparent only in recent times, few people could deny that in the 1480s no man more deserved the throne than Richard III. Thanks in many ways to Richard's own military skill, his elder brother Edward IV had maintained a pretty strong grip on the kingdom for twenty years (bar several months in exile at half-time). Having finally seen off John of Gaunt's Lancastrian descendants (securing his claim as grandson of Gaunt's little brother Edmund), Edward proved to be a whore-mongering yob of a despot. However, crucially, a discovery made by Dr Michael K. Jones during the filming of Tony Robinson's Channel 4 documentary *Fact or Fiction – Richard III* in 2004 makes it rather fanciful to dispute that Edward IV, and therefore his children, the 'Princes in the Tower' and indeed every monarch for the last five hundred years, were all complete bastards, without any genuine hereditary claim to the throne at all. Records at Rouen Cathedral made the ancient rumour that Edward was the result of his mother's knee-trembler with a Welsh archer while her husband Richard of York was away on campaign far more than gossip. When he died (quite possibly poisoned by his ambitious in-laws) in 1483, at last a true-blue descendant of Edward III could rule – the handy younger son whose personal motto had always been 'Loyalty Binds Me'.

Ricardians have worked tirelessly (and indeed tiresomely) to point out the justice of Richard's claim and the injustice of his defamed legacy for so long that the jolly depiction of the King in the Blackadder Chronicles no longer seems at all outlandish. It's universally accepted that the hunchbacked bloodthirsty baddie so indelibly glued into the nation's psyche by Shakespeare, to the delight of Henry VII's ginger granddaughter, is a bad joke. A lick of black paint on the shoulder of an official portrait here, an imaginatively damning reconstruction of his reign by Sir Thomas More there, and Dirty Dick became an official bogeyman, By Royal Appointment. Admittedly, Richard did himself few favours PR-wise by putting himself in the frame for the murder of his nephews in the Tower, but then his one fatal error was to be killed at the Battle of Bosworth in 1485. Until then, he had done all he could to secure the crown, and clear away all false claimants.

Henry Tudor himself had only the most pitiful claim to the throne, being a Welsh descendant of Henry V's widow on his father's side, and from a line of Plantagenet bastards, the Beauforts, on his mother's. He got round this by marrying Edward's daughter Elizabeth, but as the daughter of a bastard herself, she also had about as much claim to the throne as the privy-scrubbers, making the entire Tudor dynasty – right of conquest aside – illegitimate. To have thrived as King on such laughably shaky credentials, fighting off pretenders from all sides, is remarkable – but could Tudor have been hiding more? Was even his right of conquest a forgery, having simply strolled into an empty castle stacked high with the poisoned bodies of every Yorkist in line to the throne (bar the easily overpowered Lord Percy, Duke of Northumberland), and just taken over? Is it conceivable that his propaganda skills extended to convincing the whole of Christendom that an entire reign had not taken place, and that there had been no Richard IV at all?

Being a royal child in the late Middle Ages was far from being all larks. Even resembling a blue-eyed legitimate Yorkist could earn you the attentions of some disaffected nobleman, ready to claim you as his own puppet King, one of the two Princes miraculously saved from execution – and Henry VII would make mincemeat of you in the end. Lambert Simnel and Perkin Warbeck, both famed pretenders to be demolished by Tudor one way or another, established legends of their own despite the propaganda machine. It's generally believed that the sickly uncrowned Edward V may have died in youth anyway, but his hale and hearty monkey of a little brother, Richard of Shrewsbury – twelve years old at the time of his disappearance, by existing records – became a prime target for treasonous romance. It's also alleged that a bastard son of Richard III could have been legitimised on Dick's triumph at Bosworth (he is said to have lived out his life as a bricklayer in Essex), but if Tudor *had* been vanquished on 22 August 1485, and Richard III subsequently died, the teenage Shrewsbury would have been a cert for the crown. Had he been alive.

That this theoretical Richard IV could conceivably have had two sons in their early twenties (born a decade before him, by official record) is an undeniable complication. The historian J. H. W. Lloyd suggested that Henry VII's management of the switchover to the Gregorian calendar at the end of the fifteenth century explained away the apparent inconsistencies of the Blackadder Chronicles, but to imagine the ramifications of deleting at least a couple of decades of British history does tend to make the brain ache.

But then, why would the Blackadder family falsify this claim? The figure of Edmund, Duke of Edinburgh (1461–99), that emerges from their Chronicles is hardly a dashing Hotspur of an ancestor to crow about – even his famed nom de plume is accredited to a peasant, Baldrick. This naming in itself causes problems for the Blackadder history, which also records that Edmund was the bastard son of Donald, Third Duke of Argyll,* and took on the 'Black Adder' moniker independently. This is clearly at odds with the family history, which claims to trace the Blackadder bloodline back to pre-Roman Britain, and includes

---

* The nobleman's true identity has escaped public record.

the Domesday compiler the Duc d'Blackadder and inept crusader the Baron de Blackadder. Unless Argyll was a Blackadder bastard himself, it seems safe to assume that one of the few Blackadder kin who were not hiding from the dangers of the Yorkist/Lancastrian wars was also intimately acquainted with Edmund's mother, Gertrude of Flanders.* It can only be presumed that the servant Baldrick had heard of such gossip, and cunningly gave his master his true birth name by stealth.

The question remains as to why this forefather of the Blackadder who either commissioned or wrote the Blackadder Chronicles was clearly shown to be such a loser – arriving late for the Battle of Bosworth, ignored by the royal line into which he had been falsely sown, and presumably only managing to pass on his genes and create his own bastard due to some freak moment of passion involving mistaken identity. The only reason for the record of his exploits can be because, by sheer default, this Edmund was indeed King of England, although for only thirty seconds.

As the first academic to gain access to the Chronicles, J. H. W. Lloyd admitted that the endlessly revised history is an exhausting tangle of self-aggrandising lies and exaggeration peppered with embarrassing moments of candour and unintended confession, thanks to what the historian termed 'long-winded tirades where the various authors furiously insist on absolving themselves from any blame for such events as the crash of the R101, the Indian Mutiny, the loss of the American colonies or the sinking of the Lusitania. Since no such involvement had ever occurred to one, one can only assume that all these things were in some way the fault of the Blackadder in question.' It's fair to assume, then, that the Blackadder Chronicler was not overly occupied with constructing a wholly believable series of hagiographies, or lacked the skill to do so. But if these Chronicles have any one aim, it is to try to establish a strong case for the family's rightful claim to the English crown. Perhaps the

---

* You can also save yourself the bother of checking for Gertrude in the official records.

undeniably unflattering biography of the original 'King Edmund III'* was written in such a way as to add credence to his place in the annals of our history. Certainly, all subsequent Blackadders celebrated in the family journal would be depicted in a far more flattering light.

So is this one central claim as much a sham as so many of the Blackadder Chroniclers' boasts? Professor Justin Pollard, as well as being the History elf for *QI*, is one of cinema's most in-demand historical experts, having built a career on sniffing out fact from fiction for movies such as *Elizabeth* and *Atonement*, and when faced with the 'alternative history' of 1485–99, states: 'The political intricacies of the Wars of the Roses do pose substantial problems to qualified historians, problems which take on yet more gargantuan proportions when placed in the hands of the writers and putative "keepers" of the Blackadder Chronicles. The characterisation of Edward IV as "a huge, whoremongering yob of a despot" is somewhat at odds with what we know of this brilliant military leader and sophisticated statesman. Furthermore, J. H. W. Lloyd's contention that the otherwise wholly unrecorded Blackadder monarch can be fitted into the royal chronology by docking twenty years from that century fails to account for the fact that centuries have a relentless habit of lasting a hundred years, or that the Gregorian calendar did not exist before 1582 and was not adopted in Britain until 1752.'

Of course, not being allowed access to the Chronicles in full, it's only natural that many historians will take such a cynical view. It certainly takes a great deal more effort to construct a scenario in which a single word of the history of Prince Edmund could be true than it does to take Henry VII's word for it, and fall into line with canonical Tudor history. But that, it should go without saying, is just what Tudor always hoped would be the case.

---

* After two Saxon kings, including the tenth-century King Edmund, blandly named 'the deed-doer'.

Chapter Two

THE BLACK ADDER

We few, we happy few, we band of ruthless bastards!
All for one — and each man for himself!

By 1982, Rowan Atkinson was an established Prince of Comedy — indeed, the establishment took him to their hearts — and the spoils of his rise were there to be revelled in. After an extensive period of seeking a habitable castle to call his home, he gave up and settled into a handsome rectory in Oxfordshire, where he lived with his girlfriend, Leslie Ash, one of Britain's most idolised young actresses. He was the unmistakable star of the BBC's hottest comedy in a generation, and was even contracted to appear alongside Sean Connery in his shock return to the role of James Bond, in *Never Say Never Again* — specifically added to the movie at the last minute by writers Dick Clement and Ian La Frenais to capitalise on his popularity. Admittedly his eventual performance as weedy MI6 pen-pusher Nigel Small-Fawcett remains Atkinson's least favourite — 'There aren't many things I look back on with dismay, but that was one. There was something so clichéd about it. I was hoping to have done a character rather than a caricature' — but it showed that a movie career could be no idle dream for him.

There had been setbacks — his show for the 1980 Edinburgh Fringe, coming halfway between the second and third series of *Not*, hadn't sat well with the critics, many of whom saw the TV star as an interloper, as he complained to Michael Dale. 'They will tend, like the record press, to praise anyone who's unknown and pour large buckets of excreta over anyone who is known. Indeed that's how most of our media thrive and that was the first time I'd experienced the backlash of fame. In terms of the rest of the country, I was still just budding, but in terms of the Fringe I was virtually a failure.' Despite this, he was happy to accept a place on the board of directors for the Fringe, and would return often, with or without a show.

I Spurn You As I Would Spurn a Rabid Dog!

Two series bookended 1980, putting John and Rowan on the BAFTA stage for the first time, with the latter claiming the Light Entertainment Performance Award, but there was no series of *Not* for the whole of 1981. Through his live shows, the upward trajectory of Atkinson's career did not waver. November 1980 saw his Royal Variety Performance debut, and it wouldn't be long after that he was named the Royal Variety Club Showbiz Personality of the Year. A four-month UK tour in the autumn had given his fans a chance to see what he did best – as he told the *Daily Mail*, in his own estimation, 'I'm just not at my best on television, working around the clock for sketches which last two minutes at the most; all that whiz, bang, crash stuff. I much prefer the stage where I can stretch myself and really develop my act.'

The combination of well-travelled Fringe material, brand-new sketches and *Not* hits was ultimately commemorated on vinyl, as *Rowan Atkinson Live in Belfast*, recorded at the Grand Opera House in September, and rushed out for Christmas 1980. In this one-and-a-half-man show, Atkinson was of course accompanied by Curtis in the two-handers, while Goodall joined them on the road to provide the music for classic numbers like 'Do Bears Sha La La' and his solo spot, 'I Hate the French'. Ever the technician, however, Rowan always prepared his own sound-effects tapes at home.

'The Ranting Man' turned up to berate the audience for paying to see the 'rubber-faced twat', but bottoms still filled seats in their droves, with Atkinson's Oxford homecoming an especial riot. Atkinson and Curtis's sketches tended to be low-key affairs, episodes centred on the tiniest details of life, such as being stuck behind a student in the post office, but the new monologues gave Rowan far more metaphysical scope, especially the sketch eventually called 'Welcome to Hell', in which his louche, acerbic Devil, Toby, showcased the performer's unique skill with casual invective.

TOBY: Now, you're all here for Eternity, which I
hardly need tell you is a sod of a long time,
so you'll get to know everyone pretty well by
the end, but for now I'm going to have to split
you up into groups . . . Murderers, over here,
thank you. Looters and Pillagers – over there.
Thieves, if you could join them, and Bank
Managers . . . Sodomites, over there against
the wall. Atheists! Atheists? Over here, please.
You must be feeling a right bunch of charlies
. . . OK, and Christians! Christians? Ah yes,
I'm sorry, I'm afraid the Jews were right.

Toby's taunting would come in handy throughout the decade, an audience favourite cheered at the first sight of a pair of horns on Rowan's head, as the crowd looked forward to being berated just as they were by his Schoolmaster. For more general cries of abuse, they had to wait for the last of the trilogy of speeches in 'The Wedding', or 'With Friends Like These . . .' Richard noticed, as his twenties progressed, that most of his Saturdays tended to be earmarked for one wedding after another, as individuals from his troops of friends began to pair off and demand free kitchen utensils. Naturally the monotony of weekly church services gave him plenty of time to study the archetypes, and Rowan's resultant turns as a tiresomely groovy Vicar, utterly clodhopping Best Man and drunken, bitter Father of the Bride were only the beginning of the writer's obsession with nuptials:

FATHER: Ladies and gentlemen, and friends of my daughter . . . There comes a time in every wedding reception when the man who paid for the damn thing is allowed to speak a word or two of his own . . . Primarily, I'd like to take this opportunity, pissed as I may be, to say a word or two about Martin. As far as I'm concerned, my daughter could not have chosen a more delightful, charming, witty, responsible . . . wealthy? Let's not deny it . . . well-placed, good-looking and fertile young man than Martin as her husband. And I therefore ask the question: why the hell did she marry Gerald instead? . . . As for his family, they are quite simply the most intolerable herd of steaming social animals I have ever had the misfortune of turning my nose up to. I spurn you as I would spurn a rabid dog! . . . I would like to propose a toast: To the caterers!

The show settled into the Globe Theatre (now the Gielgud) in a new guise directed by Mel Smith, headed *NOT Not the Nine O'Clock News But . . . Rowan Atkinson in Revue – With Richard Curtis and Howard Goodall* – but few punters paid much attention to the latter duo. Curtis cycled from his flat in Camden to the theatre night after night, onstage for at least an hour feeding Atkinson lines, blinking in the lights and cursing his anonymity. 'My greatest hero, David Bowie, came backstage after one show, and was introduced to me. He had no idea who I was. He had been watching me for nearly an hour but my face didn't ring any bells at all – he assumed I had been the stage manager and congratulated me on how efficient the scene changes had been.' This was the final gasp of Curtis's long-held thespian dream – he admitted his job was to 'look as ordinary as possible all of the time', but the snubs got to him – one night, playing the blind man in the prototype Mr Bean sketch in which Rowan tried to change into swimming trunks without detection, Atkinson's forced absence from the stage presented an opportunity for the writer: 'I was alone, onstage, in the West End – the moment I'd dreamed of all my life. I left a big pause. Then crossed my legs. Huge laugh. Another pause. I did it again. Smaller laugh. And again. No laugh at all. By the time Rowan returned, to tumultuous applause, my desire for an acting career had died forever. So I gave up, definitely, once and for all, and accepted that writing was my game.'

The idea of this twenty-something trio on the road suggests all sorts of antics, but Goodall remembers very little in the way of debauchery; in fact the reception Rowan received on every date of the tour made the experience quite odd. 'You're touring with one of the great comic geniuses of the century, you're all twenty-two and you're three friends. So how do you handle that? Because obviously the minute Rowan walks onstage, he has three thousand people in the palm of his hand; it's an extraordinary gift. We don't really discuss it very much, but that's what's happening. I think the rest of us found it quite difficult to adjust to the fact that he was becoming very famous very quickly, and we were still who we were. So there was quite a lot of adjustment to be done, especially for Rowan. Difficult for him to get used to his friends always wondering whether he was going to buy the meal or not.'

Besides his own show, Atkinson made time for the numerous charitable gigs which called for his patronage – *The Secret Policeman's*

Other Ball found him rubbing shoulders with Alexei Sayle, Billy Connolly and Victoria Wood, appearing in more sketches with Cleese and Footlights classics like 'Top of the Form', as well as donning the surplice once again for Curtis's *Not* sketch 'Divorce Service'.

But closer ties to a new generation of performers, who already made Atkinson seem like one of the old guard, came from the *Not* team's appearance on a show in June called *Fundamental Frolics*, staged by 'Schoolmaster' scribe Richard Sparks in support of learning disability charity Mencap. A duo new to the Comedy Store called 20th Century Coyote were given eight minutes on the bill, but their blisteringly insane, inane blend of extreme violence and crap gags about gooseberries in lifts ended up stunning the crowds for more than double their allotted time. For Atkinson, this act was the most electrifying new brand of humour he'd seen since, well, his own. But for his part, Rik Mayall was happy to announce, 'We were very anti *Not the Nine O'Clock News* – we reckoned that we were the best because we were doing cabaret and not revue. Revue was a dirty word, and so was Oxbridge, we had a down on the Pythons . . . although we secretly all thought that the Pythons were great, and half of us were red-brick and university anyway.'

RICHARD MICHAEL MAYALL
BORN: 7 March 1958, Harlow, Essex

Richard Mayall grew up in Droitwich Spa from the age of three, the second son born to drama teachers John and Gillian, with two younger sisters completing the family. With his parents' background there was a certain inevitability about young Rik's fascination with theatre, but it was no guarantee of the academic skill which would put him two years ahead of his contemporaries, starting his secondary education at the King's School, Worcester, at the age of nine, and immersing himself in school drama, with and without his parents' supervision. 'I used to do shows after school with mates – it was also a way of getting off games. We used to do absurdist drama, mainly – *Waiting for Godot*, a bit of Pinter, *Rosencrantz & Guildenstern are Dead*, *Endgame*, *The Real Inspector Hound* – good fun to perform, and would have a bit of an impact on the teachers and the parents. Those plays are quite significant because you can be very serious by being funny . . . that was mainly where I developed my distaste for being serious.'

Being just another face among the freshers on his arrival at Manchester University in 1976 predictably did nothing to cow the ebullient show-off, who dripped with confidence gained from years in the spotlight. Forming an anarchic theatrical group with the more worldly Adrian Edmondson in his first year, the then five-man-strong 20th Century Coyote tried and failed to get Equity cards by putting on semi-improvised plays in the university canteen, but became famous on campus in the meantime, staging forgotten dramas such as *God's Testicles*, *How to Get a Man Out of a Bag*, *Who is Dick Treacle?* and *King Ron & His Nubile Daughter*. 'We were doing a half- to three-quarter-hour show every two weeks,' he recalls, 'so we had personas that we could do best – I was best at being angry and petulant and selfish and a nuisance and ugly and unpopular. Adrian generally played either heavies or women.'

These plays greatly honed Rik & Ade's comedic chops, while a tour of the USA with the Oxford and Cambridge Shakespeare Company sharpened Rik's straight acting skills – but this was no help in finding work after he graduated with a 2:2. 'I was living in Droitwich with my parents and working in a foundry during the whole of 1979. Adrian and I did a show every month or two; we put together a show called *Death on the Toilet* – I played God and Death, and Adrian played a character called Edwin.' Taking this play to Edinburgh that August – and actually making money – was the spark that showed Mayall that he had to leave home and start performing professionally. By now 20th Century Coyote was reduced to just Rik & Ade, but their audition to replace the popular Fundation comedy group (including a fledgling Hale & Pace) at the Woolwich Tramshed showed that the years the duo had spent honing their brand of lavatorial absurdism put them in a class of their own – until, that is, they moved on to the Comedy Store and met Peter Richardson and Nigel Planer, performing as the Outer Limits. But even among this group, Mayall glaringly stood out as a unique entertainer.

⚜

Although Ade Edmondson's brand of nihilistic stupidity made him a tricorned ginger icon of eighties comedy almost as quickly as Mayall himself, there was something about Rik's bravado, ambition and nostril-flaring, bogey-wiping demeanour which seemed to push him to the front, right from the start of their careers. He quickly found himself an agent who set him up for a flurry of tiny movie roles including a memorable cameo playing dominoes in the Slaughtered Lamb in *An American Werewolf in London*, as well as being taken under the wing of Paul Jackson.

Jackson was a comedy boss from a completely different school to John Lloyd, the son of a TV producer who had started out as a runner on *The Two Ronnies* in the early seventies and worked his way up to become producer and director of the show as well as working on a host of mainstream favourites like *The Generation Game*. He became the first producer to put his budget where his mouth was and bring the most exciting regulars at the Comedy Store to TV in their own vehicles, starting with two special shows broadcast one year apart named *Boom Boom Out Go the Lights*, which showcased Mayall's turn as an undeservingly arrogant poet, alongside Nigel Planer as a terrible hippy musician, plus Pauline Melville, Alexei Sayle and Keith and Tony Allen*.

---

* At the same time, revealing the duality of Jackson's career, Rik showed up as a guest on *The Cannon & Ball Show*.

Mayall's first fully formed TV creation, however, came via the unlikely patronage of BBC Scotland. The early eighties saw a steady stream of shows hoping to take on *Not*, offering a topical sketchbook with a limited licence to offend. A *Kick Up the Eighties* was a Colin Gilbert production – the script editor for *Not*, Gilbert would eventually score a hit with *Naked Video*, but this prototype sketch show had less of a Scottish flavour. The first series was rather unpromisingly linked by the far from Alternative Richard Stilgoe, but for the sketches Tracey Ullman headed the cast (fresh from Jackson's *Three of a Kind*), backed up by two more experienced comic performers – Miriam Margolyes, finally getting a chance to showcase her skills in visual comedy, and Roger Sloman, five years after his creation of the hideous Keith in Mike Leigh's *Nuts in May*. By the second series in 1984, they were joined by a burly Scotsman with impressive versatility, Anthony 'Robbie' McMillan.*

Entirely separate to A *Kick Up the Eighties'* sketches were the weekly 'investigations' from Kevin Turvey. Kevin's bizarre rants, centred on the mind-numbing minutiae of his life as a young unemployed self-styled investigator from the duller part of Redditch, entwined with moments of surreal surprise, made for one of the most difficult to categorise comic characters – though 'bastard son of E. L. Wisty' would be a starting point – Mayall himself told Roger Wilmut in *Didn't You Kill My Mother-*

---

* McMillan was born in South Lanarkshire in 1950, although thanks to a public-school education at Glenalmond College ('the Eton of Scotland'), paid for by his doctor father, he was ridiculed for his posh accent when he enrolled at Glasgow Art School in the late sixties. In truth, Robbie despised the public-school system and rebelled at every opportunity, even though he was also a popular figure, playing rugby for the school and becoming head of the debating society. Also, like Rowan Atkinson, at a young age he developed an insatiable passion for the internal combustion engine. His studies in Glasgow centred on painting and film, but before graduation he had already decided that the latter was his true medium, especially in front of the camera, and so began a long decade of working on the fringes of Scottish theatre and comic improvisation in Glasgow nightclubs, having taken his stage name in honour of his jazz hero John Coltrane. It wasn't until the start of the following decade that Robbie Coltrane moved south and began to pick up bigger comic roles.

in-Law?, 'My comedy is a lot less pointed than other people's – the meaninglessness of my comedy is really the message. There's hardly ever any constructive message in there . . . I don't deal in words and rational ideas. I deal in the unusual, the exciting, the very personal . . .'

Before long Mayall and Edmondson had moved from the Store to the Comic Strip, to form a solid team of new comedians, each one ready to find a place for their humour on TV, as Rik had already managed, to an extent. Kevin Turvey may be an undervalued part of British Comedy history, but he remains the one thing most people remember about *A Kick Up the Eighties*. Though several writers worked for both shows, and Sean Hardie himself was executive producer for the first series[*], none of the new pretenders could compete with *Not's* ongoing success. With the fourth series lined up for the start of '82, Lloyd and Hardie called their team together to lay out future plans.

Why Don't You Grow Up, You Bastards?

'We had an empire, we had a franchise,' laments Lloyd, 'and what I wanted to do was break into America, and I wanted to do movies, and, you know, make something that would last forever. Sean and I asked the cast to dinner, and the proposal we were going to make was that we were going to do exactly what the Pythons had done, when they started Monty Python Productions.' With everyone gathered, however, Rowan had to offer an apology – in not so many words. 'You're all very nice people,' he began, 'and I like you a great deal and you're all very talented . . . but I've talked to my agent, and he thinks that I shouldn't play with the second eleven any more.'

Jaws dropped all around the table. 'You won't get Rowan being rude to people,' Lloyd insists, 'he doesn't do rude to people. He was passing

---

[*] Plus a sublime forty-minute spin off, *Kevin Turvey: The Man Behind the Green Door*, starring Rik, Ade and Robbie

on a remark . . . He then left the restaurant and everybody else got fantastically drunk, because we all thought that was the end of our careers, basically. And we had to go in the next day and be polite to each other in rehearsal, which was pretty tricky.' The BBC's thirtieth-anniversary tribute of the debut, *Not Again*, did allow Atkinson a belated apology, when he jovially admitted, 'Retrospectively, I'd like to apologise for my high-handed attitude towards the whole thing.' But the fact remains that back in 1982 he had big plans: movies to make, and perhaps – like many a great comic keen to cement their place in comedy history – a solo sitcom vehicle which he and Curtis had already begun to toss back and forth. They were done with sketch comedy, as the third member of their trio, Howard Goodall, reflects today: 'It would have been an odd thing had he stayed in a topical weekly TV show forever. You're talking much more Chaplin, Jacques Tati-type character. Rowan needed to find a bigger, wider stage to play on. And boy, did he . . .'

Nevertheless, there were still six episodes slated to begin broadcast in February, so it was time for everyone to watch their backs, look to their own futures, and get back to work. It was more than a year since the third series had closed on a muted note – being broadcast a week after the murder of John Lennon, the screen had finally cut to black and 'In My Life' played as the credits rolled.* Despite this long time away, the fourth and final series of *Not* hit the ground running, every episode packed with sketches which were soon to become classics.

Most people nowadays only know *Not the Nine O'Clock News* as an array of differing compilations or, of course, audio highlights (many taken from the fourth series). It may be that the rights holders fear that twenty-first-century sensibilities might be offended by some of the gags in uncut episodes, which could be construed as racist or

---

* On the list was a first ever writing credit for one 'Steven Fry', who had supplied one of many quickies poking fun at the mind-blowing new technology of electric handdryers.

homophobic. There's no denying that everyone on the team was happy to offend, but what is naughty in one decade can seem scandalous in another (such as Toby's order to the sodomites in Hell, or the free use of the term 'spastic' in much of British comedy at this time). On the other hand, perhaps it's considered that a full DVD release would be a commercial flop because the topical references would mean nothing over thirty years on – as if a Britain in which a Tory government were making ruinous cuts in public spending, provoking zooming levels of unemployment and mass protest, and having a royal wedding to help distract the populace, would seem to be an alien world to modern Britons. But the original broadcasts still stand up, peppered as they are with celebrated moments (the final series' opener concludes with Curtis and Goodall's epic New Romantic lampoon 'Nice Video, Shame About the Song') and forgotten jewels (Mel Smith running a company which offers job creation schemes for human sofas, hatstands and pencil sharpeners). By the time the final sketch (the Youth TV spoof, 'Hey Wow', featuring a leotarded Atkinson as the mime artist Alternative Car Park) had descended into bedlam, there was no doubt that the *Not* team were going out on a high. The punning finale, the valedictory ballad 'Kinda Lingers' (another Curtis/Goodall original), was filmed in the cold industrial atmosphere of Bankside Power Station, and closed with Atkinson quite fittingly cutting transmission with a hefty turn of a valve. After three years and twenty-seven episodes, that was the end of *Not the Nine O'Clock News*.

John Lloyd had to let his empire kinda linger a little longer, however – a book covering the 1983 election was published, and with Douglas's help, he put out two *Not*-themed calendars. Despite their late-seventies contretemps, Lloyd and Adams did some of their best work in the eighties*, with the calendars giving birth to *The Meaning of Liff*

---

* John had also sent the internal BBC memo which led to the *H2G2* TV series, and was on standby to produce until *Not* filled up his schedule, though he received an 'Associate Producer' credit.

comic dictionaries, rated by John as his favourite creations. The odd comedy book continued to surface under the *Not* banner, with Lloyd and Hardie collaborating on *Prince Harry's First Quiz Book* as late as 1985. A vastly different US spin-off for HBO, *Not Necessarily the News*, on the other hand, ran quite successfully for several years without any input from either Sean or John.

The final gasp from the original team was the live show *Not in Front of the Audience*, a farewell concert staged in Oxford and at the Drury Lane Theatre, where on 29 April a recording was made for the last *Not* double album. This theatrical swansong came only a month after the last episode was broadcast, and was necessarily boosted in topicality due to the Falklands War, which had begun in the interim, and would be over by June. Although constructed from brand-new material (albeit including the old joke about being 'well hung'), the team allowed themselves the return of a few favourite characters and sketches, Rowan reprising his outrageous sex-obsessed French critic, an extra-foul-mouthed 'Ranting Man' and Zak, the friendly alien with a malfunctioning translator.

With the last bows taken that night, the unusual quartet went their separate ways – although Rowan would remain close to regular collaborator Mel, whose years of comically successful partnership with Griff would also lead to massive financial success with the setting up (and flogging off) of their production company Talkback. *Not* was never a love-in, and both Smith and Atkinson would have difficult relationships with Stephenson, but three decades on, Rowan's memories of the time tend towards the fond. 'What I do remember about those days was the fantastic freedom you felt at that age to do and try anything,' he reflects, 'There was none of this sort of angst which one feels later on in life, where you think, "Now is this the kind of character I should be playing at this stage in my career?" You just sort of busked it. If it worked then everybody took the credit, and if it didn't work then nobody took the blame.' He adds, however, 'I think it stopped at the right time. I think if you're going to carry on with that idea, you have to do something a little different. Either you have to bring new people in, or lose some people, or take it in a different direction . . .' His own new direction was sitcom, although taking on the might of a popular and artistic triumph like *Fawlty Towers*, even four years after its final episode, was a task which neither he nor Curtis savoured. 'For some reason we started to think about the possibility of writing a sitcom together, for me to perform or be a major character in. And I remember we both felt the sort of scourge of *Fawlty Towers*, which was, and remains, fantastically funny. And it was sort of hanging over us as something to which we were bound to be unfavourably compared. We were fairly convinced that whatever we did, set in the modern day, was going to be described as a pale imitation.'

Curtis was beginning to shape a contemporary crime series, pitched unpromisingly as '*Fawlty Towers* meets *Starsky & Hutch*', centring on Atkinson as a lawyer's clerk who turns detective after a spate of bicycle thefts in Camden Town. *Not* had already sent up the state of situation comedy back in its second series, presenting the BAFTA Award for Best Sofa in a cosy suburban sitcom, so something a little grittier than *That's My Boy* was required. As Atkinson explained to the *Sun* in 1989, 'We wanted to go the opposite way from the usual sitcoms and thought a bit of crime would give the comedy an edge.' But after a series of wrestling matches with a rudimentary script, they had to agree that it wasn't going to work. There was just something tawdry about such a low-key premise, and they thought that the more epic their idea was, the better chance it had of being a hit. Then, as Atkinson was to recall, 'Errol Flynn came to the rescue . . .'

A daytime showing of the 1938 film *The Adventures of Robin Hood* lit a spark for the duo: if it was murder and skulduggery they wanted, after years of topical sketches, what could be a cleaner break than a medieval tights-and-codpiece spoof? 'I remember the *Robin Hood* movie was a touchstone for us,' Atkinson revealed twenty years later.

81

'We thought it was definitive in terms of its way of presenting – albeit in a slightly Hollywoodesque way – the excitement of that time, of the fifteenth century.' Not that the powers that be offered them any encouragement. 'We were very strongly advised that the two things that absolutely never, ever worked – and everybody tried – was sitcoms set in heaven, and historical sitcoms,' Curtis remembers, 'but, um, we ignored the advice. The reason we did the historical one was twofold. We did it because I just couldn't imagine putting Rowan in a jacket and being anything but embarrassed by how much less funny he was than Basil Fawlty; and second, we liked the idea of big plots! Death and carnage and kings and princes and chaos, rather than just writing about your car breaking down.' The duo had form with mocking historical drama – a regular part of their live shows was Curtis's Shakespearean lecture, with all the laughs coming from Rowan's mimed illustration of every point, while Richard droned, 'At the centre of the Elizabethan world, sits the King. Upon the character of the King depends the plot, and so there are many different kinds of King. The benign King . . . The benign King with a physical defect . . . The benign King with two physical defects . . .' and so on.

Everything Rowan turned his talent to tended to emerge as a unique animal, no matter how many footsteps he was treading in, but he and Curtis must have been well aware of the rich tradition of which they were planning to become a part. What made historical comedy so verboten to comedy commissioners in the early eighties, and how could they make it work this time, and keep the Atkinson star in the ascendant?

Historical Comedy Through Comedy History

Ever since the first nomadic hunter-gatherers swapped Neanderthal impressions around the fire, it's been a reflex action, part of the subversive side of human nature, to laugh at the past. When Shakespeare depicted the fifteenth century Lollard Sir John Oldcastle as a drunken coward fit for the finest clown to play, he was writing historical comedy – although Oldcastle's Elizabethan descendants were litigious enough to compel the playwright to change the name to Falstaff after the first run of *Henry IV, Part 1*, and before long the character became the Elizabethan equivalent of Alf Garnett, Del Boy and Alan Partridge rolled into one.

Another titan of English literature, the big, bearded Yorkshireman Jane Austen, deliberately spoofed his own history tutorage in the posthumously published *History of England*, written when he was just a fifteen-year-old girl. A hundred years later Mark Twain mocked the medieval idea of chivalry in *A Connecticut Yankee in King Arthur's Court* in much the same way that Cervantes had depicted the clash between antiquity and 'modern life' in *Don Quixote* in the sixteenth century. Maybe the single most comprehensive literary send-up of British History, however, came courtesy of *Punch* magazine, which gave rise to the publication of *1066 and All That* in 1930. Combing through the annals of our island history (or 'all the parts you can remember'), humorists W. C. Sellar and R. J. Yeatman provided the template for historical piss-taking for years to come, with a combination of inaccuracy, anachronism and downright silliness which spawned a host of spin-offs.

By this time, historical comedy had already found its way to the screen, notably in *Three Ages*, written, directed and performed by Buster Keaton in 1923. In separate strands designed to be split into shorts if necessary, Keaton showed the unchanging ways of courtship from the Stone Age through Roman times to the hectic city life of the Roaring Twenties – no matter what the period, each incarnation of the long-faced clown still had to fight the heavy and please his prospective in-laws to get his girl. Keaton intended the movie as a burlesque of D. W. Griffiths's *Intolerance*, but then historical comedy is almost always respondent – if not a direct spoof of popular costume drama or historical teachings, then usually a suggestion that there's been quite enough heavy emoting in tights, and it's time to make a mockery.

The first infamous example of this reaction to the kind of early Hollywood romps which made Errol Flynn a star was Danny Kaye's 1955 musical *The Court Jester*, originally a huge flop, but rendered a TV favourite for its Technicolor (indeed, VistaVision!) spectacle and zippy crosstalk ('the vessel with the pestle' ad nauseam). But the setting was all that mattered, and the plot and characters were pure cheap fantasy – accurate English history didn't sell tickets in the Midwest, but tap-dancing in brightly coloured jerkins was a winner. One consequence of the film's total avoidance of existing lore was that the Robin Hood cipher, the brave fighter famed in song for his skills in battle, was known as the Black Fox – perhaps a tribute to Robert Louis Stevenson's historical romp *The Black Arrow*, in which the hero takes his eponymous name when he becomes embroiled in the Wars of the Roses*.

To find the real flowering of home-grown historical comedy, we need to fast-forward to the late 1960s, when the *Carry On* franchise hired a new writer to replace the trusty Norman Hudis, and Peter Rogers snapped up Talbot Rothwell – a trusty joker who had taken up gag-writing as a prisoner of war twenty years earlier, staging noisy revues alongside Peter Butterworth to drown out the sound of tunnelling. Although his first film released turned out to be *Carry On Cabby*, the script which got Rothwell the job was a tale of eighteenth-century highjinks on the high seas, *Carry On Jack*, which triggered a whole new world of period sauce for the continually buoyant series. Rothwell had a passion for historical japery which steered the *Carry Ons* from being a strictly contemporary comedy franchise to a series of irregular period parodies, with the usual team in their familiar roles, transported through time in every other film. Again, these were almost always in

---

* As Stevenson's story was adapted into a rollicking TV drama in the seventies, *The Black Arrow*'s influence on *Blackadder* seems hard to ignore.

reaction to great historical epics of the time, often even using the same costumes and scraps of sets at Pinewood Studios. *Jack* begat the hugely loved Roman epic *Cleo*, with genre spoofs *Cowboy* and *Screaming* to follow, and almost every second or third offering from Sid, Kenneth, Babs and the gang throughout the seventies was historical – the French Revolution, Dick Turpin, Edwardian England and the days of the Raj saw many of the same faces in the same positions no matter what the calendar said, each period lovingly brought to screen on the most economical of budgets.

Henry posed an alternative Tudor history, prefaced with Rothwell's apology: 'This film is based on a recently discovered manuscript by one William Cobbler which revealed the fact that Henry VIII did in fact have two more wives. Although it was at first thought that Cromwell originated the story, it is now known to be definitely all Cobbler's . . . from beginning to end.' This gave them the licence to enjoy the same bawdy set-up as ever – King Sid dealing with battleaxe wives and lusting after pert ladies-in-waiting, while Williams's Cromwell stalks the shadowy corridors, ploddingly plotting away. This being a *Carry On*, however, it's all a fun anachronistic pantomime, as light as the flutes and strings of Eric Rogers's score – when Charles Hawtrey's Sir Roger de Lodgerly is forced on the rack to squeeze out an admission to a bit of slap-and-treason with Joan Sims's garlicky Queen Marie, he stretches like toffee. The Tudor romps also extended to the TV spin-off *Carry On Laughing*, alongside a whole host of historical half-hours in the Rothwell style, which took in medieval England and the Cavalier years. The Dick Vosburgh & Barry Cryer-penned *Orgy & Bess* featured Hattie Jacques as a (naturally) matronly Elizabeth I, flirting with her favourites Raleigh, Essex and Sid James's rascally Sir Francis Drake.

So successful were Talbot Rothwell's historical romps that, just before scripting *Carry On Henry*, he was commissioned by BBC executive Michael Mills to write a brand new vehicle for Frankie Howerd. Howerd had recently enjoyed great success stepping into the sandals of Zero Mostel for the West End run of Sondheim's *A Funny Thing Happened on the Way to the Forum*, and on the plane back from his own holiday in Pompeii, Mills decided that a sitcom starring the comic as a Roman slave, tetchily interacting with the audience just as he did in all his shows, was a dead-cert hit. *Up Pompeii* was Plautus by way of Donald McGill, the desperate antics of Lurcio the British slave gaining handsome ratings and endless repeats of its two series – but it also started the ball rolling for a whole decade or more of further historical titters for Francis, with the bawdy farce spawning a cinema franchise of its own, long after Rothwell had written his last double entendres for unlikely hero Lurcio to quibble over. Ned Sherrin produced a series of movies transporting Howerd through time, from doomed Pompeii to Norman Britain, and ultimately the Great War, in *Up the Front*. Each setting saw a new incarnation for the scheming servant to get one up on his idiotic masters, though scripting duties fell to Sid Colin, backed up by the prime likes of Galton & Simpson and Eddie Braben. In 1971's *Up the Chastity Belt*, the serf Lurkalot dreams of greatness, little knowing that he's the elder twin of Richard the Lionheart, stolen from his cradle by evil barons and left to be brought up by pigs. During his epic tale, the fool Lurkalot dresses as a nun to avoid detection, is tried for witchcraft, meets a limp-wristed band of Merry Men led by Hugh Paddick's camp Robin Hood and by the end of the narrative, the crafty coward finds his way into the royal bedchamber. Despite his royal blood, Lurkalot's twentieth-century descendant Private Lurk was as lowly as ever, hypnotised into joining up to 'Save England', and getting embroiled in a series of lascivious plots which made Flanders during World War I seem like a swingers' holiday camp.

There were several less canonical entries into 'Howerd's History of England' (which itself was the title of a 1974 TV special). *Whoops Baghdad* was an unsuccessful Babylonian attempt to repeat the success of *Up Pompeii*, and the final offering, following the World War II

"THE BLACK ADDER"

by

RICHARD CURTIS

and

ROWAN ATKINSON

EXECUTIVE PRODUCER .... JOHN HOWARD DAVIES
DIRECTOR .... GEOFF POSNER

Production Office 4138 TC Ext:
4816/4817

N.B. THE SENDING OF THIS SCRIPT DOES NOT CONSTITUTE THE
OFFER OF A CONTRACT FOR ANY PART IN IT.

John Lloyd: 'These photographs [this page and following two pages] graphically illustrate how painfully slow the first series was to make.

It was shot without an audience: all young comedy writers go through this stage where they think it would be "better" without one. In my experience, this just means you don't have to work so hard to get the laughs, so it's not as funny.

Because there was no audience seating in the studio, we could have huge sets and put the cameras almost anywhere – this meant it took longer to shoot and (to be honest) none of us really knew what we were doing.

We changed all this for *Blackadder II* – small sets, all the cameras in a line across the "fourth wall", a live audience. Rowan's timing improved at once, the script was much tighter and, as we had to shoot each episode in two hours max, there was no hanging around getting bored – everyone was much too busy!'

To prepare for his time in the saddle of the far-from-trusty Black Satin, Atkinson was sent for extensive training, under the guidance of a Swedish Olympian equestrian – though he subsequently insisted that he learned more from the horse-wrangler on set. Despite all this effort, Ben Elton observed, 'Rowan falling off a horse at 200 metres is not really funnier than anyone else falling off a horse at 200 metres…'

King Brian: 'I had very strong ideas about the King – like he must be a man who never opens the door. So he knocks one down, you build another – if I could, I would like to walk through doors like Tom & Jerry!'

Natasha King, the first Mrs Adder, remembers: 'aged only eight and with my front teeth missing I was over the moon to receive a bouquet of flowers from Rowan Atkinson when filming finished – it did wonders for me in the playground!'

Frank Finlay, one of only two thespians to merit a 'Special Guest' credit in the opening titles, prepares to take the despicable Grumbledook to task.

Peter Cook, the King of Comedy, as Richard III:
'Now is the summer of our sweet content made o'ercast winter by these Tudor clouds…'

exploits of Private Potts in *Then Churchill Said to Me*, was shelved in 1982 due to the Falklands War. There was even a brace of short-lived eighteenth-century spin-offs: the ITV pilot *A Touch of the Casanovas*, and *Up the Convicts*, made for the Seven Network in Australia, which featured Frankie as early colonist Jeremiah Shirk, who no doubt had close ties to the Lurk family. The details of the Lurk dynasty are never explored, though – after all, each incarnation was only an excuse for Howerd to get into period scrapes while enjoying the comedic beard of being surrounded by busty damsels.*

The similarities between the *Up* franchise and *Blackadder* are glaring on the surface, but none of the Rothwell-inspired films and TV shows are tarred with the 'undergraduate humour' brush, belonging to a completely different comedy tradition – saucy music hall by way of the permissive society. The period sitcoms of David Croft, Jimmy Perry and Jeremy Lloyd also broadly belong to this comedy category, but programmes like *Dad's Army*, *It Ain't Half Hot Mum*, *You Rang, M'Lord?*, *'Allo 'Allo*, *Hi-De-Hi!* and *Oh, Doctor Beeching*, as well as often being genre spoofs, more pedantically come under the heading of 'Nostalgia' rather than 'History'.

A more apposite forefather of Atkinson's sitcom would be the 1959 *Beyond the Fringe* sketch 'So That's the Way You Like It'. As masterminded by future celebrated Shakespearean director Jonathan Miller and medieval historian Alan Bennett, the sketch is of course a lampoon of Shakespeare's Histories rather than History itself, taking a step back from the text and recognising its inherent silliness and pomposity – or rather, the difficulty of performing the text effectively without sounding like an idiot.

---

* There was nothing new about a comic playing different members of one vast family tree either – the first star vehicle for *On the Buses* favourite Reg Varney was a children's comedy series in 1964 called *The Valiant Varneys*, which ran for two series looking at a whole host of the cheeky chap's historical ancestors, though sadly every episode was deleted and the show is now officially Missing Believed Wiped.

MILLER: Get thee to Gloucester, Essex. Do thee to
Wessex, Exeter.
Fair Albany to Somerset must eke his route.
And Scroop, do you to Westmoreland, where
shall bold York
Enrouted now for Lancaster, with forces of
our Uncle Rutland,
Enjoin his standard with sweet Norfolk's host . . .
I most royally shall now to bed,
To sleep off all the nonsense I've just said.

One young fan of the sketch who would have the honour of taking over Dudley Moore's Fool role when it was wheeled out for the *Secret Policeman* forerunner *Pleasure at Her Majesty's* was Terry Jones, an English scholar at Oxford when he first saw the revue. His writing partner Michael Palin was the one studying History when they met at the university in the early sixties, and as the fledgling Oxford Revue gave way to budding careers in TV comedy, getting laughs out of British History was often on their minds. In 1967 the pair were hired to create filmed inserts for the live BBC comedy show *Twice a Fortnight*, one of which was the Battle of Hastings in the style of a boxing match. When given the chance to make their own comedy vehicle in between series of Humphrey Barclay's children's show *Do Not Adjust Your Set*, they expanded the idea to a whole series for LWT, *The Complete & Utter History of Britain*. One series in early 1969, posing as a History magazine programme with reports from different epochs, received short shrift from viewers and broadcaster alike, and by the end of the year Palin and Jones were glad to accept the invitation to sign up for the *Flying Circus*.

It would be several years before they would return to a similar clash of ancient Britain and modern manners, with *Monty Python and the Holy Grail*, which is in essence a series of typically silly medieval sketches, made funnier by the gravitas of Jones's pedantic eye for period direction, and Terry Gilliam's muck-encrusted art direction. 'I don't think I ever wanted to *take the piss*,' Jones insists. 'I didn't see *Holy Grail* as being a parody of Knights or anything. I just saw it really as doing silly things in a context that you recognise – and I was very keen on History, because I was into the fourteenth century at the time . . . You had to *feel* the period. But I think it's exactly like *Blackadder*, we're not making fun of History, it's making comedy within a historical context.' Richard Curtis admits that it was this approach which guided him from the start with his historical sitcom idea. 'I suppose if there was any precedent for what we were doing it was *Carry Ons* and *Up Pompeii*, and that must have been something we *didn't* want to do, to make it look as though it had just been knocked up.'

We Need Something . . . More Cunning

Having taken their cue from the Technicolor romps that fuelled a writer's procrastination on daytime TV in the early eighties, Curtis and Atkinson had no real historical spur in plotting out their swashbuckling sitcom. 'It was those sort of medieval Hollywood-type movies that seemed to have the word "black" or the colour red – *The Black Shield of Falworth* or whatever – in front of it. And then . . . God knows where "Adder" came from,' says Curtis. Where these movies starred a handsome hero fighting for honour, it was the twisted bastard anti-hero of Jacobean tragedy that piqued Atkinson's interest – the swaggering murderous wit of Middleton's Vindice, and the ugly ambition of the bastard Edmund in *King Lear*. 'Villains are always more fun to play than good guys,' he says. 'That's a well-known fact. And I enjoy characters who have a vindictiveness in them. I always have done. In the end, it's just more fun . . . You only have to go through a fairly mild public-school education to have witnessed cruelty. If you tried to do what I did, which was to establish your individuality, you become a loner and to some extent I experienced bullying and cruelty. I am a really meek person and keen to please, so I grew up terribly conscious of cruelty. Comedy may well be my way of taking revenge all these years later.'

There was only one person the duo could imagine taking their new script to – the man Curtis at that time considered 'the oldest person I know', their long-time fixer Lloyd. But he was still recovering from the rigours of producing *Not*. 'I worked far too hard on that show; I felt about eighty years old. Then Richard and Rowan came up with this pilot. The original title was *Prince Edmund and his Two Friends* – a rather weedy thing.' John was already producing Pamela's own comedy pilot, *Stephenson's Rocket*, with video director David Mallett, and couldn't commit to both projects – although Stephenson's show would fail to get beyond a pilot. 'I got big-headed,' John recalls, 'thought I was a genius because I'd got a BAFTA Award. We all thought we were geniuses and, of course, the show was absolutely awful.'

Rowan and Richard's pilot script clearly played up to the idea of going beyond the trad sitcom set-up, showing the ideal historical royal family in its very first scene: the almighty King reading scrolls, the ditsy Queen making lace, the foppish elder son Prince Henry . . . painting an apple. But somewhere in the castle, fermenting in his bedroom like any dissatisfied adolescent, is the younger son with eyes on the throne. Like *Lear*'s Edmund, this Duke of York knows that he could take the reins of power far better than his idiotic elder brother, or anyone else for that matter. Atkinson stipulated that this dark plotter was 'a tall, dark, satanic (but hopefully comic) figure in studded black leather, scowling villainously'. His bedroom was packed with horrific instruments of torture, very like the coat of arms that had been designed to open the pilot.* By the Prince's side were the two friends of the original title, idiotic sidekicks completing a trio of treasonous hoodlums. Neither part was at all well developed beyond the fact that both were fall guys:

---

* A frowning serpent circling a crown, with dragons rampant, a host of vicious weapons and emblems of skulls and torture, adorned with the motto *Veni Vidi Castratavi Illegitimos* ('I came, I saw, I castrated the bastards').

the base clown Baldrick, convinced of his own cunning despite his lowly position, and the more inbred Lord Percy, who doubled as the family retainer. Together, their inept plotting and squabbling would bring to mind a medieval Will Hay movie more than anything else: three clods with sliding scales of idiocy, getting caught up in scrapes of their own devising. So many hoary old gags could be done with this set-up: Edmund being cornered by Harry, with the other two miming answers to get him out of trouble, and of course, Baldrick's plans being dismissed and then instantly proposed by his master, to great approval.

Rather than worrying about the boss coming over for dinner or getting into a tricky situation over a pound note, however, this gang would be facing the worst that the Middle Ages could throw at them: battles, duels, the block – an extreme farce indeed. Basil Fawlty may have frequently been wound up, but he never had the option of hacking his customers to pieces.

Ed opens up a cupboard stacked floor to ceiling with every shape and sixe of sharp instrument – swords, daggers . . .

EDMUND: Thieving Scots rat. I'm going to stab him.

BALDRICK: Where?

EDMUND: In the great hall, and in the bladder. (*He is sifting through the selection.*)

PERCY: But if you stab him in front of everyone, won't the finger of blame point rather firmly in your direction?

EDMUND: I don't care. (*He is now toying with one dagger, making stabbing movements, feeling its sharpness, etc.*)

BALDRICK: I think your father likes McAngus and, if he suspected you had harmed him, he'd cut you off without a penny.

EDMUND: Yes, perhaps you're right, we need something
. . . more cunning.

BALDRICK: I have a cunning plan.

EDMUND: Yes, perhaps, but I think I have a more
cunning one.

BALDRICK: Mine's pretty cunning, my Lord.

EDMUND: Yes, but not cunning enough, I imagine.

BALDRICK: Well, it depends how cunning you mean, sir.

EDMUND: Well, I mean pretty damn cunning, how
cunning do you think I mean?

At the recommendation of John Howard Davies, the first adventure for this Black Adder to face – involving a drunken Scots lord, a Royal Command Performance and a cache of dirty letters which throw the King's issue into question – took the catholic route for sitcom of not wasting any time setting up the situation, but jumping right in (Edmund is never even referred to as 'the Black Adder'). The script was undeniably perfunctory, but there was clearly something there, and the two creators persevered without the aid of Lloyd. Luckily they had the patronage of Howard Davies, and together they mounted a pilot, with a studio date set for May.

Some elements of the casting were no-brainers – Percy was written with McInnerny in mind, and even though Tim had embarked on a promising career as a straight actor since Oxford, Curtis knew how to play to his friend's comedic strengths almost as well as he did Atkinson's. Throughout his time at university, Tim was usually in about three plays per term, as well as joining in the revue, and despite any formal training, his career in theatre was blossoming. He once admitted, 'When I left college, there were three parts I saw as benchmarks: Hamlet, Gethin Price and Jack in *The Ruling Class*' – and he played them all before he hit thirty. Nevertheless, Richard has been known to insist that 'Tim has the mind and the voice of Laurence Olivier, but he has the face and the neck of an ostrich,' and his pale, high-browed, stringy-limbed form was just what they wanted for Edmund's snooty foil. McInnerny found that the set-up was entirely to his taste, and snapped up the part. 'It was all skullduggery, swords and poison. It was like Jacobean drama, but funny. One of my favourite episodes was about executing people, whether they're innocent or not . . . It's very sick!'

Noel Gay's artist roster provided freshly graduated Footlighter Robert Bathurst, who was a natural fit for Henry,* while John Savident brought his bulk and comic dourness into play for the King, and for the Queen, Scottish actress Elspet Gray seemed ideal. The wife of famous farceur Brian Rix (he would make her a Lady when given the title of Baron Rix a decade later), Gray would be the only other supporting cast member with McInnerny and guest performer Alex Norton to survive into the actual series.

This still left the rather thankless role of Baldrick – the short serf who balanced out McInnerny's lanky fop – apparently impossible to fill. The long struggle to cast the part wasn't made apparent to jobbing actor Tony Robinson, however, to whom the eventual offer came as manna from heaven. 'I just got a script dropped through my letter box in Bristol, and it was for this new project called *Black Adder*, and there was this part for a servant in it – he only had eight lines, and none of them were funny. But it was an offer! No one just *offered* me parts at that time, I used to have to go up to London and do about nineteen auditions and interviews – and I was terribly flattered . . . All that had happened was that John Howard Davies had seen me a couple of years previously, playing a part I think for BBC Bristol, and had written me down in his book as "small and vaguely humorous", and he was so near the end of his list that he'd suddenly found me and offered me the part because otherwise they wouldn't have been able to make the thing.'

---

* The part would bag him the odd distinction of having two central but short-lived roles in the pilots of huge eighties sitcoms – *Blackadder* and *Red Dwarf*.

TONY ROBINSON
BORN: 15 August 1946, Hackney, London

In his one-man show, *Cunning Night Out* in 2007, Tony Robinson paid tribute to his late father Leslie, a talented jazz pianist from Essex who at seventeen had the dubious honour of being the Assistant Beadle in Britain's very last workhouse, before his life was changed by World War II. The diminutive Leslie was a hard-working member of the RAF ground crew, but was regularly sneered at by the lofty airmen whose lives he helped to maintain. 'He wasn't one of "the few, we happy few",' Tony revealed. 'My dad thought "the few" were tossers.' The war did, however, bring Leslie together with the equally musical Phyllis, and a year after VE Day, their only son was born – they were determined that he would not lack the nurturing which their own talents were denied. Ostensibly, young Tony was educated at the local Wanstead High School, where he eventually passed four O levels, but as a child actor, anything academic was precisely that.

Lionel Bart's musical *Oliver!* opened in the West End in June 1960, and there as part of Fagin's gang of ruddy urchins was the teenage Tony. Young Robinson impressed the management so much that he was swiftly made understudy to the actor playing the Artful Dodger, and illness soon led to him taking on that very role at short notice: 'I shouldn't say this, but I was bloody good . . . for the first four minutes.' Tony's own understudy at the time was Steve Marriott, a fellow child actor and model who was grinning alongside Tony in Fair Isle knitting pattern magazines just a few years before he founded the Small Faces – 'Itchycoo Park' was allegedly inspired by the days the two of them played truant, learning to smoke in Little Ilford Park.

Tony had a busy, successful career in his teens, appearing in the Judy Garland film *Judgement at Nuremberg* in 1961, and in the same year making his BBC debut as Stubbs in *The Man from the Moors* (earning twenty-one guineas, plus another thirteen for his chaperone). Eight years later, after many more theatrical and television roles, training at the Central School of Speech and Drama (where his tutor was Eric Thompson) and four years in rep, a BBC bigwig annotated his file: 'A comic personality. Easy and relaxed and holds one's attention and interest – a young man with a future.'

By this time Robinson, after a short stint as artistic director at the Midlands Art Theatre, had moved to Bristol, tuned in, dropped out, formed a commune and smoked prodigious amounts of weed. He had also settled down with his first serious girlfriend, Mary Shepherd, and their twenty-five-year union produced two children. Their lifestyle was not just about free love and soft drugs, however – Robinson was a highly politicised socialist and activist, with a fervour that was reflected in the work created by the Avon Touring Company, which he co-founded.

Further accolades came from his appearances at the Chichester Festival (which included Feste in *Twelfth Night*), but despite small movie roles, appearing with John Wayne in *Brannigan* in 1975, soon Robinson would become most recognisable as a star of Children's TV, part of the gang on *Play Away* and also *Words and Pictures*, with Miriam Margolyes playing his mother when he took the title role in *Sam on Boffs' Island*. As the eighties arrived, the family man and jobbing actor could be forgiven for feeling that he had gone as far as he could in his career.

One fillip had been the friendship of Terry Pratchett, who had heard Robinson in a spoof show for Radio Bristol and asked him to be the first narrator for the audiobook versions of his *Discworld* novels, which the actor had grown to love as his daughter helped him through a period of depression by reading them aloud to him. Pratchett's worldwide popularity would have made Robinson a footnote in comedy history – but at the age of thirty-six, he still wanted more.

✤

By the eighties, Robinson hadn't had an uneventful acting career. 'I'd had the lead in comedy pilots, I'd done good bits in television plays – there was a drama-doc called *Joey*, a true story about four guys who were incarcerated in a mental hospital during the war and were still there in the fifties, and they didn't have a mental illness, they just had cerebral palsy. We won the Golden Rose of Montreux with that.' But there was no denying, with a young family to support, that a central role in Rowan Atkinson's new sitcom was a very desirable job, and well worth the commute from the West Country . . .

All of which made it all the more annoying for him when industrial action by BBC technical staff that May wiped out any chance of the pilot being filmed. Of course, a vehicle for Atkinson was only ever going to be *postponed*, but by the remounted pilot's recording date, Sunday 20 June, Robinson was already in Greece performing Tragedy with the National Theatre. 'For me at that time to be asked to go to the National anyway was such a pat on the back that although I was gagging to do the *Blackadder* pilot I just couldn't get out of it. And I thought my chances of working with those guys was gone.' In the event, young actor Philip Fox would be thrust into Baldrick's jerkin, and have to make the best of it.

Fox wasn't the only new boy in the remount, however. Geoff Posner – who had been a fledgling director on the fourth series of *Not* – was drafted in to put the show together with little notice, a task which made him, in his own words, 'scared shitless. I got the script and thought, "Blimey, I've bitten off more than I can chew here!" It was a very complicated thing, and it all had to be done in the studio. But I remembered Rowan, John and Richard talking about the show towards the end of *Not*, and what it would be, and it sounded really interesting, and a great challenge.'

The BBC were not given to paying for sitcom pilots which weren't up to broadcast standard, and Posner and his crew* turned round a very impressive half-hour which, while not canonical and miles from the quality of the eventual saga, is packed with unique highlights. Atkinson's penchant for visual tomfoolery demanded two complicated set-piece sequences: a climactic duel with a trick blade (though this dashing Black Adder is famed for his swordsmanship), and 'The Death of the Scotsman'. When the plot was recycled for the second episode of the series, 'Born to Be King', the play put on for St Leonard's Day† was quite swiftly dealt with by Edmund, as he struggled to prevent the live stabbing of the Scots enemy he had just doomed to death, having heard that he carried letters proving Henry's bastardy. The original concept was far more complex – an entertainment for the Queen's birthday with Percy and Baldrick in ridiculous costumes trying to kill the enemy, and Edmund's desperate attempts to prevent the Scotsman being hanged live onstage (yes, there is a 'well hung' joke) go on for ten times the length. Atkinson and company rehearsed this violent pantomime to a clinical degree, creating a frantic dumbshow of dizzying proportions – the director's script for the pilot has several pages painstakingly breaking down even the smallest movement, to tune the farcical ballet to perfection.

It's something of a fallacy that the studio-bound format of *Blackadder II* was a miraculous development, as the original pilot is stylistically far more akin to the later series than *The Black Adder* would be – even the character of Edmund, the witty, vicious bad boy in black leather, is a

---

* Including production assistant Hilary Bevan-Jones, who had started her career on *Not*, and would stick with the *Blackadder* team for the series before becoming a successful producer, working again with Curtis on *The Boat That Rocked*.

† A hastily rewritten version of *The Death of the Pharaoh*, featuring alternative comedy icon Malcolm Hardee.

clear taste of things to come. But it seems clear why this pilot was kept under wraps for so long – it wasn't really *Blackadder* at this point, and as Lloyd himself would observe, 'It kind of wasn't *about* anything.' The wooliness of the central conceit is underlined by Geoff Posner: 'They decided that they didn't want to tie themselves down to one period. They just thought they'd make it a medieval/Elizabethan period. I remember having a discussion with the costume designer, and thinking, "This is a pilot, we don't have much money for costumes, so where shall we set it, and *when* shall we set it?" The timing of the setting was more decided by what there was available in the costume store than Richard saying, "It has to be set in 1523" or whatever. It's very vague . . . I won't say we immersed ourselves in months of historical research, because we were more concerned with getting the jokes right.' No clearer sign is needed that they were not quite there yet than to point out that in the pilot, Edmund is ultimately saved by the King's solemn interdict to spare the life of his son (whose name he actually knows), once he has begged for forgiveness. 'I know that we thought it was going very well,' Curtis says, 'and I remember sitting down in front of about six friends and watching it, and realising it hadn't quite worked. There was *something* there, but . . .' Tony says, 'It's like a signpost pointing in a particular direction, but certainly not getting there.' Posner recalls that it was felt, given the epic nature of the setting, that it seemed a shame not to expand their horizons and film some ambitious external sequences, allowing for more spoofery of BBC costume drama of the time.*

Posner would not play a part in the series again, however, as he had already signed up to direct episodes of Paul Jackson's new sitcom about a student household, and was soon preparing to start filming in Bristol.

---

* Costume dramas themselves rarely had such luxury – by the time Atkinson was filming the first series of *Blackadder*, in another studio in Broadcasting House Ron Cook was covering the same period of history by playing Shakespeare's *Richard III* with nothing but cardboard sets and painted backdrops. He only got a taste of the high-budget life when he resurfaced in the sitcom's finale as Sean the Irish Bastard.

When editing the final episodes of *Not*, Posner had been bothered by the screeching coming from the next booth, found Jackson immersed in cutting together the pilot of *The Young Ones*, and grabbed his chance to get involved with an extraordinary new branch of sitcom. It looked like Rik Mayall (with his girlfriend Lise Mayer and an old pal from Manchester University) had finally found the right TV format for the Comic Strip's manic anarchy, and with the start of Channel 4 heralding the first ever episode of *The Comic Strip Presents* (thanks to *Young Ones* renegade Peter Richardson and producer Michael White), the BBC quickly demanded another five episodes to be recorded as soon as possible.

For the full series of *The Black Adder*, however, Atkinson and Curtis would have all the time they needed – they just needed a hands-on producer. 'By that stage I'd had a bit of a rest,' John Lloyd says, 'and I remember Richard and Rowan sent me a dozen red roses and a case of champagne, saying, "Please come and do this," so I saw the pilot, and it was very funny – but it was somehow not rooted . . . I couldn't see the point of it really. My sort of contribution, if I might call it that, was to try and say, "This should be set in real history, so that you've never heard of Blackadder and Baldrick, but you've heard of the people around them." It was a missing bit of history which had been written out. Interestingly, there's a theory from Germany doing the rounds that the years 600–900, the darkest of the Dark Ages, never existed. Because there was a guy called Otto IV who wanted to be Holy Roman Emperor at the time of the millennium, so he just fast-forwarded about three hundred years, and changed all the dates. I'm reliably informed that it's bollocks, but it's a very amusing theory. As we know, Henry VII did a lot of propaganda. So I wrote all this genealogy and so on . . .'

'We thought we did quite well,' Curtis says, 'John thought we did quite badly.' After a period of pondering, and with *The Times* at that time promising extraordinary extracts from the newly discovered Hitler Diaries (and questions about their authenticity being raised by all the other newspapers), the air of conspiracy inspired Lloyd to cook up a whole new angle for the writers.

What Happened to Bernard Fripp

The task of reworking *The Black Adder* in time to start production in the new year, of course, still fell to Rowan and Richard, but first of all they had another original half-hour to film before the year's end. *Dead on Time* (also known as *Whatever Happened to Bernard Fripp?*) was a short film that could be seen as the first of Curtis's boy-meets-girl movies, but is more of an extended sketch, like one of Atkinson's live skits, on celluloid. Michael White once again stepped in to fund the film, with his girlfriend Lyndall Hobbs directing, and, of course, Howard Goodall provided the insistent, plaintive soundtrack to accompany the dynamic action. Once again, getting laughs out of death was very much the theme.

It was the tale of another Bernard, in this case Fripp, a personable but shallow bespectacled gawd-help-us who discovers in his lunch hour that he has contracted a rare disorder called Hirschman's disease, and has less than thirty minutes to live – and so, in near-as-dammit real time, he decides to try and experience everything he possibly can before his life is over. This is the natural cue for a frantic race across central London to make up for his wasted existence, but with surprisingly little in the way of visual humour by Atkinson's usual standards. Bernard is more of a sufferer of verbal diarrhoea, which isn't cured by his new desire to seize life.

> BERNARD: Shut up, all of you! What are you doing with your lives that's so damn important you can't even find me a pen? I mean, suppose you died tomorrow? Funnier things have happened – I'm dying today, for example. Then St Peter,

at the Pearly Gates, asks you what you've done
with your lives, and you say, "I've worked in
the bank at the corner of Glossop Street for
fifteen years," will he then say, "Oh my son,
you have exceeded my expectations! Step
royally into the house of heavenly peace"? Will
he hell. He'll say, "You complete prick! What
do you think I gave you a brain for?" . . . Life is
a sweet: suck it!

What the short does contain, however, is an alarmingly star-studded
cast, largely made up of actors yet to make their mark – although the
doctor who sends Bernard off on his quest was Nigel Hawthorne, already
the winner of two BAFTAs for his transformation into Sir Humphrey
Appleby in *Yes Minister*. As Bernard streaks around, trying to cram in all
the art and music he should have appreciated, find the spiritual solace
he desires, and even hopefully find love in the last few minutes of his
time on Earth, there's a famous face on every corner, few of them given
enough screen time to make the slightest impression – Ade Edmondson,
Nigel Planer, Jo Kendall, Rupert Everett, Christopher Biggins and
Rowan's girlfriend Leslie Ash all pop up, with Greta Scacchi as the
love-interest nurse who saves the day. The *Blackadder* cast was also well
represented, with Curtis himself belying his retirement from acting by
playing a tough in a cafe, plus McInnerny, Alex Norton, Joyce Grant,
and Jim Broadbent as one of the few characters with enough time to
register: a slow, syrupy clergyman who fails to understand that Bernard's
in a bit of a hurry.

Curtis and Atkinson's brief experiment in film-making came and
was forgotten with little ceremony, and the autumn of 1982 brought
them back together with Lloyd to start the scripting of the full series
of their sitcom. Just as with *Hordes of the Things*, Lloyd suggested a
strong framing context for their epic comedy, a real world surrounding

the swashbuckling gag-slinging to give every laugh an entirely new level of pathos, a depth which would mark it out in the world of early-eighties sitcom, if nothing else. He could not have picked a more perfect moment in our island's history to focus on, as few periods were quite as entangled by vipers as the roots of the Tudor reign, just a generation earlier than was suggested in the pilot. The five-hundredth anniversary of Richard III's coronation would coincide exactly with the eventual first broadcast run, with 'Born to Be King' marking the day on 6 July 1983. If ever a bubble of believable alternative history could be floated it was in that dark period, one ruthlessly vilified by Tudor propaganda for centuries, set in stone by Shakespeare, and only recently revised by committed Ricardians. Making the hero of the sitcom the son of one of the Princes in the Tower, whose entire reign was stamped out of existence by Henry VII, took the Ricardian cause to absurd lengths.

Not that a vast amount of scholarly research was conducted, of course. Lloyd is quite open about the level they were aiming for. 'There's a book that I had when I was nine or ten, called *Looking at History*, by R. J. Unstead – "In the Middle Ages, women wore wimples, and in the seventeenth century, gentlemen wore wigs!" So pretty childish, but about what anyone except a professional historian can ever remember.' They had a checklist – witchcraft, torture, sedition, Shakespeare, killing archbishops and, of course, plague and death. 'We took it back another hundred years to the middle of the fifteenth century when it could be harder and even more vicious and people were very mean and hundreds were murdered every day,' Atkinson told the *People*. 'In *The Black Adder* nearly everyone suffers and humour is about human suffering and hurt. In any humorous situation someone is always having something terrible done to them or rude said about them.' 'Real jeopardy was fun,' Curtis confirms. 'The fact that death was always around the corner was a delicious thing to be cracking jokes about. What I wouldn't give now to be able to have some deaths in my romantic films . . .' Now it was just a case of the partnership setting off to a 'hideous house' in the south of France to hammer it all out together. Or rather, as Curtis told the audience at the Cheltenham Literary Festival in 2008, 'It was a sort of, um . . . what's another word for "lie"? It was a *myth* that Rowan wrote. He was going out with Leslie Ash, so I was keen to go on holiday in the same house, with her in her bikini, so I was allowed there on the understanding that we'd write together . . . It didn't make any difference, she was repelled by me anyway.'

When they returned from rewriting British History in France, the pair found that Rik Mayall's new sitcom had begun, gradually but surely, to blow minds on Tuesday nights on BBC2. It was hugely rough stuff even given the wealth of untrained talent involved, but *The Young Ones* was at that time Curtis's big treat after a day of trying to get laughs out of fifteenth-century politics – the blend of fresh comedy with live bands was catnip to such a pop music obsessive. Lloyd too was impressed, given that he'd had an early peek at what Jackson was up to. 'I was sent the script of *The Young Ones*, and this thing arrived, you know, covered in Marmite stains and half written in pencil and full of Ben Elton's terrible spelling . . . and I could not make head nor tail of it. It was full of brilliant ideas, but so incompetently put together, you'd think, well, if I did this I'd just try and structure it, make it neat, and . . . that would have destroyed it really.'

The Young Ones gave first appearances to a huge number of comedians who would go on to establish their own legacies in the coming decade. 'It just happened to have lots of people who were at that point in their career where they were just starting out,' Geoff Posner reflects, 'most of them had stood on the stage at the Comedy Store at some point and wanted to start their own career, so getting a break was probably what it was all about, really.' Many future *Blackadder* players, from Helen Atkinson-Wood to Robbie Coltrane to Tony Robinson himself, would be happy to add *The Young Ones* to their CVs as the series continued.

By the start of 1983 Curtis had pieced together the alternative history, and the group knew where their series was headed, even if some scripts were still perfunctory. Lloyd had recalled as much of the original cast as he could, with the added bonus of John Howard Davies managing to give Tony Robinson another chance. Philip Fox was dealt a bad hand with his brief time in the Baldrick role, though Atkinson insists, 'He was very good, but when we eventually got to make the series Tony was available and we opted for him.' The Prince of Wales would now be played by seasoned theatre actor Robert East, and for the King, a revelation. Brian Blessed had been a household name for two decades, since starring in Z Cars in the early sixties, and had developed his craft in an array of successful roles year after year, from historical drama to cult science fiction, his scene-stealing bellowing as Prince Vultan in Flash Gordon sealing his reputation as a bombastic, captivatingly histrionic actor, a man to be feared and to obey in so many roles. Who better to take on the mantle of Richard of Shrewsbury, hitherto thought of only as a tiny weak golden-haired child doomed to die by an uncle's hand, than a large hairy 47-year-old with a voice that could drown out the apocalypse? Despite this being his one foray into sitcom, Blessed acknowledges, 'I can't tell jokes, but I myself, as an individual, when I'm talking to other actors, usually leave them asthmatic with laughter because of just being me. I do see life with a big smile. And even in Shakespeare, you have to find the comedy.'

Now is the Winter of Our Discontent...

The following February, the cast and crew of The Black Adder arrived in the frozen Northumberland countryside to begin bringing Atkinson's alternative history to life. Alnwick Castle had been selected as the perfect site for the filmed inserts, being already a regular on-screen from movies such as Mary, Queen of Scots and Becket, and fated to star in Robin Hood: Prince of Thieves (a return for Blessed), Elizabeth and *Harry Potter*. The wintry location would provide everyone with a crash course on the sufferings of the medieval way of life. As Atkinson recalls: 'Alnwick had this sense of openness and bleakness, particularly in the snow in February – genuinely Northumbrian winter weather of the mid-twentieth century, very, *very* cold and snowy. I just remember sort of the sense of difficulty of everything, the scale of what we were trying to do, and the number of animals, and children, and extras, most of whom you felt had a slightly miserable couple of weeks . . . And us not quite knowing what we were doing.'

The very first scene to be filmed exemplified just how up against it the fledgling sitcom-makers were. Director Martin Shardlow was admittedly an experienced pair of hands, having steered *Only Fools and Horses* through a bumpy first series as well as helming *Then Churchill Said to Me*, but at the time he was suffering from a painful slipped disc which meant that he could only direct the scenes while flat on his back. Blessed recalls that every time the director's pain dissipated, the cast would soon make him laugh and out would pop his disc again – often requiring the mighty King Brian to walk up and down his spine until it clicked back in.

The bitingly frosty weather posed challenges not just for Shardlow and the cast, but the entire crew were witness to Atkinson's first appearance as the reborn Black Adder. Rowan had gone so far as to inflict a harsh Henry V haircut on himself for the role, which made him look like he'd 'just been let out of the Belgian army'. 'Certainly the costumes got more flattering – and the haircuts in particular – after the first series. This extraordinary pudding-basin cut that I really had, my own hair was cut that way for the first series. For the three months we were rehearsing and shooting the programme I remember it was very difficult to go into shops and unselfconsciously ask for Mars bars and things.'

The series' first shot was actually for the final episode, where Prince Edmund takes leave of the loyal Baldrick (offering him a reference, in an exchange which was cut for broadcast) before setting out to take the throne by force.* Robinson recalls, 'I can remember on the very first day, Tim and I started to get the giggles, because in the previous hour we'd been subjected to *five different kinds* of snow. It was everything the North-East had to throw at us.'

As the flakes fell and the prone director called for action, Atkinson leaned over in his saddle, nose dripping in the icy air, beckoned Lloyd over, and hissed, 'What voice should I use?' Lloyd, taken aback, hadn't a clue, and deferred to Richard Curtis. '*On the day we were going to start shooting*, John came over to me with Rowan and said, "What's Rowan's character?" And we all thought, "Oh God, we don't know! We've written some funny lines but we don't how he's meant to perform them!"' The ridiculous design of Edmund's costume already marked out this Duke of Edinburgh from the earlier Duke of York, but the inbred grotesque that came to Rowan on that first day of filming was an entirely different Adder. As he admitted on-set, 'I love characters that are extreme and larger than life and very peculiar. But I like them to read consistently and real. You think this guy is a lunatic, but you are convinced you've seen him somewhere . . . He thinks he is a great swordsman and seducer. In fact he is just the reverse – a loud and arrogant failure in both departments.'†

A whole day was spent filming footage of the Black Adder proving his ineptitude as a swordsman, equestrian and adventurer for the opening titles. With no sound or dialogue to worry about, Rowan built on his character, scowling and leering as he fails to waylay a merchant's cart, trying to pull an arrow out of a trunk and bringing the entire tree

---

* Baldrick's fear that he would be lucky to get back up to dung-shoveller level was an unintended spot of historical accuracy: medieval dung-shovellers, or gong farmers, earned far more than most labourers.

† His characterisation owed much to his insane performance as mercenary guerrilla Mad Mike Hoare in the last series of *Not*: 'The enemy, soldier, are dedicated professionals, armed with 500 machine guns, dozens of tanks, flame-throwers, atomic bombs, Martian ray-guns, giant spiders and large sticks with spiky bits on the end, which they love to shove up your bottom and turn rapidly!'

down on top of himself, and tumbling from the back of his oblivious stallion, Black Satin. Even when just creeping along ramparts, or trying to run up cramped castle staircases in pointy shoes, Prince Edmund and his two friends couldn't hide the beating they were taking from the elements.

Despite the freezing conditions, the comics soon began to thaw to the extent that their producer felt that he could be cautiously hopeful, writing in his diary for 12 February 1983: 'On Monday and Tuesday, worried dreadfully that Rowan's character was a disaster, but it seems to be gelling well. Tim McInnerny is brilliant, as is Tony Robinson – quite splendid juices being squeezed from a rather shrivelled selection of lemons . . . Filming has been fantastically slow and tedious; the snow comes down on the words "Turn over" as if summoned by an incantation, and a remarkable variety of textures . . . The hailstones are as fat as mint imperials and it's so cold we had to wear our long johns in the bath.' This wasn't quite like making the epic Hollywood romps which inspired The Black Adder, with Errol Flynn and pals battling under the Californian sun. Creating a sitcom on this scale was drudgery, Lloyd admits in hindsight. 'The first series was by far the least enjoyable to make; we were all absurdly disorganised and overambitious. Rowan was sacked from any actual writing quite early in the series – he was far too busy trying to learn the lines which we pushed under his hotel-room door at four in the morning for the next day's shoot.'

Of the main cast, only the men were needed for location shooting, so the central trio were soon joined by Blessed and East – the latter playing the boyish heir to the throne at the age of forty, only seven years the junior of his screen father. Perhaps as a response to The Young Ones' surreal dimension, in much the same way that many of the jokes were now far more outlandish (the dog which Edmund kept in a cage in the pilot had now become his pet dwarf, for instance), the central characters had also taken a definite turn for the peculiar since the pilot, with Curtis making the most of Blessed's bombastic capabilities to have the King roaring, in another unused scene: 'CHISWICK! FRESH HORSES! I want to strip naked to the waist and ride round and round the castle shouting, "*I AM HE WHOSE PECTORALS FRIGHTEN THE MOON!*"'

Sitcom was a departure for Blessed, but, he recalls, a pleasing one, to be working with such fresh comic talent. 'They were a team, and they had their rules. Rowan, it's fair to say, is an incredibly serious comedian. He always reminded me of the famous Russian clown, Auguste, who was quiet and serious and sad, and would have audiences roaring with laughter. I don't know that Rowan is sad, but he seemed somehow out of place, light years ahead of everybody mentally. He has a face that belongs to all periods, from the modern age right down to the Stone Age. I would call him the History Man. And he likes mechanical things and speed, speedy rehearsals, speed of thought.' However, Blessed would soon establish his own way of working. 'Richard IV is the power base. Without the King, you cannot have a Kingdom! Rowan would be directing and giving very serious notes and so forth, scratching his head all the time – and everyone was very obedient to this except me! I was therefore like a sore thumb, and I used this, because I have an animal cunning. I felt it was my job, as the King, to fuck up every scene, to which Rowan was rather taken aback. I love him, he's wonderfully clever, but I had very strong ideas about the King – like he must be a man who never opens the door. So he knocks one down, you build another – if I could, I would have liked to walk through doors like Tom and Jerry! He's in a world of his own, he's utterly fearless, he has a wild, strange imagination, an astonishing capacity for blood, and rumpy-pumpy! And a wonderful, healthy loathing of the Turks.'* East got on famously with his screen father, but recalls that Blessed took his psychotic characterisation to such great lengths, remaining in

---

* Brian is quick to add that when climbing Mount Ararat with a Turkish party in 2008, his comrades would gleefully quote from the show, especially his line 'Love your fellow man as yourself – unless he's Turkish, in which case, KILL THE BASTARD!'

bloodlust mode at all times, that the cast learned to keep their distance. 'The BBC rehearsal rooms at that time (long since sold off, rehearsal now deemed superfluous for TV acting) were full of poles on circular bases that were used to mark the boundaries of the various sets and corridors etc. They were about six foot high and quite substantial. We were rehearsing the scene where Brian comes back from the Crusade and bursts through the door of the castle, and in order to create the appropriate effect Brian thought it entirely appropriate to hurl one of these poles across the room. It cannoned into several others and about ten poles dominoed to the ground around the room, felling several elderly actors in the process. Never one to do things by halves, our Brian.' This headstrong autonomy set Blessed up for a fall. He merrily recalls, 'The camera crews, for the fun of it, made one of the doors really solid, and bolted it and God knows what. I was breaking into the door, to get to the Bishop. You only had one take, and I had to literally break down this three-inch steel door – and I'm powerful, I bench-press four hundred pounds . . . Rowan nearly lost the use of his legs with laughter as I had to actually fucking break open the door and half of the set to get in.'

King Richard's milder elder son had his own eccentricities, being secretly afraid of spoons and openly obsessed with drains, which Blessed is sure was partly down to the actor himself. 'I always thought it was a mistake that they didn't carry on with Robert; he was a very inventive man, a lot of the things Harry did, 10 per cent of it was his own creation.' Despite being every bit the fine son that Edmund wasn't, the Prince was already a fully realised irritant, judging by these external scenes, edited out of the finished version of 'The Archbishop':

HARRY: Now that you are to be primate of all England,
            I feel that we must really grapple with the
            problems that are facing the Church today.
EDMUND: Yes, of course . . .

HARRY   For instance, where do you stand on the
            torture of talkative women, hm?

EDMUND: Well, I thought . . .

HARRY: Which side of the fence are you going to come
            down on as regards the castration of talented
            choristers? And above all, how are you going
            to get the youth involved? Burning questions,
            Your Grace, *burning questions*!

EDMUND: Yes, I think I may need to meditate on this . . .

HARRY: Ah!

EDMUND: . . . Alone.

In the same sequence, a more concerted attempt to channel
Shakespeare was also attempted (in order to justify the Bard's 'additional
material' credit), but had to ultimately be cut as it held up the plot to
have our hero soliloquising while his flunkeys hurriedly pack to flee
uncertain death, Becket-style.

EDMUND: Farewell, sweet England, and noble castle; first
            watering place in the desert of my life. And
            torture chamber, playroom of my youth, adieu!
            Farewell, gentle gibbets and sweet crenellations
            . . . and best of luck to you, noble turret! From
            which I once tossed kittens in experiments to do
            with weight. And farewell . . .

BALDRICK: My Lord?

EDMUND: Yes?

BALDRICK: Are you sure it's gonna fit on?

EDMUND: Yes, yes, on the horse, on the horse! And
            farewell, dearest gutters, down which all sorts of
            business has daily made its way. And farewell,
            spiky gates, the final resting place of the heads

of thieves, murderers, Great-Aunt Isabella, and
all those who forgot my father's birthday . . .

A huge crash, and a neigh, off.

BALDRICK: My Lord?
EDMUND: Yes?
BALDRICK: The horse has died.
EDMUND: Well, get Percy's horse!
BALDRICK: It *was* Percy's horse.

Only selected guest stars were chosen to make the pilgrimage to
Alnwick, and when Frank Finlay – a major name to feature proudly
in your opening credits then, as today – came up to film the complex
tragedy of 'Witchsmeller Pursuivant', he fared little better than the
chilly regulars. Hilary Bevan-Jones is embarrassed to recall: 'I made a
terrible mistake – it was a Friday night and one of my responsibilities
was clearing up afterwards and making sure that everyone had gone,
and I thought that Frank Finlay had gone home with the person that
normally picked him up. And in fact he hadn't, and he was left behind
on this snowy location. I was already back in the hotel, having a
brandy, and some of the make-up people came in and they'd found him
wandering, in his costume, on the way back to the hotel. I thought my
career was over . . .'

A co-financing deal had been struck with the Seven Network, the
Australian company which had for decades been paying big money to
the greatest UK comics to defect Down Under (from, tragically, Tony
Hancock, to Cook & Moore and, of course, Frankie Howerd), but
Lloyd tried to be very careful with how the money was spent. Bevan-
Jones remembers Finlay's episode being one of the bigger deals. 'There
were certainly times during the first series when you'd turn up and
it felt more like a huge feature film than a BBC comedy! Stunts and
animals and lots of make-up effects as well. We built a whole village

111

for "Witchsmeller Pursuivant"! And we set fire to it, so we weren't pussyfooting around.'

Curtis's scripts were confidently adapting to the styles of the cast as shooting continued, and it was clear by Finlay's episode that they had a catchphrase. As we've seen, the 'cunning plan' was already a central part of the pilot, but at first nobody had seen it as especially resonant. Tony Robinson, however, was all for a spot of repetition: 'I said, "Could I not say 'I have a *cunning* plan'?"' "I have a plan" is rather a flat line, but "I have a *cunning* plan . . ." – you dwell on it, it's so exciting, it's so sexy this plan, that it's bound to be fantastically good. I think even then, I thought, "Well, maybe it could turn into a bit of a catchphrase . . ."' The design of Baldrick's sack-like livery and dishevelled appearance did mark him out as the most proletarian character on-screen, but he still sparkled like a new pin in comparison to the rest of his filthy family tree. Certainly, something was needed to give some life to 'the short one' of the trio. 'He was just the servant, the kind of everyman servant. And it was only as the episodes went on, and I was after all surrounded by the greatest comic writers of their generation, that gradually his character matured and developed. And then that whole character was thrown completely out of the window, and we started again . . .'

McInnerny was in the more confident position of playing a well-known archetype – the foppish fool. It was a role he already knew well from Oxford, and would eventually get to reprise when Griff Rhys Jones directed *Twelfth Night* for the RSC in 1991. 'I loved Percy because he was extraordinarily loyal, I mean, to the point of it being dangerous to his health. What Percy reminded me of most was Sir Andrew Aguecheek, from *Twelfth Night*. He's a very similar character who's mocked and derided by Toby Belch but is immensely loyal to him throughout.' He did, however, have the pressure of history weighing on him more than most, as they were filming in the very castle which had for centuries been the seat of the real Percy family, the Earls of Northumberland – albeit as a Lancastrian stronghold, rather than Yorkist.

Despite the progress, stylistically there was still some degree of floundering – Baldrick's now familiar cry of tactical inspiration when he, Percy and Edmund (or 'Grumbledook') are seconds from being burnt at the stake for witchcraft was met with a blunt 'Oh, *fuck off*, Baldrick!' from the Black Adder in the recording, a lapse of wit which had to be covered up in the edit with a hasty cough. The finale had also yet to be completely straightened out – a sequence was filmed in which Patrick Allen's Hawk bloodily murders Prince Harry as he smells a rose, which would have made the series' conclusion far blacker than it already was.

Peter Cook's journey north to play the King came along when the land had thawed even further and everyone else in the cast was well settled. In these excised lines Cook, Blessed and East's incitements to the Yorkist army at Bosworth Field seem a case in point – Cook channels his own perversion of an arch Olivier, Blessed barfs pure bloodlust, and East simpers like a country priest.

RICHARD III:	Arms which used to wave at you, whip 'em off! Eyes that used to blink at you, whip 'em out!
RICHARD:	Hands you have shaken today, cut off! Heads that have nodded, CUT THEM OFF TOO!
HARRY:	Now, obviously a lot of you are going to get killed. But then, others aren't, so that's something to look forward to, isn't it?

Coming off the back of a miserable period in Hollywood making US sitcom *The Two of Us*, and also being up to his neck in another historical romp at the same time, Graham Chapman's *Yellowbeard*, Cook didn't especially need a trip to the North-East. But for the chance to play royalty with his favourite young comic* he agreed,

---

* It is tempting to see the moment Atkinson lops off Cook's head as symbolic of a torch being passed.

113

to Lloyd's delight. 'Peter was his usual modest self when we asked him – "I don't think I'll be good enough" – when of course he was, he was perfect.' 'He was very nervous,' Blessed agrees, 'he had a lot of Shakespeare speeches to do, and he liked just being himself. He kept saying to me in the make-up room, "What do I do, Brian?" I said, "Just play him slightly mad. Get out there as if you've got a temperature all the time, and you're almost hallucinating. As if he's got some disease." And I relaxed him . . . I think the reason Peter then made such a success of that episode was because he was so fucking scared. I think that Rowan was frightened as well. It's healthy. The best performances come from people who are vulnerable, within an inch of failure. It makes you do exciting things.'

McInnerny says the guest did go some way to make Richard III his own. 'Rowan had to be on his toes quite a lot, because Peter wasn't content with doing the lines as written on the page, there was quite a lot of improvisation going on. So Rowan had to get over his shyness quite quickly with Peter!' 'He got on well with all of us,' Lloyd says, 'and he'd known Rowan for a long time. But like so many actors who came to do cameos on *Blackadder*, we treated them appallingly because we wanted a "house style", a sort of revue way of performing rather than Great Acting.'

Cook owed Atkinson a cameo anyway. Rowan had been invited to guest-star in several programmes in his short career (giving a memorable lecture on one of his favourite topics, church organs, for *The Innes Book of Records*), but one of the unmissable offers had been to feature in Cook's own solo vehicle in 1980, an LWT special made for Humphrey Barclay called *Peter Cook and Company*. Atkinson stepped into Cook's traditional role of playing exasperating freaks in public areas without any trouble at all, but the special never led to a renaissance for the elder comic's career.

Once they returned to the BBC studios, many more hugely respected actors, what Blessed terms 'people of substance', were drafted in to feature in episodes, often with only tiny roles – Richard 'Stinker' Murdoch and the legendary 'Man in Black' Valentine Dyall only get brief lines as part of the King's council, but not all egos were as forgiving, and Wilfrid Brambell's similarly minor role, which would have been the final comic performance of a sitcom icon, had to be recast when the veteran walked out after waiting three hours to get to his line, carping about 'bloody amateurs!'.

The Vile Turnip of Sweet Richard Slain . . .

With the onerous location shooting finally complete, there was only a short break before decampment to the capital for rehearsals and studio recordings. Ordinarily the BBC would be dispensing free tickets to see the live recordings at the end of each week, but the *Adder* team had to make the decision to do without an audience – the lavish production which they envisaged left too little room in their allocated studio to fit in the bleachers where the audience sat. It wasn't an exercise in 'comedy realism' to do without a laugh track, however; the edited shows would be shown to audiences later[*].

In the rehearsal studios in North Acton, Rowan and the cast could really begin to shape their half-hour comic tragedies, and the rest of the crew could witness how the master craftsman worked. What Chris Langham termed the 'mental chemistry' of Atkinson's approach, the clinical cerebral engineering of every line and look until it is deemed amusing enough to him, could seem like procrastinating perfectionism to less tolerant co-stars, and Atkinson himself admits, 'I'm just a perfectionist, which is good in some ways because it makes you strive harder, but it's not something of which I'm particularly proud. I would agree with anyone who suggests that perfection is

---

[*] 'Canned laughter' being largely an invention of dim-witted critics, Hanna-Barbera cartoons aside.

a disease, not a quality. It reduces you to a person who worries too much and that isn't healthy for anyone . . . I don't like to take it home with me. That's why I'm so keen on my sports cars, because they are a simple, boyish interest. They relax me.' But with the equally exacting and tenacious Lloyd by his side, and the perfectionism of *Fawlty* ringing in his ears, Atkinson was clearly aiming high. 'They all put up with the interminable wrangling in rehearsal as we paced about struggling to think of a vegetable beginning with C funnier than courgette,' John recalls. 'Mostly they just sat quietly listening to the debate with a kind of aghast bemusement.' Once again, poor Frank Finlay suffered on his brief sojourn with the *Adder* team. After many hours of laboured fine-tuning holding up the proceedings, with Shardlow's and Atkinson's backs turned, Finlay crept over to Lloyd and begged, 'For God's sake, will someone *tell me what to do?!*'

Tony Robinson admits to feeling overawed by his co-star on first impressions. 'From my point of view, quite crudely, when I joined it, Rowan was a big famous person! And in his own way, though very confident, he was a very shy person, quite a stroppy guy in some ways, and *very* bright. Not somebody who you'd want to tangle with. But also he's a kind of omnivore in a way, he watches everything that's going on all the time, you know that whatever you're doing, or the lighting director's doing, or the prop man, he's always kind of running through that as well . . . So for me it was like, "I'm going to have to keep some way away from this guy."' He soon found, however, that perfectionism didn't extend to egotism. 'I can remember very early on, Rowan had a very funny line, and John said, "We ought to cut away to Baldrick after that and get his reaction." I can remember thinking, "Oh Christ, that's not going to stay in, there's no way he'll allow it to happen." But the extraordinary thing about Rowan, as far as I was concerned, was that he was so incredibly generous, he allowed me to have the kind of reactions and cutaways that most stars wouldn't have.'

Having broken the cardinal rule of sitcom by writing a new episode to establish the situation, the first Chronicle the team put through the BBC sitcom assault course was 'The Foretelling', in which we discover the depth of Henry Tudor's treachery, and witness the birth of the Black Vegetable. It's easy to forget, after four triumphant series of often absurd but generally grounded historical comedy, that *Blackadder* essentially began life as a ghost story. In fact, not only would the writers' desire to prod Shakespeare inspire them to echo Banquo's ghost by having Richard III's spectre chasing after his own head, the series would also contain instances of genuine black magic, witchcraft, demons and even a cameo from Satan himself. But then, as adaptations of an unreliable chronicle, each episode was bound to represent the superstitions of the Middle Ages, creating a world in which an old crone can conceivably give birth to a poodle, sticking your finger up a sheep's bottom on Easter Monday increases fertility, the King eats roast horse and there are any number of popes at any given time. This is lost history after all – who remembers the Swiss Invasion now?

The lavish production design underlined the ridiculous nature of this forgotten period of history, with costume designer Odile Dicks-Mireaux given free rein to add to the spectacle, with knights sporting absurd antlers and King Richard rarely seen without his golden armour. Atkinson adds, 'I remember having increasingly ludicrous codpieces, and wondering if it wasn't so lewd that your eyes were glued to it instead of the actor the entire time when it was in shot. We compromised on something that, even now, when you look at it, still looks fairly extraordinary. I'm not sure that you'd want to do that kind of thing now. But I didn't mind wearing the tights and the codpieces were, we thought, hilarious . . . these hideous but hysterical priapic appearances in my crotch.'

A post-coronation sequence in which the new royal family pose for a portrait made good use of the livery of Atkinson's strange new creation, but though it established the central characters of the series brilliantly,

117

it had to be trimmed for time.

QUEEN: Now, you two boys, since you are going to be princes, we really must settle on a coat of arms. Edmund, I was looking at your shoulder . . . Perhaps you would like something with your dear little worm on it?

EDMUND: It's an Adder, mother. A poisonous symbol of aggression and virility.

QUEEN: And what about you, Harry?

HARRY: I've been thinking of a sort of fruit motif. A golden pear rampant on a field of gooseberries perhaps.

QUEEN: That sounds nice.

The second episode introduced a surprise regular character and a double act of great import to *Blackadder*. 'The Queen of Spain's Beard' mocked the ruthless arranged marriages that powered medieval politics by matching the weedy Edmund with a Hispanic monster of an infanta, Maria Escalosa – a comedic gorgon played to perfection by Miriam Margolyes. Despite the actress's natural exuberant sweetness, she says she was happy to transform herself. 'I liked the people very much, much better than the Footlights crowd that I knew earlier . . . The main thing about the Spanish Infanta is that she's hideously ugly, and I could have felt a bit peeved at being cast in this role, because although fat, I am charming and pleasant-looking. But I remember it being lots of fun.' Nevertheless, some of the script's jokes may have been deemed too cruel – or were cut for time.

BALDRICK: I believe she came by sea.

EDMUND: Yes: they stuck a couple of sails on her and pushed her off at Cadiz.

Of this first time working with Atkinson, Margolyes recalls, 'I was fascinated to see that he had a stammer, and sometimes if that got in the way of working, he would get so furious with himself. I only saw, on the television, the superb, disciplined results of his work, I didn't realise how hard he had to try not to stammer.' A first-rate comic actor of Miriam's skill could only be paired with someone equally adept, and so Rowan and John were happy to be reunited with Jim Broadbent, who played the small but memorable role of the Infanta's interpreter, Don Speekingleesh. Since his appearance on *Not*, Jim had turned down the role of Del Boy in *Only Fools and Horses* in favour of the lesser role of dodgy copper Roy Slater (who also debuted in 1983), had appeared in Terry Gilliam's *Time Bandits*, and would further his film career by appearing in Gilliam's next, *Brazil*. But alongside these small but significant roles, Broadbent was making a far bigger commitment in joining Patrick Barlow in the National Theatre of Brent, playing the long-suffering Wallace: co-star and general dogsbody of the great theatrical impresario Desmond Olivier Dingle*.

Together Miriam and Jim would play scenes which would be among the few moments from the first series which all the *Blackadder* team agree to be classic, not least Curtis: 'Jim as the Spanish translator – I've never worked out why it's so perfect, but I think it's that he misstresses *every single word*. It's just a sort of astonishing technical feat, to get the rhythms of the English language so completely wrong.' Brian Blessed recalls, 'They'd just rehearsed it, and Rowan grabbed me by the arm and said, "Come and watch this, what do you think?" And of course I had tears in my eyes from laughter. And Rowan looked at it, and said, "You find this very funny, don't you?" I said, "Yes, yes!" And he very seriously said, "I think it's funny, yes, I think it works."' 'I'm

---

* Desmond continues to run the company to this day, but his time with Wallace signalled the height of NTOB's popularity, presenting a very different kind of historical comedy, channelled through the gob-smacking amateurism of Dingle's writing and direction.

embarrassed to say that I had no idea really of what a Spanish accent was so I just came up with this thing which I suppose is a very bad cod Italian accent, but it seemed to be funny,' Broadbent shrugs. 'Nobody questioned it, but I'm embarrassed now because I should have done my research . . . The fact that he was slightly camp seemed to fall into place from how it was written. That famous line, "Nice to have a little talk just about-a the *ly-dees*' things . . ."' 'Now I'm a specialist in accents,' Margolyes says, 'and I'm not quite sure what accent Jim was employing . . . it doesn't matter!'

Playing the leading man's child bride, when Edmund swaps the Infanta for the 'young and beautiful' (and of course, heavily anachronistic) Princess Leia of Hungary, would provide a career highlight for the eight-year-old Natasha King (now a successful businesswoman). Being a Curtis creation of course, Princess Leia bubbles over with cuteness – perhaps discounting her excitement at her husband being burned alive – and King's performance was perfectly natural, just on the right side of stage-school-style excess. 'The one thing I remember very clearly,' she says, thirty years on, 'is what a genuinely warm-hearted and very considerate cast and crew they were to work with. In particular, aged only eight and with my front teeth missing I was over the moon to receive a bouquet of flowers when filming finished from Rowan Atkinson – it did wonders for me in the playground!'

Other actors to create a number of reincarnations throughout *Blackadder*'s history were Bill Wallis, a Cambridge contemporary of Peter Cook's who would get caught up in the slipstream of the satire boom, singing 'Alan A'Dale' for *Not Only But Also* and providing voices for *Week Ending* during Lloyd's tenure and *H2G2* before debuting in 'The Archbishop' as Sir de Boinod, one of two drunken knights thirsty for the unholy Edmund's blood. Barbara Miller, a wonderful comic actress who truly embodied *Blackadder*'s performance ethos of 'more is more', also made her first appearance as one of the three witches (alongside Gretchen Franklyn) who hail Edmund King, besides playing Edmund's claimed wife during his witchcraft trial. She would return as *Blackadder II*'s Wise Woman and even have an uncredited cameo as the old crone in *Blackadder's Christmas Carol* before her death in 1990.

The influence of *The Young Ones* is tangible in *The Black Adder*'s wealth of eccentric cameos and supporting roles – in the last episode, Edmund's villainous Black Seal is entirely made up of great comedy actors, including *Young Ones* regular Roger Sloman as Three-Fingered Pete. The Oblivion Boys, Mark Arden and Stephen Frost, made their first appearances in the show playing themselves as blockheaded guards in much the same way that they'd popped up as policemen in *The Young Ones* episode 'Boring'. Perhaps the most eccentric minor character was that of the regular roly-poly Messenger, played by young actor David Nunn, who'd had a few small roles in *Not*. Where the pilot's Messenger, Rudkin, had been a straight servant, Nunn's clumsy herald was an absurd pain in the Black Adder's neck, prone to mirroring his masters' actions for no apparent reason other than to annoy them – with no discernible cause, the usually charming Prince Henry reserved a specific fiery detestation for the chubby envoy[*].

The greatest example of *The Black Adder*'s debt to *The Young Ones* came, of course, with Rik Mayall's guest spot in the final episode – once again, uncredited, just as he had been with Kevin Turvey: 'I had my name taken off the credits because I was addicted to this form of performance where the audience thought it was genuinely happening.' There was less chance of this with his appearance as Mad Gerald. The character's role essentially was a) to get on Edmund's nerves while at his lowest ebb, and b) to give the anti-hero some way of escaping imprisonment and a slow death by snail – but within those parameters, from the moment Rik showed up on set, he was in charge of the creation of Mad Gerald. This was the first time that Rowan and Rik could size each other up in collaboration, and see whose brand of humour would win

---

[*] Sadly, Nunn died in spring 2012, at the age of forty-nine.

the day.* If Rik's rotting prisoner of Philip of Burgundy was an ancestor of Lord Flashheart, then phenomenal amounts of sexy genes must have been introduced in the intervening decades. Barely recognisable in a shock wig, with massive false teeth and caked in red-raw make-up, Mayall provided the ultimate test for Atkinson's eternally irritated Prince: a stinking presence which could rival the medieval Baldrick's descendants, a penchant for rats and that endless inane laugh – all, according to John Lloyd, of his own invention. 'Rik insisted he rewrote all his lines, which is why, when he appeared, he wiped the floor with everyone else – because he took over his scenes.'

The same episode featured the last great guest spot in the series, with Patrick Allen stepping into shot from his narrator's chair to play the Black Adder's nemesis: the Hawk, Philip of Burgundy. Originally he was to have enjoyed far more screen time, disguising himself as a messenger to tell the King and Queen that Edmund had beheaded himself in a bear trap, causing clever Baldrick (who found work as a guard) to complain to Percy, 'I think we may be victims of someone else's cunning plan!' Despite his ex-servant's quick wit, however, in every version of the script Edmund – though eligible for the throne for only a few moments before idiotically poisoning himself – ends up horrifically mangled in Philip's torture machine, and the Black Adder's machinations are finally ended.

Thanks to the leather-and-mahogany tones which made Allen's fortune,† Lloyd could not have found a more perfect voice to relate the facetious historical background to every episode, introducing the entire legend of *Blackadder* from the very first shot: 'History has known

---

* They would be reunited a year later for one of John Cleese's Video Arts training films, *Oh What the Hell?* – but then most of the comedians featured in this book would crop up in a Video Arts film at some point.

† A voice that has been embedded in the national psyche for decades, not least thanks to the government's official 'Protect and Survive' nuclear attack public information films and his apocalyptic narration for Frankie Goes to Hollywood's 'Two Tribes'.

many great liars . . .' But historical comedy was nothing new to Allen, who had filled the same narrator role for two historical *Carry Ons* – *Don't Lose Your Head* and *Up the Khyber*. His physical presence for the finale was equally apt: in his long career he'd had roles in a number of historical TV thrillers of just the kind that they were lampooning – indeed, his experience went back far enough for him to have featured in the *Errol Flynn Theatre* anthology series in the fifties, providing a solid link between Atkinson and his inspiration.

May His Name Last as Long as Our Dynasty!

Patrick Allen's vocal stylings have become such an eerily ubiquitous part of British culture that it's easy to forget how they defined the cod epic approach of *The Black Adder*. Several years later, the idea of him using that authoritative, strident voice to read out complete nonsense was hijacked by Vic Reeves and Bob Mortimer for every episode of their first BBC series, and from there he could be heard belting out non sequiturs for an endless succession of shows and products – or rather, in many cases, it was a soundalike stealing his style, for shows like *The X Factor*, with the sad result that Allen's bombastic tones can still be heard some years after the one and only original died in 2006, at the age of seventy-nine.

Complementing Allen's narration was, of course, Goodall's theme music. The melody and style had come to Howard back in 1982 when he was first given the brief for the pilot: a strident, galloping slice of orchestral derring-do which could have graced the credits of any serious historical epic. There was work required to fine-tune the theme for the series, however. 'With a producer like John Lloyd, his instant reaction is to say, "Give it a try, how bad can it be?" Once we had a tune that everybody liked, it was a question of rearranging and finding other ways to do it . . . It was mock-heroic. In fact the "horse's hooves" part of the tune I wrote without the chorus for the pilot. I took

123

it into a BBC rehearsal room, and played it to John, and he said, "It's all right, but it needs a middle bit, it feels like it's just the first phrase going round and round. What would it be if it was the same rhythm as the word "Blackadder"? So I just said, "What about this? *Duhduhduh, duhduhduh . . .*" and he said, "Yeah, that." It was kind of instantaneous.' Curtis joined the pair in the pub and added lyrics, perfect for priming the audience for half an hour of thrilling swashbuckling: the sound of hooves, the deadly flashing blade (a reference to the badly dubbed sixties French series called, of course *The Flashing Blade*), and many a cunning plan. Goodall wasn't just briefed to pen the theme, though, and provided the soundtrack for every episode – far from being incidental music, his pastoral pastiches and melodramatic organ stabs energised every cunning plan, conveying as much information and emotion as every twist and turn of Atkinson's simpering face.

Bringing together all the footage for the audience's laughter, however, was a sizeable feat even for a master of editing like Lloyd. 'We never finished on time, so we had to pick up the next week and it got longer and longer. It took months and months to edit.' Whole sequences had to be cut – in 'The Archbishop' there are numerous scenes with the Plantagenet family suffering through boring sermons and King Richard raging from the pulpit at the funeral of the Archbishop he's just killed. 'They were all very over-length and very difficult to edit down to size,' Curtis says, and Lloyd confirms, 'We showed the first two episodes to BBC Light Entertainment, and they said, "I dunno, is it funny? It's very good, but it seems rather scary . . . do you think it's funny?" We said, "Yeah, we think it's really funny, but it's not meant to look, like, *obviously* funny . . ."' Tony Robinson claims to have felt less confident at the time. 'I think we all knew from the beginning that the first series was pretty dire, but it was a bit like a production line, in that once you've started it off, you can't just stop it right away. Everything was booked, you just had to go through with it and make it as good as you could. And if you think about it, no one had made the kind of historical comedy half-hour series that Richard and Rowan had got in their minds, and it wasn't until we'd started work that we could actually see what worked and what didn't.' 'My theory,' Curtis counters, 'is that no matter how hard you try on sitcoms, out of six episodes two are good, two are all right and two are weak.'

The finished series debuted on BBC1 at 9.30 p.m. on Wednesday 15 June 1983, and the *Radio Times* heralded the sitcom and Atkinson's new character ('the scummiest toe-rag in the great basket of human history') with a special investigation into the new-found Chronicles by Lloyd himself, establishing the lore of the Blackadder family. Lloyd has always been keen to shape the packaging of every project with his name on it, from press fluff to comical credits, here listing the cast 'In Order of Precedence/Affability/Witchiness/Disappearance' and concluding with the Hollywood-ribbing 'Filmed in Glorious TELEVISION'. Not for the last time, there was an unexpected episode switch to worry about as well, with Lloyd having to make the decision to swap the unready scene-setting second episode 'Born to Be King' with 'The Queen of Spain's Beard', despite the opening narration providing a date for each instalment, making a bigger nonsense of the already nonsensical historical context.

It was a knuckle-gnawing summer for the whole team as their show entered British homes, lined up for judgement by critics both professional and public. Curtis admits to snooping around the suburbs of Shepherd's Bush peering through windows at half past nine to see whether people were watching his creation or not, whereas Atkinson was saved from such embarrassing behaviour by already being in Australia on a promotional tour. Maybe the biggest impact on Atkinson of having his first sitcom starring role was that it finally forced him to officially change his occupation to 'comedian' on his passport, and admit that his dreams of staying out of the spotlight were officially dead: 'I tried to maintain "engineer" as a career for as long as possible, mainly for insurance policies. You have *no idea* of the quantum leap in the premium when I made the change.'

As was clear from the readers' letters in *Radio Times*, varying from 'Superbly brilliant, side-splitting, fabulous, hilarious and very, very funny' to 'Utter rubbish – Rowan Atkinson's facial contortions made me feel physically sick', the reaction to *The Black Adder* tended to be quite violently split between approval and disgust at the show's perceived blasphemy, lewdness and general 'undergraduate humour'. John Lloyd rightfully bridles, 'Anyone who's been in comedy will tell you sooner or later, somebody says, "Oh, undergraduate humour, I see." You mean, people who have been to university type humour? "Yes, that's right, toilets and all this kind of stuff . . ."' There may have been a number of laughs squeezed out of nether regions in the show, McInnerny concedes, but 'You have to have a couple in each episode to make a bedrock of laughter, on which to build the intellectual gags!'

Blessed says, 'I remember with *I, Claudius*, the first write-ups were quite derogatory. And within a week, they said, "Ah! I can see the style!" and apologised that they got it wrong. And I was in tears of laughter to see a review programme the night after the first *Black Adder* episode was shown, and they just thought it was a disgrace! Unfunny, silly, immature, and absolutely substandard. It's making me laugh now, the shock on their faces . . . It was terribly misunderstood. *The Black Adder* has a magic of its own. It's somehow more vulnerable, and varied in a strange way.'

'We were very proud of it when we did it,' Lloyd says today, but the general verdict on the historic first series has always tended towards the derisory from all concerned – largely in order to more grandly praise the series yet to come. Everyone has had their theories as to why it wasn't the immediate hit that Atkinson's reputation in 1983 – and of course, the unprecedented cost and ambition of the production – should have delivered. Much has been said about the lack of a live audience, which Lloyd feels 'meant the cast had no focus. Rowan is used to performing to an audience; that's what edits his performance and makes it real.'

Atkinson himself feels that it was a kind of hubris: 'We were flattered to find someone willing to spend a lot of money on the project and got a little carried away. Instead of the three sets and five actors you get with the average sitcom we filmed in snowdrifts around Alnwick with a large cast, sixty-five extras and a dozen horses. It was misguided, naive thinking on our part. Someone should have slapped us down and said "No", because it didn't really work. The action got in the way of the humour.'

'In many ways *The Black Adder* was the most ambitious of all the series,' McInnerny says, 'in that there was at least five minutes of film in every episode, there was no live audience . . . For that reason I think it should be cherished. Having said that, it was kind of rough and messy, and some things didn't work. Rowan wasn't entirely relaxed in the first series – none of us were, because we still weren't quite sure what we were doing.' To which Curtis freely puts up his hand: 'We bit off slightly more than we could chew, is the truth of the matter. And with Rowan's character we tried to do lots of things – we tried to make him sort of arrogant, scared, feeble, bullying . . . We tried to do a really rounded thing, and the truth of the matter is that it was too much for a character to hold. I think it was a conglomeration of quite a few funny things that we knew Rowan could do.' 'And an amusing costume and a daft haircut an amusing character doth not make,' adds Atkinson, volunteering that they made Edmund 'a little too despicable. Heroes of the classically successful British comedy series tend to have won a high degree of sympathy and affection from the British public, like Frank Spencer and even Alf Garnett. Basil Fawlty certainly did. To run a small business and hate your customers is very British.'

But after three decades of self-flagellation, it's probably time to steady the whip. It's difficult to appraise the show on its own merits, bearing in mind what was still to spill from the Blackadder Chronicles, but it seems highly unlikely, if *The Black Adder* had remained a stand-alone series, that it would be remembered as anything less than a lost classic by lovers of British comedy everywhere. The remarkable cast and their unforgettably silly performances would have earned the programme fans all round the world even if nobody involved ever worked together again after 1983, and despite the modest viewing figures both on first broadcast and when repeated in the autumn of 1984, the show did have the distinction of winning an International Emmy for 'The Archbishop'. Blessed grins, 'I remember Martin Shardlow rushing over here in a car – I didn't know he knew where I lived! – with tears in his eyes, saying, "We've won an Emmy, Brian, we've won an Emmy!" just weeping with happiness.'

The scene in which Baldrick reveals the going rate for the Catholic Church's pardons, curses and fake holy relics (including Jesus' own waterproof sandals, knocked up in his carpentry shop) remains a favourite among all the cast, though Curtis admits that such high points tend to give away his background. 'What used to be strong about British comedy is that people went from writing sketches to writing sitcom, and their sketch craft was carried through – some of the best things in series one are really sketches.'

The team knew that there were lessons to be learned for a second series, but their bridges were burned anyway – mutilated, tickled half to death and finally self-poisoned, King Edmund's reign was definitely over. 'That,' snarled the Hawk in another sequence cut from broadcast, 'will be the end of the so-called Black Adder!' But if that really was the case, the show could proudly stand alone, and disgrace nobody. John Lloyd admits today, 'I do think one of the hallmarks of it is that it seems better than one remembers it. On the odd occasions that I do see it, you think, "God, this is quite good, it's slightly embarrassing . . ."'

His featured role was certainly a fillip for Robinson's career, not only qualifying him for an appearance in *The Young Ones*, appearing alongside Robbie Coltrane as Victorian physician Dr Not the Nine O'Clock News (who cannot tell the difference between his elephant and the Elephant Man), but also introducing him to a completely different group of Oxford and Cambridge comics, who would welcome him into the team for *Who Dares Wins*. Being Rowan's sidekick led him to roles in the first series of *Alas Smith & Jones*, produced and directed by Martin Shardlow, with Phil Pope and Jimmy Mulville also supporting the starring double act. 'With those shows,' Robinson says, 'I had a big introduction to the entire comedy mafia of that time. Rather than playing for Dagenham & Redbridge, I was suddenly playing for Manchester United! Since *That Was the Week That Was*, before I left school at sixteen, I'd known that kind of TV was the place I could be happy and make a major contribution, but I thought it would never happen because I didn't know anybody involved in it, and I'd written countless letters to directors of various comedy shows and nothing ever happened. Then I got this lucky break . . . Mel and Griff asked me to do some bits and pieces in *Alas*, which was enormous fun to do, and at the time I was as excited by doing that as I was by *Blackadder* – for a start it was much funnier than the first *Blackadder*! And it meant I was around much more for the creative parts – the first *Blackadder* series, by and large, we acted what was written down, but with Mel and Griff it was much more about workshopping comedy. The script editor was Jimmy Mulville, and we got on very well, so he suggested me for the Channel 4 series.'

Originally piloted in 1983 without Robinson, *Who Dares Wins* was another attempt to carry on where *Not* left off, with an Oxbridge bunch reacting to the foibles of 1980s life, spearheaded at first by ex-*Not* scribe Andy Hamilton and Denise O'Donoghue. With head writers Mulville and Rory McGrath joining Oxonians Pope and Julia Hills for the full series – broadcast late on Saturday night on Channel 4 in 1984, specifically aimed at boozy youths thrown out at closing time – Tony's 'theatrical university of life' background made him an interesting performer to complete the quintet, and gave him plenty of scope for showing a little versatility after the less rewarding creation of the first Baldrick (even if he is mainly remembered as a panda, or for running around naked). 'I think I learned more from the four series of *Who Dares Wins* than almost anything I've ever done. I was surrounded by incredibly talented people at the top of their game who were constantly creating comedy, it really was a comedy factory, and you either sank or swam.'

Although never a mainstream hit in the vein of *Not*, *Who Dares Wins* did boast some of its best writers, including Hamilton, Guy Jenkin and Colin Bostock-Smith, plus Tony Sarchet, all given specific licence to push as many boundaries of taste as they dared. 'We got away with murder!' Tony says. 'And this was the time when Mary Whitehouse was watching every sketch show like a hawk.'

Luckily for Who Dares Wins Productions, latterly Hat Trick (the production company started by McGrath, Mulville and his wife O'Donoghue to make the programme), another sketch show on Sunday nights over on ITV was drawing far more flak from the nation's moral watchdogs. With the launch of *Spitting Image*, John Lloyd had moved on from Rowan Atkinson's rubber face to a cast of thousands of them, and in the process he would inspire a whole new chain of collaborations and comic legacies – starting with an early writers' meeting not long after the broadcast of *The Black Adder*, at which Richard Curtis's paranoia about his sitcom's popularity was calmed by his meeting a genuine fan, in the shape of *Young Ones* writer and budding stand-up Ben Elton.

Parte the Third:

THE VIRGIN BASTARD

With Henry Tudor establishing the most efficient internal government and secure royal line in late-medieval Britain, it's not surprising that the system inherited by his granddaughter in 1558 should have been one of unprecedented sophistication and power. Elizabeth's time on the throne would usher in revolutions in literature and warfare, but as a time of espionage and intrigue, the Elizabethan era also stands alone. Thanks to the machinations of her spymaster Francis Walsingham and the delicate balance of power between Protestant England and her Catholic neighbours, the Queen's reign was a hotbed of secrecy, plot, murder, mystery and cunning planning. So many differing and unverifiable claims can be made about Elizabeth's forty-five-year reign (Did she hide a bastard by Dudley or Seymour? Had she colluded with Dudley to kill his first wife? Was she Shakespeare? Was Shakespeare Shakespeare?) that it would be very easy for our Blackadder Chronicler to drop in a celebrated forebear, right in the heart of the Tudor court, in its first flush of post-Bloody Mary jubilation.

Especially in this early part of her rule, Elizabeth's flirting with her favourites and teasing of both her council and the Princes of Europe with promises to wed and deliver an heir ensured that there would be so many posthumous claimants to the Virgin Queen's deflowering that one more favourite (albeit one who has escaped any mention in primary sources of the period) would make little difference. However, what nobody would expect such a claimant to suggest is that Elizabeth I was, for at least the last two-thirds of her reign, a psychotic cross-dressing German called Ludwig.

The issue of Elizabeth's sexuality has been so hotly debated for centuries that the question of her actual *sex* is seldom addressed. Until the Queen was approaching her fifties, her doctors regularly testified that her reproductive organs were still capable of providing a healthy child. Although medicine may not have been the most advanced of sciences in the sixteenth century, it would be hoped that a royal physician could recognise a Prussian package when he saw one – but then who could say that any quack, violently threatened by his monarch to keep well away from the crown jewels and to report that all was well, would dare to defy her, or him?

Certainly, the bulk of the history of the Lord Edmund Blackadder (1529–66), one-time Lord High Executioner and part-time explorer, depicts the sovereign as girly in the extreme. The Lord's exact line of descent from Prince Edmund Plantagenet is never entirely settled in the Chronicles, with different claims that he was his great-, or great-great-grandson. But it's easy enough to posit that any determined bastard spawn of Prince Edmund could have convinced the wily Henry VII that his silence on the little matter of Henry's thrashing at Bosworth was easily bought, with a new title and perhaps a Blackadder Hall to call home. The next Edmund in line, identified in the Chronicles as Cardinal Blackadder, Keeper of the Privy Rolls, would have thrived in the debauched and dastardly environment of Henry VIII's court. Any noble given licence to hang around the royal toilet was in effect the closest to the seat of power in the whole kingdom, and the family thrived, until Henry VIII's death (here claimed to be murder at the Cardinal's hands) led to Queen Mary's reign of terror, and exile for the whole family, whereupon Cardinal Blackadder was said to have frittered away the family fortune on 'wine, women and amateur dramatics'. This left his impecunious but dashing son ill-suited to dallying with Elizabeth when she took to the throne, and yet here he is claimed to be her real favourite, making all but daily visits to the Queen's palace at Richmond.

Lord Robert Dudley has always been recognised as the closest thing to a real love in Elizabeth's life, but it may be telling that the dates for Lord Blackadder's time at the heart of the Elizabethan court begin in 1560 – two years into the Queen's reign, and the same year that Dudley's chances of ever marrying Elizabeth were nixed by the questionable suicide of his terminally ill wife Amy Robsart, in the summer. Perhaps with her hopes for Dudley dashed, Elizabeth turned to another intimate, the handsome Edmund, her 'Ned'. Elizabeth's numerous favourites are well documented, from Raleigh and Essex to poor Sir Christopher Hatton, who went to his grave unmarried, still proclaiming his love for the redhead ruler. Yet there is no Edmund on record – perhaps the most tantalising equivalent known to historians would be Thomas Butler, 'the Black Earl', a childhood friend of Elizabeth who grew to be a witty charmer, nicknamed 'my black husband' by the Queen. As an Irish noble, however, he is clearly not our man.

This problematic stretch of the Chronicles does suffer greatly from being dramatically at odds with the established record. Although purporting to cover the years 1560–66, Edmund's comic tragedy is studded with impossible claims for the time – Shakespeare is mentioned despite having just been born, and Raleigh himself was only a youth in the 1560s, not to return from the New World until 1581 – bringing with him sweet tobacco, not potatoes. Although it's possible that a forgotten member of the Percy family could have been at court in this time, the Chronicle also features the ever-present figure of Lord Melchett, who remains mysterious to history, while there is no mention of the Queen's constant adviser William Cecil, Lord Burghley. Perhaps the Lord High Treasurer was unwell during Lord Blackadder's visits, but the complete lack of any mention does seem fishy, as Cecil was the man to conquer, if Edmund stood any chance of wooing the Queen. Why Cecil also neglected ever to acknowledge such a favourite of Elizabeth (and a noble who allegedly discovered Australia two hundred years early, no less) is a question the Blackadder Chronicler fails to address. Perhaps the one note of verisimilitude in this passage comes from the depiction of one of the Queen's closest servants, Blanche (not Bernard) Parry, who had been in the Queen's service since birth, serving as her wet nurse, and would loudly and happily tell all and sundry, right up until her death in 1590, that she had rocked the sovereign in her cradle.

Of course, if Prince Ludwig was in power under the guise of Elizabeth Tudor, it's only natural that he would destroy every mention of the one man who came closest to vanquishing him, the 'Indestructible' master of disguise. If such a German prince had existed at this time, he would probably have to have been an unpopular son of the Holy Roman Emperor Maximillian II. Perhaps paternal neglect, being considered too short, greasy and spotty to be acknowledged in the family record, could have been enough to spur Ludwig on to killing his way to a throne, even if it did then mean spending forty years in a dress. But then, if the bloodshed of Prince Ludwig's revenge was as horrific as described in the Blackadder Chronicles, it's a wonder that anyone was ever in a position to record the death of Lord Edmund, and the real Elizabeth, at all.

But is that reason enough to dismiss entirely the theory that Queen Elizabeth I was a man, from 1566 until her death in 1603? Professor Pollard certainly believes so. 'Whilst there is the legend of the "Bisley Boy", which does indeed suggest that the young Princess Elizabeth was swapped for a man, the clue to its authenticity comes in the title "The LEGEND of the Bisley Boy" and even in the florid pages of this story there is no mention of "Ludwig the Indestructible". The Blackadder Chronicles of this date also present other insurmountable problems – the completely different make-up of the court, the failure of any protagonists from outside the Chronicles to be present at the place and time (and even age) that they are known from elsewhere and, perhaps most significantly, the fact that the only surviving manuscript of this section of the Chronicles appears to have been written in the margins of a copy of the *Racing Post*.'

This is of course sheer wilful arrogance, when discussing a time as murky and duplicitous as the Elizabethan reign. Whoever it was who gave up the ghost at Richmond Palace on 24 March 1603, man or woman, Tudor or German, they took with them enough secrets to provoke a thousand conspiracy theories, and the one concerning Prince Ludwig would surely not be the least likely of them all. Besides, from the Blackadder family's point of view, Ludwig's massacre of the Elizabethan court and successful hushing up of his transvestite usurpation was at least delayed payback for Henry Tudor's own dishonest takeover – the Tudor dynasty ending as it had begun, with one ambitious bastard, and a stack of dead bodies.

Chapter 3

BLACKADDER II

I try, Madam . . . And then, ten minutes later when I've got my
breath back, I try again

Enrolling at Manchester University in the late 1970s may not have had the same cachet as going up to Oxford or Cambridge, but the ancient academies could never have hoped to hold their position as the near-exclusive training grounds of Britain's educated comics forever, and the thriving revue traditions at institutions like Manchester and Bristol, many with a commitment to taking shows up to the Edinburgh Fringe, were sure to add to the nation's wealth of entertainers eventually. By 1979 Manchester had already turned out two of the greatest comics of the next decade, Mayall and Edmondson, who had both been conspicuous stars of the university's drama course – long-haired self-proclaimed genius Rik was going out with his tutor's daughter, Lise Mayer, and Ade, already on his first marriage, was the lead in most of the department's biggest productions, and liked trying to ride his motorbike up the stairs in Rik's student house.

The anarchic duo who staged plays about God's testicles in the refectory to try and get their Equity cards couldn't have failed to leave an impression on the freshers they left behind, but they equally wouldn't forget about one eager bespectacled writing machine from two years below – even if Edmondson claims his earliest memory of the first year in question is Mayall shouting, 'Duck! Ben Elton's coming up the drive!'

'As soon as Ben arrived, he started writing,' Mayall recalls, astounded. 'First years don't do that! He got to know everyone very quickly, and he was casting! You know, meeting people, getting to know them, seeing who the best actors are, and churning out plays, really fast.' 'I didn't *really* know them,' Elton admits, 'Rik and I were sort of pally – he used to take the piss out of me, basically – and I never really knew Ade . . . Rik was a couple of years above me, and my God, did he let that be known! He used to pretend he didn't know my name, that was his great joke, he'd say, "Oh hi, fresher, what's your name again?" I mean, we'd been working together for years. I was always the little farty fresher . . . But he came to see one of my plays, and he must have thought it was funny because two or three years later when he and Lise Mayer were starting to write *The Young Ones* and they felt they needed another element, they thought of me.'

BENJAMIN CHARLES ELTON
BORN: 3 May 1959, Catford, London

Like Rik Mayall, Elton was born to academic parents, but his father was from a more exalted scholastic background. Gottfried and Ludwig Ehrenberg, the two sons of German Jewish scholars, first came to Britain in 1939 for obvious reasons, and it was while fighting against their ex-compatriots in World War II that they anglicised their names, to Geoffrey and Lewis Elton. Geoffrey would go on to be knighted for his work as a historian, specialising in the Tudor period, while Lewis moved to south-east London, became a professor of physics, and married English teacher Mary.

Ben was one of four children – and the loudest. 'I've always been a talkaholic. My mum used to have a rule when I was little, that she had to be on her second cup of tea before I was allowed to start talking.' As he told Roger Wilmut in 1989, the family was 'Middle class, no question there. My dad's an academic, my mother's a teacher, so I suppose I had quite an academic background, but I went to ordinary schools. We went to Guildford when I was ten. I was always grateful I was brought up in a liberal household – I always felt I learned a great deal more at home than I did at school.' Over the years Elton has been criticised for affecting an estuary accent, but his state education in south-east London gave him the same vowels as his friends and siblings.

By the time Ben was settled in at Godalming Grammar School, however, the eleven-year-old Catfordian had decided what he wanted to be: Noël Coward. 'I hadn't discovered his work at that point, but I fell in love with his *life*.' Ben's other main spur to follow the theatrical life – besides an adoration of the front-of-curtain antics of Morecambe & Wise – was joining the Godalming Theatre Group (of which he was ultimately made President), and winning the role of the Artful Dodger in their production of *Oliver!*. 'I didn't even have to audition! They thought, "There's a show-off little oik, we'll have him!" I don't think they could get a boy to play Oliver, either the part was too wet, or there wasn't a boy good enough or whatever, so they cast a girl, Gabrielle Glaister – my oldest friend, really.' 'He was wonderful,' Glaister was to recall, 'because he has got a huge stage presence, and that's a fantastic part. He's so vibrant, that's the thing about Ben, he's a little thing full of lots and lots of energy.'

'I wanted to be an actor at that point,' Elton continues, 'but quite quickly my ambitions changed, and by the age of thirteen I knew that principally I wanted to be a writer.' The precocious teenager began writing plays and jokes with a characteristic verve, and did not slow his pace when he moved away from home at the age of sixteen to study English, History and Drama in the apt locale of Stratford-upon-Avon. 'I wouldn't have wanted to be out facing the world at sixteen – or eighteen, I was pretty ill-equipped at twenty-one – but at least I had quite a lot of time to meet people, to think – no pressure – and I'm grateful for that.' Having gained top grades after two years fending for himself in a Warwickshire caravan at such a young age, it's no wonder that Ben seemed so immensely confident to his fellow freshers at Manchester University in 1977.

✤

The Farty's Guide

By the time he graduated in 1980, Ben Elton had written numerous plays (including two musicals), and garnered a reputation as a safe pair of hands on the typewriter, and certainly prolific. 'That's a bit of a legend, really – well, I don't think you could go so far as to call it a legend – but it has been put about the place that I wrote thirty plays while I was at university. I certainly wrote thirty identifiable pieces, but I think about seven or eight full-length plays . . . a lot of sketches, monologues, anything. Most stuff was rubbish – you don't write your best stuff when you're eighteen.' Comic ideas overflowed from the student, and though the words poured out in his own dyslexic approximation of the Queen's English, his inventiveness, ambition and prodigious output were key to his future. *The Bear Hunt, Man of Woman Born, Musso the Clown,** all these early efforts were proffered up for undergraduate entertainment, and he simply didn't care that his ambition and 'let's do the show right here!' bravado made him a target for his cynical contemporaries. 'I was never cool – in fact, the penny dropped quite early for me, that being cool was kind of holding things in contempt, you know? You

---

* Historical drama was a speciality – the last play imagined the scene when Mussolini was captured by partisans, prior to being strung up in 1945.

hate what's going on in the world, you hate your course, etc. And I didn't – I loved what was going on!' At five foot eight Ben was hardly a dwarf, but knew it was easy for his contemporaries to look down on his enthusiasm, and had already embraced his reputation as a theatre nerd by reclaiming the term 'farty' – not just for himself, but as a kind of ineffectual everyman.

Although Manchester would remain central to his career for years to come, it was natural for the 21-year-old Elton to head homewards after graduation and equally natural that he would join his fellow Mancunian graduates to see how 20th Century Coyote were developing out in the wide world. 'I'd just left university, and I bumped into Rik – and of course Rik and Ade were into something exciting, they'd become part of what was known as the "Alternative Comedy Boom". . . I wrote myself an act, auditioned at the Comic Strip (very, very nerve-racking), and God bless Pete Richardson, he gave me a job. Then I got a job at the Comedy Store, and I very soon was able to do it, but it was always the material that was effective. People liked my material, they didn't particularly like me onstage . . . Really, for want of anything better to do, I thought, "Well, I'll have a bash. No one's reading my plays, I'd better shout my comedy to the world." I must say, of all the things I've done in my life, that decision was the most astute and the luckiest – I decided to become a comedian. It has to be said that everybody said, "Don't!"' Mayall admits, 'I was the one who said to him, "Ben, listen, I'm your friend, right? *Don't* go onstage. Don't! Because you'll have a bad time. You're a writer, Ben, you keep writing. Don't go onstage." About a week later he went on at the Comedy Store and *stormed* the place.'

Elton's early act would be painful to him now – allegedly it involved inept impressions of Ronald Reagan – but whatever he was doing was still an improvement on his first stand-up attempt at college, when he thrust on a straw boater and performed a Frank Carson set verbatim. 'There I was as a sixteen-year-old virgin, doing this sort of "grown-up" act.' In the late-night bear-baiting arena of the Comedy Store, he

141

quickly learned a survival tactic which would come to define his style – modesty was never going to ward off the dreaded gong, and so he attacked the boozy crowd at high volume, pre-empting heckling with a combative style and rattling off his painstakingly written material at a fast enough rate not to give the crowd time to get a word in edgeways. At the same time, although he was open about his motives for taking up stand-up, he realised he could not ignore current issues, and he found that he did have something to say, beyond the nightmares of student fridges and InterCity train travel. 'The eighties was an extraordinary decade. People look back, they think it was about BMWs and slicked-back yuppie hair, but the decade was one of continual conflict. The first gigs I ever did, Brixton was in flames, as was St Paul's, as was Toxteth. Y'know, I was twenty-one, twenty-two, playing in London with riots going on outside, it's going to affect your act.' Within six months the firebrand had been made compère at the Store, to some consternation but little surprise, and he admits, 'I really felt like the King of London – I was twenty-one years old, I'd just earned thirty quid or whatever, the cab was gonna cost four quid, you know? I was earning more than the dole in a night, and it just felt fantastic!'

With his great showbiz mates getting off to such a good start, there was little floundering before Ben was invited to showcase his stand-up skills on TV, and he was soon back in Manchester to be a regular on the confusingly named *Oxford Road Show* (broadcast from the BBC's studios on Oxford Road). 'I got a chance to be a bloody awful comedian live in front of a very aggressive audience. I used to think that the *Oxford Road Show* was a competition between a group of skinheads and a group of Mohicans to see who could look most bored during my act.' Nevertheless, riding the wave of popularity attached to any comic who could manage ten minutes on the Comedy Store stage was setting Elton in good stead for his desired career in light entertainment, without any further help.

On the other hand, when Mayall and Mayer sat on the tour bus for the Comic Strip tour in 1981 and had the brainwave of placing their regular characters in a student house together, Rik decided that 'little Ben Elton' was the perfect man to 'churn out the gear' – and without a moment's hesitation, Elton became the youngest scriptwriter in BBC history. When Nigel Planer's Outer Limits partner Richardson refused the role of Mike Thecoolperson, preferring to establish *The Comic Strip Presents . . .* on Channel 4, Ben was quick to offer himself up for the role, but was firmly shouted down. He nevertheless managed to play several small roles in the sitcom – a blind DJ, a stand-up cat, a Grange Hill pupil – and anyway, he had already secured himself his first acting gig on commercial TV – again, thanks to Mayall.

Rik was as hotly in demand with comedy producers in the first years of the eighties as Rowan had been a few years previously, and having been the jewel in the plastic crown of one attempt to cater to young comedy fans in the wake of *Not*'s premature end, it wasn't surprising that he was wooed by producer Sandy Ross at Granada to do the same thing for their new sketch show for ITV. In the end Mayall had to turn the offer down, but not before he'd recommended that they make use of the scripting skills of Elton – and having impressed the producers with his scripts, Ben was in a position to suggest that the best person to bring them to life was himself. So as the first series of *The Young Ones* was nearing completion, the writer was back on the train up to Manchester to meet up with the rest of the troupe for the try-out series of *There's Nothing to Worry About*. In alphabetical order, the opening credits would scream the fledgling comic stylings of Ben Elton, Stephen Fry and Hugh Laurie.

Belts Off, Trousers Down, Isn't Life a Scream?

Six years after John Lloyd picked up his degree from Cambridge, the Footlights revues were still a far cry from the salad days of *A Clump of Plinths*, despite the regular relay of big-names-to-be who continued to file through the club's portals. Martin Bergman and Robert Bathurst

143

would take over the presidency from Jimmy Mulville before Jan Ravens became the first ever female Footlights boss in 1979, but the excitement generated by *Chox* had long since abated by the time the summer revue, *Nightcap*, travelled up to Edinburgh. Even though the scripts came from some of the best writers of Footlights past and present (including Sandi Toksvig, Mulville and McGrath and even Lloyd himself), Bergman's revue would never become embedded in the national psyche. Up against Rowan Atkinson at the Wireworks, *Nightcap* amused without remark, despite boasting not just Bergman and Bathurst in the cast, but the debuts of Emma Thompson, the radiantly gifted daughter of *The Magic Roundabout* genius Eric, and a twenty-year-old Anthropology and Archaeology student who never went to any Anthropology or Archaeology lectures, Hugh Laurie.

Hugh's presence in any comedy revue was a complete surprise to himself, he admits. 'I think I made a girl laugh in a bar . . . so many stories start that way . . . It happened by sheer fluke. I'd gone to Cambridge University to become an oarsman, but I met this woman called Alison in the student bar one night. I told a joke or something and she said, "You've got to come with me." She took me to this club and said, "Here are these people doing the Footlights; you've got to audition." So I did and off it went . . .' Emma Thompson instinctively knew that rowing was not to be Laurie's real *raison d'être*, nudging a friend on her first sight of the buff blue-eyed six-footer and squealing 'STAR!' – and she would be proved right with surprising speed. Although the strapping young athlete would get his blue at the following spring's Oxford and Cambridge Boat Race, his crew would lose the race by a mere five feet, which would haunt him (at least on chat shows) for decades to come. A bout of glandular fever finally finished off any hopes he had of following his father into Olympic rowing, but that just left more room for fooling around getting laughs.

One non-Footlighter up in Edinburgh for a Cambridge production of *Oedipus Rex*, an English scholar who had gained a bit of a reputation as a handy performer to turn to when in need of an aged classical or Shakespearean king of any kind, managed to get tickets to both Atkinson's and Laurie's revues. The former would leave young Stephen Fry 'almost unable to walk. My sides and lungs had taken a hell of a beating. They had never been put to such paroxysmal use in their lives ... That is the kind of joy that can never be reconstructed, to encounter an outstanding talent for the first time with no preconceptions and no especial expectations.' *Nightcap*, on the other hand, though it made less of an impression on Fry's funny bone and bladder, would have far bigger repercussions on his entire life, bringing him face to face with his closest colleague for the first time. 'A tall young man with big blue eyes, triangular flush marks on his cheeks and an apologetic presence that was at once appallingly funny and quite inexplicably magnetic.'

To this day neither Hugh nor Stephen can agree on how the two would make meaningful personal contact beyond mumbled post-gig congratulations – whether it was Thompson dragging Fry to Hugh's home where they instantly began working on a song for the Footlights pantomime together, or perhaps Hugh rolling up at Stephen's rooms for tea, crumpets and chess – but as Fry was to affirm in his second volume of autobiography in 2010, 'The moment Hugh Laurie and I started to exchange ideas it was starkly and most wonderfully clear that we shared absolutely the same sense of what was funny and the same scruples, tastes and sensitivities as to what we found derivative, cheap, obvious or stylistically unacceptable.'

STEPHEN JOHN FRY
BORN: 24 August 1957, Hampstead, London

'One of the interesting things about being English is that people who are said to be exemplars are often curiously hybrid, as I am,' Fry offers of his genealogy. 'My father's family, the Frys, are as

English as you can get. As my great-uncle George wrote in a not highly successful book entitled *The Saxon Origins of the Fry Family*, "unlike so many so-called English families, the Frys did not come over with the Conqueror, they were there to meet him when he arrived". But my mother's family is entirely East European Jewish.'

Fry was the middle child of three born to physicist and inventor Alan and his wife Marianne, and from a very young age it was clear that he was more of a handful than his older brother Roger and little sister Jo put together. A relatively idyllic infancy in Norfolk was interrupted at the age of seven when the time came to decamp to prep school at Stout's Hill in the West Country, where he was acknowledged to be notably gifted, but equally averse to school rules and discipline – a trait which was only exacerbated when he progressed to Uppingham School in Rutland. Between a tendency towards kleptomania, which funded his hard-core addiction to sweets, and the heartbreak which came from coming to terms with his own sexuality (having fallen head over heels in love with a fellow pupil), Fry's regular rebellion led to expulsion from the school at fifteen for going AWOL in London, supposedly addressing the Sherlock Holmes Society, but indulging his love for cinema by watching *Cabaret* and *The Godfather* on a loop.

He spent even less time at his next school before being shown the door, and at the age of sixteen tried to take his own life. The failure of this attempt did not lead to any turning over of new leaves, and one year later he reached a nadir when he stole the credit card of a family friend and led police on a cross-country chase, until the law finally caught up with him in a hotel in Swindon, and the teenager was placed on remand for three months at the misleadingly cuddly-sounding Pucklechurch prison in Gloucestershire.

Whether due to the suffering of his family, or the experience of playing the 'Professor' role for his fellow inmates, who had far fewer opportunities in life than the public-school boy, Stephen left prison and marched confidently towards rehabilitation, gaining a place at City College Norwich by assuring administrators that his A-level grades would earn him a place at Cambridge – and being proved right. A short period of teaching (and mastering smoking a pipe) in Yorkshire presaged his entrance into Queens' College on an English scholarship in 1977. A sensible return to teaching after gaining his degree was his only ambition, but as his two decades of existence had already shown, nothing in Fry's life ran along conventional lines.

❖

JAMES HUGH CALUM LAURIE
BORN: 11 June 1959, Oxford

The Lauries are an ancient Scottish family, but Hugh's father, Olympic rowing hero and colonial doctor William Laurie (known as 'Ran', from his middle name Ranald), was born in Cambridgeshire and settled in Oxford with his family after serving in World War II. By the late fifties, William and his wife Patricia already had a son and two daughters, and one more addition to the family, several years on, came as something of a surprise.

Their youngest son would have his work cut out earning the respect of his parents, and the pressure of having to follow in the footsteps of his gold-medallist father, coupled with a stern Presbyterian upbringing, would not allow the baby of the family any of the swagger which prejudice would suggest comes from being the product of a privileged background. Like his father and brother before him, Hugh would be sent to the world's most elitist school, Eton College, but this exclusive environment, which had churned out world leaders for centuries, failed to instil the school's traditional sense of superiority in the youngster. In fact, his parents struggled to put Hugh through the college, and he admits, 'I went to a very posh school with some very posh people, but I'm not especially posh myself.' He was a gifted child with an innate musical ability, plus a deep love of the blues, passed down to him by his brother. Crucially, he also excelled on the sports field, which at Eton was more important than any academic achievement.

For all his gifts, Laurie describes himself, particularly in adolescence, as a 'horrible' child: lazy, discourteous and difficult, and he has underlined in the past a particularly fraught relationship with his mother, for whom he never felt any achievement was good enough. However, he credits his teenage redemption to the discovery of the works of P. G. Wodehouse, almost single-handedly converting the stroppy adolescent into a bringer of sweetness and light. Winning a scholarship to Selwyn College, Cambridge, also just like his father, Laurie may not have been academically minded, but remained determined to make Ran proud with his rowing career, before making himself useful in some far-flung corner of the Empire.

❖

Having arrived at Queens' College after a year of teaching and a period at Her Majesty's pleasure, Stephen Fry was committed to immersing himself in the world of academe, and despite a rich love of comedy from Wilde, Wodehouse and Coward to the Bonzo Dog Doo-Dah Band, Cook & Moore and Morecambe & Wise, he had no thoughts of the Footlights until he and Laurie clicked in that second year. Tall, thin and saturnine, with meticulously fluffy verbiage on tap and prone to tweed and pipe-sucking, the sudden manifestation of young Fry within the Footlights coterie like the bastard son of Graham Chapman was so smooth it's a wonder that his comic powers weren't unearthed earlier, but even after a thirty-year friendship, the Footlighter who rubber-stamped his entry only offers, 'I just delight in the way his brain works.' Both well over six feet, the goggle-eyed Hugh and bent-nosed Stephen stood out together in any crowd, and over the tops of their contemporaries' heads, the duo made a connection which has survived decades of fame, crises of depression and transatlantic career moves, to become one of Britain's most loved double acts. 'We were very traditional,' Fry says, 'he was the straight man, I was the homosexual man, which is the way it always works.'

When a comedy partnership is forged out of a deep friendship rather than showbiz accident or financial expediency, the love they have for each other tends to be returned by the public a hundredfold, although Fry has noted, 'One of the most fortunate things really for me, as a gay man, is that I never fancied him. Although he's extremely good-looking – which he is, and a lot of women could faint at the sight of him – fortunately, for some reason, that switch was never on with me and Hugh. And it would have been embarrassing if it had been, if you think about it.' Although Stephen and Hugh have flourished apart for longer than they were a partnership, for many fans, no amount of solo success can overshadow the blessed twinning of Fry & Laurie (the ampersand is significant), a partnership which began in the Michaelmas term of 1979.

The new colleagues were only credited sketch writers for the following summer's revue (Footlights' first all-female show), but by their last year, they and Thompson had formed a strong comic group, with Emma repeating her final terms for theatrical reasons, despite having already been enthusiastically signed up to the Noel Gay organisation by Richard Armitage. Cambridge comedy was not just about the annual Footlights shows at the Arts Theatre and the Fringe, and the show that was to become *The Cellar Tapes* emerged from months of charity balls, private parties and smokers.*

---

* It was John Lloyd's visit to one of the latter which led to Fry getting his *Not* credit, much to Laurie's annoyance as it meant they had to cut the gents hand-dryer quickie out of their own show.

With his allegiance now shifted from the rowing team to his new comedy chums, Laurie could be terrifying in the face of barracking and heckling, dragging one 'bijou revolutionary' out from an Emmanuel College May Ball entertainment and shaking him by the throat until the whole marquee quaked, yelling, 'Don't you dare insult my friends!' 'I used to have a lot of confidence,' he admitted on *Desert Island Discs* in 1996, 'I used to think: "I know I can do this; I can stand on a stage with virtually nothing and no idea of what I'm going to say or do, and know that it will be all right, I can make it work." And as soon as I started doing it for a living, it all changed, I don't know why. One of the strange things that happened was that hitherto I had always thought of audiences as being female in character, and when I started to do it professionally for some reason they became male. They became competitive, an adversary that had to be conquered, and I imagined rows of men with their arms folded saying, "Go on then!" I have to confess I'd get very aggressive. Stephen and I would absolutely seethe with rage if we hadn't triumphed.'

Laurie had been such a team player since his first year at Cambridge that it seemed natural for him to inherit the presidency in 1981, with Jan Ravens remaining to direct the revue he and Stephen were poised to stitch together. Fry had indoctrinated multitalented and dirty-minded fresher Tony Slattery into the troupe, although the acknowledged thespian star of their generation, Simon Russell Beale, turned down a similar offer, to concentrate on his serious craft. With Paul Shearer (who was fated to remain an unknown in British Comedy until his roles in *The Fast Show* more than a decade later) and Penny Dwyer (who relinquished comedy for a career in metallurgy before her tragic death in 2003), *The Cellar Tapes* team became without a doubt the first Footlights gang to rival the success of Cleese's generation seventeen years previously. As they rehearsed, Fry & Laurie would gaze up at the imposing monochrome icons of Footlights Past – Cook, Cleese, Garden et al. – and confirm to each other that the good times were gone. Nevertheless, *The Cellar*

Tapes would trace the same path as every previous May Week revue, plopping into the Edinburgh Fringe melting pot in August 1981. Hugh was adamant, that if nothing else, the new show would be different. 'I was absolutely determined that it should be very grown-up, in that very pompous sort of twenty-year-old way. Some of the previous revues had been very sprightly, with young undergraduates nipping around the stage, and that had rather nauseated me, so I wanted to do something . . . rather sick, in fact. And I chose Stephen. Not for the sickness reason, but because he appeared then to be about sixty.'

With hindsight, as with every single Footlights revue ever staged, it's difficult to claim that *The Cellar Tapes*, at least as captured for broadcast by the BBC, could safely be regarded as a classic. With a title giving an early suggestion of Laurie's obsession with espionage thrillers, the show was presented as a rather low-key assemblage of linguistically intricate pastiches – Victorian melodrama, Alan Ayckbourn – and darkly satirical musical spots, concluding with a haunting choral number about the National Front. There are, however, definite highlights that still showcase the revue's original appeal even today – Thompson's prophetic award acceptance speech as 'Juliana Talent', Fry & Laurie's 'Shakespeare Masterclass', and Fry's Bram Stoker send-up, 'The Letter':

STEPHEN: The day the letter arrived I was due in court on the intricate case of Melchett versus the Vatican, which was coming to a delicate and potentially explosive stage. The letter, then, came as a welcome diversion, and I tipped the delivery boy out of the window with more than ordinary generosity. Even then, I fancy I gave a momentary shudder as I unfolded the letter, but it was a cold morning, and in accordance with Mr Tulkinghorn's instructions with regard to Melchett versus the Vatican, I was naked . . .

Fry's choice of name for the man who took on the Pope of course provides an early sign of how much influence he would eventually have on *Blackadder*. Perhaps the standout moment in *The Cellar Tapes*, this monologue, revised and extended – 'I stooped, I recall, to pick a buttercup. Why people leave buttocks lying around I have no idea' – remains Fry's party piece for charity benefits and royal galas alike.

Reviews were unusually kind for a Footlights show – there's a long tradition of critics showing themselves up with bad predictions when it comes to Footlights revues, but there was an irrefutable star quality in this cast that few could ignore. At the close of one performance, Fry recalled, the applause reached an unusual crescendo which mystified the cast – unaware that behind them, in his official role as a member of the Fringe board, the unmistakable figure of Rowan Atkinson had crept onstage, and was ineffectually holding his hand up for silence. Rowan had met the cast a couple of nights earlier, and sent them into paroxysms of embarrassed joy with his praise, but this was inexplicable. 'For a moment or two I thought he had gone insane,' Fry recalled. 'His reputation for timidity was already established. It made no sense whatsoever for him to be there.' Thirty years after the event, Stephen's recollection of the speech that followed can be heard all too clearly in the *Not* star's halting tones: 'Um, ladies and gentlemen. Do forgive me for interrupting like this. You must think it very odd. You may know that this year sees the institution of an award for the best comedy show on the Edinburgh Fringe. It is sponsored by Perrier, the bubbly water people. The organisers and judges of the award, which is to encourage new talent and new trends in comedy, were absolutely certain of one thing – that whoever wins, it wouldn't be the Cambridge bloody Footlights. However, with a mixture of reluctance and admiration, they unanimously decided that the winner had to be *The Cellar Tapes*!' To be the inaugural winners of the most influential award in British Comedy was one thing, to have it sprung on you by your new comic idol, in front of your own ecstatic audience, was an unlooked-for delight.*

Already a stablemate of Thompson's, Rowan continued to play comedic Santa in Hugh and Stephen's lives, as they received their own invitations to sign up to Noel Gay. Armitage had been deeply impressed with Stephen especially, and lost no time in laying out the deal. This impressive figure with the beautiful Bentley and enormous cigars eyed up the lofty pair and asked, 'Do you see yourselves doing this kind of thing professionally? As a career?' And on reflection, they realised that they did. They were shortly to pick up indifferent degrees, with Stephen accepting a 2:1 for English, and Hugh bagging a third. 'He had been to one lecture, which gave him the material for a quite brilliant monologue about a Bantu hut, but otherwise had not disturbed his professors, written an essay or entered the faculty library. I think he would be the first to admit that you know more about archaeology and anthropology than he does,' Fry says, and here was an unexpected consolation. They were lined up for a tour of *The Cellar Tapes*, with a run at the Lyric Hammersmith and heading as far as Australia with Bergman in charge, but after that? Stephen had only considered an academic life, and Hugh was almost entirely sold on joining the Hong Kong Police; but with Emma's inspiration, the two new friends realised that whatever doomed musings about fame they may have had as undergraduates, here was a real old-fashioned, powerful agent who could make it happen for them. 'Stephen was always destined for attention,' Hugh reflected a quarter of a century later, 'he was always going to get attention in this life. I was never sure attention was something I wanted . . .'

Both Stephen and Hugh had been on television before, two years

---

* Not that everyone in the room on that comedy time bomb of an evening was ecstatic – somewhere in the crowd was nineteen-year-old struggling street performer Eddie Izzard, who took one look at the bright young things on stage and vowed that he would be up there himself one day.

earlier – Fry in the Queens' College team on *University Challenge** and Hugh presenting scraps of *Nightcap* on BBC show *Friday Night, Saturday Morning*. 'It was trying to be a sort of David Frosty-type thing, with tart comment on the week's news; and so I suppose I was meant to supply some tart comment. I didn't have any then, and I don't have any now. It's not my thing, tart comment.' Their first joint engagement for BBC TV was a filmed version of *The Cellar Tapes* that was never broadcast – Geoff Posner had seen the show, and asked the team whether they minded being the subject of his Studio Direction Course graduation piece. As his incredible track record from *Not* onwards would suggest, it was good enough for the young Posner to pass with flying colours, but the revue was eventually restaged with a live audience when the cast returned from their tour in 1982, produced by the top man, Dennis Main Wilson.

The Corporation missed the bus this time, however, as by the time the remounted *Cellar Tapes* was broadcast, the cast – with a few adjustments – were packing their bags for an extended stay in Manchester, to film their all-new sketch show for Granada. 'We were extremely lucky,' Laurie says, 'because *Not the Nine O'Clock News* was a great success, and very quickly other television companies were desperately scrabbling to get their own version of it, so suddenly young people doing sketch-comedy became a very sought-after . . . *product* is such an awful word, but that's probably how television executives would have described it. We were sort of caught up in that scrabbling.'

Pretty Much a Case of the Game's Afoot!

Congregating for the first time in the flat of Jon Plowman, then a researcher for Granada but eventually to become one of the most influential comedy executives in the business, the Footlights mob

---

* They were beaten in the final by Merton College, Oxford, in a cerebral mirroring of Hugh's Boat Race experience.

could not help but be aware of the perceived gulf between them and their new co-stars. In truth there was little in it – Scottish actress Siobhan Redmond graduated from St Andrews with an MA in English and, as we have seen, both Elton and eventual cast member Robbie Coltrane came from very comfortable backgrounds. Elton's confident prolificacy, however, was a real eye-opener, as Laurie recalls: 'Ben was just a whirlwind, he sort of blew us away, really. We had one thing written on the back of an envelope, and we'd hold it up and Ben would just smack down this forty pounds of good com.' 'Our slow, mournful and insecure rate of writing had been trumped and trampled on,' Fry confirms. 'Where our comedy was etiolated, buttoned-up and embarrassed, his was wild, energetic, colourful and confident to the point of cockiness . . . Ben would perform his, playing every part, with undisguised pleasure and demented relish. Despite our complete sense of humiliation and defeat we did laugh and we did unreservedly admire his astonishing talent.' For all the Footlighters' fears to the contrary, there was no chance of Elton indulging in inverted snobbery, as might be expected from a Comedy Store compère from a red-brick university. Whatever genuine revolutionary zeal had been apparent in the original cabal of comics at the birth of the Store had been swamped almost immediately by wave after wave of talented and ambitious performers, and besides, as Fry was to argue: 'As an old lag *I* might be said to be the most real and hard of any of them, a thought preposterous enough to show that the idea of there being a group of working-class comics threatening Castle Poncey was really quite misguided.'

Although Fry & Laurie's writing naturally extended from *The Cellar Tapes*, with their revolting suburban 'horror men' Alan and Bernard (soon to mutate into greasy businessmen Gordon and Stuart) putting in an early appearance, Elton had crafted an entire Didsbury street full of characters for the first episode, in a way pre-empting *The League of Gentlemen* by setting interlinking (and rather sick) sketches within a community. His input also provided an unprecedented blend of social comment and juvenile vulgarity, particularly in the role he crafted for Stephen – or rather, as he had rechristened his pipe-smoking new pal, 'Bing'. 'In me he saw a crusty relic of Empire and created a character called Colonel Sodom, who might, I suppose, be regarded as a rather coarsely sketched forerunner of General Melchett.' This grey old buffer lived on the same street as a tribe of yobbish Brüt-swigging 'Wallies', a sickeningly earnest group of young Christians, a tiresomely right-on couple played by Ben and Emma, and Hugh's tragic loser Mr Gannet. Colonel Sodom's main characteristic on his introduction was an apocalyptic case of flatulence which blasted a hole clean through his trousers – and although the undeniably stilted, almost dreamlike drabness of the first of the three try-outs Granada had commissioned was self-contained, Richard Armitage made it clear that he hated the direction in which his new signings were being steered, dubbing their new collaborator 'a foul-mouthed cockney street urchin with a sewer for a mind'.

These 'Other Young Ones' may have beaten Mayall and company to the screen by several months, but it wasn't just to Armitage's relief that their rudimentary offerings only ever aired in the Granada region, to a muted response. The try-out wasn't considered such a disaster that a full series was out of the question, however, with the main alteration being the replacement of the blameless Shearer for Coltrane, fresh from threatening Kevin Turvey and on the verge of taking his place within the Comic Strip team. 'Big, loud and hilarious,' Fry recalls, 'Robbie combined the style and manners of a Brooklyn bus driver, a fifties rock and roller, a motor mechanic and a Gorbals gangster. Somehow they all fitted together perfectly into one consistent character. He terrified the life out of me, and the only way I could compensate for that was to pretend to find him impossibly attractive and to rub my legs up against him and moan with ecstasy.' There was also a change of name – with the crew taking advantage of the latest lightweight video equipment, they could eschew studios altogether and go out into Manchester to film anywhere a sketch dictated, shooting *Alfresco*.

Another perhaps telling change was the introduction of John Lloyd, on script-editing duty. In truth he only cast an eye over a few of the scripts, but it was inevitable that he and this later generation of Cantabrigians would be drawn together, professionally as well as socially. Since the exodus to London, Fry especially had quickly established firm friendships with many of his idols, becoming the darling of the most exclusive parties and a regular at the Zanzibar, the Covent Garden club where almost every figure in this book would meet and drink and schmooze. Fry had already encountered Peter Cook in a restaurant as an undergraduate, and painted the town red with him, and within a short time of 'entering society' he was similarly embraced by his fellow computer nerd Douglas Adams,* and even became a confidant of his hero Vivian Stanshall. As Noel Gay's new young, erudite favourites, Stephen and Hugh were securely set up as part of the graduate comedy elite as if their places had been reserved for them, leaving them free to pop along to Soho to discover a whole new world of riches: advertising. Stephen's deep, warm tones and Hugh's puckish intonations were clamoured for by advertising executives on behalf of everything from nappies to Mexican cuisine, while there were high-profile on-screen roles for Extra Strong Mints, Alliance & Leicester, and myriad consumer goods.†

Whether due to Lloyd's limited influence or not, when the cast booked back into Manchester's Midland Hotel that autumn to start on the new series, their scripts were quite drastically different to those for *There's Nothing to Worry About*. In particular, the sudden explosion in the number of historical pastiches was noteworthy. Amid the twisted musings on the misery of Thatcherite Britain, the first episode cuts to

---

* Who described the protégé's sudden ubiquity as 'a whole cupboardful of Stephen Fries all doing things'.

† It was while recording a surreal commercial for Whitbread bitter, dressed up in military garb with excrescent moustaches, that Fry first encountered a pre-Percy McInnerny, playing a minstrel.

a World War II Stalag, exploring that perennial sketch cliché, the silly POW escape plan. *Ripping Yarns* had already got a whole half-hour out of the set-up, but there's no denying that the cast – especially future Pipe Smoker of the Year Stephen – looked the part in their uniforms (both Allied and Nazi), and the sketch would be recycled for *Saturday Live* a few years later:

MAWKINS (BE): Well, we can't just bloody sit here, can we, sir?

CAPTAIN (HL): Mawkins, I'd like a word with you. Chaps, would you mind? (*Everyone leaves.*) Look, Mawkins, nobody's worked harder on this show than you and, well, if anyone deserved a place on the first team it's you, but I'm afraid I can't let you go.

MAWKINS: But sir, I . . .

CAPTAIN: You're a bastard, Mawkins, we all hate you.

Three decades on, the extended period sequences have inevitably stood the test of time better than any of the satirical, surreal or sick contemporary sketches – although nearly all were so silly as to make little effort to cover up the fact that this was a bunch of youths with a dressing-up box. For the second episode, at roughly the time Curtis was still at the typewriter concocting his own Shakespearean comedy, the *Alfresco* team were out on location actually filming Ben Elton's, on a battlefield complete with pikestaffs, spear carriers and gaily coloured tents:

SERF 1 (SF): 'Ere, George?

SERF 2 (RC): Yars?

SERF 1: You remember yesterday as how I remarked as how it was pretty much a case of once more

	unto the breach, dear friends, once more or
	close up our wall with the English dead?
SERF 2:	Yars, I remember thinking at the time what a
	load of bollocks you do talk.
SERF 1:	Ar, that's as maybe, but the King nicked the
	whole speech! I heard him yesterday, giving it
	down word for word like he made it up himself!
SERF 2:	The bastard!
SERF 1:	He nicks all my best lines, he does. Never a
	word of credit. Never an 'As old Dick were
	saying the other night, it's pretty much a case
	of the game's afoot, God for Harry, England and
	St George', none of that, no, thank you very
	much indeed . . .

However, this conceit is quickly blown apart by Hugh approaching as a camping holidaymaker who has taken a wrong turn and gone through a time warp – despite a generous budget, all of the historical pastiches in *Alfresco* are deliberately paper-thin, with a smattering of Elton puns thrown in to try and provoke the audience into revealing their recorded presence. History was a subject Ben was regularly drawn to – even *The Young* Ones had a high number of jumps to period setting, with medieval TV shows, Coltrane as a Cycloptic pirate, Australia-bound convicts, etc. An *Alfresco* Crimean War sequence with Thompson as a vain Florence Nightingale complaining about the lack of shadow-kissing from her patients once again gives Fry an early run at the bluff General, replying to Nightingale's complaints about the conditions in the field hospital with a blustering 'Well, those are my conditions, Miss Nightingale, and you will just have to accept them!' in true Duke of Wellington style. Wellington himself pops up played by Laurie, advertising his new line in gumboots. Among sketches involving World War II pilots, the French Resistance, gossiping wiggy fops, Regency duellists and Henge-crazy ancient Britons, the team even pulled on tights for their own Robin Hood sketch, pre-empting Tony Robinson's vision by featuring Thompson as a heroic Maid Marian, forced to fight Elton's Sheriff of Nottingham after Laurie's cheesy American Robin accepts a job as a serving maid.

Fry's memoirs reveal that the team remained unsure of themselves through all this jolly dressing-up, not least because filming coincided with the launch of Channel 4, broadcasting *The Comic Strip Presents*. . . and also the first broadcast of *The Young Ones* – after a day's filming, the cast would flop into Stephen's hotel room to watch the competition. 'When Ade Edmondson as Vyvyan punched his way through the kitchen wall in the opening five minutes . . . it felt as though a whole new generation had punched its way into British cultural life and that nothing would ever be the same again.' In comparison, he felt, 'We were guilty of over-complicating everything out of a fear of being perceived as imitative and unoriginal . . . so we wallowed about sightlessly, guiltily and confusedly without the confidence to do what we did best.'

Alfresco's first series once again aired only to a bemused North-West, drawing to a close one week before the debut of *The Black Adder*. Despite being bolstered by music from half of Squeeze, and kicking off a whole host of comic motifs which would stick with Fry & Laurie (including the fatuous foreign language of 'Strom'), nobody claimed it as a hit.

Fry & Laurie had a separate stab at finding a TV vehicle the following year, when BBC2 piloted their spoof science-magazine programme *The Crystal Cube*, a kind of *Look Around You* twenty years early, featuring everyone from *Alfresco* bar Elton and Redmond. The innovative mockumentary style of the show got the thumbs down from the BBC bosses, however, Laurie laments. 'We loved *The Crystal Cube*, we just thought this was something that no one had ever done before, and there were all kinds of great comic possibilities, as we saw it. The BBC I think hated . . . would that be too big a word? No, I think that was about right, they *loathed* it.'

This early setback aired at the same time as *The Black Adder*, but the team's adoration of Atkinson aside, his new sitcom didn't impress them quite as much as Mayall's Molotov cocktail of a half-hour. 'I do remember a little tiny part of me being faintly disappointed that it was a bit of a mess,' Fry admits. 'I don't mean it was badly written or badly performed, it wasn't either of those things. I have this theory that I call the Tennis Theory of Comedy (which sounds very pompous, and indeed is, I promise you). If you watch a tennis match, and it was two of the greatest tennis players in history, it would be meaningless, wouldn't it, if you couldn't see the ball? And I think with *The Black Adder*, you couldn't really see the ball, there was no focus for the comedy, with comedy you have to see who's speaking and who's listening . . . The camera was so wide and so pleased with the rolling parkland and the horses and the guards in the castle and the reality of it all that you lost that. Plus it was filmed, and then shown to an audience, and you can always tell somehow, the audience is not there. I'm a great believer in real, old-fashioned sitcom where there's an audience there. People complain about it, but it really brings it alive.'

Though Stephen's criticism was echoed by Ben, to someone as versed in British history as one of the Elton clan, *The Black Adder* was a weekly pleasure – dense where the *Alfresco* sketches had been scratchy, earthy where their spoofs had been shallow, and Elton declared himself a big fan when he finally got to meet the writer face to face, united by the godfather Lloyd for his new ITV show, *Spitting Image*, in the autumn of 1983.

One Step Beyond

John Lloyd didn't carefully select Curtis & Elton as his chosen writers when perfecting the TV format for topical satire that the decade demanded; they just happened to be two hot names on a long list of gagsters who had impressed him over the years, from *Week Ending* onwards. Long after his failed attempts to interest Fluck & Law in a TV version of their art, the pair had independently struck out with a new scheme, swayed during a famous lunch with graphic designer Martin Lambie-Nairn. Their first choice for producer was an elder Footlighter, Tony Hendra, who had triumphed in the USA with *National Lampoon* since his days of being rude to Miriam Margolyes. Considering Lloyd's early interest in bringing Fluck & Law's grotesque creations to life, it was only fair that he in turn was brought in on the immensely complicated project, alongside Jon Blair. Throughout 1983, whenever *The Black Adder* was not diverting his attention, Lloyd and his fellow producers battled to find the right way to make a weekly topical puppet show a viable programme. Immediately prior to setting off for Alnwick there had been a very basic try-out then titled *UNTV*, with Elton as the sole writer and Lloyd attempting to voice a rubber Michael Foot. Although the show would eventually be driven by two other writing partnerships, Ian Hislop & Nick Newman and Rob Grant & Doug Naylor, Curtis & Elton's involvement did go beyond those early meetings, with both getting several sketches in the first series when it finally aired on Central TV the following spring. The ensuing years would return John to the familiar pressures of passionate, maddening devotion to TV production which had characterised *Not*, with the wrangling of puppets and writers and performers and lawyers consuming him night and day, as he broke out to become sole producer.

He was to bow out after three series,* becoming executive producer and giving Geoffrey Perkins his first taste of TV production after years of success on Radio 4, where he was still keeping the *Oxford Review* spirit going in *Radio Active* (with Curtis still chipping in with jokes), just as fellow cast member Phil Pope had crossed over to become *Spitting Image*'s resident maestro. To have made such an era-defining success

---

* On leaving the producer's chair, he was presented with his own hideous Fluck & Law caricature, which eventually found a home in Curtis's garden as a particularly horrifying scarecrow.

out of a wildly ambitious logistical (and legal) nightmare like *Spitting Image* was both a testament to Lloyd's work ethic and a vindication of his original enthusiasm for the concept. Nevertheless, he realises the madness of claiming any sole praise, telling the audience at a 2005 BFI event, 'When people used to say, "Was *Spitting Image* your idea?" I used to say, "No it wasn't," but actually it's like somebody having this great idea: "Why don't we fly to the moon?", "Yeah, that's great . . . how do we do that?" And then it takes somebody to invent the aeroplane, the internal combustion engine, the rocket, and there's a thousand things . . . and all these little insights that each person on the team – the writer, the puppeteer, a mould-maker – would bring, meant an advance.'

Not least in terms of scriptwriters and performers, *Spitting Image* became as crucial a training ground as *Week Ending* had been the previous decade, with far too many grand names to list submitting sketches throughout its twelve-year history. Few stayed on the credits for long before moving on to their own hit projects, and from that first meeting, it was clear that Ben and Richard had other topics to debate once they'd been brought together by the latex satirists – partly how much they loved each other's sitcoms and shared a taste not just for the obvious influences, *Python* and Cook, but the more mainstream humour of Morecambe & Wise and *Dad's Army*. By far their most distracting shared passion, however, was pop music – the cheesier the better (although Ben used to make Richard buy Kylie Minogue singles for him, as he was less recognisable). 'Put me and Ben in a room, and we were only interested in Madonna and Madness and talking about pop and the Beatles. We didn't care about comedy enough to waste our time talking about it,' Curtis says. 'I'd also tried writing in the same room with Rowan, and it was just so slow and boring that we'd get stuck on the jokes. So, from the start, Ben and I exchanged computer disks with each other. The only way is just to sweat it out on our own.' 'Nowadays, with email, I guess we would probably never have met!'

163

Elton adds. 'In those days I used to glue bits on, and "lift tab here, see B attached", etc., as did he.' By this time, Curtis had abandoned Camden Town for the Oxfordshire countryside, and admits, 'I had years and years that were spectacularly ill-disciplined as far as time was concerned. I lived in a little cottage in the country and used to be as chaotic and self-indulgent as writers are allowed to be: watching eight or nine hours' television a day, watching *Neighbours* twice, and often not starting work until three in the afternoon.' Another quirk shared by the two writers was an inability to do the job without having music playing – in Curtis's case, because 'I think that trying to write comedy is a bit like trying to get yourself in the mood you are with your friends at the end of a dinner party, cheerful, and the only way I can artificially bolster myself is to put on happy pop music.'

Naturally, this first meeting between the two pop addicts brought up the subject of the regular bands who played in *The Young Ones* lounge every week – a clever ploy designed to make use of the bigger budgets doled out for BBC Variety programmes. Both were big fans of the north London ska outfit Madness, who had made the most memorable musical appearance in the first series episode 'Boring' ('You hum it, I'll smash yer face in'), and would be back for a musical street riot in the second series. Geoff Posner had shared with Ben his admiration for the witty musicians' style, and had an idea. 'I felt that there was a bit of a lack of a youth-orientated comedy programme, and when Madness were in *The Young Ones*, although they were a little ill-disciplined when they recorded their bit, it was quite clear that they generated a lot of excitement, they were the group that everybody wanted to have on. And I thought that this could be the eighties equivalent of *The Monkees*.'

Curtis leapt at the chance to try and create a musical sitcom with Elton, but at this stage any spin-off had to wait, as Elton had second outings for *The Young Ones* and *Alfresco* to write, and perform. There was a final attempt to rejig the latter to find the right chemistry for a break-out hit – the original mournful credits were replaced with a jaunty comic-strip intro, setting up a zany return to the sitcom-style framing device of the first pilot. Taking their own advice to the *Blackadder* team, the cast returned to performing in front of a live audience in their new comic personas, who congregated in Bobza Coltrane's 'pretend pub'. Stephen became florid kindly aristocrat Lord Sezza, Hugh the right-wing Huzza, and Ben gave his persecution complex a physical manifestation as the prole-like Bezza. The show was edging from strength to strength, but after another six episodes it was clear that this cast couldn't be kept together for more regional engagements, and they called it a day after two series. Thompson was especially unable to commit to further shows, due to starring in the massively successful revival of Noel Gay's thirties musical *Me and My Girl*, masterminded by the composer's son, who invited Fry to pen the new book – making him a millionaire by his mid-twenties in the process.

Alfresco may not have caught on, but having failed to beat *The Young Ones*, the Granada gang elected to join them, as the sitcom's second series overlapped with the end of their run in the summer of '84. Where the first series of *The Young Ones* had built up a cult following, the second became a national sensation, not just with the students in the firing line, but their younger siblings drawn to the cartoony anarchy of Rick, Mike, Neil and Vyvyan's escapades – aided by the sudden boom in the home VCR market ('YES, WE'VE GOT A VIDEO!') which allowed fans to memorise every episode with endless re-viewings. The first outing, 'Bambi', finally brought the *Alfresco* cast, aka 'Footlights College, Oxbridge', face to face – or panel below panel – with the Scumbag University students, for a *University Challenge* contest which had originally been suggested to Ben by Stephen since they recorded in the same Granada studios as the long-running quiz show. Where *The Young Ones* had quite viciously swiped at Footlighters in the first series, the right-on anti-Oxbridge sentiment of 'Bambi' was toothless, having been suggested by a Footlighter, and Balowski family star

Alexei Sayle was beside himself with repulsion at the infringement. 'I thought, "These are the enemy!" I was out there sawing through the brake cables of Stephen Fry's car, saying, "These people are the Devil and you're inviting them onto my show!" Of course nobody else knew what I was talking about, you know – "Stephen's lovely! Emma's gorgeous!" I was a twat to go on about it really, but that's how I felt.' Sayle ultimately played a smaller role than usual in the episode, and had no need to interact with the interlopers, even though the studio for that recording was packed with one of the richest crossovers of comic talent in a generation – Griff Rhys Jones and Victorian doctors Coltrane and Robinson included. On the other hand, Tony says, 'It's only in hindsight that you are aware of the fact that it was a bit like playing the England team against Brazil or whatever, that's not what you're thinking of at the time. What I was thinking was, "I hope that fucking elephant isn't going to drag me all the way across the studio." You cannot take an elephant where it does not want to go . . .'

The end of that summer saw an even more priceless blend of comedians congregating together in the unlikely genteel surroundings of the Hampshire village of Nether Wallop. A thatched and gabled time warp that doubled as Miss Marple's home of St Mary Mead in the BBC series, Wallop became the site of an attempt to stage an arts festival to rival Edinburgh, when journalist Stephen Pile complained about the need for an overflow from the crowded Fringe. Professor Stanley Unwin, author Gore Vidal, poet Roger McGough, artist Ralph Steadman, musicians Jools Holland and Bill Wyman, and actors Michael Hordern and Jenny Agutter were just some of the artists to stand alongside the village's local talents in the festivities – and Bamber Gascoigne, coincidentally, hosted a special village quiz. The zenith of the weekend was the Sunday-night gala in a marquee, overseen by Paul Jackson and starring the cream of the *Secret Policeman's Balls*, Pythons aside. As well as Billy Connolly, new boys Fry & Laurie repeated their 'Shakespeare Masterclass', Rik Mayall brought along Kevin Turvey as well as appearing in person for a nostril-snorting rendition of 'Trouble', and Rowan Atkinson was reunited with Peter Cook – albeit not onstage. Rowan slipped back into his native Geordie to harangue the local football team's performance at that morning's match, while a glowingly inebriated Cook and Mel Smith giggled their way through a one-off display of dry-land lesbian synchronised swimming which had been hammered out with Lloyd over several pints, and half forgotten by the time they reached the stage. These top-drawer bookings were drawn to the festival largely by the sheer eccentricity of the event, but also by the fund-raising aspect – partly in aid of the church spire, but mainly for Charity Projects, an organisation set up by Jane Tewson to help the homeless in Soho. Although dyslexia prevented her from getting any qualifications, Tewson had attended lectures at Oxford while working as a cleaner, and her reunion at Wallop with Oxford graduates Atkinson and especially Curtis, there to lend his friend humorous support, would yield extraordinary charitable results.

With Rick and his bachelor boys burnt to death in a double-decker bus in the valedictory 'Summer Holiday', Posner decided it was time to put his spin-off idea into action, and Ben and Richard gladly got together to posit a sitcom format which could contain the anarchic Madness while giving them room to get into all sorts of comical scrapes. The group set up their own cabinet in a cafe in Camden Town, with lead singer Suggs as the new Prime Minister of Great Britain, and their arch-nemesis would be the cartoonish villain Dr. Maniac, played, like his nerkish henchmen, by the band themselves. The lads had a grand day out messing around with the idea, with Elton himself filling in any extra lines.

ELTON: (v/o): And now, a party political broadcast on behalf of Madness.

SUGGS: As the Prime Minister, I've been asked to give an address to the nation. And the address I've

chosen to give is Mrs Hilda Carmichael of 104
The Old Kent Road, London N3. Hilda lives
alone, and hasn't received any letters for ages.
It would be lovely if you could just drop her a
line and wish her well. By the way, thanks for
voting Madness – the party that actually cares!

The resultant rough ten-minute caper (in which Dr Maniac steals
some secret bomb plans just as the boys expect a visit from their mums)
didn't give much room for the Curtis/Elton partnership to show what
they could do, Posner admits. 'It wasn't quite what I thought it would
be. The most important thing is, it wasn't a pilot, it was a taster. We did
it on a shoestring, with the most simple kind of camera that there was
– I couldn't afford to hire any actors, it was just Madness, everything
was really basic. And of course it doesn't really hang together very well,
but I thought that somebody was going to turn round and say, "I think
there's a germ of an idea here." With Ben and Richard writing, we
could perhaps create a teatime programme on Saturday that people
would love, with Madness playing two or three numbers in the middle.
I thought the people viewing it would be a little more adventurous, but
it fell by the wayside.'

Luckily Curtis & Elton weren't holding their breaths for BBC Variety
boss Jim Moir to jab a thumb either way, as they had already decided to
collaborate on the even more thorny problem of how to reanimate the
corpse of the Black Adder, and make his cunning plans funnier than
ever.

Cowpats from the Devil's Own Satanic Herd

There was no question that Curtis knew he had to start from scratch,
having slaughtered the entire Plantagenet dynasty in 'The Black Seal',
but there was never any possibility of the small matter of all the main

characters dying standing in the way of Atkinson getting a second series. John Howard Davies had already recommended some form of reincarnation, as Curtis admits. 'That was John's suggestion, he said, "Well, you've probably done enough in that era, do another one, then another one!" Which was one of the reasons it was so delightful to work on. I think the public liked it because it kept changing.' Howard Davies also compared Edmund's journey to *Flashman*, and although that literary saga only follows the exploits of one man, George MacDonald Fraser's extrapolation of one character from *Tom Brown's Schooldays* to create the whoring, dishonourable coward Harry Flashman certainly provided an admirable blueprint for how to establish a believable fiction, interwoven with comically distorted real history.

If the Blackadder Chronicles traced the family tree throughout British History, then Curtis & Elton had at least half a millennium left to play with for their second entry in the series. 'It might have been in the back of our minds that we would change it, but obviously it was very convenient to change it, after the first one clearly needed mending,' Curtis says, 'and thereafter, it was just such a great thing to be able to jump and deal with new jokes, rather than being stuck in the same time.' Elton – who at first had been keen to make an even cleaner break, changing the characters entirely – was already enthusiastic about the era for Edmund's next incarnation, returning the show to the century of the original pilot, albeit this time rooted in fact. He may have enjoyed the first series, but admitted to Lloyd, 'I hate that period, it's muddy and filthy and horrible, and we should do the Elizabethan thing, which is dead sexy.'

'We kind of talked the Elizabethan period through,' Ben says, 'and came up with a number of things – discovery, disease, tobacco, beheading, that sort of thing – and we felt instinctively we were sort of on the right track; touching on a certain sort of half-remembered school history memories for people, and yet actually, you know, playing very fast and loose with them.' Elton was already steeped in knowledge,

169

which was only natural for the nephew of the author of *England Under the Tudors*, G. R. Elton; but still, Curtis admits, 'We wrote the whole second series without ever reading a book. After we'd written *Blackadder II*, I gave Ben a Ladybird book of Elizabethan history for Christmas and it turned out we'd covered twelve of the thirteen chapters. Somewhere in your bones, you know there was exploring, beheading, religious corruption, the invention of the cigarette and so on.' If Elizabeth I was their monarch this time round, the only status worthy of a prince's bastard descendant, which would give free rein for them to experience all that the times offered, was one of the Queen's infamous favourites – the missing link between Dudley, Raleigh and Essex.

History was one thing, but getting the laughs right was the most important element. Elton says, 'My sort of memory of it is Richard basically saying, "Look, it sort of only half worked, we think we got a lot of it right and a lot of it wrong, and would you like to come in, and *we'll* write it?" And of course, I thought "Fantastic!" The opportunity to write lines for Rowan Atkinson!' 'The very first lesson was to pick Rowan's character, to get it exactly clear what it was he was going to do,' Curtis remembers. 'There was a whole imperious, sarcastic, posh side of Rowan which we both loved, which we knew how to write, it came very naturally to both of us . . . Ben and I went through the vocabulary of the first series, and went through what Rowan could do, and decided that someone that sarcastic would be fun. We just sort of made him simpler, and he could then become increasingly complicated through the episodes and through the series.' Most important of all, however, was the agreement to return to the studio. Talking from experience, Ben urged, 'Let's get into the studio and have two wooden, cardboard sets, because the money's in Rowan's face. Rowan falling off a horse at two hundred metres is not really funnier than anyone else falling off a horse at two hundred metres, but get the camera in close, and he'll make you laugh.'

With their blueprint laid out before them, Elton had to call time yet again on the process to see to the weight of projects he had on the go.

His workaholism was fuelled by two primary bosses at this point – Paul Jackson in TV and Phil McIntyre in the live arena. McIntyre was a top rock promoter, but soon saw the appeal of putting comedians on the road in much the same way that bands like the Smiths and New Order were touring under his mantle. Elton had developed a live show originally to star Mayall, with Andy de la Tour supporting, but it soon became a fifty–fifty affair: 'Rik and I both wanted to tour, and Rik was a big star so we were able to play 2,000-seaters; he wanted me to go because we wrote together, and because I was a good support act – and because we were mates. Rik said we must have equal billing and equal money, which was probably the only time a star has ever done that! It's very difficult to write for Rik's live act because it's really an excuse for him to be brilliant, to be a hilarious person. It was astonishing to watch him do so much with so little.' Through '84 and '85 they honed their live show, even taking it to Ibiza for Club 18–30 holidaymakers, with support from Peter Bennett-Jones. 'Rik was doing Kevin Turvey in a rabbit costume,' Ben recalls. 'It was a hundred degrees in that club, and he had his Rik suit, the Kevin Turvey furry bomber jacket on top, and on top of that his rabbit suit for the first half of the set. The man was mad.'

While his stand-up career continued to flourish, Elton was put to work by Jackson on two comedy series. His script-editor role on ITV sitcom *Girls on Top* was simply a guiding hand for main scriptwriters Dawn French, Jennifer Saunders and Ruby Wax, as they pieced together an all-girl sitcom which was openly inspired by *The Young Ones*. *Happy Families*, however, was the 25-year-old's first solo creation for the BBC, planned for broadcast on prime-time BBC1 in the autumn. This time a live audience was specifically rejected in favour of thirty-five-minute filmed episodes of such blackly perverse comedy it's little wonder that critics had no idea what to make of it. Elton's style of humour remained as grossly cartoonish as *The Young Ones*, but within the context of a dark comedy serial telling the story of the dysfunctional, incestuous aristocratic Fuddle family, and the cocktail was an acquired taste. In a way, *Happy Families* was intended as something of an *Alfresco* spin-off designed to exhibit Emma Thompson's versatility, as Paul Jackson recalls. 'Ben had been sitting at home one rainy afternoon, watching *Kind Hearts and Coronets*, and he thought to himself – very Ben at the time – "Why shouldn't a woman get the chance to do a comedy like this?"' *Me and My Girl* of course put paid to any hopes of Thompson taking part, but one major link to the Granada show remained – Fry's return as the misogynistic, arrogant bastard of a family physician, Dr De Quincy.*

Jackson hadn't worked with Thompson before, so the loss of the star simply meant that he could offer the challenge of playing a host of strange characters to a comedian whose talents he already trusted, Jennifer Saunders. With Ade Edmondson starring as Guy, a mentally damaged cross between a Wodehouse Drone and the ultimate farty, his then girlfriend Saunders played a quintet of wildly different roles completing the family. When Guy's hate-filled grandma is told by De Quincy that she has nine months to live, she sends the idiot round the world to reunite his four long-lost sisters: Hollywood star Cassie, French beauty Madeleine, loopy nun Joyce and the incarcerated youngest, Roxanne. The structure of the series gave Jackson great scope for experimentation, with each sister's tale taking on different filmic forms, from the soft-focused pornography of 'Madeleine' to the Ealing-style larks of 'Joyce', but there was even greater scope in the ensemble casting, encouraged by Elton's ability to give great lines and rounded characterisations to even the most minor of characters. As with *Girls on Top*† and *The Young Ones*, no role was too small for some bright new star of eighties comedy to take; the shared casts of all

---

* Whose housekeeper happened to be the unseen 'Mrs Miggs'.

† Which featured, among myriad comic turns, Hugh Laurie being date-raped by Dawn French's character Amanda in only his second sitcom appearance.

three shows practically exhaust the entire checklist of the 'Alternative' fraternity. Naturally, several were also *Blackadder* players, with Helen Atkinson-Wood as a tour guide, Jim Broadbent once again displaying an outrageous accent as French pornographer Dalcroix opposite Rik Mayall's Nazi priest, and Elton himself playing the groovy governor of Roxanne's prison, the boss of a drug-dealing warder played by his old school friend Gabrielle Glaister. This was only a brief job for Ben though – while filming continued, the writer went back to crafting his submissions for the Black Adder's new adventures. Although not suited to its BBC1 slot, *Happy Families* did well enough to be offered a second run by the Corporation, and remains a unique creation, its pervy malevolence (surely an inspiration for *The League of Gentlemen* and others) exemplifying the freedom given to Jackson and Elton at this time.

Lloyd was very happy to have Elton on board. 'We became very good friends very quickly. Harry Enfield, Ben and I used to see a lot of each other, and get very drunk, because our girlfriends all gave us the sack at about the same time. Of all the people Richard told about Ben joining in the second series, I was the most pleased, because I thought he was a great guy and very talented.' However, the degraded machinations of the Fuddle family were certainly not the stuff to win over a man like Richard Armitage, and the suggestion that Elton would become the new co-writer of his star comic's big sitcom vehicle was not welcomed in the Noel Gay office. Atkinson knew that the stand-up had a track record second to none, but his agent's misgivings could easily have called the whole project to a halt. In the end, it was Fry who stepped forward to vouch for his friend's perfect suitability for the job. 'You can't not get on with Ben – whatever his apparent reputation may be as a bit of a yappy Jack Russell, he's the most adorable and brilliant man you could possibly hope to spend time with. So I was utterly thrilled when he and Richard got on well enough to decide to write together, because I knew that together they would make something that was absolutely of the time.' However, he was to note, 'Ben is one of the most extraordinarily gifted people I have ever met. As much as he is gifted he seems cursed with a woeful talent for causing people to disapprove of him . . . he has never been a fool and knows this very well, yet the one accomplishment he seems not to have been granted is the ability to do anything about it.' Luckily, Fry's honeyed words did the trick, and it was full steam ahead for *Blackadder II*. 'I was flattered to have my opinion so valued. My contribution to the success of *Me and My Girl*, which had made Richard the happiest man in London, and the fact that I could be taken to any weekend gathering or dinner party without letting the side down, had led him to rely on me as a kind of intermediary between his world and the brave new one that was springing up around him.'

Besides, Elton's style comprised two main threads: there was gleeful vulgarity, for sure – he admits himself, 'I don't dwell exclusively on the nether regions, but my comedy has plumbed a lot of orifices' – but his other main strength was always his deep love of toying with the English tongue. 'He was very good on the history,' Curtis confirms, 'and fantastic on the language. Ben has an extraordinary sort of Rabelaisian love of insane language . . . *Blackadder* is the fanciest thing I've ever written, and that came about partly because of Ben, and partly because we were allowed to be fancy because it was old.' Elton agrees. 'The character loves to form a fruity sentence, or to undercut a fruity sentence.' But Tony Robinson has a different take on the programme's move towards the sesquipedalian. 'If you think about where *Blackadder* came from it is actually the comedy of adolescent boys trying to impress each other. And given that it was adolescent boys, most of whom, I would have thought, weren't great on the games field, it was going to come through their banter and their competitive use of words. I don't think it's a surprise that that use of language should have been so strong in *Blackadder*.' Mellifluent dialogue and anarchic smut just happened to be also central to the first series' appeal, so it's little wonder that Curtis & Elton found the construction of the new Lord Blackadder's world surprisingly easy, resulting in a number of scripts which Lloyd claimed to be the best he had read. 'Just completely brilliant. And I was jumping up and down, as any producer is when you get a great script through the letter box.'

'Ben has this extraordinarily profligate talent when it comes to writing,' Curtis continues. 'So you say to Ben, "Wouldn't it be a good idea if maybe . . . we do Elizabeth I?" And then you say, "Let's meet again on Thursday and have another chat about it," and by Thursday, he'd written three episodes.' 'Richard and I had, I think, the best imaginable writing collaboration,' Ben adds. 'We very quickly evolved a work method that stood with us through all three series.' 'The fantastic thing was that you end up morphing into each other,' Richard says. 'You end up actually trying to write to please the other person, so you might think that I was in charge of plots and history, and Ben was in charge of knob gags, but in fact I used to write jokes to try and make Ben laugh, and Ben used to try and write plots in order to impress me.'

Curtis & Elton's one golden rule was that neither could ever question the other's edits, the junior partner recalls. 'You wouldn't fight for a line which had been cut, which was quite difficult, because often Richard would cut stuff which I thought was good, and often vice versa. The theory was, you don't tell a joke at dinner and then if no one laughs, say, "Wait a minute, you weren't listening, I just said something really funny!" You just move on. So that was very relaxing, not having to rake back through the stuff you did before.' Richard did, however, have a habit of ticking jokes which made him laugh, frustrating Ben, who admitted to sifting through notes fuming, 'What's wrong with the rest of the stuff, you bastard? There hasn't been a tick for three pages and it's all brilliant!'

'Once we'd finished the episodes,' Curtis continues, 'we'd then give them to John, he would give us all his notes, we'd take those into account* . . . Then we'd have a reading – and it's a great and depressing

---

* Ben was to dub John 'Mad Jack' for the passionate, epic nature of his annotation, which sometimes extended beyond the length of the scripts themselves.

surprise that no matter how hard you work on anything, some things just don't take wing when they're read. And there were always a couple – not necessarily the ones we thought were the best – which, because of the nature of the set-up, would just fly from the beginning, and people would laugh all the way through. And then there'd be other ones which were stodgy and incorrect, and then we'd take them off and get to work on those again.' There were teething problems – a murder-mystery episode started by Elton soon ended up in the bin – but the fruits of the duo's labours were well received, especially by the star himself.

Since completing work on *The Black Adder*, Atkinson had taken the title role in Larry Shue's West End comedy *The Nerd*, and among the usual round of Royal Variety Performances, there was a special birthday tribute for Bob Hope. Armitage had also teamed him with Fry to create a screenplay for a Jacques Tati-inspired crime caper, to be produced by David Puttnam. Stephen remembers, 'The idea was an English M. *Hulot's Holiday* in which Rowan, an innocent abroad, would find himself unwittingly involved in some sort of crime caper. The character was essentially Mr Bean, but ten years too early.' But although Rowan had happily relinquished scripting duties, the return of the Black Adder remained paramount, as he told *Time Out*, 'My future credibility with the BBC probably rests with the success or failure of this series.'

However, the team hadn't even had time to arrange a reading before news came through that the series was dumped. Michael Grade – TV high-flyer, sole inheritor of the Grade empire's fame, and new Controller of BBC1 – swung the axe. 'The Head of Comedy came in to see me, and he rattled through, another series of *Only Fools and Horses*, another series of *'Allo 'Allo*, and another series of *Blackadder*. . ." And I said, "Stop right there." And he sort of dropped his pencil and looked at me. I said, "No."' Lloyd, Atkinson, Curtis and Elton subsequently each received letters from John Howard Davies informing them that there would be no *Blackadder II* 'for this season, and realistically that means forever'.

It's Spontaneous and It's Called Wit

The fact that *Blackadder* was nearly axed is hardly an astounding source of dramatic tension – its return from the brink has become a textbook case for TV bosses, warned to give fledgling sitcoms time to develop, even though *The Black Adder* was laughingly dubbed 'The show that looked a million dollars, and cost a million pounds' by BBC insiders. On the other hand, the manner of *Blackadder*'s saving remains a bone of contention. Grade insists, 'I felt the show was kind of indulgent, and a bit lost. But I could see there was something there, and I wanted to do it again, and I laid down the condition that I would do another series, provided they came into the studio with the audience and got the show on its feet, shot it in sequence, and they'd find out what they had, which I don't think they did on location.'

'My memory is that the scripts were written, they were basically finished,' Elton argues, 'and the decision to go into studio, and to avoid the big filmic vibe of the previous series was one that Richard and I took on day one. The idea that it was a financially canny executive that sort of pushed us back into the studio is not true.' John, Richard and Ben quickly took the scripts, double-checked the excise of any sequence which required anything more ambitious than a polystyrene knoll, and rushed to show Auntie what they had in mind. Ben continues, 'John ran to Michael Grade and said, "Look, I know exactly why you cancelled it, but we knew that too! That's why we've done *Blackadder II*. This is the new thing – it's different, it costs half as much and it's three times as funny. You're gonna love it," and to Michael Grade's great credit he read it and reinstated it.' It couldn't have done any harm that Richard Armitage (boyhood friend of that other son of a famous musical act, Bill Cotton Jr, then Managing Director of BBC TV), went into TV Centre all guns blazing to fight for Rowan's return.

'Not enough laughs to the pound" was the phrase used at the time and I suppose it was quite a reasonable attitude,' said Atkinson to the

Mirror in 1990. 'Grade could think of many worthier – and certainly cheaper – shows he could put on, so to him there was little point in persevering with *Blackadder*. What nobody bothered to mention was that the second series was going to cost a third of the first . . . It was a classic BBC cock-up. The Light Entertainment department failed catastrophically to represent our interests and it could have spelt the death of *Blackadder* there and then. It was a nerve-racking time, but, fortunately, after he was put in the picture he changed his mind.' As the spring of 1985 rolled along, Lloyd was finally able to begin forming a cast and a crew, for this all-new bubble of historical slander.

Publicising the show at the time, Atkinson said, 'We really wanted to do the second series to make some of the failings of the first series into strengths and also because there was enough life still in the storyline to make it worthwhile. Edmund's the great loser, but this time he's not quite such a fool, he does get out of things in the end.' And the new writing team had presented the star with a whole new challenge. 'The two of them – rather bravely, I thought – decided quite consciously to make the central character less silly, less comic, less daft, and made him sort of rather cool and sardonic and cynical and even, in my bearded manifestation, some claimed, rather good-looking. And I think that was definitely a very important turning point, and started to provide the template of the sort of witty cynicism which so characterised the Black Adder through the remaining series.'

The first day of production involved the shooting of the few scraps of actual film seen in the series, the team pitching up at the Wiltshire manor of Wilton House on 30 May. New director Mandie Fletcher had been drafted in to cover the technical side, an experienced theatre director fresh from learning her TV trade on suburban sitcoms like *Butterflies* and *Three Up, Two Down*. 'Mandie was great,' Robinson says, 'but the role of a director varies from show to show; in *Blackadder* there were so many competing contributing forces that by and large the director was there simply to make it work for television, working out the shots and liaising with the various departments. Some directors contribute a bit more artistically, and I would say Mandie was one of those, but really John was driving an awful lot of the comic vision. In lots of other series I've been in, the producer's hardly ever there and the director does that.' 'I was put onto *Blackadder* as some kind of punishment by the Head of Comedy, I remember,' Fletcher says. 'I wasn't that experienced then, and arriving was like walking into a public school halfway through the second term in the middle of a pillow fight. They would arrive with a script that should be thirty-odd pages, but was under ten pages, which was then written during the week when I should have been rehearsing and blocking them. It was a nightmare, I'm surprised I didn't get an ulcer! I just gritted my teeth and made bloody sure that we had a show that could be shot on the night. I'm grateful, because it put the steel into my soul for everything that came afterwards. We had T-shirts made, and they had on the front "I Survived Blackadder", and on the back was a knife going in between the shoulder blades.'

Much water under the bridge later, John pays tribute: 'Mandie's an extraordinary person, she became a director at a time when women *never* directed TV comedy. She'd been assistant floor manager on *Not*, and I was very keen on her, we were good friends. She had to fight her way up the system like crazy, and was very fiery and sassy – like a principal boy, swashbuckling, with big boots and hands on hips and, "Come on, lads, let's be having you!" And the crew all loved it, because she was damn sexy!' 'We had a love/hate relationship – we had history,' Mandie says. 'He was funny and charming, and in those days I can't tell you how attractive he was – he was blond and blue-eyed and just gorgeous, and that slightly put one on the back foot. But he was the creative force, and he did pull it all together. He did need to be draconian, with so many egos around.' Lloyd continues, 'I used to say to her, "You're treating me like a disobedient puppy!" She'd snap her fingers and say, "John, come here!" Used to make me very cross. But she was the person who first started to bring a real visual style to *Blackadder* – I'd say, "That's what you do, Mandie, you do the shots, but I've got to do the script because I know these guys, and you're not going to get a better line out of them because you don't know how to." It was a co-production, but we squabbled like mad, like two naughty kids.'

Along with new costume designer Annie Hardinge (who would stay with the show until the end) and Rowan himself, Fletcher helped to sculpt a louche anti-hero so closely modelled on Michael Kitchen's charming Edmund in Jonathan Miller's 1982 BBC *King Lear* that it could only be deliberate. Fletcher admits that the results were striking. 'The moment that Rowan stepped out of the make-up caravan at Wilton House, dressed in all that garb, all us girls went "Ooh!"' and Elton begrudgingly concurs, 'I think we were all surprised at how well Rowan scrubbed up – particularly when he was in bed with the prostitute, nearly nude. Honestly, all the girls kept sort of whispering, "Gosh, he's actually quite good-looking, isn't he?" There was a lot of that going on. We made him sexy!' 'I deceived everyone into thinking I was half decent-looking,' Atkinson laughs. 'I thought I looked like the Yorkshire Ripper. It's exhausting playing a great lover, but I must say I did enjoy it. As Edmund, I'm ambitious to have a good time – especially with Queen Elizabeth.'

Despite the star's modesty, the sequence they were there to film did cast him in the role of lover, in a rare instance of wilful anachronism, advertising Tudor love songs in a style defined in the script as a 'very naff Woolies ad'. The writers promised themselves that the cheap laughs afforded by playing around with historical inaccuracy were off-limits. 'We were not allowed to say, "What's the time? Oh no, they haven't invented watches yet!" That sort of joke,' Elton says. 'The whole thing was, basically, that Blackadder *was* the wristwatch that hadn't been invented, he kind of had the attitude.' Curtis adds, 'That was resistant to the two traditions that there were at that point, the *Up Pompeii* and *Carry On* tradition, because whenever the *Carry On* people did the past, the whole thing was about anachronisms.'

The 'Tudor Love Songs' insert did, however, highlight another boon of the Elizabethan period – more Shakespeare-ribbing. With the series set in the early part of Elizabeth's reign, 1560–66, Shakespeare was mewling and puking in his nurse's arms at the time, but that didn't preclude digs at his crap jokes, and 'Bells' directly references *Twelfth Night*, as the dishy Edmund falls in love with his pageboy, Bob/Kate. The first character to accompany Rowan in the series therefore was Gabrielle Glaister, who had enjoyed success in the hit musical *Daisy Pulls It Off*, and the two of them echoed the quandary of Duke Orsino and Viola as they strode around the Earl of Pembroke's gardens. For Glaister, the spoof element provided a clear template for her character. 'Viola's got everything Bob's got really. Presumably Viola is quite sexy, as one hopes Bob was, and feisty, holding her own in a man's world. And deceiving people.'

While at Wilton House, Fletcher took the opportunity to make the most of the elegant surroundings. 'I won't take credit for much of *Blackadder*, but I will for the closing title sequence on series two. We had a day's filming in His Lordship's garden, so we put the camera back to the window, locked it off, and everyone came up with an idea of what the minstrel could do, and what Rowan could do to the minstrel, and it just worked a treat.' Comic actor Tony Aitken had already been booked to mime the minstrel's part, and would return to the studio for further Shakespearean spoofs, referencing Edgar's madness for the episode 'Money', though he admitted, 'I didn't really understand the reference to *King Lear* and Poor Tom, the Fool and all the Shakespearean references. I could go back to university and spend three years studying *Blackadder* scripts and get a lot out of it.'

Naturally, Howard Goodall had been given crushing deadlines to get the new music ready so early. 'It was fun doing those songs at the end, although my memory is that Richard would give us the lyric about a minute before it had to be recorded, so it was always a bit tense to be honest, because we were never quite ready to do it . . . I feel slightly nostalgic about it, because these days you couldn't do credits like that. First of all, you're only allowed a tiny amount of time at the end of a programme, and second, they're showing you the next programme over the credits and talking over them.' The opening credits would also continue the sexy trend, blending period instrumentation with rock. 'All the way through, I wanted to play with the idea of what you would expect to hear, and what you might then get, and I think I suggested a Renaissance-sounding band, and then a kind of crazy guitar solo. I actually wanted, rather like in *Red Dwarf*, for the guitarist to go madder, but it's quite hard to get a really top session guitarist to play something that doesn't seem to fit.' With the original series' opening histrionics replaced by a modest serpentine title sequence spoofing *I, Claudius* (although this adder needed more direction), the form of the new show was established, and it was time to fill in the gaps.

Turnips, Cabbages and Queens

'With the second series, we started to establish the repertory company,' Atkinson says, 'not only a sort of claustrophobic and dramatic setting, but also quite a small and neat group of people who had a lot of natural creative empathy with one another, which continued until the end.' Perhaps the simplest reincarnation in *Blackadder II* was that of Percy Percy, whose Elizabethan guise just made the Sir Andrew Aguecheek comparisons blatant. McInnerny's long, lissom form seemed made to personify the Renaissance dandy, with ostentatious ruffs bringing to mind 'a bird swallowing a plate'. 'I think one of the things that made *Blackadder* so superb was the amount of research that went into both the props and the costumes. There were real absurd fashions at the time, where things were taken to huge extremes, so it's not so outlandish an idea.' Percy's role as Blackadder's emotional punchbag was to earn him the viewers' love, and Glaister nails the appeal: 'He's like the runt of

Good Queen Bess and her saucy Ned. Atkinson's expression would surely have been even sourer if Brian Blessed had worn the red wig and the dress, as he threatened.

Camera rehearsals in the miniscule royal court. 'Someone once said this lovely thing about series two,' Curtis says. 'They were talking about the other series, and they said "I miss the 'ee's!" And Ben said to them, "What d'you mean you miss the ease?" And they said, "Well in series two it was Percy, Nursie, Melchy, Queenie…" they were like a friendly bunch of schoolchums.'

Love with young Bob came only fleetingly for Lord Blackadder, 'which is a bit sad really,' Gabrielle Glaister says, 'because I think Blackadder and Kate would have made rather a nice couple!'

'You have a woman's... beard, my lord?' Everyone's favourite Doctor was a welcome presence on set in June 1985 – though he still insists that he should have had his Equity card revoked for his celebrated scenery-chewing.

The combustible cream of a comic generation. 'There was a sort of gang feel and it was fun,' Elton says. 'For heaven's sake let's not say it was cliquey, but it was people who liked being together and working together, and I think perhaps the fact that everybody is still friends might be unique.'

Edinburgh, August 1981:
An Oxbridge convergence like no other, as the final ingredients of the *Blackadder* chilli are located. Fry: 'Hugh nudged me; a man had walked on stage from the wings behind us and was coming forward, holding his hand up for silence. His presence only encouraged more cheering. It was Rowan Atkinson. For a moment or two I thought he had gone insane…'

The Elizabethan Bilko, and cohorts. '*Blackadder* worked the way it did because someone was at the top and someone was at the bottom and there was a real threat of punishment or death'.

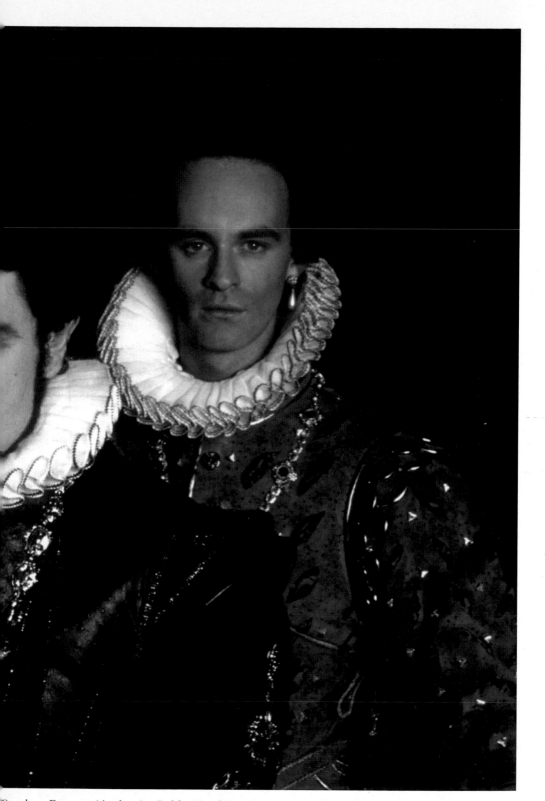

Stephen Fry says. 'And as in Goldoni and Ben Jonson, you don't always find that the one on top is the smart one… that tradition connects all the way up to Jeeves & Wooster of course.'

In a lifetime's worth of hard-man roles, Arthur the Sailor must be the high point in actor John Pierce Jones' long career – it's certainly one of the most celebrated one-scene-wonders in the *Blackadder* canon. 'Now how much do you charge for a GOOD – HARD – SHAG?'

Long after Baldrick's last cunning plan, Robinson has perennially been happy to ease back into the stinking trousers over the years, largely for Comic Relief – his Christmas Card is now a collector's item.

the litter, you want to kick him, just because he's so desperate to please, you want to say, "Oh, go away!"' 'I remember people asking me at the time whether Percy was based on anybody,' McInnerny says. 'He just naturally grew out of the rhythm of the writing. Every time you looked at Richard's writing, it was just there and very clear.'

Tony's return was as much a transformation as Rowan's, albeit in the opposite direction – Baldrick was about to embark on a course of devolution that would make him the nation's favourite dullard. 'In order to make Blackadder's character work,' Robinson recalls, 'he needed to be surrounded by people who were clearly much stupider than he was. And the problem with having a Baldrick who was brighter than he was, was that *everyone* was brighter than him, so where's the comedy? There was no subtlety about it, no duality about it. So one of the ideas they came up with was that Baldrick should be the *stupidest person there'd ever been in the history of the world.* And it took me a long time to get him as stupid as was required – he was still fairly bright in series two, he was quite chipper in many ways. By series four, he was the living dead, but I'm not quite sure that that was in some ways as good as he was in *Blackadder II*.' Both writers had a deep love of sitcom idiocy, admits Curtis. 'The very, very stupid character is a sitcom tradition, it's a lovely thing to have total idiocy.' This new Baldrick balanced out his loss of mental agility with a whole new level of Curtis-inspired cuddliness, and the stirrings of a crucial trait spearheaded by Elton. 'I can remember Ben bouncing up to me and saying, "I've got a great idea, Tony – Baldrick loves turnips!" I said to him, "What's so funny about turnips?" And he said, "You know, they're shaped like that, and they go to a point at the end . . ." And I said, "Ben, that's parsnips!" And he said, "Whatever, it's really funny, believe me." I said, "Ben, really, it's not going to get a laugh, it's like the most unfunny thing in the world." Which proves how little I know about comedy, and how much Ben knows. But on the other hand I do know much more about root vegetables.'

'It's rather impressive, I always think, how both Tim and Tony manage to be stupid in different ways. Usually stupidity is rather a one-note song, but they have their own brands,' Stephen Fry says admiringly. But his own entry into the *Blackadder* brethren, though hardly the shrewdest nob in Christendom, would provide some contrast. With Edmund and his two friends back in the saddle, a new court had to be built up around them, and Elton always intended the Black Adder's new nemesis to be played by his *Alfresco* comrade, even named Melchett in honour of Fry's famous monologue. Elizabeth needed 'a sort of William Cecil, Lord Burghley figure, all forked beard, forked tongue and fur-lined cloak' to cheaply personify the extensive council who would have filled the royal court, and Fry lost no time in accepting the role, even though he recalls his friend apologising, 'I won't lie to you, it's not like the greatest character in the world – he and Blackadder hate each other. He's a kind of chamberlain figure, you know?'

With Melchett as the Queen's right-hand man, a space was reserved on her left for that Shakespearean staple, the jolly Nurse, and the Ashford-born seasoned actress Patsy Byrne perfectly fitted the role. Though proud to prove to everyone that she could still do the splits on command, the 52-year-old diminutive, cuddly Byrne was the real veteran of the team. Her time with the English Stage Company at the Royal Court under George Devine in the fifties saw her originate roles directed by Lindsay Anderson and John Dexter, and Aunt Mildred in N. F. Simpson's comedy *One Way Pendulum*. 'We were all theatre-trained. I remember Tony Robinson's Feste in *Twelfth Night* at the Chichester Festival, it was very good – he was a classical actor!' Byrne's own theatrical experience dovetailed perfectly with requirements, with roles including *Twelfth Night*'s Maria for the RSC, plus *I, Claudius* and historical epic *The Devil's Crown*, and most fittingly of all, playing the Nurse in an ITV production of *Romeo and Juliet* a decade earlier, giving her a trial run at Bernard the Tudor Nurse's combination of matronly dotage and treacly idiocy. 'I played the Nurse about three or four times

– it followed me around, that character. So Nursie was a good part for me! I added just a little kind of colouring. She's an earthy character and I think you've got to have a certain roundness – perhaps to the vowels, though she'd probably think more of the bowels than the vowels . . . I was completely at home right from the start with Nursie – innocent, scatological, and most incredibly stupid with a very warped and weird view on life, and just so sweetly gormless, but a rather loving creature. I mean, I liked her.'

The producer was delighted with the new trouper, and her ability to be 'naughty and saintly by turns, and utterly lovable on screen and off', and for Byrne the public's love for her character would be the cherry on top of a long and successful life in the business. 'It was six weeks' work in, I'm quite happy to admit, a fifty-year-long career, but that six weeks made an enormous difference. For years I'd done some not high-profile but very interesting, rewarding work, and I'd done quite well. Suddenly I became almost, even in the very small part of Nursie, a household name! I still now go to Sainsbury's and about eight times, every time I go, people say, "Hello, Nursie!" I enjoy that . . . I've often been asked, "Could you come to a party and bring your udders with you?" I say, "I don't keep them in the wardrobe!"' Miriam Margolyes says, 'I'm still great friends with all of them – particularly Patsy Byrne, for whom I'm often mistaken! People often think that I played Nursie but I have to say, somewhat sadly, that I didn't, but that I know Nursie and I will pass on the good wishes. She was a glorious fixture in *Blackadder*, I was just a recurring guest artist.'

The budgetary restraints had turned an opulent royal court into a cosy family, but with Blacky, Percy, Melchy, Nursie and Balders all signed up, the team still faced the biggest challenge of all – it seemed impossible to find a Queenie, the all-important authority figure for the Black Adder to slither over. The most startling suggestion was Brian Blessed, who had early talks with Martin Shardlow about sticking on a red wig and playing the Queen himself – the idea being that where he never knew Edmund's name in the first series, in the second he would be so obsessed with Blackadder that the star would be in constant terror of sexual attack. Luckily (or tragically), however, Blessed's availability did not match with the recording dates, though he would remain friends with Rowan, who appeared on Brian's *This is Your Life* in 1984, bowing and scraping. In lieu of Blessed, at least forty female actors (including many famous names who can of course never be specified) were rigorously auditioned, but found wanting. Curtis and Lloyd were in despair, until 'a scruffy, slightly distracted-looking girl with unwashed hair', a redhead of the exact same age as Elizabeth herself in 1560, changed everything.

MIRANDA JANE RICHARDSON
BORN: 3 March 1958, Southport, Lancashire

Miranda was the younger of two daughters born to Marian and marketing executive William Richardson, coming along several years after the birth of her sister. Growing up in a cosy corner of the North-West, young Miranda discovered the two all-pervading loves of her life while still very tiny – performing, and four-legged friends of all varieties.

Her original hopes of becoming a vet, however, were abandoned, thanks to the undeniable skill she showed onstage and in the classroom as a talented mimic. After her O levels Miranda's first port of call was the Bristol Old Vic Theatre School, where three years of study were followed by the then indispensable training ground of repertory theatre. Glowing notices from her work at the Library Theatre, Manchester (where she was also assistant stage manager), led to a West End debut in the play *Moving*, in 1981. In the same year, she had a small role in the ITV sitcom *Agony*, and further success in television roles had by 1985 led to her first starring role in a film, playing Ruth Ellis, the last woman to be hanged in Britain, in *Dance with a Stranger*.

✤

'Miranda seemed very willing to muck in,' Rowan reflects. 'She did effectively become a member of the repertory company. She had such a sort of brave and eccentric creative curiosity to her, it meant that she didn't really care what she did or how she did it, she was going to enjoy exploring all the possibilities, and that's where her Elizabeth came from.' In the summer of 1985 Miranda Richardson was already mulling over the lead in Hollywood thriller *Fatal Attraction*, but having recently had such success playing one romantically deranged murderess in *Dance with a Stranger*, she felt that historical sitcom would offer a greater challenge. 'I had a glorious opportunity to go off at a tangent, you know? I hate being boxed and labelled, so if somebody had just gone, "Oh, serious drama!" I'd have been a bit disappointed. I'm an actor and I like to be as flexible as I possibly can be, so I was given the opportunity immediately to go and do something really quite wild and wacky . . . The scripts were very detailed and arcane. It was the combination of, if you like, Ben the yobbo and Richard the scholar. The same elements are all in *Monty Python*. It was scholarly, wide-ranging and mentally adept as well as wild and woolly. That sort of anarchy is very English.'

Curtis was delighted with the new addition. 'Everybody did it in a very two-dimensional way, and then Miranda came in and she was just completely bizarre – a strange mixture of sort of woman–child–nymphomaniac–tyrant. And I remember that, in a way, every line got changed afterwards. She could do what we wrote, but we actually then wrote something much more in her direction.' This is not to say that the completed core cast instantly gelled. Tony Robinson remembers the crisis in the air: 'For the first week we were really, really frightened, because Richard and Ben didn't know how to write for women. I don't think they'd met a woman until that time. It was only when Miranda came in and did this fantastic performance that they knew how to write for her. Miranda is an extraordinary actress, and Richard knew that she was, and brought her in because of the quality of her acting, he was so captivated by it. But the part that had originally been written was half baked, and if the Queen Elizabeth character didn't work, then the show wasn't going to work.' The situation wasn't helped by Lloyd's admission that 'her well of creativity is so bottomless and so brimming with such mysterious liquids that directing her is pointless'. It was down to Richardson herself to find a way to play the Queen, a world away from Glenda Jackson, Bette Davis and a hundred other Elizabeths. 'I think I knew that this was somebody with a lot of power but far too young really to deal with it. I thought of her like an infanta, somebody who everybody was kowtowing to and saying "yes" to, while politicking like mad in the background . . . It's within court, which is a very small, bejewelled world, you know, and there are these little people in there who think they rule the world, but of course it was only me that ruled the world. I thought of her as someone with too much, too soon, far too young. She's quite prone to sending people off to be trimmed – a small nip and tuck, involving their head usually, if she feels a bit moody that day . . . and she's a girl. Girls get moody.' But that wasn't the whole picture, this was a young Elizabeth, freshly crowned, and not entirely virginal. 'She was obviously somebody who had crushes – because I mean, let's face it, I don't think she did anything of great significance with boys. It was sort of like the pony club and men in tights – perfect combo for her . . . big bulbous tights. But nothing ever came to fruition, so she was always in that sort of suspended state of not-quite-adolescence.'

The eureka moment came when Richardson discovered the exact lisping delivery to convey this weird infantilism, a voice which had made the cast of *Dance with a Stranger* howl in between takes. 'I know I was referencing a friend I had at school, we'd talk in this sort of silly language to each other, and go into a sort of exacerbated sweet, slightly girly sort of baby voice.' 'Midway through that first week,' Robinson says, 'suddenly Miranda discovered this young woman who's on the cusp of ponies and sex, as it were. And I remember the scene when she got it; John Lloyd was leaping up and down with excitement, going "Yes, that's it! That's it!" And from that moment, that series took off. Miranda has this ability to make what she does look entirely spontaneous but it's virtually always really thought through. And it's as though by thinking it through, she can then allow herself internally to have a whole kind of 5 November firework display going on inside her head, because she's confident in the structure that's she's already created.'

The rest of the cast were bowled over by Richardson's transformation. McInnerny admits, 'It was very frightening what Miranda did with Elizabeth – turning her into this kind of psychotic.' And her sidekick Byrne would concur: 'She gave a performance of sustained imagination – and she's just so clever!' 'It ought to have been deeply weird, pervy, peculiar, wrong, Queenie's relationship with Nursie, but instead of making the Queen less dignified, it somehow made her more so,' Fry says. 'The essence of caprice in a monarch that Miranda played is one of the most joyous experiences of my life, to be standing next to her watching these incredible contortions and writhings, and hearing these phenomenal squeaks and squeals and noises coming out of this incredible woman.' To complete the circle of mutual admiration, Miranda was eventually to pay tribute in return, in her own way: 'Stephen is fantastic . . . much older than his years, he had this extraordinary gravitas and maturity, that's what I remember. And his marvellous height! His presence added to the extremes, you know – you've got Nursie who's sort of practically spherical, then I'm like this little firework or something in the middle, and Melchy's this wonderful lugubrious long streak of piss next to me. His character reminded me a bit of something I used to watch all the time, Noggin the Nog. He reminded me of Thor Nogsson, so I was very taken with him.'

All this extraordinary backslapping, however, was in the future, as the *Blackadder* company repaired to the 'North Acton Hilton' for rehearsals, preparing to go into Studio 6 at BBC TV Centre, for the show's first exposure to a live audience.

Tweaking the Nose of Terror

'It's a bit like doing Shakespeare in front of an audience – it's not at all like doing sitcom,' Mandie Fletcher was to claim about those Sunday-night recordings, but to the returning trio from *The Black Adder*, this stressful new system came as a shock. Early-summer 1985 was given up to this recurring nightmare, six intense performances, each the result of a week of equally intense rehearsal and argument. In *The Fry Chronicles*, Stephen traced the process: 'On Tuesday morning we would read through the script, with Richard and sometimes Ben in attendance . . . Mandie would make notes and build up her camera script, and John would grimace and sigh and smoke and pace and growl. His perfectionism and refusal to be satisfied was part of the reason *Blackadder* worked. Every line, plot twist and action was taken, rubbed between his fingers, sniffed and passed, rejected or pulled in for servicing and improvement.'

Close proximity to this gaggle of perfectionists had caused problems for guest stars in the first series, but now the stakes were higher. The scripts had already been feted as the best Lloyd had seen, but greatness could be polished further, and even at this relatively early stage in *Blackadder*'s evolution, the wrangling could become fraught. Fry says, 'Hours would pass and packets of cigarettes would be got through and huge quantities of hideous polystyrene muddy coffee would be drunk, in an effort to try and get the scripts right.' 'I remember Stephen at one point just scraping his chair back and striding around the room,' Richardson adds, 'this enormous person striding round, and he came back to the table, grabbed a pencil and piece of paper and put it in front of me, and it just said "Fucking hell!"' Amid this comedic ruck, while sharing tea-making facilities with David Jason and Nicholas Lyndhurst, Atkinson must have occasionally envied them their straightforward approach to John Sullivan's *Only Fools* scripts. 'Sometimes it was very tense,' he says. 'I remember some very difficult times when we appeared to be just sitting around for two and a half hours bemoaning the lack of writing clarity in a particular scene and desperately trying to think how that might be reorientated to work.' On the other hand, Fry says, '*Only Fools* was a success because it was real and not trying to be anything other than set in a world Sullivan and his cast knew – a kind of antidote to our smart-arse "Oh look at me I've been to university" school of comedy.'

Patsy Byrne says, 'Miranda and I would play Scrabble at the side while the boys all conferred with John on the script.' When it comes to favourite scenes, she offers, 'I think I remember visual moments more, and I really crack up whenever I see them. Perhaps my most favourite is the moment when Baldrick is discovered in a corner, trying out his costume for the party, with two pencils up his nose . . . and I liked that really disgracefully dirty scene, with the sailor who "loved his mum", and then asked for a quick one.' 'Patsy was delicious,' Fry says. 'She seemed happy to let us get on with it and rewrite all the time and there wasn't a line she couldn't get instantly. She completely understood her character. An unsung genius.'

When the big recording day arrived, the natural warm-up for the relaunched show was of course Elton himself, never short of a gag, topical, scatological or historical – although often in rapid enough succession that Fletcher had a job to shut him up for a take. He would also put the episode in context for the crowd, which Fry recalls as being vital, as 'there was always a detectable air of disappointment emanating from the audience. No part of the current series would yet have been broadcast, so they would be staring at an unfamiliar set and fretting at the absence of the characters they had known from the previous series. When they came to *Blackadder II* they were sorry not to have Brian Blessed there as the King; when they came to *Blackadder the Third* recordings they missed Queenie; and when they arrived for recordings of *Blackadder Goes Forth* they wanted to see Prince George and Mrs Miggins.' The role of the warm-up is a crucial one, with the audience's participation central to the proceedings, even if the slog of some TV recordings can prove torture to the general public. Elton didn't give them time to grow restless, urging, 'Do try and make new friends during these pauses, you know, use the time properly – we'll be passing some joints around later, maybe linking arms, I'll be doing some mime in a leotard . . . Middle-class comedy, go go go!'

With the Elizabethan set-up established, Elton would then introduce the cast. 'Which didn't make you feel less nervous, actually,' McInnerny says. 'Very, kind of, American, it felt like. Everybody applauding and you thought, "Oh no, now I've got to live up to that!"' Robinson continues, 'Then Rowan would come out, so embarrassed, walking like someone with a tragic physical illness, and they'd all think he was being comic, and it was just his nerves. And he would kind of squeak, turn his back on them and go onto the set.' The set itself was split into three, with Lord Blackadder's home occupying the left-hand space, the throne room in the centre, and on the right, that week's one allotted special location, all designed with an eye on simplicity by Antony Thorpe. Rowan was to reflect, 'It is hugely ironic that, having set out to make the first series of *Blackadder* as unlike *Fawlty Towers* as we could, by the time we got to the second series and rejigged it, we did end up with three sets, and something quite claustrophobic and hierarchical. So we learned the error of our ways: there are good reasons why sitcoms tend to have the shape that they do.' Lloyd went further: 'Despite our efforts to disguise the provenance of the series, there are in fact only seven plots, and in many ways *Blackadder* is actually *Fawlty Towers* in tights, with Rowan as Basil perennially poking Tony's Manuel with a pencil.'

'Rowan would deliberately forget his words so that he could do the take again, McInnerny laughs. 'He'd use his stammer if he wasn't happy with a take, so he could redo it. Whereas we weren't allowed to, we were only allowed to do retakes if they got the camera wrong!' But the show's star, despite his triumphs with audiences for a decade or more, was having to adjust to the sitcom recording experience. 'That sitcom tradition is very strange, when you're performing to both a camera and an audience at the same time. It's a discipline that some actors find quite difficult to adjust to, and to find the best compromise between what performance you're going to give. In the end, you are just performing for the cameras, and the studio audience have to pick up whatever they can.' However, he has no doubts about the benefits of the process. 'It made a tremendous difference. It was just a joy to have real people in the room and to be recording it like a theatre show – we did rehearse it all week and then we put on a show for two hours. Admittedly only half an hour of programme came out the other end, but it felt like what it was, a live performance. People even now are rather surprised when you tell them that we had a studio audience; they just assume that either the audience had seen it later, afterwards, or that it was canned. And even though, when I look back at *Blackadder* now (which I don't do very often), I can see moments when I, you know, stammered a bit, or the pause was a bit too long, and you think, "God, how frustrating that we did it on the hoof, and how much better it would have been if we had got every little pause and every little inflection absolutely right in a filmic way of doing take after take after take." And yet, you have to pay that price of slight inconsistency and fault lines to get the energy and the feel and the joy of a live performance. And in the end, I think it was probably a sacrifice worth making.'

'Head' was the perfect series opener for this return – in some ways the closest to a pilot that the show had, with no guest stars, besides the return of Bill Wallis as Ploppy the Gaoler, son of Ploppy the Slopper. All the characters were reintroduced, with Baldrick's loss of wit perfectly summed up by the opening maths lesson ('To you, Baldrick, the Renaissance was just something that happened to other people, wasn't it?'), and the plot itself was a testament to Elton's populist tastes and the series' swerve towards the traditional, with the most frenetic farce yet attempted. *The Black Adder* had farcical situations aplenty, but the new Lord High Executioner's desperate bid to save his own head provided the ultimate clash of sitcom scrapes with deadly peril. 'It's a very rigidly hierarchical world,' Fry says. 'You've got real threat – Blackadder is going to have his head chopped off at any moment. It's perfectly possible this mad capricious Queen really could say, "This time I mean it!"' However – and despite Percy's decision to shave off his beard during the second episode causing a blatant continuity problem – it's clear why the decision was taken to reverse the two opening episodes for broadcast, as 'Bells' called for the return of Rik Mayall, in his first major post-*Young Ones* role. 'I was surprised when they asked me,' Mayall says, 'very *honouring* that they should ask me . . . I was thrilled to pieces, what a great part! The ultimate crazy Errol Flynn shag-rat. And he wasn't on for long – he used to come on, steal the show, then run away again. Usually with a bird.'

Ben and Rik's comedic symbiosis would suggest that getting him to return would be automatic – after all, Richard notes, 'This was a time when there was really no BBC casting department – you simply cast people you'd either fancied or fallen out with at some point.' And Ben adds, 'We were young and sort of hip, and as long as John was in charge we were pretty much given free rein.' But the meeting with Mayall at – where else? – the Zanzibar showed that he had lost none of his unrestrainable passion for making a splash. He told the writers, 'I'm only doing it on the condition that I can be funnier than Rowan. Every line has to be funnier than the funniest line of Rowan's in the whole thing.' With Mad Gerald a deranged memory, they concocted a legendary figure more akin to 'the Hawk' – a childhood friend of Lord Blackadder who was never less than ten times the man he was in every regard. Mayall's creation of Flashheart was his own escape from the fartiness of his 'Rick' persona in much the same way that Atkinson was escaping the drippy Edmund – but, as ever, for Mayall it had to be on a grander scale. He worked with Costume to ensure the character was just right, insisting on glamorous blond locks threaded with seashells, and, of course, an outrageous moustache. 'I would like to praise and congratulate the Costume department,' he was to ooze, 'I mean, look at the fantastic costumes they gave me, gave everybody, in the Elizabethan one. I could make jokes about my codpiece and things, and it was just *gorgeous* gear.'

'Rik was a particular joy,' Curtis recalls, 'he would not say a not-funny line. He's so exuberant and noisy, and Rowan is constitutionally rather calm and quiet . . . he just gently stepped back during that week and did his homework in private, while we indulged Rik's magnificent firework personality. And then Row would step forward once Flashheart had buggered off.' Fry has theorised at length about the opposed forms of comic genius which Mayall and Atkinson had at their fingertips in the 1980s – the former a gross exaggeration of his own personality, the latter a far more intangible talent which seemed to grow out of him 'like an extra limb': 'It was like seeing a Vermeer next to a Van Gogh, one all exquisite detail with the subtlest and most invisible working and the other a riot of wild and thickly applied brushstrokes. Two utterly different aesthetics, each outstandingly brilliant . . . I am as capable of envy and resentment as the next man, but when you are in a room with two people who possess an order of talent that you know you can never even dream of attaining, it is actually a relief to be able to do no more than lean back and admire like a dewy-eyed groupie.' The chemistry which resulted from the clash of these two elements on 16 June 1985 produced an unexpectedly resonant comic explosion. Throughout rehearsal, Fletcher says, 'Rik would nod sagely as I said, "Perhaps you should do it this way . . ." "Yeah, fine!" And do it perfectly, but the instant he got in front of those cameras he went berserk! And if you look at the scene, you will see that everyone's standing around on that set, looking completely amazed at the force of nature that's just arrived.' 'Whenever he arrives in something he always gives it a good kick up the behind, so everybody has to look up and pay attention, and actually look to their own game plan. And improve it,' Tim says. 'Rik decided not to watch how everybody was working, he decided to make everybody work the way he was working . . . Rowan had to find his way around Rik's style of acting, which I thought was very amusing. Always fun to watch other people react to other actors.' Tony agrees: 'When Rik gets in front of the camera, you just kind of keep out of the way, basically . . . Part of Rik's whole strategy is to ensure that he gets the best snog. So Gaby Glaister was obviously a very clear target. But quite honestly, if you'd put a dog's bottom in a dress, Rik would have snogged it.' Rowan has never been less than glowing about Rik's comic powers, but Mayall openly admits, 'Of course there's a rivalry there! Because I'm thinking, "He's funny, and I don't understand *how* he can be funny." Maybe he's thinking, "That bloke shouts a lot louder than me." I could hit him, I could shout about myself, I could talk about my genitals . . . whereas Rowan could get his laughs from just two words, or just a raised eyebrow, or just his stasis. I can't do that.' Elton concurs: 'Rowan knows how to pause. He said after seeing me do stand-up in 1987 that I had enough material in one show to last him a lifetime.'

As the smoke cleared, with the flimsy paper doors hanging off their frames and Flashheart eloping with the hero's girl for the first time in recorded history, the injection of Flashheart into the annals of *Blackadder* lore showed to Lloyd that 'Bells' would be a dynamite return for the much-mocked *Blackadder*. 'And at the end of it,' Robinson smiles, 'Rik said, "Did I win?" Which isn't really in the spirit of the ensemble, is it?' 'Of course I haven't counted,' Mayall says, 'but I got three and a half rounds of applause and Rowan didn't get one.'

Lap Dogs to a Slip of a Girl

Far from being threatened by Flashheart's explosive intervention, Atkinson says, 'People thought I was crazy to give him a part because he got so many laughs. They reckoned it was professional suicide and said he would wipe the floor with me. But I can't understand to this day what they were on about. By coming on like a whirlwind and wanting to sleep with all the women he helped me tremendously because it enabled Blackadder to look even more icy and cynical.' Furthermore, he insists, 'I loved it when people used to come in and be extremely funny, because I always regarded my role in nearly all the *Blackadder* series as a bit like a master of ceremonies, it was a bit like saying: "Ladies and gentlemen . . . " and then I put my hand up and greet the next extremely funny performance. And it was fantastic being able to delegate, if you like, so much of the responsibility for the comedy and for the acting to others. It was great that Tony was always so good and so funny, and I felt that our double act always worked so well. It was just lovely being able to share that responsibility, which of course in a programme like *Mr Bean* I was far less able to do, it's far more of a one-man show, and it's a horrible responsibility which I don't particularly enjoy. But *Blackadder* was, as work goes, almost enjoyable.' Stephen was just one of many to be given their share of the limelight as these New Elizabethans recreated the glory of the Virgin Queen's reign 420 years on, and says, 'It's funny that Rowan has this reputation for being the great rubber-faced clown, the great performer, which he is, but he's also a magnificent straight man. And in *Blackadder*, part of its success I think was his simple generosity – he was the star of the show, and television sitcoms are littered with stories of people like Tony Hancock, who couldn't take Kenneth Williams getting more laughs than him. Well, Rowan was never like that. So if Baldrick or Percy got a great laugh Rowan was thrilled, and he would help build on it by being the best straight man you could ever work to . . . He could just watch with

197

a Buster Keaton stony face and then come out with a single word, and be brilliant.'

The bustle of the Elizabethan court gave more scope for Lloyd's idea of having Blackadder clash with real historical figures, and yet the series would boast only one, with Simon Jones, who appeared in *H2G2* and *Monty Python's The Meaning of Life*, landing the role of Sir Walter 'Ooh What a Big Ship I've Got' Raleigh in 'Potato' – another superman for our anti-hero to thumb his nose at, who peppers Blackadder with so much belittlement the new editor, Chris Wadsworth, could pick and choose from them, excising his remark that Edmund is 'the sort of moist scallop whose feeble posturings I went to sea to overshadow'.

A despicable cheat of course, our Lord does not sit around and suffer any demotion in rank among the Queen's favourites, and is soon plotting with his friends to put to sea himself – even though Percy, savaged by a turbot as a child, hides in a box to save his skin, in a scene truncated for broadcast.

EDMUND: Oh hello, Balders, where the hell's that idiot Percy, you haven't seen him, have you?

BALDRICK: . . . Yes, my Lord, he's hiding in the box!

EDMUND: Come on, jellybrain, hurry up, otherwise we'll miss the tide! Whatever that means . . . (*Exits.*)

PERCY: I was just trying it out for space! I thought it might come in handy as a lifeboat. (*Opens box.*) What went wrong?

BALDRICK: It was the force of his personality.

PERCY: Damn, of course!

He strikes his forehead, the box lid thunks down on him.

Portraying Wally Raleigh gave Jones some of his finest on-screen moments, and yet the undeniable force of Tom Baker's other-worldly personality blew everyone else out of the water, his Captain Redbeard Rum, 'a huge bearded pirate with every cliché attached', being the closest thing in this series to Blessed's epic bluster, with a wealth of twaddle to match, as in this out-take:

PERCY: I mean, why do you think it's called the Cape
            of Good Hope?
BALDRICK: Why?
PERCY: Because you've got no hope, it's a joke, it's a
            sick joke!
BALDRICK: Cheer up, my Lord, it's not the end of the
            world.
RUM: No, we'll know we've reached the end of
            the world when we fall into the jaws of the
            gigantic mouse . . .

Roaring into the plot with a textbook example of Lloyd's insane 'house style', Baker chews the scenery magnificently, electrifying the court and even stealing Nursie's heart, to Byrne's joy. 'Anyone who pays attention to her in a slightly flirtatious or sexy way, she crumbles with delight! I think she thinks Rum is quite extraordinary, even if he is legless.' Baker himself was not quite so pleased with his performance; while claiming it as the oddest TV role he's played (more so than a two-hearted time-travelling alien), he has also complained, 'I keep getting money because they repeat my appalling *Blackadder* performance . . . for which someone should have taken away my Equity card. It was terrible and the buggers keep playing it.' Fry begs to differ: 'His performance was superb, and he himself was entirely charming. While a scene that didn't involve him was being rehearsed he would disappear and return with a tray fully laden with sweets, crisps, chocolates, sandwiches, nuts and snacks, which he would hand round to everyone in the room, often nipping off again to reload . . . He had a way of gazing at you with grave bulging eyes that made it rather hard to determine whether he thought you an idiot or a god.' Despite being repeatedly hit with a boomerang in the episode, McInnerny was to declare, 'He's my favourite Doctor, so working with him was a fabulous week! One of my favourite weeks on *Blackadder*.'

Technically, the role of the Bishop of Bath and Wells in fourth episode 'Money' was not a true historical figure, but there is something slightly fishy about the fact that the official records for holders of the exalted ecclesiastic post record two of the few extended vacancies in the 800-year-long history of the diocese during the late sixteenth century – it's probable that a bishop who was a self-confessed baby-eating 'colossal pervert' would be expunged from all documents. The late Ronald Lacey, despite being a doubly well-known face, as the greasy Harris in *Porridge* and the Nazi Toht in *Raiders of the Lost Ark*, was lost within the ruddy folds of fat that enveloped his despicable bishop. So infamous was his grotesque depiction, indeed, that when the present incumbent the Right Reverend Peter Price took up the post in 2001, he felt obliged to tell the House of Lords in his maiden speech, 'In the aftermath of the *Blackadder* television series, there are always perils for the bishops of Bath and Wells. I am constantly reminded of the alleged activities of one of my predecessors as a baby-eater . . . Entering Your Lordships' House has proved no exception, and the greeting from the doorkeeper on my first day was capped only by the Bishop of Southwark seeing my five-week-old granddaughter arrive and remarking, "The Bishop has brought his own lunch!"'

The penultimate caper 'Beer' (rated as least favourite by the team, but highest rated by viewers) was another ramped-up farce, introducing a new branch of the Blackadder family to make Edmund's life a misery – and providing a celebrated return for Miriam Margolyes, as the violently Protestant gorgon Lady Whiteadder. 'For a Jew, as I am, to be covered in crosses was a complicated experience,' Margolyes says sweetly, neglecting to acknowledge the pleasure she gained from treating Atkinson and McInnerny to repeated physical abuse without recourse to stage-fighting, the latter laughing, 'I think that she would say that there was no way of faking it . . . but it really hurt, actually.' Fletcher adds, 'In rehearsal, Rowan got a bit fed up with this, and actually it was very funny. He said, "Would it be all right, Miriam, if you just didn't do it *quite* so hard?"' But as the original directions called for the mad Puritan to *hit* Edmund rather than slap him, perhaps they got off lightly. Margolyes insists that people still request slaps and cries of 'Wicked child!' from her in the streets, to her bemusement, but above all, she says, 'I remember being quite surprised that the director was a woman! Mandie was very good; I hadn't been expecting a woman to be directing comedy, I don't know why, I suppose I came from that world where comedy was always completely dominated by men. It was just terrific to see the authority she had. We laughed all the time, and worked very hard.' 'I used to crave the times when we had women performers on, like Miriam,' Fletcher returns, 'not that we had many, we were terribly outnumbered, but we were often at the lunch table together.' Margolyes's screen husband Lord Whiteadder would of course have been a fitting return for Jim Broadbent – almost entirely silent where his Interpreter had found it impossible to shut up – but Jim's unavailability gave the part to the stony-faced Daniel Thorndike, nephew of Dame Sybil, who would go on to feature in A *Bit of Fry & Laurie*.

The episode's real place in history, however, comes from the *Blackadder* debut of Hugh Laurie, stepping in to fill the minor role of merrymaker Simon Partridge, alongside William Hootkins and *Spitting Image*'s Roger Blake. 'I had the strong feeling at the time that someone had backed out at the last minute . . . But of course it was thrilling, because by that time Stephen had been doing the second series, Melchetting and all that stuff, and I had pangs of jealousy! And it was a real thrill to get a ticket onto that ocean liner.' This characteristic self-effacement belies the fact that Hugh was already in place to be the final guest star of the series, providing our anti-hero with his ultimate nemesis, Prince Ludwig the Indestructible. It's interesting that Laurie's first involvement also coincides with an emphasis on cast-led script enhancement, defined by Lloyd as 'plumpening'. Fry says, 'The first four scripts which Richard and Ben presented were simply perfect, we barely changed a word, they really were marvellous. I guess, flushed with the excitement of working together and doing something completely new, they really honed them. I'm not saying they got lazier for the last two, but maybe we were more confident with our characters so we were adding a bit more.' Whether it's therefore fair to apportion blame or not, 'Chains' is perhaps the one episode which most betrays the writers' avoidance of historical logic – in a time when Elizabeth was constantly fending off either France or Spain or both, our heroes are finally brought down by a German (albeit with a Spanish torturer). For once, Edmund got to swing into action Flynn-style and save the day, even if it was only his own hide that concerned him . . .

And there Curtis & Elton were content to leave the Lord, victorious and adored by his Queen (not to mention finally managing to catch the taunting minstrel and give him a dunking), until John Lloyd put his foot down, and decided, 'No, let's not get stale, let's move on another two hundred years!' As a coda, where every other episode was to sign off with a jolly cha-cha-cha, once again a royal court was piled high with bodies, for a tragic ending which allowed the producer to note in the Radio Times that 'Chains' was a 'very funny last episode in which the court get horribly murdered at the end again'.

The Filthy Genes Resurface

Despite the long delay between the end of recording in July and the eventual first broadcast of Blackadder II the following January, the slickness of the studio recordings, thanks to the simplicity of Fletcher's direction, made for a far smoother post-production job for Lloyd and his team. Any slight flabbiness was tweaked as career-defining performances from the extended family of performers played out on the edit suite: Baldrick doing favours for sailors; Bernard the Nurse wearing her dead lover's beard; Melchett's glorious golden comedy breasts (as presented to Fry for the twenty-fifth-anniversary tribute); Edmund's attempts to finish the song about goblins; the alchemist Percy's miraculous discovery of how to make a splat of the purest green;* Lady Whiteadder chomping on a turnip 'as nature intended' . . . Lloyd had no doubt that the finished series had been well worth the distraction from the pressures of *Spitting Image* – the new show was cheap, sexy, and *windingly* funny.

A full quarter of a decade after Edmund's debut, the official press release would warn, 'The filthy genes of the Blackadder family have resurfaced in the melting pot of history,' as the rogue landed in the same slot, Thursdays at 9.30 p.m. on BBC1. Atkinson busily went to work to remind the British public about his historical alter ego, recording special trailers for the series† and telling the *Radio Times*, 'I'm actually happier with this series and believe it has wider appeal. It's zappy and anarchic.' On *Wogan*, he mulled over ideas for future incarnations of his acerbic noble, positing the World War I flying ace the Baron von Blackadder, and the space-age adventurer Star Adder.

But though he was open about his hopes for the show to catch on, Atkinson had already gained the most important thing in his life from his time on *Blackadder II*. Sunetra Sastry was the make-up artist detailed to glue on the Melchett beard for every recording and, Fry admits, she had quite an effect on him: 'From a Brahmin-caste Indian family, she was bright, funny and as captivatingly alluring as any girl I had met for years.' Although describing himself as '90 per cent homosexual', Fry

---

* 'We could probably have made a fortune by creating lots of bits of green and selling them to the public,' rues McInnerny. 'Maybe I could still do that now . . .'

† 'He lived rough, he talked rough, he wore . . . a ruff'.

had created a rod for his own back when he wrote a short article for the *Tatler* admitting that sex was one of the things he 'didn't do', but despite his self-imposed evasion of romance, he claims that the make-up artist gave him pause for thought. 'I was quite seriously considering asking her out on a date, when Rowan timidly approached me one morning during rehearsals for the second episode and asked if I would mind swapping make-up artists with him. Since he had grown his own beard for the part, unlike me, who had to have my large excrescence glued on with spirit gum every week, I thought this rather odd: his make-up sessions lasted as long as it took to powder the tip of his nose . . .' Fry eventually decoded his diffident co-star's meaning, and with his blessing, Atkinson finally plucked up the courage to ask Sastry out. Despite taking her to a Dire Straits concert on what was reportedly a disastrous first date of Bean proportions, Sastry was smitten, and Rowan's bachelor days were over. Fry continues, 'They now have two children and twenty years of marriage behind them, but I still sometimes wonder what would have happened if I had been bold enough and quick enough on my feet to have asked Sunetra out straight away.'

The critical response to *Blackadder II* was markedly warmer than it had been for the first series, but still the praise was not entirely thunderous, Ronald Hastings in the *Telegraph* begrudgingly admitting, 'The first series was so variable, all right, so awful, that the BBC must have been reluctant to make a second. It is good that they did, for this is a great improvement.'

John, Rowan and the team were certainly vindicated for fighting for *Blackadder*'s return and yet, especially for its mainstream slot, the second series was no breakthrough hit on its first broadcast, with ratings as modest as the critical appreciation. Tony recalls, however, 'It was around about the repeat of the second series that I began to get an inkling of quite how popular it was. It also coincided with the time I was bringing up my children in Bristol and so it wasn't as if I was popping in and out of the Ivy and the Groucho Club. I was dealing with things like queuing up outside primary schools and driving children to the next games field. I remember going to Alton Towers with my kids one day and we were unable to go round it. My presence there caused chaos. I suddenly thought, "I have to recalibrate what my life is!"' These BBC2 repeats, at 9 p.m. during the glorious summer of 1987, opened up the *Blackadder* history to a whole new audience, not least the millions of children who would have been tucked up in bed for the first airing. A third series was already a certainty, but thanks to being prefaced by the triumphant repeat run, Edmund Blackadder was finally gaining the place at the heart of British society which he had always felt his absolute right.

By this time of course everyone in the cast had moved on to different projects, in film, theatre and especially comedy. But the biggest project of them all, which would unite most of the cast for years to come, began to take seed right back in the summer of '85. As Stephen recalled, 'The Saturday after the taping of the last episode of *Blackadder II* Richard held a party at his house in Oxfordshire. It was a glorious summer's day, and, as we all wanted to watch television, he unwound an extension cord and put the set on a wooden chair in the shade of an apple tree. We sat on the grass and watched *Live Aid* . . .' Before the party was over, having witnessed the magnitude of what could be achieved in the name of charity, Curtis and his friends began to form a plan. By the time their newly wrapped series was actually broadcast, Comic Relief would already be a red-nosed, stonking reality.

PARTE THE FOURTH:

THE GEORGIAN BASTARD

While it's not surprising that Ned, the Lord Blackadder, sired bastard issue, it does seem unlikely that any kind of continuity in the Blackadder inheritance should have been possible. With Ludwig in drag on the throne, no Blackadder heir would have dared to claim their title, and so there is no notable clash with monarchy for much of the early Stuart reign, until the ennoblement of Sir Edmund Blackadder by Charles I.

The Blackadder Chronicler not only insists that Sir Edmund was the Privy Counsellor, Royal Master of Revels and a close friend of King Charles, loyally hiding him from his enemies, but also that he was his friend and monarch's executioner. Once again, the mysterious historian has seized on one of the greatest questions in British History and answered it – there is no official record of who severed Charles's head on a freezing January morning in 1649. When the chief executioner Richard Brandon publicly refused to behead his King, the streets of London were scoured for an anonymous replacement, with two masked men being paid £100 for the job. Although the most likely suspect remains Brandon himself (letting it be known that he refused to commit regicide, but then doing it anyway), Sir Edmund Blackadder may as well join the roll-call of the accused.

Sir Edmund's confession to betraying the infant Charles II and cosying up to Cromwell did not apparently dent the dynasty's standing in the restored court – perhaps because Charles II was actually nineteen at the time of his father's beheading. The Chronicles even insist that a dukedom was conferred on the family in the reign of Queen Anne, and yet little is told of the Duke, or why the title was so short-lived –

and indeed, the next head of the family to be extensively biographised was nothing more than *Mister* Edmund Blackadder Esq. (1762–1828), butler to the Prince Regent in the late eighteenth and early nineteenth centuries. He could lay claim to being a gentleman but, although closer to the seat of power than any of his ancestors had been in centuries, he was no nob. Volume XIV of the Chronicles, which details the exploits of 'Mr B', still qualifies for its claim to be 'a giant roller coaster' of a story (this is the first known use of the term in the English language) because, as well as being 'crammed with sizzling gypsies', the narrative also describes how this Blackadder finally achieved what Prince Edmund only managed for thirty seconds – he took the crown.

The scandalous assertion that King George IV was a Blackadder in borrowed robes is perhaps the Chronicles' most audacious, perverted and stupid claim of all. Even in the twenty-first century, George IV easily won a BBC poll to find the most hated monarch in our history, beating King John and Richard III thanks to a life of gorging himself on the nation's wealth. So why would any Blackadder lie, to claim such infamy for themselves? Admittedly, an impostor taking on the duties of Prince George would have had to behave as like the pampered epicure as possible, but after centuries of waiting for a Blackadder to rise to power, and despite the Chronicles' ludicrous suggestions that this 'George IV' 'started the British Museum, the National Gallery, the Police Force' and 'legalised trade unions', the fact remains that this Blackadder, if the rumour is true, proved to be a very bad king, leaving the worst legacy possible.

The chronology of his mooted usurpation makes for one of the most tangled webs of impossibilities in the entire saga – the Chronicle places Pitts the Elder and Younger in direct succession as Prime Minister, while surrounding the great Dr Johnson (whose Dictionary was first published seven years before George's birth) with Byron, Shelley and Coleridge – a prospect akin to H. G. Wells crossing Abbey Road with the Beatles. They also heavily suggest that this Blackadder was the same age as his royal master, born in August 1762 – but if the two had even a passing resemblance, Mr B must have been of the 'extremely rotund' school of butlers. Everything about George Augustus, Prince of Wales, was rich and bloated. Escaping from a childhood of sadistic austerity imposed on him by his father George III, who then cruelly prevented him from pursuing his dream of a military career, 'Prinny' could only rebel by diving into a life of excess, becoming celebrated and pilloried for his passion for life's richest bounties, with an egregious penchant for food, wine and laudanum, outrageous military fashion and amply girthed ladies,* not to mention a bad reputation for gilding everything in sight in his ruinously expensive architectural projects, especially his home for much of his life and Regency, Carlton House.

That famed mansion was pulled down by George (or Edmund) himself in favour of Buckingham Palace in 1825, however, and there are no existing records to show that an Edmund Blackadder was ever in the Prince's retinue. Prince George had a number of extremely close aides throughout his life: Colonels Gerald Lake and John McMahon were both prized private servants, entrusted with the Regent's most secret affairs – paying off mistresses, bribing publishers to throw unflattering cartoons on the fire and so on – but both were father figures to the Prince, not contemporaries. Either the butler Blackadder knew too much for his existence to be known to the general public or, of course, the first thing he did when taking his master's place was to destroy all evidence of his former life (his dogsbody S. Baldrick was immediately sent to Australia), only revealing the truth to his own bastard offspring for posterity on his deathbed.

The ostentatiousness of the proposed usurpation is heightened by the suggestion that the real George was shot by the Duke of Wellington – a war hero and future prime minister who was on record as a staunch

---

* George illegally married the positively circular Catholic Maria Fitzherbert at the age of twenty-three, and had a number of aristocratic lovers of the 'Rubenesque-plus' variety.

opponent of duelling. If their duel took place before the Battle of Trafalgar, as is claimed (Trafalgar being a battleground allegedly suggested by Blackadder himself), then Arthur Wellesley would still have been several years away from becoming a field marshal, let alone a duke. By this time Prinny had been compelled to marry and impregnate – and subsequently become instantly estranged from – the equally repellent Caroline of Brunswick, and their only daughter, Princess Charlotte, would die in childbirth a few years after the official start of the Regency. With no issue from 'George IV' therefore, Blackadder may have made himself King, but failed not only to secure the throne for his family, but even to raise the bastards he had sired to their previous nobility.

The evidence certainly mounts up to support the suggestion that Volume XIV is the biggest load of untruths in the entire Blackadder Chronicles, and Justin Pollard agrees. 'There are two main stumbling blocks to entering this particular volume of the Blackadder Chronicles into the accepted historical record. Firstly, and as is the case throughout the Chronicles, we are presented with the fact that none of the Blackadders central to the narrative appear in any other official documents – at all. This is despite the Hanoverian household being remarkably well recorded in every other respect. Secondly, our assessment of the source material is hampered by the fact that the curator J. H. W. Lloyd will only allow his fellow historians access to the document if they agree to be blindfolded and heavily sedated. I did, however, find the section on "sizzling gypsies" strangely gripping.'

Convincing stuff – and yet it's hard to suppress a slight chill of doubt when some details of George's behaviour later in life are brought to light, unbecoming in any prince and not at all in character for the gluttonous despot which people think of in Gillray's cartoon, sneering over his voluminous belly and picking gristle from his teeth. Despite the infamous exotic opulence of the Brighton Pavilion, which was George's main passion in later years, the Regent was said to enjoy secretly dressing as a butler, with a flair for baking bread and expertly carving a joint to share with his servants in their own quarters, down below the sumptuous banqueting halls. As *Niles Weekly Register* reported in March 1819, 'We are assured that, a few nights ago, the Regent, in a merry mood, determined to sup in the *kitchen* of the pavilion . . . The whole of the servants, and particularly the female part, were, of course, delighted with this mark of royal condescension!' Were old habits hard to shake off for this frustrated impostor?

CHAPTER 4

BLACKADDER
THE THIRD

*It's no life for a man of noble blood, being servant to a master with the
intellect of a jugged walrus and all the social graces of a potty.*

It must be a source of eternal befuddlement for Richard Curtis that he
has so often been identified as the sole instigator of Comic Relief, when
a great number of people worked together to make it the institution it
has become – not least Peter Bennett-Jones, roped in early on to bring
his organisational flair to bear; promoter Peter Crossing, who dreamt
up the red-nose motif; Alan Yentob, who brought the idea to BBC
TV; and especially Jane Tewson, who was the real visionary. In setting
up Charity Projects, she was taking the *Secret Policeman's Ball* benefit
concept to its charitable conclusion, creating a fund-raising business
that aimed for funds first, and worried about the most deserving
recipients of the aid later. In the wake of *Live Aid*, with the human
tragedy unfolding in Ethiopia and the Sudan unavoidable throughout
UK media and Bob Geldof already a scruffy, saintly icon, Tewson's old
Oxford friend Curtis pledged to help out with the charity's next step.
'It was a horrible mistake to start with, in so far as Jane was a friend

of mine and was asked by Save the Children, I think, to go out to the Sudan because she ran Charity Projects . . . I offered to go with her, just as a friend, because I was sort of instinctively interested in it, and I thought that she could do with the company.' In the end, the charity sent Jane elsewhere, leaving Richard bound for war-torn East Africa at Oxfam's expense, 'sent off with no purpose or plan to Ethiopia for three weeks'. While on the road between Addis Ababa and Desei, Curtis amused himself with the idea of Cliff Richard duetting with his number-one fan, Rick, and the rest of the Young Ones. The tragedy Curtis found around him required many remedies, but it was clear that extra injections of cash for relief supplies could only do real human good – and who wouldn't pay to see a duet like that?

Wild-Eyed Loners Standing at the Gate of Oblivion

The spotty quartet had of course burned to death in a bus crash at the end of their last series, but besides surviving in print thanks to the book *Bachelor Boys*,* the repulsive students had already been squashed by eclairs and stampeded by medieval knights and lived to tell the tale, so they could rise again – and all it would take was a few phone calls. While Curtis's inherent and oft-praised *niceness* was unquestionably one factor which made (and still makes) so many people give in to his demands for Comic Relief, there clearly needed to be a will of solid iron under that fluffy exterior to turn Tewson's inspiration into a genuine laughter-and-cash-generating entity. The scheme was launched on Christmas Day 1985 in the unlikely surroundings of Noel Edmonds' *Live Live Christmas Breakfast Show*, and when Cliff and the Young Ones' rendition of 'Living Doll' hit the number-one spot the following March (remaining at the top for

---

* In which Vyvyan Basterd's 'History of the World' claimed that after the Vikings' exit, 'The world was now a pretty boring place apart from a few wars, and even some of those were about stupid girly things like roses.'

three weeks, and raising three-quarters of a million pounds in the process), it showed that perhaps the whole nation could be tickled into giving, and giving in to a new form of vast rag week led by the young graduate clowns.

In the wider national consciousness, these 'Alternative comedians' had largely been seen as foul-mouthed communists, by the kind of conservatives who thought that describing the new blood as 'the alternative to funny' was witty. John, Ben and Stephen appeared together on a special *Central Weekend Live* show at this time, however, for a debate pitched as 'Alternative vs Old School', up against Barry Cryer, Neil Shand and Michael Bentine, and the production team's hoped-for grudge match turned out to be a feast of mutual appreciation. Of course, none of the young trio had any involvement in the original creation of the comedy movement which became labelled 'Alternative' (a term which was already a meaningless cliché) and their move into the mainstream, typified by Comic Relief, simply widened the gulf between these acceptable young comics and their more politically puritanical brethren. Alexei Sayle was just one comedian who volubly declined to offer support or entertainment for the new cause (and certainly wouldn't allow himself to be seen emoting on-camera while a Sting song played in the background), when he felt the problems faced by the charity's beneficiaries ran deeper than just a shortage of cash, and that it should be down to the government to fight suffering in the UK, not a gang of celebrities. Elton himself admitted to *Smash Hits* at the time, 'I'm ambivalent to charity because I think in the long run you need a change in the system, not just to give people things. On the other hand you can't just fiddle while Rome burns . . . As Geldof's fabulous work last year proved, it helped but it *changed* nothing. People will starve until we believe we are a community on Earth and not out for our own private gain.' However, Curtis says, 'I don't think there are so many cynics. If you expected anyone to be cynical then it would be the comic community. But they understand it. I've only met a few people over the years who said "no" to me and that was because they tended to be hard-core socialists who believe that you have to get the state to pay for change. And I respect them for their opinion.'

The thorny issue of exactly what Comic Relief's famous supporters were getting out of their involvement was central to Helen Fielding's first novel *Cause Celeb*, loosely based on her experience as one of the charity's first documentary producers. As an old flame of both Curtis and Lloyd,* Fielding was well placed to observe intimately the foibles of the 'Alternative' stars, and saw at first hand the disparity between the suffering of refugees in the Sudan and the neuroses of the British media darlings flown out to front the appeal. At the other extreme of seeing charitable celebrities as self-serving egotists, however, was the accusation of being a bleeding-heart liberal. In response, Curtis told the *New Humanist* in 2007, 'I think "sentimental" is a complicated word. A lost word. What is wrong with being touched by what goes on around you? I am very touched by what is good and true. It's a family characteristic . . . But what struck me when I went to Ethiopia was the lack of sentiment. I thought the nurses and the water engineers there would be highly charged, highly emotional, with tears in their eyes. But they weren't, they were bluff northerners with beards busy drawing maps. They were doing something they did well for other people. And when I came home I decided to use my own skills in the same way, to see what I could achieve.'

The Utterly Utterly Merry Comic Relief Christmas Book was already being put together by Douglas Adams and Peter Fincham,† but the obvious next step was the traditional West End benefit – staged at

---

* And also co-author with Curtis and Simon Bell of the 1987 book *Who's Had Who*, a guide to famous infidelity, well worth a reprint.

† The eventual seasonal lucky dip contained input from Curtis, Atkinson, Lloyd and Fry, though items such as 'The Young Ones' Nativity' nearly caused the book to be uncharitably pulled from shelves, thanks to Christian pressure groups.

the Shaftesbury Theatre in April, broadcast on Yentob's *Omnibus* strand shortly after, and masterminded, like Nether Wallop, by the industrious Paul Jackson. 'At that time comedy was so hot hot hot. I mean, they're all big stars now, but at the time it had a kind of cult, happening feel about it, and you had this, I suspect, un-regroup-able bill of comedy talent.' The *Comic Relief* show was quite consciously not just about the young ones though, with the *Omnibus* broadcast introduced by comedic PM the Rt Hon. Jim Hacker, and Ronnie Corbett mingling with Atkinson, Billy Connolly, Lenny Henry, the *Spitting Image* puppets and Cliff and his Bachelor Boys. The show provided numerous memorable moments for future clip shows (including Rowan duetting with Kate Bush on 'Do Bears . . .?'), but the reception given to Ben Elton was the most electric of the evening. Despite the odd job on Radio 1 and presenting a regional culture show, *South of Watford*, his motormouth style had only had limited exposure to the general public, and yet the white-hot welcome the long-haired farty received at *Comic Relief* is unavoidably reminiscent of Graham Chapman's Brian Cohen, awaking to a multitude of devoted disciples which he never asked for, ready to hang on his every word.

The main gig to have drummed up this level of Elton fandom was his slot on *Saturday Live*, the first series having staggered to a close a few weeks before *Comic Relief*. A conscious move by Jackson to crib from the successful *Saturday Live* format, the one-hour live broadcasts for LWT had been going out on Channel 4 throughout the winter, but the changing host format made for a changeable show. It was a coup for Jackson that he was able to draw on Elton's scarily appreciative right-on young following every week, alongside the permanent sketch team, which Jackson had asked Fry & Laurie to join during the *Happy Families* filming in Stoke. They were to feature alongside the Dangerous Brothers Rik and Ade, plus less frequently, Mark Arden, Stephen Frost, Lee Cornes and Paul Mark

Elliott, known as 'The Wow Show', plus Simon Brint and Rowland Rivron as Raw Sex, and the new boy, Harry Enfield.*

Despite their close friendship, Fry & Laurie had never struck out as a duo before. 'We conferred nervously with each other in the bar that evening,' Stephen wrote. 'Hugh and I wondered if we would stick out like sore and inappropriately tweedy thumbs. Despite our characteristic fears and forebodings we decided that we should do the show . . . somewhere at the bottom of our churning wells of nonsense we knew that we could and should do comedy together.' The duo dared to test out their material at the relatively new London club Jongleurs, but however they fared in that boozy atmosphere, it couldn't prepare them for the ramped-up pressure of those Saturday nights. 'Transmitted live from the biggest studio in LWT's South Bank Studios, it featured a large central stage, side stages for the bands, random giant inflatables floating above and a vast arena for the audience of groundlings . . . Hugh was convinced that they were more interested in how their hair looked on-screen than in anything we might be saying or doing to try and amuse them.' 'There was a guillotine hanging over everybody on that series, including the show,' Elton adds, 'I mean, series one was in danger of being axed daily, because it wasn't doing very well.'

IF YOU CAN'T BE GOOD, BE CAREFUL

The experimental melting-pot atmosphere of Jackson's venture just added to the stomach-churning high of the live recordings. 'I always knew Hugh hated it and was always very nervous,' Ben recalls, 'but you would never know onstage, you couldn't believe it. Stephen, Hugh and

---

* A *Spitting Image* protégé of Lloyd's, Enfield's rise was augmented by the support of two witty neighbours, East Anglia University dropouts Paul Whitehouse and Charlie Higson – their plastering work on a house in nearby Dalston, occupied by Stephen and Hugh, led to the creation of zeitgeist-collaring monster Loadsamoney. Hugh admitted, 'They were so funny that it actually made me think, "Well either they're really funny or I'm just simply not, and I ought to now become a plasterer."'

Harry always seemed so cool – I imagine I probably did too, I certainly never went around going "Ohmigodohmigod!" Although I always talked *Young Ones* talk then, and DHT – *Deep Humiliating Troub'!* – that was what we'd say: "We've got no material, we're all crap, thank God we've got some bands on!'" But for all the self-confessed toilet-pebble-dashing, it was this core team which would survive to the series' second outing one year on, with Elton being promoted from regular topical ranter to full-time host. With this rejig, after all his attempts to bring the new wave of comics to the screen in a cabaret style, Jackson had found the right formula, with himself in the control room and Geoff Posner on the show floor.

Although 20th Century Coyote had morphed into the Dangerous Brothers before *Saturday Live* began, Rik & Ade already had plans for a new sitcom mutation of their personas at Jackson's behest. They refused to deliver a third series of *The Young Ones*, and besides, in 1985, while Rowan was wooing his future wife, Rik flew to Barbados to happily wed his own make-up artist, Barbara Robbin. They remain happily married three decades later, but the tabloids homed in on the gossip surrounding the dramatic end of Mayall and Mayer's relationship, and though Rik and Lise were reconciled as friends, their writing partnership was over. Despite this, Jackson brought together many of the same team for a '*Young Ones 2*', and it was naturally assumed that Ben and Rik would knock the scripts into shape together again. Not that Mayall or Edmondson were averse to writing,* but Elton, as ever, could be relied on to 'churn out the gear'. 'I had this basic idea that I wanted to live in a flat with Ade, so I went to Ben and said, "Let's write it together." Ben being the kind of writer that he is wrote 95 per cent of it, so I had my name taken off the front.'

---

* With Rowland Rivron, they had just completed their own joint *Comic Strip* movie, *Mr Jolly Lives Next Door*, taking their 'Dangerous' chemistry into even darker territory as two hideous alcoholics, neighbours to Peter Cook's titular blood-spattered hitman who is hired to 'take out' Nicholas Parsons.

Having been successful TV comedians for a number of years, they were done with mocking students, and now decided that their natural target had to be the tacky world of showbiz, and Light Entertainment, as they experienced it from the inside. *Filthy, Rich & Catflap* would be a flop in comparison with *The Young Ones*, but for all its faults, it would stand as a singularly pungent skewering of old-school celebrity. In time, as the high of youthful arrogance wore off, it became common for Elton and his contemporaries to downplay the extent to which their wave of comedy reviled the less enlightened golfing stars such as Jackson's old friends the Two Ronnies, to an extent though far more so Benny Hill, Bernard Manning and 'Tarby', but the evidence is all there – these guys did despise the easy laughs which their elders got for rolling their eyes at a huge pair of breasts, and for their new sitcom, they sharpened their rapiers, and dipped them in effluent. 'I think it's the most nihilistic piece of telly we've ever done,' Mayall said at the time, 'it's completely anti-television, it's anti-fame, it's anti the media generally, and anti-privilege.'

With Rik starring as the talentless TV has-been Richie Rich (a right-wing egotist with no discernible act beyond greasily repeating non-catchphrases like 'If you can't be good, be careful' and 'Look after Mum, kids, and try and steer clear of the loony left!'), Edmondson playing his mindless minder Eddie Catflap, and Planer as Richie's despicable free-loading perverted agent Ralph Filthy, the six episodes broadcast on BBC2 at the start of 1987 had carte blanche to rip into every element of seedy showbiz, from desperate quiz show celebs to sexist BBC executives waddling around a BBC bar which resembles the last days of Sodom, to Rik getting his own back on muck-raking tabloid journalists and the union-busting villainy of Rupert Murdoch.

Whether due to the lack of Curtis's grounding good taste or the tailoring of the scripts to suit Mayall & Edmondson's combination of Beckettian absurdity and extreme nihilism, *FR&C* remains perhaps the most savage and relentless comedy ever written by Elton, no matter how much back-pedalling may come with the mellowness of middle age. The show's gags – be they joyfully infantile, cheap, shocking or even scathingly witty – simply pour out without pause, and are constantly derided by the stars breaking the fourth wall at all times, having their cake and eating it by criticising old-school double entendres while using them at every opportunity, to Eddie's cries of 'Oo-er! Sounds a bit rude!' It's also tempting to suspect a personal anger running through the series, from the overachieving young writer who had wilted under the gaze of some of his own comic heroes in the BBC bar. Ronnie Barker, then known simply as 'the Governor' in BBC comedy circles, had praised Stephen Fry's comedy warmly at one BBC function, before turning to Elton and frowning, 'Don't like you very much, I'm afraid.' As a fan, this crushed Elton, but Ronnie Corbett would be quick to point out that Barker was to regret the admission, and even befriend Elton.*

In truth, scripting *FR&C* was a literally painful experience for Ben, who was in hospital with a hernia for much of the show's composition. 'It was the most unhappy experience of my life, writing that show,' he would tell Roger Wilmut in 1989, 'because I never really knew where I was – was Rik writing it with me or not? In the end he said, "I haven't written a word, so you'd better have the credit," but by that time I'd spent four months trying to write something as part of a team, so it wasn't easy. Having said that, I'm very proud of it. All right, it's loud, it's dirty, it's noisy, but there are some good bits in it – we got more fan mail than for *The Young Ones* – we also got the most vitriolic critical panning . . .' But as ever, Elton was not interested in looking back – by the time his sitcom was either delighting or disgusting the British public, he was back in DHT on the second series of *Saturday Live*.

---

* Elton in turn invited Corbett to revive his armchair monologues on *The Ben Elton Show*, following in the footsteps of Spike Mullins and David Renwick by penning Ronnie's shaggy-dog stories himself.

Quite Frankly, Mr Perkins . . .

While *Blackadder* thrives by being untied to its decade of origin, *Saturday Live* did such a spectacular job of capturing the spirit and the comedy scene of the mid-eighties that shallower viewers of the twenty-first century could find it hard to see past the forest of mullets and appreciate the excitement of the phenomenon at the time. Elton was the perfect frontman for Jackson's aim to bring together variety and youth culture – volubly denouncing the latest machinations of Thatcher's government, while wearing a sparkly suit that radiated a kind of ironic showbiz pizzazz. Although it was his job to get material out of the top stories, being cheered to the rafters by the fashionably right-on punters with every pump of his fist, Elton was never comfortable with the whooping reflexes his attacks on 'Thatch' inspired, regularly chiding the crowd with rapid disclaimers and put-downs, reminding them that 'This isn't a rally, it's a comedy programme'; laughing 'Don't clap, you sycophants!' when the crowd got overexcited and ate into his allotted time; ominously admitting, 'I put myself down so I don't give you a chance to do it'; and of course, sending himself up with a piss-taking 'Little bit of politics, ladies and gentlemen, yes indeed . . .' The vast majority of Elton's material concerned everyday insecurity, not satire – the arch-satirist John Lloyd was relinquishing control of *Spitting Image* at this time, and would lament, 'I think satire changes perceptions, but I don't think it changes the actuality. When I left *Spitting Image* I certainly felt that we'd achieved nothing but possibly made the government slightly more powerful than we had found it.' It was a time when the government positively *invited* attack, but Elton's weekly diatribes, though heartfelt, were ultimately just 'a little bit of politics'.

Even this mid-rant self-deprecation would eventually become a stick with which to wallop the comic for his detractors, who felt they saw through his honest style, considering him a bourgeois pretend socialist. But it was his duty, as a comic with a platform, to reflect what was going on, and he worked tirelessly at it, writing fresh material every week and sweating through laugh-free weekly rehearsals with LWT's lawyers to see if his up-to-the-minute jibes were broadcastable. 'The audience loved it,' Jackson observes, 'the audience at home picked up on it, he was saying intelligent things, he was making them laugh but he was making points. And he also, I have to say, did it against the most difficult circumstances.' Lee Cornes adds, 'I remember seeing him on *Saturday Live*, thinking, "He's taken on so much!" Almost single-handedly stepping out and saying what he wanted to say. He's a very nice bloke who likes to be liked though, so the aggressive persona was never quite who he was.'

Despite having such a solid team powering the second series, the experience of recording the show remained terrifyingly chaotic. '*Saturday Live* was a bit of a party,' Elton says, 'and meant to be like a party. If I hadn't been terminally terrified for the whole of it, I'm sure I'd have enjoyed it,' and even a quarter of a decade on, Fry concurs: 'By about Wednesday we were sweating blood, by Thursday we were vomiting, by Friday our bowels were completely loose, and by Saturday we were just simply barely alive.' The sketch format, however, can be a very comforting thing, and the spirit of *Alfresco* (not to mention a few verbatim sketches) pervaded the moments when all the team came together. Elton recalls, 'I loved the sketches, I wrote a few. Those were the moments within the live broadcasts that were least horrible, because you weren't on your own, and you could sort of almost relax.' Further comfort came from the friendly faces of Robbie Coltrane (who also appeared in an extended spoof of *The Third Man* with Miranda Richardson), Emma Thompson, and indeed Rowan Atkinson, who showed up in series two, performing his country song 'I Believe' and remaining silent as the Rev. Sebastian Kryle in a sketch with Hugh and Stephen, as the Dalston Christian Community Club, Ben introducing Rowan with: 'He broke America; he was the king of Broadway for all of two days!' The inspiration for that jibe rewinds the story to the start of 1986, as the star's all-new tour began to be pieced together.

Atkinson was so pleased with the scripts for *Blackadder II* that he decided to make his new show another Elton/Curtis collaboration, and the development from the 1981 material was striking. It would seem rather too neat to suggest that the revue was heavily steeped in the dark, acerbic *Blackadder* spirit, if it weren't for the fact that Rowan took his bows to the sitcom's theme at the end of every night on the tour. Subtly accepting his small share of applause beside him every night was Angus Deayton, taking time out from *Radio Active* to inherit the thankless role of sidekick, which Curtis had finally forsworn.

The New Revue would tour the UK, kicking off at the Shaftesbury Theatre,* and taking in Edinburgh for Atkinson's last time on the Fringe. The UK shows were a run-up for his first real attempt to make inroads into America, fittingly at the Brooks Atkinson Theater on Broadway that October. 'I know that it is a potential graveyard for English comics,' he confided in the *Express* beforehand. 'It's something I must plan very carefully and I hope they turn out to see me.'

Where the humour of his earlier shows tended to be of a more low-key, almost dreamlike nature, the sketches and monologues written by Curtis & Elton were a far punchier (and notably sicker) collection, bristling more than ever with egregious helpings of people called Perkins. Atkinson's array of bastards was more devilishly offensive than previously, with one of the most celebrated two-handers, 'Fatal Beatings', more morbidly amusing than anything in earlier shows.

HEAD: Mr Perkins, Tommy is in trouble. Recently his
behaviour has left a great deal to be desired
. . . he seems to take no interest in school
life whatsoever, he refuses to muck in on the
sports field, and it's weeks since any master has

---

* *Comic Relief* provided a brief hiatus during the run – some proceeds from all the performances went to the charity.

received any written work from him.

PERKINS: Oh dear me.

HEAD: Quite frankly, Mr Perkins, if he wasn't dead,
I'd have him expelled.

PERKINS: I beg your pardon?

HEAD: Yes, EXPELLED! If I wasn't making allowances
for the fact that your son has passed on, he'd
be out on his ear!

PERKINS: Tommy's dead?

HEAD: Yes . . . He's lying up there in sickbay now, stiff
as a board and bright green. And this is, I fear,
typical of his current attitude.

The Geordie football manager who has to explain to his team *what a ball is* has a shade of Edmund teaching Baldrick 'advanced mathematics', a peace camp soldier sings Gilbert & Sullivan's 'A Wand'ring Minstrel', and an actor forced to pick up an award for a colleague who has beaten him seethes, 'What is it about Johnnie that sets him apart from other actors of his generation? Well, I think we all know the answer to that one – syphilis. And what a great and heart-warming thing it is that he has already started passing it on to a whole new generation of younger actors.' The LP of the show, *Not Just a Pretty Face*, was recorded at the Alhambra Theatre, Bradford, and augmented by extra links produced by Atkinson himself – with a coda underlining the despicable Adder-like criminality of the show's star.

ANGUS: . . .Would they be applauding quite so
rapturously if they knew that Mr Atkinson was
in fact none other than the notorious gangland
chief Ronnie 'Hatchet' Atkinson, wanted in
connection with nefarious crimes including
murder, arson, cattle-rustling, escorting a

> minor across a state border, and parking on
> those zigzag lines you get either side of zebra
> crossings? Well I'm now gonna see how Mr
> Atkinson responds . . . Mr Atkinson, this is
> Roger Crook from Central Television, I'm here
> to talk to you about one or two allegations . . .
> Is it true *The Black Adder* isn't funny? Is Ned
> Sherrin right in claiming that *Not the Nine
> O'Clock News* was simply a rehash of *That Was
> The Week That Was*, Mr Atkinson?

ROWAN: I'm not answering these questions, go away!
F—k off, you f—king f—ker!

However, the Broadway debut of the show, even including the best material from previous tours, failed to impress the most influential voice in the city: *New York Times* critic Frank Rich, 'the Butcher of Broadway'. On 15 October, the first night of the revue was viciously dismissed as 'the interminable proof that the melding of American and English cultures is not yet complete. As long as the British public maintains its fondness for toilet humour, there will always be an England . . . The writing, by Mr. Atkinson and various cronies, is stunningly predictable. Were *Rowan Atkinson at the Atkinson* to be edited down to its wittiest jokes, even its title might have to go.' No amount of fake villainy could rally the team from this conclusive blow, the first indisputable setback in a career which had seemed charmed since Oxford, and the show closed in two weeks, losing backers £500,000. Atkinson swore to the *Daily Mail*, 'The only way I'll go back is if I can take out insurance against that man coming anywhere near me . . . The only good thing to come out of the whole venture is that now I will be home for Christmas.'

'At least a third of it was as funny as I had been anywhere,' he later said on Radio 4's *Loose Ends*, 'and if he didn't like that there was

nothing I could do – lavatorial or not – that would have pleased him.'
Fry was part of the regular team on the brand-new Saturday-morning
magazine programme-cum-plug fest,* and from his position around
Ned Sherrin's green baize table, he expressed his own fears about the
fate of *Me and My Girl* on Broadway. However, he and Armitage need
not have fretted, it would run for three years, and pick up a handsome
collection of Tony awards.

Sadly, Richard Armitage was not to live to see this continued success,
as his sudden death at the age of fifty-eight in November 1986 robbed
both Stephen and Rowan of the man who had been their greatest
supporter and crucial guide to the perilous world of show business.

Delving into the Past

Stephen Fry had excitedly embraced every offer of work from Radio
4, becoming an admired rookie player of games such as *Just a Minute*,
I'm Sorry I Haven't a Clue and the fledgling *Whose Line Is It Anyway?*
before he hit thirty. He wouldn't get his own self-penned show until
the ingenious *Saturday Night Fry* in 1988 (with regular guests Laurie,
Thompson and Jim Broadbent), and while Deayton was aping Roger
Cook for Atkinson's LP, Fry's main wireless persona was David Lander,
the presenter of another crusading investigative programme, *Delve
Special*, created by Tony Sarchet. Kicking off in 1984 with an exposé
of corruption in the building of 'London's third airport' in Shifton
(a village near Birmingham), Lander's inept and often physically
damaging investigations went to great lengths to establish a believable
spoof, despite boasting famous voices including Dawn French, Harry
Enfield, Philip Pope and even Tony Robinson. The show ended in
1987, but there was a TV transfer the following year, *This Is David*

---

* Where he originated the aged characters of the unworldly Professor Donald Trefusis
and the wistfully barking Rosina, Lady Madding.

Lander, with Robinson reprising the role of a porn-obsessed victim of police corruption. As part of the *Who Dares Wins* team, his return for the TV version was only natural, *This Is David Lander* being the first official production from Mulville's newly rechristened production company, Hat Trick.

His TV work alone would have kept Tony busy after discarding Baldrick's jerkin, but the greatest progress in his career had been his venture into writing. He had a long association with children's TV, and on *Jackanory* had displayed a revolutionary zeal in his ability to tell a tale with unbridled enthusiasm, but after narrating and co-writing Debbie Gates's award-winning CITV series *Tales from Fat Tulip's Garden*, he gained the confidence to create his own stories. He was aided and encouraged by Curtis, who had already co-authored the children's book *The Story of Elsie and Jane* and even been instrumental in originating the swaggering, abusive character of Roland Rat for TVAM. Richard would co-write Tony's books and TV retellings of *Theseus* and *Odysseus: The Greatest Hero of Them All*, before Robinson found the confidence to write alone. 'I actually learned to write through being involved with the people in *Blackadder*,' he admits. 'Not that I learned the answers to writing, but I learned the questions to ask, and that was what the environment was like in rehearsals, it wasn't much to do with acting . . . I went to a publisher with the idea of writing the *Odysseus* books, and they said, "Yes, that's fine, we'll commission you." And I said, "Great!" and walked away . . . and then, when I got home, I thought, "I don't know the first thing about writing, what am I going to do?" So I went to see Richard and said, "I can't do this," and he said, "Yes, of course you can. I'll tell you what we'll do. You write it and keep coming to me, and we'll knock it into shape." So that's what we did, I would drive up to Oxford from Bristol and Richard would say, "For a start you can cut the first two paragraphs, and that isn't a character it's just a cipher, what can we do to beef this character up? And those jokes are very good, why do they run out here . . .?" And he would write a couple of paragraphs and fit them in, and that was how we wrote those books.'

These diverse frenzies of career progression did not make it easy for Lloyd to regroup the usual suspects for the third incarnation of Edmund Blackadder. He recalls, 'We had two-year gaps between series and at the time of *Blackadder II* none of us had many strings to our bows – apart from Rowan who was red hot at the time. However, between series two and three Ben had *Saturday Live*, Richard had Comic Relief, I'd done *Spitting Image* . . . The net effect was that we had bigger egos and were more used to having our own way, so we were much more reluctant to surrender any territory.'

Nevertheless, Richard and Ben had already found time between rhapsodising about Stock, Aitken & Waterman to settle on the next period for their comedy, doubling the distance between series to leapfrog the seventeenth century entirely. Moving on so dramatically allowed for an entirely evolved British society to send up – although Robinson insists that the choice of Regency England was a brave one. 'I think my favourite series is *Blackadder the Third*. Partly because of Hugh's performance, but also because I think it's so audacious to create a six-part comedy series about a period of history where virtually none of the viewers can remember anything about that period!'

For much of the Georgian era, this concern would make sense – from the dramatic end of the Stuart reign to the late eighteenth century, the nation boringly fermented under Hanoverian rule, with each German George less interesting than the last, but by the latter years of George III's reign, so many revolutions were afoot – Industrial, American and French, to name but three – that few periods of our history could have contained such rich material for *Blackadder*. From *The Madness of George III* to *The Scarlet Pimpernel*, the cusp between Georgian and Victorian Britain has always been such a magnet for dramatists that the writers needed to do little to no research to bring a bewigged Blackadder to life. Also, as with the previous two series, they could also draw on yet another BBC costume drama, as Peter Egan had portrayed the infamous 'Prinny' in 1979's *Prince Regent*.

Because in the Regency period, where would Blackadder be but as close to the Regent as possible? With both writers as devoted to P. G. Wodehouse as they were to Kylie, the fresh epoch inspired a central set-up indebted to the Master, making their anti-hero the Prince's closest retainer. 'What I think it did was that it made it a very different dynamic,' Curtis says. 'You could have had it about the King and then Blackadder would have been a Lord again, and we'd have been back in the same situation that we were in before. It's the whole Jeeves thing, isn't it, the idea of somebody actually being much cleverer than the person above them.' 'Rather than being a lone wolf as he was in the first series,' Elton adds, 'it made life easier to actually give him a position, it meant we could find things for him to do. He sort of dropped a class every time, from royal to courtier to butler to sort of lower-middle-class officer. He'd have ended up a trade union leader if we'd done the 1950s!' Fry continues, 'The fact is a lifetime of prep school, public school, prison and Cambridge had given me, and most of us, a tremendous acuity when it came to the nuances of British class and hierarchy. *Blackadder* worked the way it did because someone was at the top and someone was at the bottom and there was a real threat of punishment or death. And as in Goldoni and Ben Jonson, you don't always find that the one on top is the smart one . . . that tradition connects all the way up to Jeeves and Wooster too, of course.'

Robinson believes that the butler Mr B's world was a step towards Lloyd's ambition for simplicity, and containment. 'I think one of the things that we were always striving for in *Blackadder* was more focus, more discipline, really to concentrate on every single little joke, every scene, every concept. So *The Black Adder* goes hurtling all over the place, loads of extras, loads of horses, loads of characters. Series two is reduced from that, but by series three, that was the time when I really felt that we were focusing on what we really wanted to do.'

Where previous series had taken cues from Shakespeare, there was an equally celebrated vein of Restoration and Regency theatre to inspire the new show, with sesquipedalian verbiage aplenty, and a tradition of complicated farce, from the French. 'I don't think we consciously crafted these supposedly "brilliant" playwright-type structures,' Lloyd says, 'but we were certainly trying to make *Blackadder* more than a mere extended sketch. We could see that, if he was a butler, for example, he'd have a different attitude, a different turn of phrase and so on. Those things are taken on board and to some extent dictate the action . . . In the first series he talks like a lord; butlers don't talk like that. He has to be in a different relationship, so we had to unlearn all those things and start again.'

It was established that there would be an 'upstairs/downstairs' feel to the new Edmund's life, with the ineffable Jeevesian servant in Antony Thorpe's BAFTA-nominated gilt royal quarters reverting to type by the time he reached Baldrick's kitchens – although his reduced circumstances would, if anything, intensify his feeling of entitlement to the throne. Atkinson muses, 'He's got a ladder to climb, but he's so cynical about climbing it. And he's also cynical about those who are climbing up towards him. He's just a fantastically cynical man. He wants the fast track, and yes – he's trying to get up there . . . or at least to get out.' It's mildly disturbing that Atkinson has claimed in the past that Mr B is the one incarnation which most closely resembles himself, as the butler is probably the most ruthless of all Blackadders: seemingly urbane, but happy to commit or commission bloody murder to achieve his aims. On the other hand, Mr B is the first Edmund to be 'respected about the town', despite being just as duplicitous, ambitious and cowardly as his forebears.

One other side effect of Edmund's lowering in status was the natural adoption of 'Blackadder' as a surname, which would lead to all sorts of people claiming that the character's name came from them – but their surname is derived from Scots Border country, where the River

Adder runs, and as we know, Edmund's darkly serpentine roots reach far deeper. Still, Tony says, 'Blackadder was certainly a name that Rowan was familiar with, being brought up in Newcastle. Right up as far as Edinburgh I've seen plaques in churches dedicated to so-and-so Blackadder. They were a wealthy minor noble Borders family, stretching way back.' Atkinson says, 'Various men named Blackadder have erroneously been thought the inspiration, including the BBC doctor at the time that we were making the series and a "scout" at my old Oxford college, who died in the early seventies. I only became aware of the presence of the name in the Scottish Borders long after we began to make the programmes.'

It's fair to surmise that it was equally purely coincidental that Mr B was not the first eighteenth-century Blackadder to star in his own BBC series. Nearly forty years earlier, John Keir Cross had authored a swashbuckling radio serial, *Blackadder*, set during the Napoleonic Wars, in which the mysteriously villainous figure of the pirate/spy Blackadder looms large (this Blackadder was, it can be assumed, no relation).

As ever, frugality was important to the sitcom's creation, and so the main set, above and below stairs at the Prince's home, Carlton House, would house George's enormous entourage, slimmed down to just two, Blackadder and Baldrick – Edmund and his two 'friends' recreating *The Frost Report*'s 'Class Sketch' trio two hundred years early. However, as the show's set-up was beginning to take form, Edmund's original first 'friend' informed the team that he was out – Tim McInnerny insisted that Percy's bloodline had to be ended. 'I didn't want to get stuck with being seen as this one character. However ground-breaking it is, it's still a sitcom.' When publicising the movie *Severance* in 2006, the actor explained, 'The genre doesn't actually make a lot of difference to me, as long the character's interesting and has a journey and the acting's a challenge, that's all I'm concerned about. The jobs I don't want to do are the jobs that are easy. When I get up in the morning to go to work, I want to be excited and also a bit scared about whether I'm going to be able to do what I'm required to do that day. And I want to feel that every day.' Before *Blackadder II*'s burst of popularity, McInnerny had managed to balance his comedic and dramatic careers, with a critically acclaimed role in *Edge of Darkness* helping to make his name even before recording *Blackadder*'s second series. Percy's popularity, however, had begun to weigh him down, as he discovered when playing Hamlet for the National Theatre. 'We did lots of school matinees, and I had to win them over. They thought they were coming to see Lord Percy . . . The idea of it being fun, and friends together making something, you know, that we'd enjoy even if other people didn't, had snowballed into such a huge success that I felt it was getting in the way of the public's perception of me, and my perception of myself as an actor, and I didn't want it to overpower other things I was doing.'

This was a disappointment for Lloyd at first. 'When I heard that Tim wasn't going to do it, I thought, "Oh dear, this is a bit of a disaster," because he'd become so much a part of the second series, and if Tim had wanted to do the third series, and had he been free, he might well have played the Hugh Laurie part. In some ways, Hugh's character is a sort of Percy, similar sort of twittish type.' But with Fry nannying *Me and My Girl* on Broadway, there was nothing more perfect than for Laurie to step into the sitcom 'family' – and the fact that he was a tall wiry actor portraying one of British History's most ridiculed human balloons would be entirely ignored. 'I was conscious of filling the great Tim McInnerny's shoes,' Hugh says, 'and in comic terms, he takes a size 22. He's very big-footed, comically. I suppose George was sufficiently different, rather than being a sidekick of Blackadder's, the dynamic was different.' 'I thought it was brilliant,' Tim happily returns, 'and it worked terribly well – it wasn't the same as Percy anyway.'

Laurie had always specialised in playing repellent Middle Englanders in the past, or anyone with a stupendously silly accent, but his first chance to give an extended performance of inbred aristocratic idiocy would land him with a certain level of typecasting trouble himself in years to come. 'Hugh's Prince Regent should be celebrated more,' Elton says, 'I mean, a truly brilliant performance of a foppish Regency idiot.' Curtis agrees: 'When Hugh plays stupid, there is nothing behind the eyes. I think we took Percy, who hadn't been clever, and scooped out the final teaspoonful of brains, and presented Hugh Laurie. That utter thickness was something that was fun to put Blackadder against, and different from Miranda's sort of dangerous childishness.' 'It's that utter sort of gullibility,' Atkinson says, 'the perfect sponge for whatever anyone says. Anyone can take him in any direction at any one time. He has no resolution of his own. In the hands of the Blackadder, he is complete putty.' 'Underlying all this stupidity,' Robinson adds, 'there's a desperate loneliness; the reason why I think he craves Blackadder so much is that it's somebody who'll talk to him on a level that won't make him feel too threatened, even though Blackadder is manipulating him shamelessly.'

Hugh was also to bring with him an air of modesty stretched beyond breaking point into neurotic pessimism which, allied with Atkinson's perfectionism, would only escalate the team's exhausting obsession with 'plumpening' every script into perfect shape, to Elton's admitted chagrin. 'They got into overanalysis, but you'd have two actors, Hugh and Rowan, and I know they'll forgive me for saying it, but they were both very, very intense people, you know, the two of them together could get very gloomy about things and talk themselves into a great deal of a "This is awful, we're awful, who are we kidding?" sort of world. Particularly Hugh, but I think Row would always go along for the ride.' 'Hugh wears his heart on his sleeve; he doesn't conceal anything. If Hugh is nervous or depressed you see it, it's all over him,' Lloyd affirms, adding, 'I remember saying to Hugh in rehearsal one day, "Why aren't you a world-famous actor? You're so good," and as he does, Hugh said, "Oh, I'm rubbish . . ."' and Robinson laughs, 'Hugh would be beating himself up, going, "Oh God, oh God, I'm so unfunny, I'm the least funny person in the world!" They must throttle him on *House*, mustn't they?' However, he continues, 'What we had always concentrated on was getting the work right. Nobody was more po-faced about the work than we were. Virtually all of us thought we were the worst thing in it. Stephen thought he was rubbish. He's probably right! Hugh thinks he's the least funny person in the entire world. Miranda always felt she was an outsider. What a bunch of neurotics.'

Elton had learned to minimise his time at rehearsals to avoid dealing with the ensuing contretemps when Laurie would attempt a line only to pull a face and carp, 'Do they actually read it back once they've written it?' so Curtis had to be the one to take the blows and rework the lines accordingly. 'He'd often speak to Ben on the phone in the evenings,' Lloyd remembers, 'saying, "I'm so fed up with what they're doing, they're making a mess of it." And then when the show would come out eventually, Ben would ring Richard and say, "I can't understand it, it seems exactly the same!" He'd forgotten the details. Ben's got a rhinoceros skin – if it's getting funnier, Ben likes it. He's not precious.' It was Lloyd's job to maintain diplomacy, but he admits, 'The majority of the second series' scripts were extraordinarily good, despite them having utterly different writing styles, but later on the first drafts wouldn't be very good. They'd be cobble jobs of Richard's fluffy sentimentality, all fluffy teeny-weeny-nosey, and Ben's whacking great huge arse gags. I'd be going through the scripts, saying, "I think this knob gag's too rude," and they'd both be, "Well we like it," and I could see in their faces that they'd had a conference beforehand – "Ben, that knob gag has got to go." "Well, if I can't have my knob gag you can't have your fluffy gag!" My role was in smoothing out their writing styles in rehearsal so the end result would seem like the work of one writer.' This did on occasion lead to rescripting entire scenes himself. 'If I write, I'm generally doing a technical job. For example, in *Blackadder the Third*, Blackadder wants to stand for a rotten borough and become the MP for Dunny-on-the-Wold, and I said to Richard, "Most people won't know what a rotten borough is so you'll have to explain it – but for God's sake, don't make it a boring history lesson." He said, "Well, how can you do that? It's just boring – 'A rotten borough is . . .'" So I went home that evening and wrote that scene where Blackadder goes on about the electorate being a small dachshund called Colin, and the Prince Regent, confused as usual, going, "What about this robber button, then?" and doing chicken impressions. It's a neat piece of technical writing, going from A to B, very enjoyable to do, and in the pleasure of doing it these things occur to you – we've got to say that rotten boroughs had very few electors so you just exaggerate that . . .'

Forming the third corner of what Hugh calls Edmund's 'cretinous triangle' was, of course, Baldrick, devolved further from his wily original, with class separation finally making his relationship with his dark master more of a double act than ever, underlined by the increase in violence shown towards the stinking subordinate. Tony says, 'Baldrick puts up with all the physical and mental torture that he receives from Blackadder because he thinks that's the way of the world. He suffers pain and he accepts it because that's what people do to people like Baldrick. He doesn't notice it most of the time. It takes a long while for pain to get from any part of his body up to his brain, and by the time it gets there it's tired, and doesn't really register very much.' For all his deepened idiocy, this generation's Baldrick continued his surprising ability to play *deus ex machina* when the plot called for it, easily rounding up a lynch mob to save Blackadder from being filled with lead. This incarnation also introduced a burgeoning rebellious side to the downtrodden; with revolution in the air, 'Sod Off' Baldrick becomes keen to mutiny against the 'lazy, big-nosed, rubber-faced bastard' who keeps him subdued with his wit, and fists – even though he soon realises that he cannot cope without him.

The dogsbody's increasing repulsiveness in reverse trajectory to the improvements in human sanitation over the centuries was down to the make-up artists Ann Fenton and Victoria Peacock, to whom Tony paid tribute in his one-man show in 2007. 'You might be thinking he slapped a bit of brown on his face, thirty seconds, easy. But you're forgetting Baldrick's boils. They were created by the make-up artist the night before we recorded each episode, on her kitchen table at home. Basically she got a little round plastic ball of modelling putty and she got her thumb and put it in the middle of the ball, and then she'd tease and squeeze out the top and put it onto the kitchen table so it looked like a little pink bowler hat, then she'd get this sticky yellow stuff and squeeze it into each of the holes, stick a needle in the bottom so that a little bit leaked out and it looked like it was weeping. It was fairly disgusting – in fact during the entire run of *Blackadder*, her husband refused to eat off the kitchen table. But then we'd go into the studio, and she would glue these things onto me, which I suppose was fairly sensible, except we finished taping the show at ten o'clock, the BBC bar closed at ten thirty. At ten past ten, Stephen would be up in the bar with a gin and tonic in his hand regaling his adoring fans, Hugh would be playing the piano, Rik would be *under* the piano . . . at twenty to twelve I would still be in the make-up room desperately trying to claw off these boils, dying for a drink! But I did get my retribution in a kind of way, because during the rehearsals for each episode, Rowan would discover that he'd got reams and reams of over-elaborate dialogue to learn. I had about seven lines. And they would be going "rabbit rabbit rabbit", and I'm thinking "what do I say next? Oh yes, I remember: three, two, one . . . *I have a cunning plan!*" It was easy!' However, he continues, 'I think one of the useful things about Baldrick in that series is that he provides a breathing space. Everyone else is talking at nine hundred miles an hour in the most dazzling vocabulary, using words that often most of us don't understand, or think you may understand but aren't *quite* sure you know what they mean. And then in comes Baldrick – much slower tempo, much less to say, whatever he says, you're going to get it. And I think that helps you to feel comfortable about the series – it's certainly how I felt being in among all those dazzling minds in the middle of rehearsals!'

The central cast then was slimmer than ever, but a third regular set was needed, unless every plot was to somehow unfold at the Prince's home. In eighteenth-century London, the natural place for a man about town like Mr B had to be the coffee shops where the cream of society's thinkers, roisterers and artists would meet, plot, and debate the hot topics of the day. Finally, Elton's mysterious Mrs Miggins, the paraplegic Elizabethan pie-shop owner – or rather, her descendant – would graduate from being an off-screen funny name into an on-screen funny character. A regular female role was a must, and although by this stage any comic actress would have been glad to join the *Blackadder* team, there was a natural candidate for the role, in Rowan and Richard's long-standing collaborator Helen Atkinson-Wood.* Besides being part of the team on the ill-fated adult *Tiswas* spin-off O.T.T., Helen had only had small roles in shows like *The Young Ones* and *The Comic Strip Presents: Consuela*, and *Radio Active* was still two years away from transferring to BBC2 as *KYTV*, so when Lloyd contacted her to propose the regular role, she admits, 'I think I probably said, "Yes please" before he actually got to the end of the sentence.'

Blackadder II did of course boast its own well-seasoned female dullard, but Atkinson-Wood was trusted to bring to life her own tribute to the toothless fishwives and frilly grand dames of Georgian fiction. 'Parts for women were so thin on the ground that it was tremendous to be one of the few,' she says. 'There was Queenie, and Nursie . . . and then who? The women brought a different texture to *Blackadder*. Mrs Miggins was a very warm-hearted character: different from Blackadder, who was so oily, and different from Baldrick, who was . . . well, fiddling with his turnips; and different from the Prince Regent, who was so barking!' Being the only other regular female on the core team besides the director gave Helen an insight into the difficulties of Fletcher's

---

* Completing the connection, while performing at the Edinburgh Fringe with the *Radio Active Roadshow*, Helen had befriended Ben Elton, there as part of his Mayall tour, 'in an airing cupboard during a game of sardines'.

position. 'It was a pretty exposing place for Mandie, being surrounded by all these people who knew each other well, very hard for her to hold the whole thing together – which she did brilliantly – surrounded by a lot of very strong personalities. The gender is immaterial, but it was very nice for me, having another woman around.'

'Helen of course had always been part of the gang,' Tony says, 'just as Helen Fielding always had, so working with her didn't feel strange in any way. We were criticised quite a lot at the time for using what was called "the Oxbridge Comedy Mafia", but there was a real issue here, which was that because we didn't make acting decisions until very late in the day, people who weren't used to working that way could be dreadfully insecure – like Wilfrid Brambell. You don't want to duplicate that experience very often, because it just takes too much time. So actually if you worked with people you knew, there was no aggravation, there was no problem, you weren't having to deal with their anxieties, they knew something would come out of it at the end of the day.' 'Why work with anyone else, other than the people that you know and like? If you're in a room with people you'd be perfectly happy to be on holiday with, the whole thing just bowls along in a blissful way,' Helen adds.

'I don't think she was originally going to be a Northerner, on paper, but my roots are in the North, and I'm a great lover of cooking – it's no coincidence in a way that Mrs Miggins was the ideal character for me, given that I love pies and cakes and buns . . . I think in another guise I'd be president of the WI.' Besides her Cheshire upbringing being a help in playing 'a no-nonsense, Northern character', the attractive actress had a history of portraying the most grotesque crones imaginable in the name of getting a laugh, so the whole team knew that the role of Mr B's hostess, the hideous nincompoop who could be relied on to buy into every new craze that the period threw up (not just spearheading that week's plot but giving the butler another chance to pour scorn on the times and her personally), was in good hands. In time, Miggins would have a cult of her own. 'I still receive tons of fan mail for Mrs Miggins, and it just constantly amazes me, the fan base that's out there. So much so that I think I'm going to have to start thinking about opening a cake or pie shop, in the not so distant future.'

THE WALRUS AWAKES

The first time this new team entered the 'Hilton' to bring Ben and Richard's scripts to life, Atkinson-Wood recalls having 'that Christmas-morning feeling in your tummy. Comedy and laughter, we all feel better for it, so it is a great thing to be around. It's not like you're going in to rehearse Ibsen; you're going in to have the time of your life.' Ultimately, however, the process wouldn't be such a breeze. At this stage, the scripts still followed the Elton pattern of having simple titles – 'Dictionary', 'Actors', 'Rotten Boroughs', 'Highwayman', 'Scarlet Pimpernel' and 'Duel', in that order – but it wasn't until after recording that Lloyd, the master packaging expert, had the brainwave of giving each episode Austenian monikers, from 'Ink and Incapability' to 'Duel and Duality'. It's one more way in which the series had more of a workshop feel to it than any other, and John admits, 'Sudden changes of direction like this, right up to the very last minute, were commonplace. They brought both unforeseen delight, and perennial problems.'

As ever, this way of working was highly testing for all the guest performers, but if any of them were up to the challenge, it had to be Robbie Coltrane. Keen-eared viewers of 'Chains' may have been perturbed by one insistent grating guffaw from the audience – a sound not unlike a pirate forcing someone to walk the plank. This was Coltrane, supporting his *Alfresco* comrades in their new venture, and it was no surprise that he was to become one of the extended *Blackadder* family, with two memorable roles. However, the week of pernickety rehearsals for 'Dictionary' left him little time to really get under the skin of the noted man of letters, Dr Samuel Johnson. This first episode to be recorded was in a way the inspiration for the whole series, as Elton recalls. 'I can remember Richard saying, "I've had a great idea. Did you know it took Dr Johnson twenty-five years to write his Dictionary? How about he finishes it, lends it to Blackadder, Baldrick puts it on the fire, Blackadder's got a weekend to rewrite the Dictionary?" And I just thought, that is such a brilliant conceit. A lot better than writing three knob gags, which is what I was sort of trying to do.' Curtis says that the scripts were bound to be considered open to suggestion when he admits, 'With Ben and me it was absolute bliss, because you could be irresponsible, you could be a lazy writer. You could say, "Well, I've got some scenes here but I don't really know how to make the plot work." And you'd basically give up on the plot and write some funny stuff. Or you'd get the plot right, but put in brackets "Must be lots of jokes about a party here." So each one would be like a challenge to the other person to fill in the bits that you hadn't bothered with.'

However, the writers never bargained for the battles awaiting them – and with such a literary plot, the text was to be debated more than ever. 'People fought for their patch!' Laurie says. 'Nobody just toed the line and stood where they were told to stand and did what they were told to do, everyone stood up for themselves and for their characters. Let's just say it was very free. "Just read it out!" Richard said . . .' At such times, as Fry puts it, 'Richard, who finds it very hard to be anything other than extraordinarily nice, would look slightly miffed, which for him is like a real temper tantrum, and then we'd start again.' McInnerny remembers that in his time, 'Richard was there all day every day, writing, rewriting, taking it on the chin when everybody said, "Well, that's not very funny though, is it?" You weren't allowed to rewrite it, Richard always rewrites.' And Tony adds, 'John, Richard, Hugh and Stephen conduct themselves in a very affable way and when they talk about *Blackadder* now it all seems like it was a bit jolly: slightly sticky sometimes, but basically fine. I don't really remember it quite like that, it was *hard*. Everything took a lot of work, every day, huge numbers of ideas would go by the wayside. The tension that there was between the writers and the performers was that we had gone too far in excising stuff that they thought was very good – because the writers would be there on day one and not back again until day five. And the further we went, the more that tension grew.' He argues, however, that it was an inevitable part of the show's growing popularity. 'By the time we got to series three, *Blackadder II* had been such an enormous success that I don't think it weighed heavy on us, but it gave us a great deal of confidence, that our vision for how *Blackadder* could be was right. So we just worked very, very hard on making it as perfect as we possibly could. By that time, I don't think any of us could have articulated it, but we knew what felt right.'

As a result, Lloyd regrets, 'Robbie had this huge part which he had to learn in the last few hours really, because we never got the script perfect until late. But what we didn't do with him was think of what his character was! He'd come in and do the lines, and somehow make something of them. He never complained about it though, he's such a nice bloke.'* 'That was always the lot of any actor who came in to play the supporting roles, if one can describe it as that,' Atkinson adds, 'that they had very little time or rehearsal, and they had to sort of cope. And Robbie coped extremely well!' By the Sunday-night recording on 5 June (with warm-up this time provided by Clive Anderson, in Elton's stead), the cast may have been flying by the seats of their breeches, with rudimentary scene-blocking and improvised physical business, but every one of the episode's memorable slews of linguistic nonsense was perfect to every syllable – 'compuntious', 'contrafibularatories', 'interphrastically' and so on, Blackadderisms designed to drive Johnson mad, described by Rowan as 'Complete codswallop, and yet you can see the Latin or Greek roots of all the words.'

---

* Six years later, Coltrane would finally get a chance to put more meat on Johnson's bones, with John Sessions joining him as Boswell for a BBC2 dramatisation of their *Tour of the Western Isles*.

The appearance of Shelley, Byron and Coleridge in Mrs Miggins's coffee shop provided a chance for a different duo to step into Arden & Frost's guest spot – pioneering comic improvisers Jim Sweeney and Steve Steen, with the trusty Lee Cornes (who originally stood in for Frost in 'Chains') completing the 'romantic junkie' trio. Cornes recalls, 'I found it very interesting to watch these two very fine comedians at work – Rowan very precise, very meticulous, both technical and analytical, whereas Robbie is just a great comic force, a raconteur and storyteller and a funny bloke generally, not just on set. It was interesting to see them using very different techniques to come up with equally superb performances on the night.' The poets' appearance also highlighted a quirk of the series which perhaps lends credence to Tony's claim that the Regency period was a blank to most viewers – the apparent need for copious historical guest stars. Where every other period of *Blackadder* history relies surprisingly seldom on showing real historical figures, with only one or two per series, *Blackadder the Third* would put Edmund up against *eight* historical icons – nine, if you include Phil Pope's return as Nelson in *Christmas Carol* – to which Robinson responds, 'That's intriguing. I don't know what that's about, other than that we really wanted to root it in the times, and help people understand what that historical period was all about.'

With such a small regular cast, there was room to fill the series with more guest stars than ever, Helen recalls, 'It was a very thrilling thing to be part of. Every rehearsal was full of your favourite people or those you admired. It drew together, I suppose, the cream of all the comedy talent at the time.' The famous faces gave each plot a certain epic scope, but as Lloyd was continually keen to impress on the writers, the best sitcoms tended to be confined, and more character-based. *The Third*, if anything, was proving to be the freest, silliest series of all, sneaking in anachronistic gags aplenty. It has been argued that all historical productions belie the times in which they were made, but this is largely untrue of *Blackadder* – most episodes, if shown to a media student with no knowledge of the programme or the actors involved, could be deduced as the product of any decade since the arrival of colour television. And yet shades of topical humour* were more in evidence this time than in the other series, while an even more blatant wink to the modern audience was Edmund's lament that he deserved to have his life dramatised and played out weekly at half past nine.

The second recording would give Elton his one cameo appearance in *Blackadder*, sending up his reputation as a radical ranter by playing a Luddite revolutionary who disrupts the actors Mossop & Keanrick's play (which seems to be a revival of Prince Edmund's 'The Death of the Pharaoh') to try to blow up the fat, stupid Prince. The thespian duo themselves continued the show's deference to the comedy old guard, giving *Carry On* stalwart Kenneth Connor and *Round the Horne* star Hugh Paddick a chance to show the youngsters how it's done. As Julian and Sandy, the openly gay Paddick and Kenneth Williams were one of the most loved comedy duos of the 1960s, their campery suggesting a fine fit for the frilled pretensions of the villainous Georgian actors, however Williams's old comrade Connor made a fine alternative, and became one actor to bridge the gap between the historical japeries of *Blackadder*, *Carry On* and *'Allo 'Allo*.†

A neat and drastically historically incorrect joke about the adolescence of 'Pitt the Younger' (who actually entered high office at twenty-four, fifteen years after Pitt the Elder's ministry) inspired the third recorded episode, fated to introduce the series on broadcast, as

---

* From Murdoch's takeover of *The Times* to David Steel's 1981 exhortation to the Liberal faithful to 'Go back to your constituencies, and prepare for government' being mangled as Edmund's order to Baldrick, 'Go back to your kitchen sink, you see . . .'

† Mossop & Keanrick's painfully repeated superstitious incantation, every time the impertinent butler says 'Macbeth', has been a bone of contention for a quarter of a century, even being misquoted on DVD subtitles, but let the record show that any thespians hoping to exorcise Scottish demons should say the following before tweaking each others' noses: '*Hot potato, Orchestra stalls, Puck will make amends!*'

'Dish and Dishonesty'. Being recorded just one week after another Thatcher victory in the 1987 elections, the team could be forgiven for throwing in more anachronistic topical material, including the casting of the late political commentator Vincent Hanna as his own ancestor, a town crier who was originally intended to be seen only through the hustings window frame as a form of eighteenth century TV. Satirising the complexities of Whig and Tory politics at the turn of the nineteenth century was such a tall order that few *Blackadder* scripts were as heatedly wrestled with in rehearsals as 'Rotten Boroughs' – particularly pertaining to the perennial issue of filth. 'The great thing about putting knob gags in Rowan's mouth,' Curtis says, 'is that he's the cleanest spoken, most puritan person one knows, so he had this profound sense of disapproval at all the jokes.' Lloyd adds, 'Rowan has not had to compromise, he's done pretty much exactly what he wants to. The compromises he's made have generally been so's not to upset his mother, you know, not to say too many rude words because she might not like it.' 'I am not prudish,' Atkinson protested in 1989, 'but I tended to be the one to say "Keep it clean." The others know some extremely rude jokes and I had to step in occasionally, but I was nearly always overruled by the rest of the cast – they would mock me and tell me not to be such a wimp. My mother was certainly a factor. I think she finds *Blackadder* a bit rude and a bit harsh. She hasn't really been pleased with my work since I was Mephistophilis in the school play in 1970. Like any good mother, she defends me to the hilt, but deep down I know she would rather I was doing something she could discuss over tea with the vicar.' In the case of 'Dish and Dishonesty', a Mrs Slocombe-esque line concerning Blackadder's cat-skin 'ermine' robes caused a notable stand-off, as rehearsals ground to a halt over the star's refusal to say, 'Never in my wildest dreams did I ever think that one day I would be up to my neck in Lady Hamilton's pussy.' 'And he *wouldn't* say it!' Tony Robinson rues to this day, adding, 'I would have!'

A New Freckle on the Nose of the Giant Pixie

Since the Emmy won by 'The Archbishop', gongs had eluded the Adder, with *Yes, Prime Minister* riding high and the Comedy Performance category at every BAFTA ceremony seemingly proving to be an embarrassing race between Nigel Hawthorne and Paul Eddington. This was to change partly thanks to the Silver Rose of Montreux-winning 'Highwayman' episode – first entitled 'Cape and Capability', and ultimately 'Amy and Amiability'.

Miranda Richardson had no more desire to let a regular sitcom role stand in the way of her acting career than McInnerny, but was very happy to return for one week, leaving Elizabeth behind and finding a whole new way to depict dippy sweetness, as the wealthy industrialist's daughter, Amy Hardwood. Her bluff idiot father was Warren Clarke,* largely recognisable at this stage in his long career as a supporting player in serious drama and films as well as a regular on *Shelley*, one of ITV's superior sitcoms, and Lloyd says, 'I think he really dropped into it, Warren, of all the people who came from nowhere, he really got the spirit of it quickly.' Clarke had recently played screen husband to Atkinson-Wood in the pessimistic 'state-of-the-nation' drama series *Tickets for the Titanic* (a collection of self-contained stories, one of which starred Tony Robinson as a vicar embroiled in trouble at Greenham Common, in a script by Andy Hamilton), and as with most of the *Blackadder* players, his involvement came tangentially. Helen says, 'I'm not bigging up my part in becoming a casting director for *Blackadder*, but I would go so far as to say that I suggested Warren Clarke to John – we were having lunch, and I mentioned that Warren and I were working together, and the thought germinated that he would be a wonderful addition to the company.' As for the character of Mr Hardwood, 'They just left it to me,' Warren remembers. 'I do a lot of overacting most of

---

* He also provided the voice of the notorious Shadow, modelled on James Mason in *The Wicked Lady* – the 1945 film that inspired the episode.

the time anyway. Les Dawson was a mate of mine, so I thought I'd do it like Les. I can still be in the middle of nowhere in some strange town and somebody will come up to me and say, "I love my daughter more than any pig, and that's saying summat!"'

Another notable feature of the episode was John's increasing delight in the use of ridiculous sound effects, with the squeak of a dead squirrel (or the squelch of a large ripe frog) so pleasing that he edited in reprises at the end of the closing credits. 'I love sound effects, and radio in general. People may tell you that anyone can edit film, but the really tough thing, particularly with studio audiences, is the sound. Making a hundred radio programmes over five years, I got very good at it, and very concise. I do think in sound a lot, and it's very funny, it's another dimension – there's words, performance, the visual side, and there's sound. I think everyone should be trained to work in television by working in radio first, and they rarely are today.'

By referencing both *Dick Turpin* and *Cyrano de Bergerac* the following week, Curtis & Elton ticked off two historical heroes in one episode, but basing their French Revolution yarn on Baroness Orczy's *Scarlet Pimpernel* was to backfire to some extent, with the character's complicated copyright preventing 'Nob and Nobility' from being broadcast in America, and requiring the removal of Baldrick's quoting of the famous Pimpernel rhyme for many repeats. It did, however, supply a chance for another old friend to play a flying visit, with McInnerny escaping Percy by effectively crafting three characters at once – the foppish Lord Topper, Le Comte de Frou-Frou and, after a fashion, the Pimpernel himself.

By striding in to show up Blackadder for the coward he is, Topper could have been the closest Regency successor to Flashheart (especially with Nigel Planer turning up to play his best friend Smedley), but there was no chance of Mayall showing up for this run – he was already in cahoots with Laurence Marks and Maurice Gran, cooking up his own sitcom vehicle, which brought his particular perverse charisma to the world of *Yes Minister* via the creation of scruple-free Tory sleazeball Alan B'Stard in *The New Statesman*, which began airing on ITV only four days before *Blackadder the Third*'s premiere. By giving Marks & Gran carte blanche to delve into the darkest recesses of his personality in creating the evil backbencher, Rik created a monster which made the murderous Edmund seem almost affable, and the attacks on Baldrick were slapstick where B'Stard's methods of torture for his own dim-witted sidekick, Michael Troughton's lovable Piers Fletcher-Dervish, were twistedly sadistic. But then, unlike Blackadder, B'Stard's sheen of charm only enhanced his hatefulness, and the modern, yuppie context made the Tory's every crime doubly despicable. The ITV series continued well into the nineties,* but thanks to theatrical revivals, B'Stard remains a terrifying splinter of Mayall's persona to this day, a kind of anti-Flashheart, with all of the caddishness and boorishness of the Lord, but none of the redeeming heroism.

With Francomania rife in Miggins's coffee house, garlicky cuisine and all, the stage was set for *Blackadder*'s first Francophobic jamboree. Baiting the French had been a regular motif in Atkinson's work from the very first, and with *Blackadder* reflecting English history, our Gallic neighbours, England's closest sworn rivals for centuries, were never going to get off lightly – ironically, seeing as the programme had been created on French soil in the first place. The team were carrying on a strong English tradition by suggesting that the French are smelly, effete, snobbish, and – worst of all – Anglophobic, with Goodall even going so far as to record a single of the Curtis/Goodall/Atkinson song 'I Hate the French' in 1980:

> *They're pretty cocky 'bout their games in the dark,*
> *They think with girls they light a special spark,*

---

* Fry & Laurie popped up in the first series, as a moral vacuum of a City boy and the waiter he reduces to destitution.

But look what the bastards did to Joan of Arc,
That's why I Hate the French . . .

But as the lyric 'All I resent is that they're so good in bed' suggests (though furthering another stereotype), the song – just like any withering reference to the French, and even the Belgians – is intended to mock the nation's long feud with Continental types. Goodall says, 'It's on YouTube, with a lot of rather angry French people making comments about it. I think what a lot of people have never quite got about that song, which English people do get, is that it's a song that makes fun of xenophobia. A lot of French people saw it as a purely racist song – I love France, and the French! The reason one makes jokes about them is that they're our neighbours.'

Representing the Rosbif-hating Frog, 'hung like a baby carrot and a couple of petit pois', was Chris Barrie – another stellar talent shared by Lloyd in *Spitting Image* and Paul Jackson in everything else. Within a few months of playing the Ambassador in 'Nob and Nobility', the talented mimic would land the job of completing the unholy trinity of eighties sitcom bastards alongside Blackadder and B'Stard, being chosen by Jackson, Rob Grant and Doug Naylor to play the neurotic, bitter hologram, Second Technician Arnold J. Rimmer in their sci-fi comedy *Red Dwarf*. The programme only made it to screen by using the BBC Manchester slot earmarked for *Happy Families 2*, but rapidly became an international sensation – and for Barrie, the opportunity to craft a true icon of sitcom bastardry was a well-deserved coup considering the wealth of talent who auditioned for the role of Rimmer, which even included Hugh Laurie.

The final reunion of the broadcast series was the appearance of Fry as Arthur Wellesley, the Duke of Wellington – a truly irresistible casting choice, despite the historical anachronism required, and the difficulty of arranging a date for the guest's availability. 'It probably was due to *Me and My Girl* commitments that we did the Wellington episode when we did. It was pleasing though, as it was the last of the series anyway and ended in a great heap of bodies.' Despite the inconvenience, Fry continues, 'I was delighted, especially as it involved hitting Hugh, which was a thing that I'd become very expert at. As anyone who's done that kind of slapstick knows, the skill is not in the person punching or throwing a slap, it's always in the person receiving it, and Hugh is an absolute genius at being hit. Something about those enormous blue lagoons of eyes and their sorrowfulness makes it all the funnier, because he doesn't really understand why he's being hit. Both Rowan and I had a great time punching him in one scene, and kicking him and generally yelling at him. Very enjoyable.' 'I remember him arriving to do the violent slapstick stuff with some trepidation,' Laurie says, 'because I'd done things with Stephen before, physical things, where he's had to act punching me, and his acting . . . well, how can I put it? He's punched me, basically, he's just punched me. There were scenes where you had to judge your distance quite carefully, and be looking at the marks on the floor, thinking, "Well, he's got quite a lot of reach, if I just dip forward here I could catch one in the chops."'

The finale's one other special appearance* came from Gertan Klauber as Mad King George III – the veteran Czech-born actor being another regular (though minor) player in the *Carry On* series, as well as *Up the Front*. Mention of the porphyric monarch also gave a presentiment of things to come, as Fry's week with the old team saw him instantly settling into the old style of 'plumpening'. Given the line 'The King, your father, is mad,' he politely sidled up to Lloyd and Curtis to posit whether the line 'Your royal father grows ever more eccentric and at present believes himself to be a small village in Lincolnshire with commanding views of the Nene Valley' might be slightly more delicious. The tragic denouement of the episode – and in a way, the

---

* Besides Atkinson himself, echoing the plot's 'duality' and keeping the Scottish bloodline alive by guest-starring in a pre-recorded sequence as Mr B's equally crown-coveting Highland stereotype cousin MacAdder.

final achievement of all the Blackadders' aims, the taking of the throne – was ridiculously revelatory and rapidly tied up at least partly due to the extent of the 'plumpening' which was to be expected with the finicky Hugh and Rowan being backed up by their loud comrade – although it was already decided by the writers that, for the first time, Edmund would escape destruction and prove the real villain.

Sadly Miggins's presumed death up on a lonely Scottish crag signified the end of Helen's time on the show, with her character reduced to just a vague mention in a music-hall song in the following series. The actress, however, would soon be starring in *KYTV*, John Byrne's *Your Cheating Heart*, and in 1992 her own historical sitcom, *Tales from the Poopdeck*, in which she played terrifying female pirate Connie Blackheart. Further members of the Miggins family would have been a treat, but she says, 'I was always just so dazzled by the construction of the scripts, it's fair to say I didn't give a thought as to what was going to happen to Mrs Miggins next, it was just such a delicious twist for her to be setting off with MacAdder.'

The last day of filming was only the beginning of Lloyd's crucial packaging process, comprising the exquisite literary credit sequence in which the butler stalks through a library to Goodall's baroque theme, rejecting books such as the *Encyclopaedia Blackaddica*, *Landscape Gardening by Capability Brownadder*, *From Black Death to Blackadder*, *Blackadder's Book of Martyrs* and *Blackadder's Bedside Cockfighting Companion* in favour of the lurid romance novel bearing each episode's new name, with the dashing Edmund caught in a different passionate embrace on every cover. Howard's desire to surprise came to the fore again in the end credits, where, the final tableau frozen into a historic engraving (a familiar convention from BBC costume dramas such as 1985's *Pickwick Papers*), the composer delivered an exotic Empire-inspired interpretation of his melody, which Elton suggests 'might have been because Paul Simon had just come out with *Graceland* . . .' 'John likes making credits more than he likes making shows,' Robinson says, and the series' painstakingly detailed Regency playbill sequence, 'For the benefit of several viewers' and 'To conclude with Rule Britannia in full chorus, No money return'd', accompanied by Howard's nautical beat, suggests Tony might be onto something.

A Much Admir'd Comedy

Some producers could have been tempting fate by calling their programme 'much admir'd' in their own credits, but Lloyd knew there was little risk of calumny – *Blackadder the Third* debuted to widespread delight in the autumn of 1987, with audiences still warm from the *Blackadder II* repeat. It was accompanied by the first academic investigation into the Blackadder Chronicles, written for the *Radio Times* by Lloyd himself, the 'loafing Professor at the University of Camelot'. This early appraisal of the dynasty lost no time in damning the entire family, from prehistoric times to the most recent achievement: 'A dinner party in Chelsea in 1968, where the present Edmund Blackadder had the distinction of being the first man to scoff at flared trousers.'

With such instant acclaim, Blackadder and Baldrick were to become entrenched in the national consciousness as the Regency duo for some time, the despicable schemer and the pitiful dungball becoming a kind of British Don Quixote and Sancho Panza – quite fittingly, as Curtis had written a successful theatrical adaptation of Cervantes' novel in the early eighties. Atkinson would muse, 'It's odd where the inherent comedy of his situation is rooted, because basically he's a bright and able man and yet things go wrong for him in a way that we try to make funny. He wasn't a buffoon, he just tended to over-think things, didn't he, to out-think himself. Or maybe it was just bad luck! And of course, fatally, he always allies himself with Baldrick. It's strange, that inter-reliance, you'd think someone as bright as the Black Adder wouldn't spend any time with Baldrick, and yet he does. It is like Basil Fawlty and Manuel, why doesn't he just sack Manuel? There is some way in which they need each other. And the Black Adder and Baldrick need each other – not only to allow us to make jokes about him.'

Of the two, it was Baldrick who would be most likely to pop up on his own unexpectedly, spreading his stench in the CBBC broom cupboard for Comic Relief or even going so low as to appear on-screen with Noel Edmonds, showcasing a package of *Blackadder* bloopers on *Noel's Saturday Roadshow* in 1988, defending the errors in Noel's 'Clown Court'.

JUDGE: I have before me one of the most repulsive individuals that has ever appeared in this court.

BALDRICK: Hello, Mr E!

JUDGE: Name?

BALDRICK: Baldrick, Your Honour.

JUDGE: First name?

BALDRICK: Drop-dead.

JUDGE: I beg your pardon?

BALDRICK: That's my first name. I think it is, anyway, 'cause when people see me they shout out, 'Drop dead, Baldrick!'

JUDGE: Do you have any explanation as to why [Blackadder] has failed to appear?

BALDRICK: Er, no, Your Honour, but he did give me this note . . .

JUDGE: 'From Edmund Blackadder to Lord Chief Justice Edmonds. Dear Sir, the reason I can't be present is because I've got far better things to do with my time than turn up at your stupid court, you overdressed beardy weirdy.' . . . Mr D. Baldrick, of 17 Rubbish Row, London – I condemn you to death.

BALDRICK: Thank you very much, Your Honour. It's too
good for me.

Thanks to Tony's performance, somehow the stinking plotter had actually become *cute*, and, as he observes, developed something of a cult all of his own. 'It took me a long time to realise just how successful the series was. Then it hit me – Baldrick had become this little comedy god. People would send me turnips through the post. Believe me, I've tried every turnip recipe known to man.' Lloyd goes so far as to say, 'In my opinion it's Baldrick rather than Blackadder who gives the show its enduring mainstream appeal. Baldrick is everyman – the decent, sensible downtrodden drudge saddled with a boss who is both too clever by three-quarters, and nearly always wrong.' 'He's a pretty dim everyman,' Atkinson laughs, 'I'm not sure I'd like Baldrick to represent me in the canon of human existence. But he has an attitude to life which is uncorrupted by expectations or class structures or education or anything, he just takes things at face value and deals with them as he finds them.' 'A lot of people say they see Baldrick as an everyman,' Robinson concedes, 'and, if that's true, then I don't think it says much for the British character.'

The double act was back together the following autumn, to support the BBC's Children in Need appeal, not just on the telethon itself, with Baldrick offering the kiddies his own beloved childhood toys – an old stick and some clumps of mud:

MR B: For those of you who enjoy laughing at the
afflicted, here is your host, Mr Wogan . . . to
introduce his next guest. Thank you.

WOGAN: Thank you very much.

MR B: Um, you're very welcome, sir. If I may just
make a suggestion? I will ring this bell if I feel
that the interview ought to terminate, or if I

feel that the public are tired of your discutatory peregrinations . . . your 'chat'.

WOGAN: Ladies and gentlemen, it's now my great pleasure to introduce to you a young man whose popularity seems to increase with every passing century. The man they simply call – Baldrick!

BALDRICK: (*Enters, chewing on a rat.*) Evening, Mr T!

MR B: (*Steps in, rings bell.*) Right, I think that's enough, don't you?

The pair even fumbled their way through a whole special hour of fund-raising on Radio 4, violently taking over *Woman's Hour* to link a series of items looking at the struggle for sexual equality through the ages:

MR B: Right, Baldrick, stick the gag on. Good afternoon, ladies, allow me to introduce myself. My name is Edmund Blackadder and this is my servant . . .

BALDRICK: (*Muffled.*) Baldrick!

MR B: Baldrick, the gag goes on the women . . . As I was saying, ladies, today I am trying to raise money for Children in Need. So far I have myself generously donated the entire contents of Baldrick's wallet. As you know I am very fond of lovely little children. I've even brought a poor, sweet, needy little tiny child to the studio here today.

BALDRICK: Goo goo.

MR B: Oh for heaven's sake, Baldrick, stick your back into it. Cheques can be made out to

'Edmund Blackadder's Children in Need
Appeal', but right now I want you to phone
in and pledge lots and lots and lots of money.
Major credit cards welcome. Give them the
number, Baldrick . . .

BALDRICK: Right, and the number is zero, two, big
number, two, three, big number, big number,
three, big number, big number.

MR B: Oh good grief . . . Right, start coughing
up, ladies. Meanwhile I'm sick and tired of
continuously hearing whingeing women
whining on about the problems of life in
1988 so we're going to take you back in time
to see how really awful life could be . . .

In sound only, the duo transcended their most recent incarnations, becoming a strangely immortal pair who seem to have been bickering for centuries – but then, this was just for charity.

Fortunately, I am Not a Man of Honour

Blackadder and Baldrick's appearance for Curtis's own special cause several months earlier was an altogether more cogent offering – after two years of preparation, the first Red Nose Day and Comic Relief telethon was ready to go, and nothing was more likely to get folk tuning in and reaching for their credit card details to give to Mike Smith up the Post Office Tower than an all-new tale from the Blackadder Chronicles, plugging a gap in the lore by leapfrogging back a century and a half to witness the skulduggery of Mr B's great-great-grandfather.

The audacious pilot scheme went ahead on 5 February 1988, with millions of schoolchildren and charitable grown-ups encouraged by the young comic generation to buy red noses and do something stupid to raise funds, with the reward being a whole evening of non-stop comedy on BBC1 – a celebration of laughter in the depths of winter. These jolly, ragged early marathons, presented by Lenny Henry, Griff Rhys Jones and Jonathan Ross, were nowhere near as slick and glamorous as the titanic Comic Relief nights of the twenty-first century – that first evening even devoted a whole prime-time half-hour to a repeat of *Dad's Army* – but it's *because* of that rudimentary quality that those first Comic Reliefs were more exciting and, indeed, funnier. With Richard devotedly scribbling the hosts' scripts as the evening wore on, the several hours of that evening's proceedings (when not taken up with flubbed studio links, unexpected invasions from Ken Dodd and heart-rending documentary features) were filled with brand-new sketches and skits from every corner of Curtis's comedy fraternity and beyond. A huge stockpile of sketches had been pre-filmed a few weeks before transmission, but two bastards provided the highlights, with Rik Mayall facing Thatcher as Alan B'Stard for one persona-bending *New Statesman* skit, and *Blackadder: The Cavalier Years* forming the centrepiece of the evening.

Covering one of the single most epochal events in British History, and managing to do it in a fifteen-minute slot involving a grand total of two sets and four speaking roles,* *Cavalier Years* is a masterpiece of disrespectful brevity. Baldrick's kitchen at Blackadder Hall and Charles's cell at Whitehall provided the meagre backdrops to yet another dastardly Blackadder lie, as Sir Edmund hides and then double-crosses and executes his old friend Charles before handing Baldrick and the doll-like infant Charles II over to the Roundheads and, as ever, switching to the winning side. Presumably there was Melchett blood in the Stuart family, allowing Fry to have his turn on the throne, albeit briefly, as one of his numerous appearances on that

---

* Not including Harry Enfield, who gets his one *Blackadder* credit as Patrick Allen's stand-in for the historical introduction.

night's bill (which also included dunking Philip Schofield in a gunge tank, abetted by Hugh). Fry portrayed Charles as a kind of dithering tree-hugger (a blatant mimicry of the King's namesake great-to-the-power-of-eleven-grand-nephew), while Warren Clarke was perfectly suited to take on the mantle of his warty republican counterpart Cromwell, managing to convey a unique brand of manic perversity – even going so far as to caress Baldrick and call him 'My proud beauty' – in a slight and sketchily written role. 'They are jolly tricky, these short sitcom specials,' Curtis says, 'we've done about fifteen of them on Comic Relief. But that one just found its own natural rhythm. I suspect that had we ever done the period officially, we wouldn't have wanted Stephen to do the Charles impression – one of our big things being not allowing any anachronisms . . .'

The Cavalier Years was only a small footnote, a few months after *Blackadder the Third*, not in any way eclipsing the Regency comedy's popularity with the public, and the characters of Blackadder and Baldrick remained much the same – in fact, Tony says, 'All I remember about it is the damn wig, I was fighting the wig for the entire recording. It was the wig of the oldest hippy in the world.'

So resonant was Edmund's Regency incarnation that the 1990 ITV sitcom *Haggard*, following the antics of a despicable squire with a grotty servant, came in for criticism for aping *Blackadder the Third*, even though it was based on a character created by the journalist Michael Green more than a decade earlier. Similarly, media myths about an uncredited American 'remake' of *Blackadder*, the short-lived 1992 CBS sitcom *1775*, centred on comparisons to *Blackadder's* third series more than any other, through historical necessity if nothing else. Ryan O'Neal starred as cowardly Boston innkeeper Jeremy Proctor, with a stupid lackey called Bert and a regular customer in a twittish British governor played by Jeffrey Tambor – plus Adam West as George Washington. But this Proctor is a pretty decent family guy surrounded by sassy daughters, so even if the show had been a hit, there would be no grounds for Atkinson to sue. Another US show to be dubbed 'the American *Blackadder*', 1998's *Secret Diary of Desmond Pfeiffer*, fared even less well, with only four episodes broadcast detailing the 'hidden history' of Chi McBride's eponymous character, a black English lord who becomes valet to Abraham Lincoln (and who also has a dungball for a lackey). The show was rapidly pulled after mass complaints about slavery gags, as well as a scene in which Lincoln pioneers sex chat via telegraph, but the episodes that do survive have more of a flavour of *Blackadder the Third* than any other *Blackadder*.

So no US equivalent of *Blackadder* ever took hold, but the four series remain popular among comedy connoisseurs in the USA, not least thanks to Atkinson's encouragement to the ex-colonies to buy the real thing, back in 1988. Interviewed for the programme's first run on the A&E channel, he suggested, 'Certainly from series two onwards, the hero is quite a cool character, and most English comics or comic heroes are not cool at all, they're kind of gimpy, middle-class suburban put-upon husbands and putting-upon wives, uncool characters. Whereas Americans I think like their comedians to be quite cool – Eddie Murphy and Steve Martin – all these kind of guys, they're cool, they're in charge. They get into sticky situations, but they get out of them in a fairly cool way. And Blackadder is a pretty hard, cool, cynical character.' He also assured colonial viewers that there was still more to come, revealing plans for a Victorian series four, before a fifth series in the twentieth century. 'We are already projecting actually, we're doing a Christmas special soon in which we momentarily look into the future of The Black Adder, and we see Frondo Blackadder, who's dressed like some kind of ice warrior with lots of muscles and long black ringlets of hair, who has basically killed everyone else off in the universe and is having a very good time in AD 3000. I think there is a major future for the Black Adder.'

Parte the Fifth:

LIONS LED BY BASTARDS

In the aftermath of Mr E. Blackadder's alleged usurpation of the Hanoverian throne, little evidence is given to suggest that the family benefited from the ruse, and the nineteenth century saw the descendants of 'George IV' snaking off into disparate, more lowly areas of society, often as awkward cogs within the almighty mechanism of British Imperialism. Besides obscure references to non-eminent engineers, physicians and scientists, pictorial evidence has been discovered of a likely family member in the Empress Victoria's service at the Indian Raj, but who this was and what cunning plans they were cooking up behind the scenes remains a mystery (although a Dr Blackadder is also cited as being present at Victoria's death). One popular black sheep of the family was music-hall performer 'Elegant Eddie' Blackadder, but no footage or notation of his celebrated song 'Let's Shove, Shove, Shove (a Bayonet Up a Frenchman)' has survived.

The only remaining book of substance in the Blackadder Chronicles covers the final years of rather a lowly descendant, a Captain Edmund Blackadder (18??–1917), whose war diaries form an extensive part of the last Chronicle. But what was it about this middle-class officer that marked him out for such emphasis in the family history? When the Archduke of Austria–Hungary got shot in 1914, a relay of international aggression was unleashed which resulted in the untimely deaths of a still incomprehensible 35 million people, so even though the Blackadders had a reputation for cowardice stretching back for centuries, why should the sacrifice of this one obscure officer have become such a major event for the Chronicler?

George Augustus Frederick, the Prince of Wales: as thick as a whale omelette,
but with a wig like an exceptionally attractive loaf of bread.

'Toffs at the top, plebs at the bottom, and me in the middle making a fat pile of cash out of both of them.' Fine words for any budding politician.

Mr E. Blackadder's dogsbody, The Lord Baldrick, with intellectual equal.

The Prince and the Pauper – the porpoise, presumably, being just out of shot.

Fry could have found a regular role for himself in Regency England, but says, 'It probably was due to *Me and My Girl* commitments that we just did the Wellington episode. It was pleasing though as it was the last of the series anyway and ended in a great heap of bodies…'

Lord Smedley: a perfect example of the milk-livered Restoration fop, as Nigel Planer's colleague, the seasoned actor Nicholas Craig, could tell you.

The immortal Miggins. 'I think when Richard and Ben were creating the character,' Helen Atkinson Wood says, 'the fact a horse's willy got mentioned is no accident, me being the keen horsewoman that I am...'

Two of *Alfresco*'s finest reunited in a historically impossible, but humorously crucial, sticky situation. Coltrane would get to reprise the role of Dr Johnson in a little more depth for *Screen Two* a few years later.

The Braveheart of the Clan MacAdder: evidence of the Scottish roots of the Blackadder family, or just an excuse to stick on a skirt and a ridiculous ginger wig?

Once and for all, let the record show, only the phrase 'Hot potato, orchestra stalls, Puck will make amends!' with relevant nose-tweaking gestures, will ward off the evil spirits of The Scottish Play.

'Hand over the loot, goat-brains!' Mr Blackadder learns the crucial lesson, never to fall in love with a criminal who sounds like James Mason.

'I want to be young and wild, and then I want to be middle-aged and rich, and then I want to be old and annoy people by pretending that I'm deaf.'

The Captain's war diaries, after all, contain little to turn the accepted history of the Battle of the Somme on its head – the official record admittedly places the conclusion of action on the Somme in 1916, but it is still the case that most World War I front-line operations inspired tales of suffering, filth, incompetence and tragedy, and Blackadder's is no exception. The odd stray unswallowable detail may be littered throughout his memoirs,* but Captain Blackadder generally paints a picture that is by now the largely accepted image of the horror of trench warfare in World War I.

There are historians who seek to deny this consensus, to argue that the Great War was not only inevitable given the balance of power between the royal houses of Europe in the early twentieth century, and therefore beyond lamentation, but that Field Marshal Douglas Haig (who *was* actually known to friends as 'Dougie') has been libelled by generations of military historians, who have portrayed him as tantamount to a heartless strategic simpleton. Blackadder's primary source would be no help to these revisionist historians – for once, the Blackadder take on history chimes entirely with the accepted version. The military record contains such startlingly bestial displays of insanity in that environment (from the well-documented and widespread shooting of innocent shell-shocked men, or even teenage boys, for 'cowardice', to court-martialling soldiers simply for refusing to wear a helmet) that nothing the Captain could invent could be more mind-boggling than the truth. Some innocent conscripts, executed on the strength of Earl Haig's signature, have only begun to receive their pardons now, one century later.

Lies, however, remain central to the mysterious figure of the Captain himself. He claims to have been a professional soldier for fifteen years by the time of his arrival at the Somme in the autumn of 1914, and

---

* There is no evidence that Oscar Wilde was ever officially the Heavyweight Champion of the World or wrote a book entitled *Why I Like to Do It with Girls*, for instance.

yet this soldier's one badge of honour, his reputation as the Hero of M'Boto Gorge, receiving the Military Medal for 'selfless action in blowing up a heavily defended mango dump when under fire by a hail of wortleberries' (also described by some military historians as 'massacring the peace-loving pygmies of the Upper Volta and stealing all their fruit'), was alleged to have taken place in 1892, seven years before he joined up, while the Chronicles insist that he entered the army in 1888. Given that he could have been no younger than fifteen at the time, that would put him in his mid-forties at the time of his apparent death in 1917 (neither he nor any of his named fellow soldiers were mentioned in dispatches, or ever identified among the dead).

A Lt Blackadder was also quoted at the Battle of Rorke's Drift, dying with the words 'Oh, just keep the bloody place then!' on his lips, so the family had experience of the Anglo-Zulu war, but clouds of mystery still surround the details of M'Boto Gorge – which is another way of saying that no geographer, cartographer or military historian has ever heard of the place. It's possible that military code disguises the battle's real location, but the only lead we have is the suggestion that the young Edmund became hero of the hour by saving the life of Haig (then only a squadron commander) from a native with 'a viciously sharp piece of mango'. Haig's biographers may quibble with this suggestion, due to him beginning his soldiering in India, where he spent most of 1892 – it would be several years before his infamous career took him to the Sudan and, by the turn of the century, fighting in the Boer War, both possible battlegrounds for Blackadder's brave fruity encounter with the junior officer. The open-minded historian can only surmise that the dates in Captain B's war diaries were smudged and mud-spattered, and the Chronicler simply took a punt.

Other historians would beg to differ, however, and Professor Pollard is one of them. 'One of the defining characteristics of this section of the Chronicle for me is the copyright symbol and legend "Property of the BBC" which appears at the top of every page much in the way one might expect if the Chronicle were actually a BLOODY TV SHOW. I shall be dealing with this and every other historical travesty promulgated by these frankly fake Chronicles in my new book *The Blackadder Chronicles: The Anatomy of an Historical Fraud.*'

Like Pollard, some historians question the validity of Blackadder's experiences on the Somme front line altogether or, even further, the ultimate conclusion that the sacrifice made by hundreds of thousands of British soldiers in No Man's Land was a travesty, and an avoidable tragedy. However, even with a hundred years between us and the World War I, to visit the final reputed resting place of the Captain in northern France, to gaze across the overwhelming lines of white gravestones stretching out as far as the eye can see in every direction, each one denoting a human being wiped out in the prime of life on the whim of the ruling and upper classes, such historical revisionism seems distastefully beside the point. When it comes to the futility of warfare, Captain Blackadder was telling the truth, if ever any Blackadder was capable of such a thing.

Chapter 5

BLACKADDER GOES FORTH

If I should die, think only this of me . . . I'll be back to getcha.

As John Lloyd has established, the end of each series of *Blackadder* was the cue for everyone to go off into individual frenetic displays of creativity. Elton's career as a novelist began with the publication of *Stark*, an Australian odyssey that took him ten weeks to get down on paper: 'In 1988 I sort of decided I'd try and write a novel, I'd have a bash at it – that's how I do everything, because I feel like doing it . . . *Stark* was my first piece of extended prose, and I found that I enjoyed storytelling very much, it gave me a chance to concentrate more on the story than the gags.' *Stark*'s setting was no surprise – when touring Down Under with Mayall in 1987, Elton had met Sophie Gare, saxophonist with the boys' support act, the Jam Tarts, and they were married a few years later with Mayall as best man, beginning a lifelong association with Australia which led to Ben's gaining of dual citizenship in 2004.

The tale of a farty Pom caught up in an ecological conspiracy theory was an instant hit, launching a long and fruitful career, as well as a 1993 BBC TV adaptation, starring Elton himself (although he had to audition). The continued topicality of Elton's subject matter has been a defining element of his career as a novelist, but he insists, 'be it *Stark* on the environment or *Dead Famous* on the nature of unearned fame, it's not that I'm desperate to exploit or prove my point or say something, it's just that the stories come to me, the jokes come to me. I'm just interested in the world! I think most people are, actually . . .'

It Must be Love

Richard Curtis, meanwhile, had finally made the step into cinema that he had been coveting for years. After regrettable early experiences,* he made the decision to keep his film career as British as possible, and would go on to work closely with UK film-makers Working Title, helping to propel them from modest critical triumphs such as *My Beautiful Laundrette* to being one of the most successful production companies in the world.

Admittedly, Curtis's first script to make it to the big screen did make some concessions to a US audience, with Jeff Goldblum given the central role and the name being changed from *Camden Town Boy* to *The Tall Guy* to appeal as far afield as possible. Despite this, he says, '*The Tall Guy* was not autobiographical, but pretty close to it. I wanted it to be not misinterpretable, not something that could be taken out of my hands and turned into something else. I wanted it to be just a small, acute observation of things I absolutely knew, and I think I've stayed in that mode.' To that end, trusted friend Mel Smith made his directorial debut, spending the summer of '88 shooting Richard's personalised romance of Dexter King, the eponymous lanky Yank – a love-struck comedy stooge forced to kowtow to a self-professed 'major comic talent', the star of a West End hit entitled *The Rubberface Revue*,

---

* He pitched one film about a nervous father and son called *Four Eyes and Fat Thighs* to a team from MGM who claimed to love it, but then tore the screenplay to shreds. And then there was the Hollywood producer who only saw Curtis because he thought he had written *Gregory's Girl* . . .

called Ron Anderson. 'When I first sent Rowan the script,' Curtis says, 'the character that he eventually played was at that point called Rowan Atkinson, just as a joke, and he rang me up and asked me which part I wanted him to play.'

Rowan had been playing around with the idea of a villainous alter ego for a long time (the programme for *The New Revue* laid all blame for any signs of ego on Rowan's twin brother Mycroft), but nothing could be nearer to the knuckle than his fictional depiction in *The Tall Guy*. Smith explained to *Film 89*, 'Ron Anderson is a loud, foul-mouthed, bigoted nasty person, which Rowan certainly isn't . . . but he's having a fairly good crack at it.' 'People will realise my part is grossly exaggerated,' the star said, which his old partner Richard only partially backed up, admitting, 'The only true bit was where Jeff gets sacked, and in the interval they have a party for him, and Rowan's character produces a sort of quarter-bottle of champagne. I remember we did seventy-two dates around England, and at the party afterwards Rowan had bought one of those cherry slices that you used to get on British Rail – for eight of us . . . * But I never heard Rowan shout in all the years we were together.' Alternatively, he said, 'The only thing in which Row was naughty during the stage show, was that he did have a lot of trouble describing it as anything but a one-man show . . .' Angus Deayton once stood alongside Atkinson on Shaftesbury Avenue as they sized up the hoarding for *The New Revue*, and as he noticed that not one mention had been made of himself, despite his being onstage for most of the time, his suggestion to the star that 'something wasn't quite right' was met with complete agreement – the lettering should be in green, not yellow.

Angus would eventually get some reparation via his *Tall Guy* cameo as an actor mulling over offers from Steven Spielberg while Dexter has

---

* Lloyd made a similar dig in his one chart hit, *Spitting Image*'s 'Chicken Song' B-side 'I've Never Met a Nice South African', with the lyric 'I had lunch with Rowan Atkinson when he paid and wasn't late, but . . .'

to make do with adverts requiring a tall American (that is, until the hero gets the title role in the musical version of *The Elephant Man*, entitled *Elephant!*), but even then he gets no actual lines in a film bristling with great cameos and comic performances, with Emma Thompson providing the main love interest and Curtis getting a walk-on/walk-off role as 'Man Coming Out of Toilet', besides finally having his chance to work with Madness when the band provided a surreal musical interlude performing their version of 'It Must Be Love' – an anarchic sequence unlike anything in Curtis's subsequent mainstream hits.

The Tall Guy proved to be only a minor success on release in the spring of 1989, but in the UK at least it was Atkinson's daringly villainous turn that drew the crowds, and got many of the best lines:

RON: Listen, Dexter, is there something troubling you? Something you want to talk to someone about?

DEXTER: Well, yeah, actually, as a matter of fact, there is.

RON: Then for fuck's sake talk to someone about it, will you? And sort it out before I sack you and hire a lobotomised monkey to play your role, OK?

DEXTER: Thank you, my friend!

Jerry Lewis's turn as Jerry Langford in *The King of Comedy* had nothing on Atkinson's willingness to satirise his own career, creating a monster who dresses as a gorilla to advertise chocolate, bores everyone to death about his friendship with Prince Charles and even dares to steal the hero's girl, requiring Dexter to kidnap and imprison his ex-boss as part of a mad climactic dash to declare his love (a Curtis movie staple in the making), provoking the trussed-up major comic talent to whine, 'This sort of shit never happened to Charlie Chaplin!'

Compliments of the Gorging Season

Atkinson's one other major job that year was a return to theatre, playing several roles in a staging of Chekhov sketches, self-confessedly undertaken to feature in something that his mother could discuss with the vicar. But by the autumn, any thoughts that the *Blackadder* team had about a Victorian series were diverted by the upper echelons of BBC Comedy. 'There is a sense in which a Christmas special is a kind of accolade,' then-Controller Michael Grade said. 'Your series has made it if you are asked to do an hour-long Christmas special. You may not do it, but you just want to be asked to do it. They did deliver in fact, which was great.'

As was understandable, considering his devotion to *Oliver!* and love of everything Dickensian, Elton was already sketching out ideas for a nineteenth-century murder mystery directly spoofing Dickens, just as Shakespeare had got it in the neck in earlier *Blackadder*s. 'For a long time I kept thinking about a Victorian setting, with Dawn French as Queen Victoria. Like Queen Victoria, she is very small and round . . . ish. But unlike Queen Victoria, she is very amusing.' Although Curtis wasn't keen on the direction Elton was taking, he did note that there was a certain inevitability about exploring the most wonderful of Christmas-special clichés by retelling Dickens's greatest story once again, except with one cunning alteration: 'Again, a brilliant Richard idea,' Ben acknowledges, 'why don't we play *A Christmas Carol* in reverse? Make him start off good and turn horrible. A brilliant plotting idea, and I think we wrote a great script.' Dickens's basic set-up of a detestable misanthrope who abuses his lackey and travels backwards and forwards in time was just too uncanny for the partnership to ignore, with the idea of Rowan playing a soft-spoken, virtuous Blackadder, sunk so low as to be barely scraping a living selling fake face fungus, being an undeniable draw.

Besides, their only other seasonal idea, Richard recalls, could have led to a some undesirable controversy. 'The *Blackadder* Christmas Special

That Never Was! Blackadder ran the inn when Mary and Joseph came by, so he put them in Baldrick's bedroom.' 'Blackadder in Bethlehem' is a very curious oddity, featuring a talking turkey which objects to Baldrick's attempts to pluck it, a Miggins-esque sidekick called Rachel, festive entertainment featuring close-harmony shepherds, and a modern-day scene in which the unbeliever Blackadder is turned into a stuffed hedgehog by Jehovah. Besides Rowan and Tony playing Arabic ancestors of the central duo, the only other regular specifically included in Curtis's rough script was Stephen, who was marked down for the first of the Three Kings.

KING 1:   I'm sorry, I've been outside. Just inspecting the skies. Lovely evening.

BLACKADDER: Thank heavens you speak the lingo. So far I've construed that you are looking for a messiah . . .

KING 1:   He shall be a babe, wrapped in swaddling clothes and lying in a manger. Lovely word, 'swaddling', isn't it? I love the idea of swaddling someone. Would you like a swaddle?

BLACKADDER: Well, look, I can't say a totally clear picture of your situation, your desires or your mental health, is emerging, but if you'd like to bed down for the night, we can look into it all in the morning. It so happens we have three very expensive rooms available, did I say expensive, I meant excellent, they are of course expensive as well, but hell, you're three kings, if you can't afford it who can, quite frankly . . . If you could just fill this form out . . .

(They sign. One normally, one upside down, and the other with a huge signet stamp. Baldrick is in attendance.)

BLACKADDER:	Excellent. Any questions you'd like to ask me?
KING 1:	Yes, we were wondering whether you knew if a child is being born anywhere in the region . . .
BLACKADDER:	Ah – no – we have a rabbit coming out of a hat – but no sign of a child. (*Baldrick is surprised at this.*)
KING 1:	Very well – we shall be back later. Come, let us continue our search. (*They exit.*)
BALDRICK:	Why did you lie?
BLACKADDER:	Look at it this way – what would you think if you were booking into a hotel and someone told you the stables were presently in use as a maternity ward?
BALDRICK:	Yes, it's not a very nice idea.
BLACKADDER:	It's a positively disgusting one. 'Yes – we had an excellent night, apart from the sound of a woman in labour for six hours.' I would hardly define it as the height of in-house entertainment to listen to a midwife shouting 'push' for seven hours.
BALDRICK:	I suppose you're right. Still, it's a sin to tell a lie.
BLACKADDER:	Who says?
BALDRICK:	It's in the Bible.
BLACKADDER:	Dearest Baldrick, sweet little, naive little dung-for-brains Baldrick – you don't still believe in that mumbo-jumbo?

BALDRICK:	Of course: Moses came down the mountain. With the commandments.
BLACKADDER:	Yes. Stop there – you think it likely that a very old gentleman with a beard went up to the top of a mountain and God stuck his hand out of the sky and gave him a list of ten naughty things that good boys shouldn't do?
BALDRICK:	Stranger things have happened.
BLACKADDER:	No they haven't. All that old religion was developed by the tour operators to keep people occupied on the long journey to the promised land.
BALDRICK:	I suppose you're right. But what about David who was born in this town? He was a man of God.
BLACKADDER:	He also rogered Bathsheba and got her husband killed.

'It's not very legitimate because I never sent it to Ben,' Richard admits. 'It was begun in 1988, and then abandoned for fear that it would cause too much offence . . . On rereading it, I suspect it was also abandoned because it's like a strange mixture of *Fawlty Towers* and *Life of Brian* – both of which are too good to measure up to. So we returned to Dickens.'

Having decided that 'Ebenezer Blackadder' would be visited by a spirit which showed him previous Blackadder incarnations – bar *The Black Adder*, which was already considered best forgotten, especially given the time constraints of a special only extended by fifteen minutes – Lloyd was faced with the perennial problem of reuniting his team of in-demand stars, and it was to prove a bigger headache than ever. McInnerny was still shy of returning to sitcom, so the writers knew to work around the absence of any Percys, but even then, the programme would need to be recorded on separate evenings just to accommodate the plot's scope, and on a tight schedule – with the finished episode in that year's Christmas *Radio Times*, BBC1, 9 p.m. on the day before Christmas Eve, less than a fortnight after the recording.

So there would be less room for plumpening and argument than before, but that didn't mean the writers' original scripts would reach the screen untouched, as the unedited version of Hugh's jovial introduction alone would show:

> In the reign of Good Queen Vic, when little boys lived up
> chimneys and caring mothers drank four bottles of gin for
> breakfast, there stood in Dumpling Lane in Old London Town,
> the moustache shop of one Ebenezer Blackadder – the kindest and
> loveliest man in all England. Here is the story of what happened to
> him one very special Christmas . . .

For all the dramatic time constraints, with the writers' plan to revisit two past Blackadders as well as creating two brand-new ones ramping up the pressure, the best cast imaginable was assembled to bring the life-changing visions of Christmas to life. The New Zealand-born sitcom stalwart Denis Lill was reincarnated from the crusty Sir Tolbert Buxomley in 'Dish & Dishonesty' into the fat Beadle;* Patsy Byrne of course returned as Nursie as well as creating Bernard, her far-future descendant; Robbie Coltrane made his last guest-star turn par excellence as the Spirit of Christmas (a hairy giant who might have caught the magpie eye of writer Jo Rowling when she began to construct Hogwarts, inspiring the lovable caretaker Hagrid); and the greatest coup of all had to be the reunion of Miriam and Jim, once again displaying the most preposterous accent in the role of Albert to Margolyes's pitch-perfect Queen Victoria. 'I played Victoria subsequently in a documentary

---

* The first series' insane Messenger David Nunn also returned as one of his greedy charges, alongside *Grange Hill* icon Erkan Mustafa, and David Barber, who found fame as the 'Fat Bloke' in *Harry Enfield's Television Programme*.

about the restoration of the Albert Memorial,' she says, 'I'm fascinated by her, always have been, and I'm the same size and shape as she was . . .' As another Dickens fanatic, it would have been unthinkable to leave Miriam out of the proceedings, not least as this time she got to play a syrupy fun-bundle with only a hint of the gorgon. Add to these returning players all-new wonderfully revolting turns from Comedy Store veteran Pauline Melville as Mrs Scratchitt and *Dr Who* pin-up Nicola Bradbury as Ebenezer's irritatingly loud Godniece Millicent, and it's little wonder that the forty-five-minute episode required three nights of recording to get in the can.

The flashbacks to the days of previous Blackadders was perhaps made more of a challenge by the change of director, with Mandie's tenure ending, to be succeeded by budding sitcom director Richard Boden*. The tension between producer and director remained, however, John admits. 'When we got Richard Boden on board, we went to the pub and I said, "Now look, Richard, we've done three series now and it's a success and you're lucky to get the job – if you want to do it, the deal is, if I say I want a two-shot I don't want to argue about it, is that OK?" And he said, "Absolutely, John, of course, I quite understand and I'm pleased to be asked." A very nice, decent, civilised guy, Richard. And then on the first recording, in the camera rehearsal during the day, about two hours in, I said, "Richard, you know, shot 37, that should be a two-shot with Baldrick in the background if you don't mind." And he said "Oh, so you want to direct this, do you . . .?" "Richard, can you come into my booth . . . ?" He got up, and I said, "I won't say this in front of the crew but the answer to your question is yes, I do want to direct it and if you don't do what I ask without fuss, I *will*." And I never heard another peep out of him! It's a long-suffering job and he did it extremely well. It was frustrating for the directors, because they wanted

---

* (Fletcher's career would flourish and she stayed true to sitcom, directing Dawn French in *Roger and Val Have Just Got In* and Jennifer Saunders in *Jam & Jerusalem* and *Absolutely Fabulous*)

the power, and they weren't going to get it from me. I would consider myself the representative of the group, I would say, "Nobody is working for me, I am working for the programme and I am the programme's representative on Earth!" It's a priestly role, it's an intercessor. It's not an ego thing. All three were very nice, competent, good directors – but they walked into a room full of arrogant lunatics who wanted their way! It must have been awful for them. I'm sorry, guys!'

Editor Chris Wadsworth was still a crucial part of the crew, abetted by Lloyd's eye for painstaking editing, snipping out the tiniest exchanges to keep up the pace and squeeze everything in.* One sequence to receive a special slimming-down was the vision of Christmas Yet to Come, to tone down the writers' (and Lloyd's) understandable excitement at getting to spoof the worst excesses of the science-fiction genre. Note the switch of the name 'Frondo' to Stephen Fry's preposterous intergalactic aristocrat, and the excised reference to TV colleagues Geoff, *Only Fools* producer Gareth, and Alan:

A splendid reception chamber from the furthest reaches of time.
Four mighty figures stand in state.

ALL:	HAIL, QUEEN ASPIXIA SUPREME MISTRESS OF THE UNIVERSE.
ASPIXIA:	And hail to you, my triple husbandoid. Frondo, Mighty Birdlord of Thribble.
FRONDO:	Hail, Luscious Sovereign.
ASPIXIA:	Pigmot, Majestic Prince of Frumpity.
PIGMOT:	Hail, Empress of the Volepeople!
ASPIXIA:	And Bernard, Grim Overbeast of Yourbrav.
BERNARD:	Hello, dear.
ASPIXIA:	It is for no mean ceremonial that I rouse you

---

* Such as Mr B's original response to Prince George's claim to love Charades: 'I think you're confusing it with strip rummy, sir.'

from your pedpodules. I summon you here to
groupgreet our swift imperial navies home. . .

EDMUND: Majesties, this much greeting . . . Today we
celebrate the ancient feast of Harrodsale.
When tradition says that the great prophet
Jesus Christmas did manifest himself on Earth
and was born in a mango in Bethnal Green.

PIGMOT: We know all that but what of the foul
Marmidons?

EDMUND: . . . They're dead, if that's what you mean. I've
also wiped out the Posners, the Gwenlans and
the vile Yentobs.

The conclusion to the special proved especially tricky to pin down, once Ebenezer is returned to his rightful villainy, with a number of alternative endings being included in the studio script. When the reformed shopkeeper has sent away Victoria and Albert more offended than they have been in their entire lives, the writers suggested either a cheeky way to turn the Blackadder–Baldrick relationship on its head:

BALDRICK: But Mr B, that was the Queen come to give
you £50,000 and a title.

EBENEZER: Why didn't you tell me, you poxy little runt?
(*Thump, crash!*)

BALDRICK: I'm sorry to do that, Mr B, but sometimes you
push me too far.

Or alternatively, with Baldrick displaying the Queen's royal seal to prove to his master what a mistake he has made, there was a more convoluted but traditional display of seasonal violence from the newly despicable moustache vendor:

> EBENEZER: Yes, like that one. Ah. I see . . . This is clearly all your fault, Baldrick, but don't panic – if I climb up Mr Froggitt's drainpipe, sprint across the roofs of Pimlico, shin down Marble Arch, get a real speed up and skid the length of the frozen pond in St James's Park I may just be able to catch them before they reach Buckingham Palace, and tell them that the person who insulted them was in fact my identical twin brother. Of course, if I don't, I will come back and kill you with the poker. (*Ebenezer exits to the shop. And then reappears.*) On the other hand, thinking realistically, I'm not going to make it, am I?

He calmly stops and returns to hit Baldrick with the poker – swings to hit – freeze/engraving.

Ultimately, the producer decided to freeze the action at Blackadder's moment of realisation, and leave Baldrick's inevitable punishment to the imagination.

It was an incredible feat of comedy production to get this complicated special ready to broadcast to the nation's eggnog-sated families, but they watched in their millions with great approval as Advent drew to a close – the Black Adder worming his way into the nation's hearts even during the season of goodwill. Which makes it all the sadder that every subsequent broadcast of *Blackadder's Christmas Carol* capitulated to a minority of complaints about one of the funniest exchanges, as Baldrick details the pitfalls of recasting the role of Baby Jesus in the workhouse nativity play with a frisky dog named Spot – Blackadder's kindly concern for the orphan audience originally received Baldrick's chirpy reply, 'Nah, they loved it! They want us to do another one at Easter – they want to see us nail up the dog!' 'I have a lot of experience of being right on the edge of bad taste,' Lloyd says. 'I flatter myself that

I have a good-taste meter, I know exactly where the line is. And I can almost guarantee that in rehearsal I would be saying, "This is too strong, it's going to upset a lot of people and we're going to have complaints," and Ben saying, "Don't be so pathetic, Jack, it's just a gag." God knows how it got through the censors – I think because there was no censorship, there weren't compliance people. So it probably went through on the nod and then got a *lot* of complaints . . . It's breathtakingly cruel and very dark. And you don't just get the Jesus lobby, you've got the dog lobby as well!' Nonetheless, besides the unpleasant taste in the mouth which is inevitable when artists bow to viewer complaints, be they for reasons of animal cruelty or blasphemy, the swift edit required to cut the end off Baldrick's line has always stuck out like a giraffe in dark glasses trying to get into a polar bears-only golf club. That the gag remains excised from the DVD releases is one reason why the *Blackadder* box set's 'Ultimate' branding has a faint whiff of humbug.

One other planned festive treat has remained safely locked away in the archives: to accompany the Christmas special, Curtis, Goodall and Robinson collaborated on a Christmas single, along the lines of 'Grandma, We Love You', entitled 'Baldrick, We Hate You', complete with cherubic choir singing abuse to the stinking guttersnipe as he revels in his repulsiveness. There was a time when sitcom spin-off singles were not unusual – Steptoe & Son, Manuel and Mr Humphries all made assaults on the charts – but Goodall recalls that it was decided that Baldrick's song was just too much for the British public. 'It sort of died a death. No one would allow us to do it because it was very rude, although it wouldn't seem that rude now. I think it was mainly suppressed because it wasn't very good.'

Soupy Twists and Turns

Despite their absence from *Friday Night Live*, Fry & Laurie's live sketches had cemented a professional partnership which seemed to have crept up on Stephen and Hugh despite their close friendship, but which was seen as a done deal to everybody else. The Fry & Laurie brand, as it were, had a sophisticated but frequently outrageous charm all of its own, and they were more than ready to take on the decade's other young TV double acts, Smith & Jones, French & Saunders and Hale & Pace, as they strove to plug the holes left by the tired Two Ronnies, feuding Cook & Moore and much missed Morecambe & Wise. When the BBC finally learned from their mistake in pooh-poohing *The Crystal Cube* and offered the chaps the chance to pilot their own vehicle, the pair decided to outdo their competitors in one crucial area, as Hugh recalls: 'We just decided that we were going to write them all. All the other sort of sketch shows that were around at the time were all more or less being written by the same people, and so we felt that the thing we have going for us, if we have anything, is that this is personal, this is our personal view of the world, it's not a corporate machine that's just sort of generating thirty minutes of a sketch from here and a sketch from there, and these two guys will put on funny moustaches and do it . . . There are lots of times when we didn't make anyone else laugh, but we were always amused by ourselves.' This belies Dawn and Jennifer's gleefully slapdash creation of their own world in *French & Saunders*, and Victoria Wood took the crown for her solo authorship of every episode of *As Seen on TV*, but with their joint moulding of *A Bit of Fry & Laurie* the Footlighters had finally stepped out of the script-producing shadow of the whirlwind Elton. After a successful pilot in '87, much of the following year was spent with the two of them cursing into a word processor, but between sessions Hugh was settling down with new wife Jo and starting a family, while Stephen was in the West End making his first appearance in a Simon Gray play, *The Common Pursuit*, with Rik Mayall playing a firebrand narcissist to Fry's gentle academic. Although he claimed never to have seen any of these young stars' TV shows, Gray would develop a particular attachment to Fry, casting him in the central role of his 1990 TV play *Old Flames*, alongside Simon Callow and Miriam Margolyes, playing curious siblings.

In addition to their scripting feat, the first series of *ABOF&L*, which began on BBC2 only a few weeks after *Blackadder's Christmas Carol*, only relied on one regular third hand for sketches, with *Yes, Prime Minister*'s Deborah Norton as their female foil. Their return just over a year later was even stronger and more ambitious, with a number of guest stars, including Atkinson (credited as 'Nigel Havers'), who offers his condolences after Stephen punches Hugh to death for repeatedly singing about lost coffee-jar lids:

> ROWAN: He was an immensely dangerous man. A very dangerous actor. Whenever he was around, there was always this feeling of, ooh, anything could happen! . . . Hugh Laurie, on the other hand, was one of the dullest men I've ever met.

Hugh was probably the most voluble nit-picker in the *Blackadder* cast, and in their own programme he and Stephen chiselled away at their own comedy with the same level of perfectionism. Though their show would come to an abrupt end in the mid-nineties, *ABOF&L* amassed a multitude of obsessive admirers, with its 'vox-pop'-punctuated comedy world which, unlike so many other shows, made no great attempt to skirt around the Pythonesque, being packed with surreal skits, cross-dressing, 'amusing and unusual names' such as Ted Cunterblast and Peter Cuminmyear, and sketches which regularly dissolved into punchline-free silliness. There was also, inevitably, a memorable emphasis on the sesquipedalian, Fry positing, 'I thought language for language's sake was funny. That simply saying certain words at speed and with a kind of rhythm could be entertaining.' 'Stephen has the most terrific facility with the English language,' Hugh says, 'I mean, he takes a genuine poetic pleasure in the feeling of a good sentence.' Nevertheless, the scripts were a fifty–fifty affair, and Laurie's half of the equation is too easily forgotten. No matter how successful an actor he may become, he remains one of the most under-sung writers of completely barking comedy this country has produced.

Alongside the new series, Fry had also taken a leaf from Cleese and Curtis's book, to become a fund-raiser for a timely cause of particular import. His *Hysteria* benefits for Aids charity the Terence Higgins Trust in some ways capitalised on the *Saturday Live* fan base (with Enfield's Stavros a highlight of the first show and both Posner and Jackson getting involved), but his style of revue also took its cue from the good work still being done by the *Secret Policeman's Balls*. In lieu of Rowan's appearance, Fry, Laurie, Coltrane and Elton were mainstays of the 1987 and 1989 Amnesty benefits, witnessing Cook & Moore's final live sketch performance together. Rowan was, however, game for all *Hysteria* shows, performing new vicar monologue 'Tom, Dick & Harry', acting as a human prophylactic for Hugh and Dawn French, and for the second outing, performed at Sadler's Wells on 18 September 1989, even starring in a brand-new historical sketch with Laurie. Author Richard Curtis was so proud of this piece he could only hand it over to Stephen saying, 'That's yours. From me. But take it now so I'm not tempted to use it for Comic Relief . . .'

Veni Vidi Non Vincere

The *Who Dares Wins* team were also regulars at the *Hysteria* shows, though Tony was only with them for the first outing, playing a director who has to coach Julia Hills on how to have an orgasm. The final series of *WDW* aired at the start of 1988, and elsewhere Tony's storytelling skills remained to the fore, with series on Boudicca and Bible stories, and plans for writing a children's comedy series all of his own – which meant breaking his deal with Curtis. 'I phoned him up and said, "Richard, I don't need to schlep up to Oxford, because now I've heard your voice so often that I know what you're going to say before you say it, so I incorporate it. So would you mind if I stepped out on my own?" And he said, "Don't you realise that this is the moment that I've been waiting for since we started doing this work together?" So I was given tutorage from the best possible comedy writer I could have, without even being aware that I was doing the learning.'

The first series of *Maid Marian and her Merry Men*, written by Robinson for Children's BBC, was filmed in the leafy environs of Exmoor National Park in Somerset in the summer of 1989, and followed the heroine's silly struggle to free the muddy peasants of Worksop from Norman oppression. The inspiration for the sitcom came from the writer's own daughter, Laura, star striker for her school's football team and a spirited girl who had nursed Tony through periods of depression earlier in his career. Feeling that there was no female role model on TV with even a fraction of Laura's pluck, Tony created his own 'secret history', turning the medieval legend of Robin Hood on its head by showing the hero to be nothing more than an idle, vain tailor who took all the credit for Marian's freedom-fighting. After years at the bottom of the heap as Baldrick, he bagged the role of Marian's despicable nemesis, the Sheriff of Nottingham,* for himself. 'It did cross my mind that I might like to be Robin Hood, but quite honestly I've always thought that Robin was a bit of a wally, so I decided that what I'd like to do most was be the baddy. Having played sweet little Baldrick for so long, it was wonderful to be sarcastic and vitriolic.' But although this was a departure for Tony, the Sheriff was still ultimately the most put-upon character in the show, outwitted by Kate Lonergan's spirited Marian, let down by his moronic henchmen Gary and Graeme, and browbeaten by the infantile bully King John. John was played with terrifying abandon by Forbes Collins, who had been a peasant in *The Black Adder* (a complete

---

* In a strange twist, the actual holder of the post at the time, Nottingham's first black Sheriff, was also called Tony Robinson.

coincidence, Robinson insists), but besides Collins, *The Black Adder*'s Mr Applebottom, Howard Lew Lewis, as brainless beast Rabies* and Ramsay Gilderdale playing a Guy of Gisborne even wetter than the pathetic halibut Ralph in *Christmas Carol*, there weren't many links to be made between *Maid Marian* and *Blackadder* – at least not until Patsy Byrne cropped up as Marian's embarrassing mother in a later series, a deliberate piece of casting by her old colleague which saw his dastardly baddie seducing the cuddly old lady via a romantic samba. He says, 'There was never anyone I wanted for that role other than Patsy, I knew she would be perfect.'

Despite being aimed at a teatime audience, part pantomime, part playground-style rough and tumble, Tony says, 'We got away with murder, we said things we could never say on children's television nowadays. I remember there was one line Marian has, which was: "Men: they promise you the world, then you end up flat on your back servicing their muckspreader."' The writer had extensive experience of children's TV, and would soon be hosting his own cartoon compendium, *Stay Tooned*, but Robinson had learned from Baldrick's popularity with kids that there was no point in writing down to the viewers. 'I think I knew that I was writing for an audience who would be very au fait with *The Young Ones* and *Blackadder* and Dawn and Jennifer and Alexei's programmes. I knew a lot of nine- to eleven-year-olds at that time, and that was their world, that was the television they really cared about. They didn't care about children's television at all really, apart from cartoons. So I knew that if I was writing out of my experience of *Blackadder*, there was no need to shake that off, I just needed to write it in my own way, and I knew that my target audience would get what I was doing. I couldn't help but be informed by the comic rhythms I had been working on over the previous ten years or so.'

---

* With Danny John Jules's Rasta Barrington and Mike Edmonds's Little Ron completing the merrie band.

Being warmly remembered for its many pop-music pastiches, as befitted the anarchic nature of the show, a constant stream of modern-day allusions which the kids would get made it clear that the twelfth-century setting was not to be taken seriously – the Sheriff's expostulation, 'Wait a darn-tootin' minute! I have an idea so tasty you could coat it in sugar, stick a raspberry on top and serve it up on *MasterChef*!' not only exemplifies this, but shows that the writer had no problem with throwing in the odd *Blackadder*-esque extended metaphor, usually reserved for his own character's long speeches, which made up for years of Baldrick's monosyllabism. Despite the silliness of it all, however, *Maid Marian* complemented its gleefully childish spirit with an overtly political stance, mocking Wayne Morris's woolly royalist Robin and packing every story with suitably right-on rhetoric – a foreshadowing of Robinson's move into party politics.

While Tony was only just beginning to sketch out Marian's exploits, the Hat Trick team were branching out into sitcom themselves. Mulville had starred in the Humphrey Barclay-produced sitcom *That's Love*, but he and Rory McGrath had their own idea for a sitcom vehicle – and it was historical. *Chelmsford 123*, as the name suggested, was set in second-century Essex, and followed the frayed relations between new Roman Governor Aulus Paulinus (Mulville), and Trinovantes Chieftain Badvoc (McGrath). As a *Who Dares Wins* spin-off, a part was earmarked for Robinson, who was at first invited to play Gracientus, Aulus' slimy brother-in-law, but Tony recalls, 'I think Denise O'Donoghue said, "Actually everyone thinks it would look too much like *Blackadder* if you played that character, so we're going to ask Phil to play it."' Philip Pope ultimately put in perhaps the best performance in the show, but he wouldn't be the only *Blackadder* player to feature – the bestial Emperor Hadrian, who spoke almost entirely in Latin, was played by Bill Wallis; Helen Atkinson-Wood was a British housewife; Howard Lew Lewis's Blag allowed him to portray yet another moronic man mountain; Robert Bathurst got his sitcom pilot hat-trick; and Angus

Deayton and Geoff McGivern also joined the roster of Oxbridge guest stars littered throughout the two series. Although Britain was firmly in the firing line,* one other similarity between the two historical sitcoms was a taste for Frenchie-baiting. Indeed, the entire saga ended on such a dig, after Gracientus' despicable suggestion to Aulus that he displace Hadrian as Emperor lands everyone employment as galley slaves:

AULUS: If you hadn't suggested going back to Rome this would never have happened!

GRACIENTUS: It would never have occurred to me to have gone back to Rome if Badvoc hadn't kidnapped the Emperor in the first place!

BADVOC: Listen, don't blame me, if you Romans hadn't invaded Britain in the first place, it wouldn't have occurred to me to kidnap the Emperor.

AULUS: Hang on, if you Britons had put up a better fight in the first place we wouldn't have invaded you!

MUNGO: Oh no, you can't blame us for that. If the French had put up a better fight in Gaul, you'd never have got the chance to invade.

ALL: . . . Bloody French.

Although unfairly damned by comparison to *Blackadder*, the knockabout *Chelmsford 123* took a wholly different approach to historical comedy, using the set-up to make every anachronistic gag imaginable, with Blag regularly making 'they haven't invented it yet'

---

* The original press release ran 'In AD 123, Britain was a cold miserable dump populated by beer-swilling hooligans . . .'

gags, the whole cast turning up in a modern-day sequence as their schoolboy descendants, and even a brief toilet stop for the Doctor as the Tardis materialised in the background during the very first episode. Nevertheless, Mulville and McGrath knew that they were bound to be compared to Atkinson's team – and, of course, felt they were more than equal to taking them on. While insistent that there was never any bitter division between the two Oxbridge camps, Robinson admits, 'As with any ambitious people in their twenties, there's always petty ambitions and cattiness, but I think that's just part of the deal.' Besides, *Blackadder* was not such a sitcom Goliath for the *WDW* team to face when they first piloted their Roman comedy in 1988 . . .

By early 1989, Curtis & Elton had already agreed on the setting for Edmund's fourth full incarnation, moving into the twentieth century, and the team were contracted to begin recording in late summer. With McInnerny back in the fold, as well as Fry & Laurie being full-time players, the new line-up was just one way in which the latest series would be the ultimate distillation of everything that had gone before. There was no question of this being a finale, and yet by bringing the Blackadder family so close to the modern day, everybody involved knew that this would not just be any other series.

One of many differences for this all-new passage from the Chronicles was the fact that, with the World War I in their sights, the writers decided that historical research was a necessity, for the first time. 'With *Blackadder* two and three, we weren't particularly respectful of the periods, but I don't think we were really into any blatant howlers,' Elton says. 'Obviously, with World War I we had a very different approach.' Ribbing the attitudes of centuries gone by was one thing, but finding humour in the deaths of 35 million people within living memory was not a task that anyone connected to *Blackadder Goes Forth* could countenance taking lightly. 'We read lots of books about it,' Curtis says, 'Ben knew it all, I read a few books. They were interesting, because all the stuff we wanted to write about, which was sort of the clash of the classes, and getting stuck in a small confined space, *was* funny. All the people coming from communities where they'd never bumped into posh people, and vice versa, and all being so gung-ho and optimistic and enthusiastic . . . The first hundred pages of any book about the World War are hilarious – and then everybody dies.'

'Of course there was a long tradition of World War II comedy from *The Army Game*, with Bootsie and Snudge, through to *Dad's Army*,' Stephen says, 'with the American equivalents *Bilko*, *Hogan's Heroes*, *M*A*S*H*, etc. Radio too, with *Much-Binding-in-the-Marsh* and the *Navy Lark*.' In World War I terms, however, besides *Up the Front*, and perhaps the greatest pacifist treatment of the tragedy, Joan Littlewood's *Oh What a Lovely War*, the Great War had featured in sitcom format in Dennis Pitts's 1972 comedy *No Peace on the Western Front*. This *Comedy Playhouse* one-off began with genuine archive footage, prefacing a farce starring Warren Mitchell and Ronald Fraser as 'the original odd couple', a German and a Scots soldier who share a dugout on the Somme in 1916 and help each other to shirk their duty.

But the younger generation were far more cautious about causing offence. Laurie says, 'It was a really peculiar and bold thing to try and make a comedy out of, but I think ultimately a very sympathetic and respectful one. Even though the characters were absurd and moronic at times, it never disrespected their courage or their sacrifice.' 'It was a big gamble and we did get some complaints,' Atkinson adds, 'but of all the periods we covered it was the most historically accurate. We may have exaggerated the characters and what happened to them but it is very difficult to exaggerate the absurdity and horror of World War I. People thought we were really going over the top . . . It may sound ridiculous for someone to face a court martial for shooting a pigeon, but madder things happened in reality. Towards the end of the war thirty soldiers were court-martialled and shot in France by our own side for not wearing a hat in the trenches. It is so absurd nobody would ever believe it.'

Blackadder's *raison d'être* from the start was to draw humour from death and tragedy, but Elton for one was concerned that the closeness of the Somme bloodbath required caution – and nobody in the team was more aware of the seriousness of the subject matter than him, as both his grandfathers had actually been there, fighting on opposite sides (his father's father had even won the Iron Cross, which was hastily buried in the back garden when the family migrated to Britain). But he was adamant that the war was ripe for comic treatment. 'I was very anxious to do World War I; it's a period I'm very interested in and have read a lot about. From the beginning Richard and I were absolutely committed to being extremely respectful, and aware of the unimaginable human tragedy . . . I hope no one was left in any doubt of the respect I think everybody on the team had for the sacrifices made and the honour of the people involved. But it was a damn silly war, and if ever there was a subject requiring satire, it's people, no matter how honourably and how nobly, blindly going to war. Those awful policies, of what were called the Pals Brigades, because in 1914 people joined up together, whole gangs, the pub, a cricket team – or the tiddlywinks team as we said in *Blackadder* – would all march to the recruiting station, they'd all go together because the idea was that they'd fight together and for each other. And of course this industrial war didn't really have a lot of time for people who'd fight for each other because people would be mown down in an instant . . . It was respectful to all. Yes, we had some fun with the old "lions led by donkeys" idea, but that's legitimately part of our world experience as Britons and Europeans inheriting the memories and the history of our forefathers in that war.'

Lloyd goes further: 'People don't stop making jokes because somebody was killed just round the corner. In many ways – as people who've actually been fighting in real wars say – life becomes very precious and pumped up . . . I think it's manifest right from the beginning that nobody's making fun of people. Quite the reverse, it's entirely sympathetic to the poor bastards who were put in this appalling situation.'

But John had an extra reason for being glad of the setting. As Robinson says, 'We'd always said that more than anything what we'd like to do would be to create a series that was very claustrophobic, where the five or six of us who were the performers were trapped in a space. And what better way to feel that notion of claustrophobia than to set it in the trenches?' 'We wanted a place and a time that could reproduce, to a certain extent, the claustrophobia and the sordidness of medieval England,' Atkinson says, 'and the best way to do that is to set it in the middle of a war.' 'Good sitcoms, so the wisdom goes, are set in places where people can't get out,' Lloyd continues, '*Porridge* in prison; in *Fawlty Towers*, Basil's trapped with a ghastly wife that he can't escape from and a business which is obviously going bust but which is his only livelihood. And we set ours in a trench dugout where there's only two ways to escape – one is forward to the German machine guns, the other is backwards to the British firing squads.' However, he adds, 'I used to bang on to Richard and Ben that to do a proper sitcom, it has to be a situation in aspic, with a set number of characters who interact, and you find out more and more about them. So when they came along and said, "World War I, that's the idea – three people in the dugout, two people in headquarters and that's it, there are no other people," I said, "That is brilliant." But when the first three episodes came in, one was set in a flying school, one was set in hospital and the other one was set during a concert party. I said, "Guys, what's happened to this three in the dugout, two in the headquarters idea? Where's that gone?" And they said, "Well we couldn't do that, it's too difficult."

Your Country Needs YOU

Having begun the entire dynastic saga by chickening out of active service at Bosworth, finally a Blackadder was going to war, whether he liked it or not. This didn't actually make Captain B brave, just in the wrong place at the wrong time, although Atkinson did sense a change with each dynasty. 'In the first series, Blackadder was just an idiot. In the second series he was dashing but weak. As the butler, he became cleverer and nastier. This time he is less cruel and more careworn.' In his Flashman-esque pomp, fighting for the Empire, the Captain may have been as villainous as ever, but faced with heavily armed Germans, all he had left was what Fry calls 'a strong belief, almost raised to the pitch of religiosity, that his skin and well-being were more important than that of anybody else'. The anti-hero's traditional contempt for his surroundings was magnified by peril, in Boden's view. 'He was the person that could see the madness all around. He saw the madness in his own trench, let alone what was going on outside and in No Man's Land.'

Curtis penned special service history profiles of all the regulars for *Radio Times* on the series' broadcast, which detail how far from power the Blackadder family had fallen: 'Captain Blackadder is a lifelong soldier, pipe-smoker and moustache-grower. He joined the army to escape the rigours of civilian life, and distinguished himself sitting in armchairs and ordering drinks across three continents, making it his particular business to avoid enemies who actually possessed guns . . .' Baldrick, however, had fallen still further: 'Christian name uncertain, Private Baldrick is a graduate of the Turnip Street Workhouse, where he majored in gutter-sweeping and potato peeling . . . It is impossible to pick up any textbook on rare skin diseases without coming across pictures of him.' Despite the batman's devolution to 'amoeba level', though, Fry identifies how the change of context lent a new kind of nobility to the fetid dwarf: 'Baldrick makes his absolute apotheosis as the Tommy; he can make the best of everything, he can turn things to his advantage however ghastly, he can find a better puddle to go to.'

'One of the things I love about series four,' Curtis says, 'is that strangely I think Baldrick gained meaning. You know, he'd just been a fool and a butt the whole way through, but there was a remarkable thing that happened right at the end of that series, when he did suddenly seem to represent the working man.' 'I had the privilege of performing a part that represented the ordinary lives of the grandfathers of an awful lot of people in the country in which I live,' Robinson says, 'but really it was for them to imbue Baldrick with that notion rather than me – I was just a bloke who couldn't make coffee.' Baldrick's signing up also gave Robinson inspiration from a new quarter: 'There's a character called the Good Soldier Svejk, in a novel which came out in the First World War, who is as stupid as Baldrick. And you never actually really know whether he is incredibly stupid, or whether he's just pretending to be stupid. That was kind of my inspiration. But rather than "I have a cunning plan, sir," he says "Beg to report, sir!"'

Hugh Laurie says, 'Baldrick is the hero really, because wherever you go, every school or organisation, every shop or whatever has got a Baldrick. They just loved that character.' The audience were used to Hugh completing the central trio, and so George had to be reincarnated, with the Prince's oafishness depleted, but not one ounce of brain being inherited along the way. 'I think the kinship of stupidity between Baldrick and George was a very heart-warming one. They were companions on the great road of idiocy.' Lt George the Hon. Colthurst Barleigh was conceived as a Woosterish silly ass (Hugh even experimented with a monocle until he discovered how hard it was to keep on), but his lack of guile made him perhaps the most sympathetic character of all. The actor suggests: 'George's sort of happy-go-lucky, "home in time for tea" attitude was especially tragic. His ideas about war come from games; George could only see real warfare in those terms. He genuinely was a lamb to the slaughter.' In Curtis's own words, George embodied the innocence lost in World War I, 'Dying for a good scrap, he's always the first to volunteer for a tricky escapade, and the last to duck.'

In taking over the all-important role of Blackadder's death-dealing superior, Laurie's partner, despite the General's surname, had far more of the Wellington about him than Lord Melchett, and though he had no short supply of mad military commander forebears to inspire him, Fry became the first of the team to craft an all-new character – General Sir Anthony Cecil Hogmanay Melchett, although undeniably Colonel Blimp-ish, would go on to personify the dangerous ignorance of World War I high command like no other comic creation. Despite mistaking Cambridge for Oxford, Curtis's service history for the General encapsulated the bullish buffoon perfectly: 'Cousin of the Melchett who sent off the Light Brigade, Hogmanay Melchett is described by an uncredited captain as "having a skull that is such a perfect vacuum, it's a constant surprise his moustache doesn't get sucked up his nose". Educated, using the word at its loosest, at Oundle, where he was one of the great fag-beating team of 1877, he went on to break wind for his college at Oxford, and then joined the army to protect the British Empire and shout at the lower classes in a very loud voice.' It was the thirty-year-old Fry's portrayal, however, that made this crusty old dinosaur such a memorable monster. With characteristic modesty, Fry says, 'Young people playing old people are funny. Because I was young and I was playing a General, it was somehow funnier than if I'd been the right age to be a General, which I am now . . . Most of what I do isn't terribly hard. I don't have to "disappear" into a character in some terrible way. With *Blackadder* the last thing you want is to take it too seriously. The audience relishes the sight of an actor enjoying himself. They like to see the gargantuan imbecility of it.' He adds, however, 'The Melchett in series four was a very different character to the one in two, he was much, much more aggressive, much more insane, much more powerful. He was really, for almost the entire series, *the* source of power. And he represents the absolute insanity of the war. Without being too pompous about *Blackadder*, it does I think illustrate perfectly the nature of that grotesque war, the genuine insanity if you like, of the way the war was practised, which however much it may have been justifiable, to us it is now clear that it was a moment of madness in human history that one would never want to repeat again, so it's wonderful to concentrate some of that madness into a single being.'

Since the Cambridge days, when his Shakespearean kings tended to incorporate extraneous senile noises into every speech, Fry had entertained his friends with his own unique loud bleating, which could act as a greeting, an agreement, or even a threat. 'It was done as much as anything to amuse Rowan and Hugh, this rather bizarre way of speaking, and barking. You knew he was coming just because you heard a "Beh!" noise somewhere in the background. I would try and make Rowan laugh by sometimes sitting down and going "Ach!" and only Rowan knew it was because I had these apparent piles.' The haemorrhoidal subtext to Melchett's madness was gifted to Fry by Brian Blessed – an apt gesture, given that the General was the closest thing to Blessed's Richard IV in three series.

McInnerny was brought back into the fold with the promise of the series' second all-new character, essentially filling Fry's previous role, of Blackadder's weaselly and sycophantic equal. 'Darling and Blackadder are kind of the same really,' Elton says, 'lower-middle-class sort of semi-gentlemen. But obviously one of them has managed to connive his way onto the staff, and the other one's bad-lucked into the trenches.' As Tim recalls, this was about the size of the role. 'The whole idea of doing the fourth series . . . I mean, it took a great deal of thought, as far as I was concerned, but doing Darling was a kind of way of hoping that everyone might forget a little bit about Percy. To play Darling, who hated Blackadder, and throughout the series wanted him to go on the front line and be killed, was quite extreme.' However, he adds, 'In the initial rehearsals, he wasn't even called Darling, he was called Captain Cartwright, which is kind of dull. I mean, I didn't even know who he was and couldn't get an angle on him.'

With only a partial twinkle, Rowan says, 'Tim, unlike the rest of us, is a proper actor . . . I like to think,' and it's certainly the case that of all the cast, he took the job most seriously. Lloyd says, 'Tim, as well as being a very funny guy, is a real actor's actor. He wants to know what the haircut is, what kind of walk the character has – he's brilliant at it . . . Darling is, I think, one of the great comic creations, and it came from an actor's determination to carve himself a place here. Tim said, "I've been dragged in here for this teeny weeny part, and where's me laughs?" And then Stephen chimes in, "Yeah, and Cartwright's a really boring name, isn't it?"' Fry continues, 'Tim was a bit distressed because his character seemed to be nothing. He was called Cartwright, and I suggested, in a rare moment of brilliance, that maybe he should have a really silly name that was a constant torment to him . . . And suddenly this character was born out of nowhere, just because of the name! For the next three days, his name was changed to Darling, and we all fell about. Then I remember we actually had a vote, and said, "Look, is this Darling joke going to run very dry, and is it going to seem really embarrassing after the third episode, or will it sustain?" And Tim said, "Oh no, please let me keep it!" Because Tim being the wonderful actor that he is, he knew how to play someone who all his life had been called Darling in a sarcastic way.' 'We thought the name Darling was funny,' Tim admits, 'but it really didn't occur to us that people would pick it up in the way that they did. Which was very stupid of us, obviously. We just thought it was a silly, embarrassing name, we didn't realise what it would mean for the other characters . . . The scene where Melchett is getting ready for dinner with "Georgina", and the whole misunderstanding of him practising his speech to her, and calling her "darling", but at the same time I think he's talking to me, I think is brilliant, it's a fantastic piece of writing.' 'The character punches way above his weight. You watch him acting his socks off when Stephen's doing the talking, it's wonderful. Because acting isn't just about delivering lines, it's about being there and being real,' John says, adding, 'Darling hates Blackadder because he's jealous of him. He's a real man, a front-line soldier.' But there was more to Kevin Darling than that, with a bizarre homoerotic undertone to his hatred of Blackadder being just one ingredient which made up the neurotic 'sort of spotty squit that nobody really likes', his frustration betrayed by the pulsating squint in his left eye. 'The twitch stayed with me for months actually,' McInnerny says, 'I did get quite scared that it was never going to go, and that I'd have to start writing my own spin-offs, because I wouldn't be able to get rid of the twitch and I'd never get another job.'

McInnerny's transformation into the Captain completed the strongest line-up of any *Blackadder* series, but as the writers may have reflected even at that very early stage, Darling's genesis did not augur well for a smooth production from their point of view. When *The Times* visited the team in rehearsals, the first inkling of the finality of the new show came when Richard told them, 'If you're making a lemon sauce, all you need is a bit of lemon. But if you're making chilli everybody can shove bits in, and *Blackadder* is a very rich chilli. Everybody on the show thinks they can put in good jokes, despite the fact that Ben and I think there are already quite a few good ones in there to start with. It does usually end up funnier, but it's time to do something over which I have more control.'

Pack Up Your Troubles . . .

'One of the great things about *Blackadder* was you used go whistling in to work, because it was so funny in rehearsal. What would happen was just so very, very entertaining, and the rehearsals were often funnier than the shows,' John Lloyd remembers through rose-tinted spectacles, but Stephen has a clear memory to the contrary: 'I remember saying to Hugh and Rowan and John, "What will happen in six months' time when a taxi driver says to you, 'Oh, those *Blackadders*, I bet they're fun to make, aren't they?' Will you go 'Yes, marvellous fun!'?" And they all said, "No! We'll be honest and say they're absolute hell!"'

'The producer is supposed to be the person who makes sure that inspiration doesn't turn into complete filthy anarchy. Unfortunately, we had John . . . ' Tony Robinson says. 'We were workshopping all the time, we workshopped every bloody word, every exclamation mark! Although we didn't have the twelve writers that you would have for *Taxi* or *Cheers* or whatever, actually, you had people in the room who were doing exactly the same kind of thing that those writers on an American show would do. So by the end of the week the whole thing was really lean and spare. Everything, any ounce of fat on it, would have been challenged and hacked away. Virtually all of us who were involved in the performance were writers and, outrageously, we decided that we knew just as well if not better than Richard and Ben what the words ought to be. So we were constantly challenging every single gag, the structure of every scene – we even put additional characters in sometimes! So there was a lot of tension between the writers on the one hand, and the producer on the other, who was, as it were, the representative of what the actors were saying. And it was very healthy and very good, but it could be quite upsetting sometimes.'

Robinson continues, 'The legendary coffee scene is an example of the improvisation that we all used to do in the rehearsal room. Because in the original script, the only line was about the fact that the coffee was made out of mud. And then somebody said, "Why don't you add sugar? Dandruff!" and we all giggled like the naughty late adolescents we really were.' A glimpse of the tweaking/plumpening process was captured by the BBC series *Behind the Screen*, which bearded the troublemakers in their lair, agonising over Captain B's struggle with telephonic communications in the last episode. Rowan's dialogue is perfected word by word, to group frustration – what colour should the mis-ordered curtain material be? In which direction is the taxicab meant to travel? As the diatribe is painstakingly recited in full by the faltering star, Fry and Robinson egg him on with a desperation born of hours of sluggish progress, and cheer when he reaches the end . . . only for Lloyd to then cause groans of misery by apologetically griping: 'I hate to raise this, having worked on it for three hours, but do you think it's a very good joke?' To which Atkinson admits, 'I'm still labouring under the belief that no one ever ordered anything by the phone in 1917!' During the same tortuous session, the *Radio Times* reported Rowan sitting with two pencils up his nose (a piece of grotesque tomfoolery which had long been in his armoury), occasionally plucking one from a nostril to make further notes as the brainstorming continued.

By this point, Blackadder's skill with an extended simile was something of a trademark-cum-millstone, and a definite trap for the team when rehearsing. John says, 'It was an area where real creative madness could go on and on, and then it was the trick of trying to find which were the best aspects of that simile, and pull it back so it wasn't over-weighted.' The writers could hardly quibble on this point either, as Curtis admits, 'The most difficult thing was definitely thinking of the similes. Ben and I used to put that off forever, so Ben would send it to me and the line would say: "You are as stupid – as my knob." That's what it would always say. We couldn't use "my knob", so I'd have a go at it, and then he'd have another go at it, and when we got into the rehearsal room everybody would have a go at it.' 'John, Hugh and I in particular would rewrite until the final moments,' Fry adds, 'we endlessly had "epithet moments" as we called them, "Sticky the stick insect", all those sort of jokes. Somehow there was never enough time to get them absolutely right. We used to wriggle about screaming with adolescent laughter whenever we did those.'

Tony was not to be put off by his comic company, and admits, 'I love them all, but when I'm with them, I suddenly want to win. I don't want them to put me down . . . I can't tell you how profoundly competitive that environment is, but I contributed like mad. I think whenever I'm in a corner I always get noisy. Being the only grammar-school boy among that incredibly talented group of highly articulate performers, and having left school at sixteen, and not having been to university, there was a sense in which they always felt very different from me, really rather exotic, and yet in a way, not really kind of tuned in to the real world, because they all talked so elaborately. And I think that probably helped me with Baldrick – in a way it doesn't matter to Baldrick whether or not a hierarchy exists, because they're all up above him, dancing around in some way or another, and I suspect there's a bit of me that felt like that myself.'

'We were working with an extraordinarily creative group of people, and you know, to expect Stephen and Hugh not to chip in "wouldn't this be a good idea?" or "wouldn't that be a good idea?" would be madness, obviously the actors had a real part to play,' Elton said many years later, but as ever, he was seldom there to take the hard knocks, while Curtis says, 'I've never been able to understand non-involved writers. I think they have much happier lives – those who don't go to rehearsals all look younger than me. But I've always gone to every part of the process, right up to the edit . . . John was never happy unless everything was fabulous, so it was a very argumentative and passionate rehearsal room. But in some ways it always was – Ben and I were used to arguing about what was funny, so already by then it had been through lots and lots of drafts. We always had a read-through a month before, and two or three episodes would just be wiped because they weren't funny enough, so it was no surprise that we kept on arguing until the final moment . . . It was very difficult and testing, but the pain in the arse about it was that it was effective.' Ben, however, says, 'I think I was able to maintain friendships more consistently, because Richard did all the bloody work – he went in and I didn't. I just couldn't handle it. Sometimes lovely ideas emerged on the floor and they were marvellous, and sometimes they were completely ridiculous! Like, "What are you all discussing?" I said to John. "This sort of relentless anal worriting over each syllable can sometimes mean that you miss the whole." They'd end up doing the line as written in the first place anyway, and half a day would have been wasted, in this sort of pained panic. I thought it was *nearly* as counterproductive as it was productive.'

These final fraught plumpening sessions may have bruised some egos, but Tony insists that Richard's presence was the reason that nothing ever spilled over into full enmity. 'He's such a loving bloke, and because of him that deep competitiveness was swathed in affection, the sort of environment where everyone remembers everyone else's birthday.' And while paying tribute to the writers, Lloyd himself was happy to tell journalists at the time, 'The producer is basically someone who has no talent whatsoever, except the talent to criticise everyone else's talent . . . I have to say that the writers are saintly men who put up with an awful lot of brutality.' However, he was also to admit, 'The key to *Blackadder* is that it's about the writing: that is where all the difficulties come from. Because Ben and Richard are professional writers, I'm a writer pretending to be all the other things, and pretending *not* to be a writer . . . and there were more writers in our rehearsal room than would be in any sitcom. The scripts had always been the source of passionate disagreement between both the writers themselves, and between them and me, but when this widened to include the actors on a regular basis, it became clear that the team would not survive another series.'

A united front was put on when the team decamped to Cavalry Barracks in Colchester, in full regalia, walrus moustaches and all, to be joined by the 3rd Battalion the Royal Anglian Regiment ('the Pompadours') for the first *Blackadder* location shoot in four years. As ever, Lloyd's credits were to be meticulously crafted, with the full cast on parade in the opening credits, marching to Goodall's new military arrangement of the theme – which pleasingly resulted in the melody becoming a permanent favourite with brass bands across the nation. 'It was all very last minute,' Howard recalls, 'and it's quite hard to get a military band from the army at two weeks' notice, virtually impossible. We just happened to get in touch with someone who was a friend of a friend, and they managed to sort it out with a band which doesn't now exist, the Royal Anglian.' The end credits, which were originally to feature the ranks whistling the theme, convincingly recreated mottled archive footage, complete with militarised credits courtesy of Prd. 597602 Lloyd, J.

The march past of Blackadder's regiment, however, was to have featured the top brass mounted on horses – a plan foiled by Fry's extreme discomfort as an equestrian. 'Stephen Fry on a horse is one of the least convincing sights you will ever see,' Atkinson laughs, but Fry recalls the reality being more serious than his chums could conceive: 'The Colonel said, "Oh, I think my mount will do for you very well. Meet Thunderbolt!" This enormous horse, twice the height of me . . . I walked once around the parade ground, but then the band of the Royal Anglian Regiment strikes up "The British Grenadiers", and my horse went vertical. It was like some painting of a rampant horse. And it started to charge and go round and round the parade ground. Hugh and Tim got off their horses – not to help me, but so they could roll on the ground wheezing and barking at my predicament, which was horrific! I was screaming! I was twelve foot off solid parade ground, I was going to die!'

'We got on very well with the army,' John remembers, 'I think they thought we'd all be a bunch of communist poofters, and we thought they'd all be chinless wonders. We had lunch in the mess, and they made Baldrick sit on a stool – he had to eat baked beans out of a tin helmet.' In fact, thanks to *Goes Forth*, despite UK troops' entertainment usually being the domain of Jim Davidson, an obsession with *Blackadder* became the norm in the military. Rowan says, 'You can see why they enjoy *Blackadder* so much, it's such an enjoyable teaching tool for them, as a representation of hierarchy and humanity, which I think is what the army is, you can see how it rings all the right bells.' As Lloyd is proud to repeat, around half of all regimental goats tend to be called 'Baldrick', and in the first Gulf War, all the British lines were named after characters from the series. One week after the filming, a serious IRA attack on the Colchester barracks nearly forced a last-minute change of credits, but the team decided to go ahead with what they had, as they left the 'North Acton Hilton' once again and went into the studio.

Who'd Notice Another Mad Man Round Here?

One surprise for this final series was that with Elton busy putting together his first solo TV vehicle, *The Man from Auntie*, for producer Geoffrey Perkins, warm-up duties fell to his partner Richard Curtis. Having a style more like a jolly holiday rep than a stand-up comedian, Curtis's patter centred on the show, their plans to release a scratch 'n' sniff Baldrick poster for Comic Relief (or maybe even speciality Baldrick coffee), and a regular airing of past *Blackadder* scenes on studio monitors every time the audience had a long wait for a scene to be set up.

Equally surprising was the extent to which the first episode, 'Captain Cook'* served as a real series opener, establishing a peaceful status quo with the Captain contentedly puffing on his pipe before becoming embroiled in the latest laughable scheme from the top brass – it's no coincidence that this was the first time that a series recording had begun with the first broadcast episode since 'The Foretelling'. This first plot meanders amiably without ever really tackling any one subject, and the eventual pay-off was not only hastily put together by the team on the Saturday night before recording on 20 August, it was even simplified further from the suggested scene, which would have required a special set in addition to Blackadder's dugout, No Man's Land and Melchett's chateau:

---

* The team worked together to provide the military-themed titles, which were originally down as 'War Artist', 'Court Marshal', 'Concert', 'Flying', 'Spy' and 'Over the Top'.

In a hot kitchen, all with Italian moustaches, Blackadder supervises
Baldrick. Taking it easy.

GEORGE: Bally well done, Geraldine!

EDMUND: One thing puzzles me, Baldrick – how did you
              manage to get so much custard out of such a
              small cat?

BALDRICK: I'd rather not say, sir.

EDMUND: Fair enough, well, it only remains for me to say
              – Bon appétit, mon Général!

Warming up for a later episode, Curtis would tell the audience, 'The line was, "How did you manage to get so much custard out of such a small cat?" but when we got the cat, it was absolutely enormous, it could have filled a whole crate full of custard bowls! So we found this absolutely tiny terrified little kitten, who I think you'll notice gives a spectacularly good performance. It doesn't do anything else though, it can only find kitten work.'

Less frivolous peril awaited the Captain in the second story broadcast, pitting him against the inhumanity of the military justice system after his shooting of Melchett's precious pigeon, 'Speckled Jim'. Fry claims it to be his favourite episode for the Lear-like extremity of the General's emotions, but its popularity did lead to some terror for the actor years later when he found himself being hounded through the streets by a fan who he thought was screaming that he was a 'fucking pigging murderer!' – rather than excitedly quoting Melchett's denouncement of Captain B as 'the Flanders Pigeon Murderer'.

One inevitable result of the increased cast input was that every episode had a higher rate of excised dialogue than in previous series, be it extra references to 'gobbledegook', or Darling's demolition of Baldrick as a character witness:

DARLING: Sir, I must protest! Not only is the witness a mental defective, he's a famous long-term accomplice of the accused, and his general bolshy demeanour and extraordinarily unpleasant turnipy sort of smell have undermined morale right across the Western Front!

MELCHETT: Quite right! We don't need your kind here, Private, get out.

Or a much longer drinking session between the victorious Lieutenant and the Private:

GEORGE: I think a toast, don't you? To Captain Blackadder and Freedom!

BALDRICK: Captain Blackadder and Freedom, sir! (*They drink.*)

GEORGE: Oh yes, and to my sister Celia as well!

BALDRICK: And her lil horse. (*They drink again.*) And your Uncle Rupert!

GEORGE: And Auntie Madeleine! (*They drink more.*) Oh and I'll tell you who we've missed out – Toby Barraclough!

BALDRICK: Aw, Toby Barraclough! (*They drink yet more.*) Who's Toby Barraclough?

GEORGE: He used to be my fag at school. Remarkable fellow, he used to make wonderful eclairs. He'd drink milk, and blow whipped cream out of his nose.

BALDRICK: Whipped cream up his nose, sir! (*They drink deep.*)

The trickiest edit of all, however, was the need to dub the name 'Massingberd' to cover up the prisoner's praise for the high-flying lawyer who supplied his sponge bag. Just as Curtis smuggled in a reference to his neighbour William Greaves in 'Money', the name of Atkinson's lawyer friend Bob Moxon-Browne was sneaked into the script, only for a last-minute change to be required when this was deemed to be advertising.

There was also a blast from the past present in the cast for 'Corporal Punishment', with Blackadder's firing squad (including Corporal Jones and Private Fraser, in a deliberate *Dad's Army* tribute) very nearly comprising the whole Wow Show team, with Jeremy Gittins standing in for Mark Arden. Jeremy Hardy joined them as the chirpy northern prison guard named, irresistibly, Perkins, and recalls, 'I can't remember why I was cast but I was very pleased – I think there was some surprise that I decided Perkins should be slightly camp and northern, like a young Tom Courtenay. The Wow Show guys were used to improvising in comedy clubs and were very happy to bring ideas, but the full-time actors were more serious, and Rowan was very painstaking. I had a scene with him about an omelette, which he got nervous about because it was quite strange and tangential. I thought it was going to be really good but he seemed to panic rather and said, "Let's just cut it," rather than take a chance on it. I suppose it was very much his show and he wanted to be certain about everything. And I was biased because the scene featured me very prominently.'

Having Steven Frost taunt the prisoner Blackadder just as he did in 'The Witchsmeller Pursuivant' highlights one of the features of this fourth incarnation – the ability to show history repeating itself from series to series. John may have only suggested in jest that the programme only ever had seven plots but, more than ever, *Goes Forth* would prove that Edmund and his cohorts were inextricably linked in a series of repeated sticky situations, described by Lloyd as 'some ghastly karmic prison sentence, being trapped in a cycle, yoked to this scrofulous servant'. Consider Blackadder, usually with Baldrick, languishing in a cell waiting to hear about a fate worse than a fate worse than death from some mad foreigner; standing trial on a laughably unjust charge; being compelled to mastermind a theatrical entertainment against his will; having to risk death and undertake a lethal mission to prove himself against a tiresomely popular brave hero of the hour; Baldrick relishing the chance to get into a dress and possibly marry into the aristocracy; and of course, one or both of the duo ultimately facing an all-but inevitable bloody death.

Two episodes which made extensive use of this reincarnation loop were 'Major Star' and 'Private Plane', which may have been recorded two weeks apart, with 'Corporal Punishment' in between, but which told a single story: the elopement, once again, of Lord Flashheart and the beautiful cross-dresser Bob. As Melchett's unconvincingly disguised driver Private Parkhurst, Gabrielle Glaister made a welcome return to the team, even though it was George's dragging up as 'the Gorgeous Georgina' which won Melchett's heart, cuing an excess of double entendres when the General requests an assignation:

EDMUND: As her director, I'm afraid I could not allow it . . .
MELCHETT: I could always find another director who *would* allow it!
EDMUND: . . . Before a show. After a show, why not? Um, however, I should warn you, sir, that she is a shy and delicate flower, who needs careful nurturing.
MELCHETT: You can rest assured, Blackadder, that I shall pluck her gently.
EDMUND: Quite. Well, I'll see what I can do . . .

'Major Star' also allowed for a roasting of Charlie Chaplin akin to Lord Blackadder's damning of Shakespeare's comic powers, as the writers rushed to make the most of all the twentieth-century inventions and references, from aeroplanes, telephones and gramophones to suffragettes, limbo dancers and music hall, which comprised the latest fads in Blackadder's world. Although Atkinson was to portentously insist, 'If I had been a contemporary of Chaplin I feel I might have been able to exploit myself to the full. I am a visual animal,' in his 1992 mock lecture for BBC2, *Laughing Matters*, he argued that Chaplin's popularity was a mystery to most modern audiences, while Buster Keaton's comedy continued to be as funny as ever, suggesting some sympathy with Edmund's view of the Little Tramp.

Rik Mayall's typically bombastic re-entry into *Blackadder* lore showed that the Flashheart family remained everything that the Blackadders weren't, and the Edwardian Flash was even more famed and adored than his Elizabethan forebear – to Blackadder's disdain, but Atkinson's joy. 'In the fourth series, when Rik played the Royal Flying Corps pilot, I thought it was the performance of his career actually, I thought he was absolutely hysterical. And even though a lot of it was me just putting on a sarcastic face while he did his extremely funny stuff, I just loved it. And when I look at the episode now, I really do think, from Rik's point of view, it was one of the best things he ever did.' Mayall paid as much attention as ever to his character's look, and praised the costume and make-up staff: 'The First World War – you don't kind of think of it as sexy, but Flashheart comes on and his gear is just so sex! Total, *two hundred per cent* sex! It just made me move . . . With Rowan and me fighting in the trench, the only thing that worried me was my moustache. But the make-up operative who fixed that moustache – it doesn't move an inch! And my face is going all over the place, and I'm cascading with sweat, because the costume was so gorgeous I didn't want to take the coat off.'

Mayall raised the bar for everyone in the studio that Sunday night, but besides a cameo from future comedy writer Hugo Blick, 'Private Plane' also gave Rik's best friend Ade Edmondson his one chance to join the *Blackadder* team, playing the legendary Baron von Richthofen, one of only two historical figures to pop up in the series, albeit without any attention to historical accuracy.* Between Flash's derring-do and the quality of the guest stars, 'Private Plane' is surely the most exciting episode of the series, with an audibly electrified audience cheering on the ensemble. Robinson, however, remembers this being as much down to everything that went wrong, as what went right. 'Things went wrong in front of the live audience all the time, it was torture for them! None of us ever knew our words, because we never did any rehearsing, all we ever did was argue about the script, all week long! So poor old Rowan, when it came to the night of the performance, he was just winging it really, and he used to dry about forty-seven times per half-hour. He had every justification for doing so, but it can't have been much fun for the audience.' In this episode, Rowan says, 'I remember the one we had trouble with was "Battersea Dogs Home". In the live recording, in front of the audience, I had trouble saying . . . well, I'm having difficulty saying it now . . .' With the on-heat Bob and Flashheart loudly letting off woof-woofs at every turn, Blackadder's bitter observation that 'It's like Battersea Dogs Home round here' ground the recording down as the star stumbled on the B on every single take until, within a hair's breadth of losing the atmosphere altogether, Lloyd called down from the gallery. *Tell him to say Crufts!'* 'Of course it got this huge and totally disproportionate audience response,' Atkinson says, 'an absolutely astronomic laugh because they loved the fact that I'd finally found a way round the stammer.' 'The audience went *insane*,' Fry laughs. 'But isn't that brilliant of John? What other line is there, except for "Battersea Dogs Home"? Superb on-the-wing producing.'

Their time on *Blackadder* completed, Rik and Ade were just on the verge of launching their own massively successful, typically revolting comedy juggernaut, *Bottom*, while Glaister was only months away from

---

* The real red Baron was shot down in battle, aged twenty-five, in the spring of 1918, and had little interest in the mechanics of toilet humour.

a celebrated stint on the soap opera *Brookside*. Some of the regular cast had no day of rest, though – despite being a Monday, the evening immediately following the recording of 'Private Plane' was earmarked for the filming of *Hysteria II*, and Rowan and Hugh were required for Richard's non-canonical return to Tudor times.

To Be a Victim, or Not to Be a Coward

The genesis of 'The Shakespeare Sketch', otherwise known as 'A Small Rewrite', clearly lay in the difficulties facing the *Blackadder* writers as the group brainstorming got out of hand. After one particularly grievous spot of fixing had been carried out on one of the scripts, Richard turned to John and complained that nobody would ever have done the same thing to Shakespeare. 'I think I would have,' Lloyd replied after a pause, 'some of his stuff was far too long.'

Putting his anger to good use, this gave Curtis the inspiration to see just what the Bard did have to put up with from the Tudor equivalent of Mad Jack Lloyd. Laurie was happy to drop the inbred toff act to take on the more naturalistic role of a morose, arrogant 'Shakey', while Atkinson, still sporting his World War I tache, made very little effort to disassociate his character from the Blackadder family.

PRODUCER:	Bill! Bill, good to see you.
BILL:	Sorry I'm late – traffic was a bitch!
PRODUCER:	Good to see you. Well, the play's going well, isn't it? Looks like we've got a bit of a smash on our hands . . . They always seem to go for the ones with the snappy titles: *Hamlet*! Perfect! Perfect.
BILL:	Act Three may be a bit long, I don't know . . .
PRODUCER:	Act Three may be a bit long . . . In fact, generally, I think we've got a bit of a length

	problem . . . It's five hours, Bill, on wooden seats, and no toilets this side of the Thames.
BILL:	Yeah, well, I've always said the Rose Theatre is a dump, frankly. I mean, the sooner they knock it down and build something decent, the better.
PRODUCER:	Exactly. So that's why I think we should trim some of the dead wood . . . some of that stand-up stuff in the middle of the action.
BILL:	You mean the soliloquies?
PRODUCER:	Yeah, and I think we both know which is the dodgy one.
BIL:L	Oh? Oh? Which is 'the dodgy one'?
PRODUCER:	Er . . . 'To be . . . nobler in the mind . . . mortal coil', that one. It's boring, Bill. The crowd hates it. Yawnsville!
BILL:	Well, that one happens to be my favourite, actually.
PRODUCER:	Bill, you said that about the avocado monologue in *King Lear*, and the tap dance at the end of *Othello*. Be flexible!
BILL:	Absolutely not! You cut one word of that, and I'm off the play . . .
PRODUCER:	Bill, Bill, Bill . . . Why do we have to fight? It's long, long, long. We could make it so snappy . . . you know, give it some pizzazz. How's it begin, that speech?
BILL:	'To be a victim of all life's earthly woes, or not to be a coward and take Death by his proffered hand.'
PRODUCER:	There, now I'm sure we can get that down!

Between Atkinson's arch, anachronistic characterisation and the sitcom's preoccupation with Shakespeare, it's little wonder that the sketch was taken as a lost Blackadder Chronicle by everyone who saw it until Curtis specifically confirmed that it was completely unconnected.* That *Hysteria II* came right in the middle of the biggest burst of *Blackadder* creativity made erroneous links inevitable, especially when the sketch had to be hurriedly presaged by Stephen, lager can still in hand, due to his 'ex-friends' deciding that 'it would be amusing to get pissed instead of going on and doing a carefully rehearsed sketch'. The *Hysteria* benefits would continue to be an occasion for *Blackadder* congregation, with the final show in 1991 featuring Rowan and Hugh reuniting to perform sophisticated safe-sex vignettes (alongside Helen Atkinson-Wood's boyfriend at the time, Craig Ferguson, and the sole female performer, TV presenter Emma Freud, who was by that stage Richard Curtis's girlfriend, and remains so to this day).

More reunions were in store the Sunday following *Hysteria II*, as Miranda Richardson resurfaced to take her place in Blackadder's War, as Nurse Mary Fletcher-Brown. In yet another echo from the past, for her third incarnation Richardson was to play a fluffy funbundle of a lass who ultimately reveals a darker side to her personality, more palatable to the Captain. The big difference in 'General Hospital', however, was that for the first recorded time, Edmund got the girl – only to immediately lose her again, thanks to his own surfeit of cunning. Bill Wallis also made his final appearance in the show, as the unconvincing spy Brigadier Smith – the second red herring in the test case for Operation Winkle.

Despite the deliberate limitations of the trench warfare set-up, then, *Blackadder Goes Forth* managed to expand and enrich existing *Blackadder* lore, from the field hospital to up-diddly-up in the sky with

---

* Nobody seemed to inform BBC Worldwide, however – the sketch is included in the *Blackadder* audio box set.

the 20-Minuters.* But, as Curtis acknowledges, there was only one place the series was ever going to end up. 'It was the condition on which we wrote the series. In a way it had been the arrow shot off at the beginning, that it was always going to land in No Man's Land . . . In a way, that set us free to be as disrespectful as we wanted to be at the beginning, because we were going to be respectful, or at least truthful, at the end.' And McInnerny recalls the looming threat of the final big push: 'The world-weariness of Blackadder was something kind of extraordinary. He was beaten down, he wasn't necessarily going to win every time, and knew he wasn't. Which gave it a kind of darker edge, I think . . . The extraordinary thing was that there really was only one plot, which was "how can we get out of here?" I mean, every episode. But at the back of your mind, you think, "They can't get out of it every week, they're not going to be able to get out of it . . . Oh, they're not going to get out of it."'

Good Luck, Everyone

Goes Forth contained two musical motifs – 'A Wand'ring Minstrel', with echoes of *Blackadders* past, and Weston & Lee's 1915 hit 'Goodbyeee', the full lyrics of which, telling the tale of 'Brother Bertie' on his way to the front, not only have a surprisingly biting irony, but could almost have been written for Lt George himself to lustily and brainlessly sing at an annoyingly loud volume.

> Goodbye-ee, Goodbye-ee,
> Wipe the tear, baby dear, from your eye-ee
> Tho' it's hard to part I know,
> I'll be tickled to death to go . . .
> Bonsoir, old thing, cheerio, chin, chin,
> Nah-poo, toodle-oo, Goodbye-ee!

---

* The filmed flight sequence was expertly pieced together from stock World War I re-enactment footage by the editing team.

As a valedictory theme for the Black Adder's last reincarnation, swapping the military rank-related episode titles for 'Goodbyeee' was an inspired move, leaving little doubt in the minds of those who read the synopsis for the conclusion in the TV listings before settling down to watch on Thursday 2 November 1989, several days off Remembrance Day, that this was the end of the road for the anti-hero. And yet, as Blackadder's last desperate escape plan unfurled (pretending to be mad by putting two pencils up his nose and his underpants on his head), there was still hope that the scheming cad could somehow pull through.

For the cast and crew, however, the knowledge that such hope was fruitless made for a uniquely difficult week of recording. Laurie recalls, 'It had as its backdrop the greatest tragedy of modern man, and that gave the thing a poignancy and a texture that few other things I've been involved in have had, or could have had. We had various histories of the First World War lying about – I don't know who supplied them, where they came from, I suppose the designers wanted photographs – and in an idle moment I think we were all sort of gradually soaking up these absolutely heartbreaking details of life in the trenches, and the loss of that generation.' Atkinson, despite being well versed in dying at the end of the series, concurs: 'I do remember throughout the whole week of rehearsal leading up to "Goodbyeee", and indeed the recording of the episode, having this nasty knot in the pit of my stomach, which reflected the dilemma of my character. It may well be that if you're a serious actor then you experience that kind of thing all the time, you acquire the mentality and the physicality of the character you're playing, but I'd never experienced it before. It was very, very odd, and it was only in that episode . . . The feeling that you were going to die. This was not like your normal pratfalling comedy death either. There was just this extraordinary feeling of dread that I've never felt before.' And even the usually unflappable producer had to admit, 'I went on the trench set for the first time on the last episode. I was usually sitting up in the gallery with the director, and I actually went on the set for some reason, and it was really scary, a really odd feeling, even with an audience there and everything.'

Nevertheless, there was the best part of half an hour of laughs to be had before any conclusion, and at last, the episode attained the truly claustrophobic atmosphere desired by Lloyd for so long, as the old comrades awaited their fate.* Even then, one final guest star joined the cast for this 'last waltz', with sitcom icon Geoffrey Palmer receiving the first star billing in the opening credits since Frank Finlay six years earlier. Palmer was an inspired spot of casting as Field Marshal Haig, carelessly shovelling toy soldiers off the map (a nightmare to reset when a take went wrong) as yet another attempt to move his drinks cabinet six inches closer to Berlin was set in motion. The veteran actor's presence did nothing to alleviate the episode's feeling of claustrophobia, however, only having one scene, far from the trenches.

Atkinson and Palmer would eventually appear on-screen together six years later, in *Full Throttle*, an episode of the BBC drama series *Heroes & Villains*, dramatising the lives of great Britons. In the only dramatic TV role in his career, Atkinson played one of his own heroes, maverick pioneering interwar racing driver Captain 'Tim' Birkin (an ancestor of his friend, the TV director John Birkin), with Palmer playing his despairing father. Even then, the shadow of World War I played a part, allowing Rowan an unabashedly straight reflection on the bloodshed, as the daredevil looked back on his life with his biographer:

TIM: (*examining photograph.*) That's my elder brother, Thomas. He didn't survive the War. So many didn't, Burn. I was one of the lucky ones.

BURN: You were a pilot, weren't you?

---

* As ever, the sitcom was drawing on dramatic forerunners – in this case, R. C. Sherriff's 1928 play *Journey's End*, another tale of time idly running out in the trenches.

TIM: Yes – flew Sopwiths. Still do occasionally! Of
course, for your generation, memories of the
War must be vague, but when I was your age,
I'd known nothing else. And the prospect of
a life confined by the four walls of an office
seemed awfully dull. But I was lucky: I had
money. And I was able to seek an occupation
which brought with it the same excitement
as war, with the same chance of unexpected
disaster, the same need for perfect nerves, and
the same . . . exhilaration, of living in the
shadow of death.

Ben Elton had personal reasons for steering the final episode away
from gay banter towards real tragedy, having famously been contacted
by his historian uncle Geoffrey Elton before the series had even been
completed, haranguing his nephew in 'high dudgeon'. 'He thought we
were taking a cheap shot at the British Army and the suffering of the
soldiers during the war. He served in the army as a Jewish refugee . . .
In his letter he said, "Your father, who sired you (bit of a tautology)
would not be here today if it wasn't for the British Army." And I was,
and am, damn well aware of that, and feel exactly as he does about
the debt we all owe to the sacrifice of the past. I was stunned that he
had this reaction, because I thought the satire was loving, and took
into account the bravery . . . My hand would wither if I was guilty of
disrespect. I wrote back to him and said I had every bit as much respect
as him, and I was quite aware of how much we owe Britain. By which
time he'd watched another episode, and realised he had been a bloody
idiot. He wrote back and said I shouldn't be so sensitive to criticism.
He was clearly a grumpy old man by that time.'

Ben continues, 'It was brilliantly performed, great dramatic acting
– although I think there was worth in the script, and we're proud of

it. That emotional moment I think came from the fact that everybody involved has some sort of sense of the tragedy of World War I. And everyone gave their best – the acting, the writing, and particularly the editing and directing at that point. It was a very brave decision to take them over the top – we wrote, "They put their first step on the ladder . . ."' Twenty-two years on, the finale of *Goes Forth* has in some ways been affected by over-saturation, having come so high on so many 'Top 100 TV Moments' shows, being aired as often as Del Boy falling through the bar in *Only Fools and Horses*, but to a generation of viewers used to *Blackadder*'s silliness, and flippant attitude to death, the resoundingly profound final sequence's power to shock and move was a punch to the gut which still aches. Elton himself admits that there wasn't exactly anything new in a sitcom – or any 'light entertainment' – having some kind of weight to it, when paying tribute to past greats: 'Galton & Simpson really proved that the sitcom – whatever that means – is a medium for real drama, and the more dramatic and, in a way, heart-rendingly serious, bleak it gets, the funnier it can be. Obviously they weren't the first to discover that comedy is very close to tragedy, but goodness gracious, in terms of sitcom, they probably showed us and exploited that fact more effectively than any other writers have done.'

As the doomed soldiers waited for dawn, there was the traditional excess of jokes which would be trimmed out of the broadcast version, such as the celebrated debut of Baldrick as war poet:

EDMUND: Hang on, Baldrick, you can't even write!

BALDRICK: I remembered it in my head, sir.

EDMUND: I cannot believe that there is room in that tiny cavity for you to remember both your name and a poem.

BALDRICK: I think there is, sir!

EDMUND: All right, fire away, Baldrick.

BALDRICK: Who's Baldrick, sir?

EDMUND: *You* are Baldrick!

BALDRICK: Oh yes, that's right – Bald-rick!

EDMUND: Now, recite the poem.

BALDRICK: What poem would that be, sir?

EDMUND: No, look, forget who you are. (*He does so.*)
             Now let's hear the poem.

BALDRICK: . . . 'The German Guns', by . . . Me.

'When Ben gave me the script with Baldrick's poem on it, I just went, "Thank you!"' Robinson grins, and Fry adds, of the Tommy's proud rendition of the word 'Boom' fourteen times, 'It is fine poetry; this was the age of modernism, after all. So Baldrick was perhaps the leading modern poet of his age.'

Then there was the high-level debate as to how the war began, and what it was all for, showing once again Baldrick's Bolshevik tendencies, finally demanding to know why they can't all just stop killing and go home:

EDMUND: The reason, Baldrick, is that HQ have let it be
             known that if anyone even thinks about saying
             'No more killing', they will instantly be shot
             by the Military Police.

GEORGE: Well, there you are, you see, I knew there was
             a perfectly good reason! Well, bravo for Britain
             and a gin and orange for St George! Oh, to
             think that in just a few hours we'll be off, sir.
             Not that I won't miss all this of course, we've
             had some good times, eh? We've had some
             damnably good laughs.

EDMUND: . . . Yes, can't think of any specific ones
             myself. But who knows, there's a couple of
             hours before I have to make that phone call,

> perhaps it will be wall-to-wall solid gags 'til then.
>
> GEORGE: Yes! Oh, yes, um, here's one! Ah, haa, er, no, um. Er . . . Hmm.
>
> EDMUND: Or perhaps not.

Of course, Darling was as doomed as anybody, and it's a testament to McInnerny's performance that even a blotter-jotter as detestable as he could win the audience's sympathy, as Melchett's final brainless/ heartless act was to send him to his death. The actor says, 'My final scene with Stephen, before going to the front line, was brilliant. It is very funny, but it's *awful*. And it was also beautifully shot. I mean, long shadows and high camera angles, which added to the whole drama of it.' 'Tim's a very, very fine actor,' Richard adds, 'and so's Stephen, and just that idea of definitely condemning a man to death and him not being able to object, was moving. There are a few things in that final episode that feel very apt . . . Someone in Rowan's office once told me that 93 per cent of the mail he got – I can't believe he even got a hundred letters, but anyway – 93 per cent was about the final five minutes of *Goes Forth*. I do think it was one of those lucky occasions where we got it mainly right, and where each of the little lines that come before they go over the top has a particular point to do with defeatism and optimism . . . '

Lloyd continues, 'Suddenly they're all together, except for Melchett, and enmities have to be patched up, because at the end of the day, they're all probably going to get killed. The comedy starts to drain out of it in the most horrific way, there was this very odd feeling that you've lost control of it.' Right up until the very final few lines, with the four unlikely comrades lined up before the trench ladders, there's still hope that a typical Blackadder – or even Baldrick – cunning plan could be waiting around the corner (conceivably, in 1989, each character could even have still been alive), until Darling's breathtakingly tragic outpouring of misplaced joy, 'Thank God! We lived through it! The Great War: 1914 to 1917 . . .' finally knocks the wind out of the hopeful viewer.

For the final big push, an extra £10,000 had been spent on creating No Man's Land in a separate studio, away from the audience who could only watch on the monitors. Lloyd remembers, 'The actors were alone, in the dark, with a single assistant floor manager, and had to go over the top, with real explosions going off around them. After the first, shocking take, the studio audience and the production team were stunned into silence, but Richard Boden and I felt it could be done a bit better.' Robinson says the polystyrene scenery was at least partly to blame, as each actor bounced as soon as they hit the ground. It was five to ten, and they had one last chance to get the shot right. John spoke into the floor manager's earpiece, but the reply came from Rowan himself, in 'shattered' tones: 'I'm sorry,' came the voice, 'b-but we can't do another one, it's just too horrible.' 'What do you mean, you're not going to do it?' 'It's really the most frightening thing I've ever done, and we've all agreed we're not going to do it, and I'm very sorry.' And with that, the line went dead.

'It was one of the lowest points, I think, of my television career,' John admits, 'thinking, "The end of this amazing series, and I've just screwed it up!"' Seeing the raw footage of the cast stumbling towards the camera, awkwardly striding towards eternity, it's easy to see why the editing team had worries. However, John says, 'Each person in that room, as I remember, made at least one contribution to the ending sequence.' Chris Wadsworth was chief among them. 'It was so obvious that we had so little material to work with, we had to really slow the pictures right down in order to stretch them in time, but that produced an incredibly good effect with the flashes which were going over on the right of the picture, and the debris that falls over Rowan. In slow motion, this suddenly achieved a grandeur which was not obvious in the full motion.' 'We didn't know if they were supposed to die or not. It was meant to be ambiguous,' Lloyd continues. 'In the editing suite we played the tape of Howard Goodall playing the theme on a piano, recorded in a gymnasium; a liquid, lonely sound. Then the editor said, "What if we played this shot in slo-mo?" "Oh, that's a good idea." "And if the music's slowed down as well it suddenly becomes stronger." Someone then suggested taking out the colour, draining it out to black and white. And the production secretary said, "I know. We could have some poppies. I know where there's a slide of poppies."' Boden had always hoped to end on a poppy motif, and helped to select just the right still of bucolic peace, while someone from sound selected birdsong to complete the effect. Wadsworth recalls the first time he mixed between the drained battlefield and the poppy field, and says, 'It was a Yes immediately – this was a *moment*.' So, John proudly says, 'There were about five or six people contributing bits and when you put it all together, blow me down, it's the most moving thing you've ever seen. It's something no one person can claim credit for. It was a group effort, a well-knitted, bonded team of people who really believed in what they were doing. And luck, too. You watch it and it's like being in church. There's the sudden sense that you've touched something that isn't usually touched. A kind of epiphany, I suppose. It's extraordinary and to this day I feel a fantastic privilege that I was allowed, as it were, in the room where something as wonderful as that happened.

'When I cut the last episode, I took it home to show my then girlfriend, now wife, Sarah. She watched it sitting with her back to me as I watched it in the kitchen of our little open-plan flat, watching over her shoulder. When the episode finished, the tape simply ran out, and she simply sat, unmoving. Fearing that I'd shocked or offended her (or worse, that she'd dozed off), I crept round to look. She was sitting silently, shoulders shaking, looking out into space, her face streaming with tears.' Tim felt similarly moved. 'I just cried. Partly because it was so beautifully done, it was as well done as any scene like that in a drama, and you're also saying goodbye to your character at the same time, it was a very odd feeling . . . I thought it was a kind of groundbreaking thing for comedy.'

And so, with the series beginning broadcast just as these final touches were being put in place, the team could breathe a sigh of relief that the *Blackadder* legacy would not be tarnished – but they couldn't have predicted the unparalleled reaction *Goes Forth* would get from the British public, who hadn't anticipated that the series would reach its apotheosis on such a note of pathos and sincerity. 'I think it was always the idea that that last episode would be this kind of tragic thing, with all the colour draining out of it slowly,' Lloyd says, 'but I don't think we ever decided that it would be the last series. And I suppose in many ways,' he adds, 'we still haven't decided.'

We Will Remember Them

Richard Curtis had helped to prepare the public for Blackadder's last outing by penning a special war diary 'discovered' by the *Radio Times*, setting the scene for episode one.

September 1914 Arrived at the front today. Made contact with General Hogmanay Melchett – a very curious cove. To describe him as mad as a hatter would be to cast an unforgivable slur upon the mental state of hatters all over the world. He is accompanied by an irritating aide-de-camp called Darling. I have resolved to see as little of them as possible. Melchett's idea of a good wheeze is walking slowly towards the German guns in broad daylight wearing a sign saying 'Boo Sucks To You Fritz!' The rumour is that the war should be over by Christmas. The rumour-mongers, however, neglect to tell us which Christmas. The only good news is that I am to be joined by a truly remarkable young batman. His name is Private Baldrick. I look forward to his arrival.

October 1914 Sorry to note the continued existence of Private Baldrick . . . without doubt the least well-equipped human being on God's earth. All I can say, to his credit, is that since this is the worst, ugliest, and vilest place on God's earth, he is at least the right man in the right place at the right time. Must stop now. Rat stroganoff for dinner. With boiled potatoes. Or are they? The only light at the end of the tunnel is that I am to be joined by a splendid young lieutenant, the Hon. George Something-or-Other. Can't wait for his arrival.

December 1914 Just thought I'd grab a spare moment, away from the mindless chatter of George Blancmange-for-Brains. He is the definitive example of English inbreeding. If English aristocratic families don't stop making a point of pointing their members at other members of the family, all will be lost . . .

December 1916 Two years of war – and if I ever knew what we were fighting for, I've forgotten long ago. I'm now fighting for the right not to spend any more time with General Melchett, Captain Darling, Lieutenant George and Private Baldrick. Surely that's not too much to ask?

•

Six weeks later, the same periodical was to reflect the astonishing audience reaction to Blackadder's last push, with one of many letters speaking especial volumes – that the writer was one John Lloyd, the producer's namesake from West Lothian, was pure coincidence: 'It certainly touched the teenagers in the school where I teach, many of them were stunned at the sad ending to the characters with whom they empathised. This comedy, more than any serious programme they had watched on the Great War, affected them deeply. It was a great moment in television history. The impact on young people in "Poppy

Week" can only be guessed at.' It is true that a generation of youths now gazed up at World War I memorials with a new respect and curiosity, but the sacrifice of Blackadder touched a nerve with every age, right up to the last remaining veterans of the Somme. Elton concedes, 'Clearly it is an absolute nonsense, but it has a certain historical integrity, and is done with a great love of British history. *Blackadder* does remind us that there is so much colour and splendour in our history, how filled with madness, love, hate and intrigue it is.'

Over the years, videos and DVDs of the show have been used as teaching aids for History, English and Drama teachers, with episodes being shown as rewards or on the last day of term as a treat. Curtis says, 'I think *Blackadder* is taught in schools, definitely the World War I series is. I think *teaching* might be a slightly rich interpretation of it; I think it is background atmosphere. I've got a feeling that when they do the Regency or the Elizabethan period, at some point after exams or a particularly hard prep, the DVDs go on. What is great is that they don't think, "Oh, here's a hideously old-fashioned thing with people with mullet haircuts." They think, "Here's some comedy I like set hundreds of years ago."' *Blackadder* surfaces in other areas of education too, Richard continues. 'I was judging a poetry competition at my son's school – they were doing, you know, Rudyard Kipling and Roger McGough and lots of other serious long poems – and then one of the boys stood up and said, "This poem is called 'War', by S. Baldrick," and just said "Boom!" ten times. I felt very proud, I didn't realise that I'd contributed to English culture in that way. Well, me or Ben or whoever came up with it. That feeling, that you've left something behind, that was a pleasure to do a long time ago, and it's still rumbling on, is a nice thing.'

The British press in the aftermath of the first broadcast of *Goes Forth* went into *Blackadder* overdrive, as news leaked out that 'Goodbyeee' really would be the team's swansong. 'I think we have gone as far as we can go with it,' Atkinson told the *Sun*, 'It's a shame because the audience was enjoying it most when we were enjoying it the least. It's like selling a car – the best time to sell it is also the best time to keep it.' Thus began years of cajoling for the *Adder* alumni to regroup, and endless press speculation as to when the next series could be set. None of these would come to anything, but a year after *Goes Forth*, Curtis did unveil a new generation of the family, in an entirely new format, with the publication of the 1991 *Comic Relief Comic*.

Now a precious collector's piece, the comic was put together by Curtis, with a bizarre plot co-written with Neil Gaiman, Grant Morrison and others, utilising the talents of the greatest comic artists, ensuring cameos from every Marvel and DC superhero imaginable, plus the stars of *Dan Dare, Judge Dredd, Doctor Who*, the *Beano*, the *Dandy, Viz, Peanuts, The Simpsons*, and even the *Teenage Mutant Hero Turtles*, besides comic cameos from generations of comedy icons, including the Young Ones. In roughly connected absurd strands, the Red Nose trio Lenny, Griff and Jonathan were faced with the discovery that Griff had been taken over by evil Numskull-type spirits, 'projections from the dark side of the human unconscious', who feed on negativity and ignorance, while Ben Elton and Dawn French mutated into gigantic Godzilla-sized warring creatures (Ben becoming 'Student Fridge Sausage Man'). The primary thread, however, was another Scrooging for Edmund Blackadder – in this case, 'Mr Edmund Blackadder OBE', a powerful contemporary businessman who begins by snidely pooh-poohing: 'Comic Relief? I'd rather have a Rottweiler doing hunt-the-liver training inside my underpants than watch that. Hmmm. In two thousand years of recorded history, no Blackadder has ever given one badly forged farthing to charity. And I'll be a scrofulous monkey's somewhat embarrassing uncle if we're going to start now . . .' However, he ultimately saves the world from Griff's misanthropic spirits by donating a splendid shining 50p piece to the charity (the Christmas bonus for a punky Baldrick in footman's livery), thanks to the guidance of a disabled little girl who takes the selfish tycoon on a journey through the areas of society where the money raised on Red Nose Day brings the most relief.

The press thirst for more *Blackadder* was natural, considering the official garlands rewarded to *Goes Forth* on top of the public applause – the BBC certainly saw the weight of awards taken home by the makers and, in great contrast to their rejection five years earlier, made it clear that the *Blackadder* team would have carte blanche to return with whatever historical escapade they could cook up. Curtis & Elton, however, would not be drawn, and had turned down a number of joint movie offers – which, as they were of the calibre of *Police Academy: The London Beat*, was a wise move.

The 1990 BAFTA ceremony provided an embarrassment of riches* for the collective trophy cabinet: in a fitting relay of triumphs, Warren Mitchell was the man to hand over the Best Comedy Award and – ten years after picking up the same gong for *Not* – Atkinson's own golden mask for Best Light Entertainment Performance was presented by Frankie Howerd, Lurkio garlanding Blackadder with fitting ceremony. Atkinson was to pay especial tribute to Lloyd, who batted away the flattery, poured a drink and removed his tie with relief. 'Then, in the background, I heard Princess Anne talking about someone whose career sounded a bit like my own. Suddenly I realised I was being given a Lifetime Achievement Award and nobody had warned me. I went up onstage in a most dishevelled state with no speech prepared, although in the end it seemed to go OK. Princess Anne was fantastic about it, although I felt impelled to apologise to her and her mother for *Spitting Image*.'

On accepting the Desmond Davis Award, John proudly paid tribute to the BBC, announcing, 'I'm very glad to have this totally unexpected opportunity to bore everybody stiff about the values that that great organisation stands for, and to have had the honour for the last ten years to have worked in the most innovative, most exciting, most honourable broadcasting organisation in the world.' But by this stage there was already a feeling that his work was done at the corporation.

---

* Tony also collected the gong for Best Children's Series, for *Maid Marian*.

Despite hosting the pilot for Hat Trick's *Have I Got News for You* (then called *John Lloyd's Newsround*), John was massively relieved to see Angus Deayton finally step into the spotlight by landing the job in his stead,* and he similarly turned down an offer to present the *Holiday* show. Besides stepping in front of the camera for a *South Bank Show* comedy special, Lloyd had begun to move into directing commercials back in 1987, and indeed it was on the set of one madcap advert with Harry Enfield that he discovered he was going to be a father. Shortly after came the BAFTA. 'I remember going home, BAFTAs held aloft, thinking, "I'm the happiest person alive." Life couldn't have been any better at that moment. I had everything I'd ever wanted: the wife, the family, the career, the house in London, the cottage in the country, the cars, the money, the awards. I'd won so many awards that people had actually started booing when I went up to collect them. But from almost the very next day, things started to go wrong . . . Then one Christmas Eve I was forty-two years old and the whole point of anything disappeared. It was just like somebody pulled the rug and I found myself feeling alone and terrified . . . as if some steel curtain had come down with the words "The Life of John Lloyd – that's the end of the first part". I woke up the next day and started the descent into a dark pit . . . it felt as though I was surrounded by poisonous snakes. I found myself thinking, "What's the point of it all?" I'd achieved everything I'd set out to achieve. What was missing from my life was any sense of meaning.'

Fatherhood and solid domesticity was in the offing for most of the *Blackadder* brethren, with Rowan and Sunetra marrying in the Russian Tea Rooms in New York one day after he picked up the Royal Variety Award for *Goes Forth*. With respect for Curtis's wedding allergy, Stephen Fry was chosen as best man, and the groom told reporters,

---

* Although he did jest, with reference to his one-time girlfriend Lise Mayer, that 'Angus walked off with my life, my salary and my girlfriend'.

'I didn't want a massive wedding – so I kept guests to just the one close friend. It was a very cosy affair and I'm absolutely delighted.'

Despite the onset of family life for John, Richard, Ben, Rowan and Hugh, it was a birth of a very different kind which ensured that Atkinson and Lloyd's comedic fortunes would be diametrically opposed in the new decade – only a few weeks after Blackadder went over the top, ITV aired the first ever sighting of the alien known as Mr Bean, on New Year's Day 1990, and a new era began.

Parte the Sixth

A BASTARD ON THE THRONE

It should go without saying that the twentieth-century descendants of Captain Blackadder were to enjoy a considerable upswing in their fortunes, as the inheritors of the ancient bloodline continued to navigate the ladders of the British Establishment. Numerous relatives bagged themselves important roles in the military and the civil services, and built up a greater family fortune than ever before – all during a period when most aristocratic families were losing all power, relevance and, of course, cash, as deference died and the modern United Kingdom evolved. The details of the family's latter-day history, and the biographies of living and more recently deceased family members, however, remains the private business of the present inheritor of the Blackadder legacy, which is as it should be.

Nevertheless, even with the admittedly meagre sources available for research purposes, it is hoped that this history of the family has at least shown that British History is essentially a dialogue, with one half of the equation silenced, and only the winner's voice remaining on record. Henry Tudor, the primary villain of the piece, was surely only ever to be trusted in exact ratio to the distance he could be thrown, and his granddaughter Elizabeth equally thrived on secrets and lies, while perhaps the Hanoverians were, it is fair to argue, equally unfit to rule over this sceptered isle.

The history of Britain is infinitely studded with forgotten heroes, but perhaps it is time, in the twenty-first century, to finally give the four Edmunds kept alive by the faithful documentation of the Blackadder Chronicles and their 1980s BBC TV dramatisations, whose sad lives all ended with true victory just beyond their grasp, their rightful places at the heart of our nation's story. Propaganda may have always been the greatest weapon in any ruler's armoury, but occasionally the suppressed truth can be re-established for all to see – and especially under today's modern, open administration, under a monarch of such honest nobility as our own current sovereign.

So while it's fair to conclude that lies and propaganda may be history in modern Britain, I remain considerably indebted to those whose historical researches and philosophies have enriched my examination of how such lies have malformed our understanding of the past – the great Terry Jones, the venerable J. H. W. Lloyd and, of course, the brave Professor Justin Pollard.*

The truth remains that when a new king is crowned, what he says is the True History, becomes the True History.

GOD SAVE THE KING!

---

* To whom this True History is at least partly dedicated, he having very sadly accidentally beheaded himself flossing his teeth, before publication. He is a great loss to outlandish historical conspiracy theorists everywhere.

Chapter 6

BACK AND FORTH

Chaos theory tells us that if a butterfly so much as breaks wind,
it could cause a cataclysm . . .

You have to hand it to Rowan Atkinson, his career has been exceedingly punctual, with new challenges and projects clicking into gear with precision engineering. *Mr Bean* had a long and complicated gestation period, and at one point John Lloyd was down to be producer of the irregular series, but by the time the original programme went out on the first day of the 1990s, Atkinson had flitted to the third channel, with John Howard Davies directing and producing the debut. It was a coup for Thames TV, who had enjoyed great success with Benny Hill's internationally popular variety shows, but with Hill's brand of saucy humour finally judged to be officially past its sell-by date by Howard Davies himself, Atkinson was poised to step into the vacuum. His own company shared the production credit, Tiger TV – and, latterly, Tiger Aspect – being founded on the basis of an agreement between Atkinson and Peter Bennett-Jones, made in the wake of the loss of Richard Armitage.

Some remnants of Rowan's original idea of using the *Blackadder* powerhouse for his new creation survived for the first special, with old

Curtis material like the 'blind man on the beach' and 'falling asleep in church' sketches being recycled, alongside an exam sequence by Elton which had its roots in a sad monologue from Neil in *The Young Ones* about wasting his entire examination time arranging a selection of good-luck gonks. With that being Ben's sole contribution to the Bean legacy, the core *Blackadder* team dissolved. Curtis himself would step back from being Bean's primary puppeteer as the awkward disaster magnet's career flourished throughout the decade, his burden gradually relieved by regular *Smith & Jones* player Robin Driscoll, as Bean's five years of TV specials began to lead to international acclaim.

The Ever-Growing Bean

Despite the debacle of his Broadway debut and turning down a multimillion-dollar offer to star in a US sitcom, Atkinson continued to make more modest inroads into the transatlantic market, with a successful tour of the *Not Just a Pretty Face* show being captured for posterity live in Boston* but it was the unearthly overgrown schoolboy in the dilapidated green Mini who changed everything. Obviously the near absence of dialogue in Mr Bean's world would be a major part of the character's huge success all around the planet, and within just a few years Rowan could genuinely be said to have attained the status of international comedy icon – even, finally, in the USA. In fact, the one country where Bean always garnered a mixed reception is back home in Blighty, where Atkinson's fan base missed the verbal gymnastics of *Blackadder*, and despite the popularity of the shows, British critics could never bring themselves to applaud Atkinson's move towards all-inclusive family entertainment with as much aplomb as their foreign counterparts: 'I have to say that it is difficult to think of examples

---

* Plus, for Canada, there was a quick job providing links on a *Just For Laughs* Montreal special as a Mountie called Casey Rogers, scripted by Lise Mayer and Jon Canter.

where the gulf between popular perception and the media's perception is as wide as it is with *Mr Bean*,' he was to muse, rejecting the elitist critics who sneered at Bean's proletarian popularity. 'It's because it has no intellectual conceit, or irony or subtext whatsoever. It's the sheer manifestness of it, I think, which is sort of irritating to those who tend to look for more depth in comedy.'

Atkinson took on the form of Mr Bean more devotedly than any other character as the decade wore on. 'I did strange things – like appearing on chat shows in character. I remember going to a book signing as Mr Bean, and I just wrote "Mr Bean" in the book rather than Rowan Atkinson . . . it was a fantastically kind of freeing experience, because I could just submerge myself in this character and behave however I liked.' Videos, books, a hit number-seven single, 'I Wanna Be Elected', Easter eggs, lunch boxes, video games, toys – Bean became, and remains, a major industry, the weirdo's life extended far beyond the run of TV specials by his becoming almost a mascot for Comic Relief, regularly featuring in most Red Nose Night marathons, until Atkinson relinquished the role's taxing physical demands and Bean joined the highest echelons of comedy characters, like Laurel & Hardy and Inspector Clouseau before him, by becoming a cartoon. Mr Bean was certainly no angel, but Atkinson could hardly have got further away from the arch, cool sesquipedalian character of Blackadder in the decades following *Goes Forth*.*

With Atkinson having already co-starred in one Oscar-winning short film, Steven Wright's *The Appointments of Dennis Jennings* in 1988, Mr Bean first began inching his way into the American consciousness via cinema shorts based on the TV show – but despite Bean's tongue-tied nature, a move into features was always on the cards, with 1997's *Bean: The Ultimate Disaster Movie* and the following

---

*   The first link between the two comic universes came in the cartoon, where Bean's antics in Buckingham Palace in the episode 'A Royal Flush' featured subtle portraits of Lord Blackadder and the Prince Regent adorning the walls.

love letter to Jacques Tati, *Mr Bean's Holiday*, doing great business on release. There was a mooted UK invasion when the shorts were made, with Lenny Henry starring in Disney's *True Identity* and Rik Mayall on fine form in *Drop Dead Fred*, but although the latter film can claim a cult following, neither comic shared Atkinson's doggedness in making it big in the States, persevering even if it meant playing smaller roles in films such as *Hot Shots! Part Deux*, *Scooby Doo* or *Rat Race*. It was unexpected, however, that Rowan's movie triumphs would not come along until after his long-time partner had already been feted by Hollywood.

Four Weddings and a Funeral would not set Richard Curtis on the road to becoming a romcom 'brand' until 1994, and then Atkinson would only have a cameo, once again donning the vicar's surplice. A couple of years earlier, however, perhaps the writer's most charming feature had once again cast Rowan as the bad guy – though it remains a sadly uncelebrated part of his oeuvre, being made for TV, broadcast on BBC1 on 23 December 1991, and never repeated or commercially released in the UK. *Bernard & the Genie* was co-produced by Talkback and directed by Paul Weiland, who had helmed *Alas Smith & Jones* after Martin Shardlow's exit, before moving into movies with a turkey of disastrous proportions, *Leonard Part 6*, starring Bill Cosby. Alan Cumming made his heroic debut as the sweet loser Bernard Bottle, whose life begins to fall apart on Christmas Eve until he discovers an ancient lamp containing the bombastic good-time genie Josephus, played by Lenny Henry on full throttle. Atkinson's weaselly millionaire art dealer Charles Pinkworth – 'a very large turd in a horrible pink shirt', in the Genie's summation – is another exemplary bastard, a heartless boss in need of a Scrooging which never really comes, with a bizarre line in camp, florid abuse. Having discovered a priceless collection of Old Masters belonging to two sweet old ladies (and then offered them half of the proceeds), the promising young art dealer with the suitably alliterative name receives the first of many Christmas surprises:

CHARLES: I like the cut of your jib, Bottle. I've been watching you, and I've been thinking about your future with the firm . . . I'm already assessing the prospects for the staff, and so naturally, my thoughts have turned to you . . . and I've made a big decision.

BERNARD: What's that, sir?

CHARLES: You're fired.

BERNARD: Sorry, sir?

CHARLES: Fired, Bottle. I sack ye! I want you and your philanthropic little ARSE out of this building pronto, or I'll arrest you for loitering, and probably throw in a charge of sexual harassment into the bargain.

BERNARD: I'm not with you, sir?

CHARLES: Not any more you're not! And if I have anything to do with it, you won't be with anyone else either . . . Farewell, Bottle, and never darken our doors again. This is a profit-making organisation, not Help the Aged.

BERNARD: Wait a minute. This isn't just a lovely joke before you promote me to Head of Department, is it, sir?

CHARLES: (*Pause, smiles.*) No. Bugger – ye – off!

Curtis's own brand of warm-hearted wonder made the TV movie a Christmas treat which would be fondly remembered by many, perhaps only slightly marred in hindsight by the instantly dating topicality of the pop-culture references (when the Genie grants real wishes to children disappointed by a drunken store Santa, one young boy's transformation into Gary Lineker made perfect sense in 1991, but has jarring connotations for the modern viewer, while a line from Howard Goodall's opening music, when Bernard is on top of the world – '*He's higher than high, if he was a girl he'd be Princess Di*' – seems grimly inappropriate in retrospect). Unsurprisingly, Curtis has kept the screenplay in circulation ever since, with other writers including Linehan & Mathews reworking the script from time to time, to no avail – but then the chances of hitting quite the same note with a new cast are slim. Certainly there's no replacing Denis Lill's show-stealing performance as Bernard's compulsive liar lift attendant confidant, Kepple.

But as Curtis learned the hard way, a hit screenplay is not something you can rush – by the time *Bernard & the Genie* was on TV, he was already years into agonising development on the follow-up to *The Tall Guy*, entitled *Four Weddings and a Honeymoon*, the ultimate manifestation of the writer's irritation with Saturdays spent throwing confetti and listening to drunken speeches. Emma Freud was now her boyfriend's script editor, and proved to be a hard taskmaster. 'She's a very ruthless, almost unpleasant script editor. The thing I dread is the bloody letters CDB, which stand for "Could Do Better". I used to think: "But I've worked on that for a week!"' However, it was his old collaborator Helen Fielding who first steered him away from the whimsical fluffiness plaguing his second film script, urging him to cut a sequence where the hero Charles stalks the object of his affection on her honeymoon, and advising the writer that it was 'time to grow up'. The injection of tragedy into what was otherwise a light romance revolving around a gaggle of toffs was perhaps the strongest element* which turned *Four Weddings and a Funeral* into the smash-hit romcom of 1994 – at the time the highest grossing British movie in history, released in America with a publicity budget of zero cents, but ultimately grossing nearly a quarter of a billion dollars, besides garnering Oscar nominations and BAFTAs. Rowan only had a small role as Father Gerald, but his popularity still

---

* Besides the casting of Hugh Grant as Curtis's on-screen avatar for the first time – and the dress worn to the film's premiere by his then girlfriend Liz Hurley.

made him prominent in all the movie posters that summer – while the only film to rival *Four Weddings*' success that season was *The Lion King*, in which Rowan played Zazu the pompous Polonius-styled hornbill, duetting on the pleasingly Adder-ishly titled 'I Just Can't Wait to Be King!'

Despite the popular estimation of Curtis as a romantic comedy writer fit to stand alongside Nora Ephron, Woody Allen and Neil Simon, he says, 'I didn't know what a "romcom" was! It wasn't like it is now, a form which every young actor has done three of. I thought I was writing an idiosyncratic, autobiographical film about a group of friends, with a bit of love in it . . . but it transpired it was a textbook romantic film. Then I *did* write a textbook romantic film with *Notting Hill*, but then it was because I wanted to; I'd always wanted to turn up at a friend's house with Madonna. Then *Love Actually* was a kind of joke with myself, trying to write ten of them at once.'

From Dibley to Gasforth

Not content with becoming the UK's most successful screenwriter in 1994, a few months after *Four Weddings*' release, Curtis's first solo sitcom debuted on BBC1. With the long overdue ordination of women vicars by the Church of England becoming official in 1993, French & Saunders were the first comics to capitalise on the news, with a sketch in which Dawn donned the traditional garb of dog collar, bad teeth and dandruff – and as Saunders had recently launched her own solo vehicle, *Absolutely Fabulous*, French was the ideal star of Curtis's new series, even if it took the natural clown a long time to accept what was for her a relatively straight role.

During the usual interminable relay of wedding Saturdays, Curtis had reflected on how women registrars seemed to be far more suited to the job than crusty old male vicars, just as he felt that it was the women in his life who had steered him through his most emotionally fraught periods, and he decided that if he could do something to further the cause of women priests, he would. The eccentricities of his own rural Oxfordshire home had already struck him as ideal sitcom material, and marrying the two ideas presented him with his first domestic sitcom set-up, after years of rejecting anything remotely cosy in favour of death, battles and rewriting British History.

Like the majority of the *Blackadder* team, Richard had no religious faith to inspire his new venture, telling the *New Humanist* in 2007, 'I stopped believing before university. This is going to sound facile. But I thought if God is worth worshipping then he must be at least as intelligent and knowledgeable as my own dad, and yet Dad would always forgive me for the mistakes I made. There is no way in which he would look at all the pressures and temptations on a person and then still say that he should be punished. So I thought, well, either God doesn't exist or he is thoroughly nasty, in which case I am not interested in worshipping him.' But *The Vicar of Dibley*'s brand of Anglicanism was more concerned with humanist charity than theology, and as the years went by, the series would double as a mouthpiece for the writer's social conscience and campaigning spirit. Curtis has also admitted that *Dibley* was a specific reaction to years of perfecting Blackadder's lip-curling cruelty. 'I was very interested in writing about the problem of niceness. A lot of sitcoms are about nasty people losing their temper a great deal. And I think most of us in life come across more comedy by attempting to be nice; we're endlessly caught attempting not to offend this relative, or that person, making arrangements we don't want to make, going to places we don't want to be . . . You write a play about a soldier going AWOL and stabbing a single mother and they say it is a searing indictment of modern British society. It has never happened once in my entire life. Whereas you write a play about a guy falling in love with a girl which happens a million times a day in every corner of the world and it's called blazingly unrealistic sentimental rubbish. It has always been that way. Nobody has really written anything intelligent about Shakespeare's comedies. People prefer to write about tragedies because they can't get to the bottom of happiness or comedy.'

On the other hand, being presented with a flock of such incredible freakishness as the pillars of the Dibley community (Hugo the lovable posh dimwit, Jim the stutteringly negative geriatric babe magnet, Owen the creepy livestock lover, Frank the world-beating bore and Mrs Cropley the creator of the Marmite chocolate cake), French's Reverend Geraldine Granger still filled the Blackadder position of being the relatively sane centre of a ridiculous world, perhaps sharing the weight of the inanity with the right-wing head of the parish council, David Horton. It's surely forgivable, however, to see the greatest *Blackadder* echoes in the relationship between Geraldine and her sweet but utterly brain-free verger Alice Tinker. *Blackadder* obviously has no monopoly on stupid sidekicks, but it would be no surprise to see Emma Chambers's Alice cropping up in Baldrick's family tree.

GERALDINE: . . . Alice, can I just share a private thought with you?

ALICE: Oh certainly, Vicar – as long as it isn't about tampons, 'cos I don't understand them at all.

GERALDINE: No, no it isn't. I'd just like to share with you the fact that, well, I hate the people of this village.

ALICE: Oh dear.

GERALDINE: Yeah. Every single one of them. Self-righteous, small-minded, senile, chocolate-scoffing gits and that's true.

The phone rings, Alice answers.

ALICE: Hello, Geraldine's phone. Well, not actually her phone, because the phone can't speak, but Geraldine's phone meaning

Geraldine is usually the person on the
phone – even though actually this time it's
Alice – so I might have said 'Alice's phone,'
but I didn't because it's not mine.

GERALDINE: Who is it?

ALICE: I don't know, they just hung up.

It would be wrong to over-egg the *Blackadder* comparisons, of course, not least because, having set up his new situation in the pilot, Curtis was quick to bring in new co-writers to help him pen the programme, including Kit Hesketh-Harvey and, above all, Paul Mayhew-Archer. Besides remaining loyal to radio production (helming both *Radio Active* and *I'm Sorry I Haven't a Clue*), Mayhew-Archer was a mainstay of family sitcom, with mainstream fare like *Nelson's Column*, *An Actor's Life for Me* and *My Hero* on his CV, and for most of *Dibley's* thirteen years of existence, he and Richard developed such a seamless partnership, a kind of invisible collaboration where Elton's work with Curtis had been explosive, that it became impossible to tell who had written what.

Perhaps one of the few remaining *Blackadder* parallels, as with *Mr Bean*, was the musical input from Goodall, whose reputation grew as he complemented his career as a composer by moving in front of the camera, as the authoritative but playful presenter of his own programmes, including *Howard Goodall's Choir Works* and *20th Century Greats*. Having specialised in devotional music, his rearrangement of 'The Lord Is My Shepherd' for *Dibley* came naturally, but as the maestro for a wealth of shows including *Red Dwarf* there was little he couldn't turn his hand to, so it was natural for Ben Elton to turn to Howard when he needed a jolly, whistled theme tune for his solo sitcom venture, *The Thin Blue Line*.

It had been the best part of a decade since Elton had created a new sitcom, but since *Saturday Live* his TV work had gone from strength to strength, with his stand-up vehicle *The Man from Auntie* lasting for two series, despite a jocularly acknowledged loss of credibility after standing in for Terry on the early-evening chat show *Wogan*. As a writer, although his novels continued to appear with insouciant regularity, the nineties had seen a new career as a playwright bloom for Ben, with Laurie perfecting his insufferable yuppie businessman persona in 1990's *Gasping*, in which executives attempt to corner the market in designer oxygen. In 1991, Elton finally got his chance to craft a role for Dawn French, as the eponymous gossip columnist in *Silly Cow*,* and in the following years his novels *Popcorn* and *Blast from the Past* would both successfully be adapted for theatre, the former receiving an Olivier Award for best comedy. His new sitcom in 1995, however, was a concerted return to traditional light entertainment. 'I wanted to write a sitcom I would enjoy to watch, and although I love *Seinfeld* and *Frasier*, and gritty abrasive stuff or whatever, my favourite of all is *Dad's Army* – although I'm not so arrogant as to think that I can write something like *Dad's Army*.' On the other hand, he adds, 'I don't know whether it's traditional, there's a lot of stuff in it that isn't.'

Elton would never have had any trouble interesting the BBC in a new sitcom, but as Fry suggests, the one crucial ingredient would be its star. 'Essentially, all you have to do is go in and say, "It's a sitcom for Rowan Atkinson and Rowan wants to do it," that's the only thing you need to do to pitch it!' After half a decade on mute as Bean, Atkinson jumped at the chance to craft a new sitcom role, taking it to the BBC under the Tiger Aspect banner (like *Dibley* before it), with Geoffrey Perkins co-producing alongside Elton, and with Rowan's usual knack for timing, *TTBL* debuted on pre-watershed BBC1 less than a fortnight after the final *Mr Bean* TV special, in the autumn of 1995.

Examining the friction between the uniformed plods and deluded

---

* The role would eventually be taken over by Helen Atkinson-Wood, with Elton remaining as director.

 342

detectives of Gasforth (a godforsaken town within the Thames Valley, motto: 'It's not as bad as you think!'), *TTBL* was any character comedian's dream, but Atkinson was to be the heart of the show, even prefacing each episode with a *Dixon of Dock Green*-style monologue in series two. The mirroring of Blackadder's status – this time, rather than being the only modern voice, Rowan played 'an old-fashioned stick-in-the-mud in a modern situation' – meant that there would be no mistaking Inspector Raymond Fowler for any Edmund, although perhaps his strained politeness may have had a tang of Ebenezer Blackadder. It might be taking it too far to suggest that Fowler's anoraky bumbling made the character closer to what Atkinson could have been if he had not been famous, but he was happy to admit, 'I liked the part immediately because Fowler is a man with some amusing contradictions. He has to live in the modern world but he wishes it was different. Fowler rings bells with me, I can identify with his point of view . . . The common link between my parts is that they are establishment – soldiers, vicars, policemen – which must relate significantly to my upbringing. You can believe in the establishment but, by gum, there's a lot to laugh at about it.'

Initial moans from critics expecting instant *Blackadder* levels of brilliance centred on the sitcom's reliance on broad humour and innuendo in the Croft & Perry vein, and also the unoriginal setting, but Elton argued, 'In comedy the obvious is often very good. You've got a vast wealth of background knowledge of television police stations that have gone before. You don't have to establish anything. It's just a sitcom full of completely flawed and fumbling but basically decent people . . . Thank goodness Rowan said yes. I'm always at it like a terrier, but he's more selective about what he does.' The humour's broadness was of course deliberate, and it certainly struck a chord with the average 11 million viewers who tuned in.

Just as he had slipped *Dad's Army* references into *Goes Forth*, there was a certain level of homage to the classic in *TTBL*'s central cast.

Fowler's pomposity of course put him in the Captain Mainwaring role, while his begrudging comradeship with CID boss Derek Grim made the latter reminiscent of ARP Warden Hodges, with a parallel pairing of two mutually loathing leaders who are both on the same side.

GRIM: This afternoon officers from this station – CID officers – led by Detective Inspector Grim – i.e. me – will deploy ourselves operationally in a suspect arrest scenario vis-à-vis and apropos of a terrorism containment action in conjunction with operatives and personnel from Special Forces.

FOWLER: . . . And for those English speakers amongst us?

GRIM: Me and Special Branch are gonna nick a mad bomber. Right, that is all. Kray, Crocket, follow me. (*Exits.*)

FOWLER: Well, we can only hope that their endeavours are crowned with success. There was a time when I was destined for Special Branch, you know? Oh yes, that was very much what my instructors at Hendon had in mind for me – the drug war, counterterrorism, that sort of thing.

GOODY: What happened, Inspector?

FOWLER: What happened, Goody? A little thing called ordinary policing, that's what happened. A little thing called the day-to-day business of protecting the public and keeping Her Majesty's peace. Not glamorous, I dare say. Not 'sexy'. But what we do in this station every day is every bit as important as preventing a bomb attack!

GOODY: We're all part of the Thin Blue Line, isn't that right, Inspector?

FOWLER: That's right, Goody – the only difference being that your bit of the Thin Blue Line is slightly thicker.

The relationship between Fowler and clownish Constable Goody was clearly another to be placed in the Blackadder & Baldrick pile, but there was also a shade of the silly boy Pike about the rookie bobby, while Trinidadian veteran PC Gladstone could be compared to either Jones or Godfrey, as the most senior thorn in Fowler's side. With Atkinson getting his lips around regular long decorative speeches composed for him by Elton, every episode of *TTBL* had his usual stamp of quality, but the star had some competition for laughs against David Haig's astonishingly nuanced portrayal of the dangerously frustrated Derek Grim, with his own show-stopping rants about Fowler's 'wishy-washy, diddums, half-cock, up-yer-social-worker, fol-de-rol, blame-it-on-society, psycho, sicko, socio-claptrap-crap!' Nor was it possible to ignore James Dreyfus as Kevin Goody, debuting a brand of heightened sitcom campery which belied the character's longing for Mina Anwar's Constable Maggie Habib, the one real voice of reason in Gasforth.

The richness of this police line-up was a potent enough recipe for continued success beyond the second series (and a Christmas special featuring Ben as a modern-day Joseph), and the show also garnered a British Comedy Award, but Atkinson decided to lay Fowler to rest at the customary two-series mark. For Elton, *TTBL* was an undeniable step towards the conventional (the first episode even has Fowler forgetting the anniversary of his relationship with sexually frustrated desk sergeant Patricia Dawkins), but he described the show as 'the thing I have the most special love for'. In the BBC's 'Britain's Best Sitcom' rundown, viewers voted *TTBL* in at number 37, which, arbitrary though these polls are, did put Fowler ahead of sitcom legends like Reggie Perrin, Rab C. Nesbitt, Alan B'Stard and Brian Potter. A concerted campaign by *Dibley* obsessives, however, zoomed that series in at a flabbergasting number 3, only to be fought off by John Sergeant's urging to give *Blackadder* the crown – which was ultimately pipped to second place by the nationally beloved *Only Fools and Horses*.

Fry was one other person who was glad for *TTBL*, as Atkinson was happy to offer his best man his first return to sitcom in six years, popping up at the end of the first series as the blatantly Melchettian Brigadier Blaster-Sump, a dangerous lunatic in a kilt detailed to assist Fowler in leading a camping expedition for criminal youths:

BRIGADIER: My name's Blaster-Sump, damn you! Now, you play a straight bat with me and you'll find we'll rub along pretty well together. Use a bent bat, however, a wobbly bat, a bat with a hole in it and bits sticking out of the end, and by thunder I'll crush your young testicles beneath the hard granite of the Mull of Ben Craggy!

HABIB: And those of the party who are not equipped with testicles?

BRIGADIER: The victims of tragic accidents, you mean?

HABIB: No, I mean girls!

BRIGADIER: Fortunately I've never been called upon to discipline a girl! No, quite the other way round, as a matter of fact . . .

FOWLER: Brigadier Blaster-Sump?

BRIGADIER: Yes, young lady?

FOWLER: I'm a trained orienteer, as are two of my officers. We wish only to use your equipment.

BRIDAGIER: DAMN YOU, YOU BITCH! Are you telling me I'm orf the team?

FOWLER: Reluctantly, sir, yes.

BRIGADIER: Oh well, probably just as well. I like to sleep naked when I'm out of doors. Don't want you

young ladies getting all flushed and dampened,
do we?

As the Brigadier frightened off the campers with a terrifying lift of his kilt, this evening's work became not just an episode-stealing cameo appearance, but a crucial step towards comedic rehabilitation for Fry, during what was turning out to be an overwhelming decade for the high achiever.

A Lot of Fry & Laurie

Together and apart, the early nineties was a conveyor belt of creativity for Fry & Laurie, both of them featuring in Martin Bergman and Rita Rudner's sadly maligned *Cellar Tapes* reunion movie *Peter's Friends* – sharing the distinction of being directed by Kenneth Branagh with Elton*, Stephen also joined Ben in adding 'novelist' to his list of careers, with early offerings the quasi-autobiographical *The Liar* and *The Hippopotamus* garnering especial plaudits, and Hugh followed suit with *The Gun Seller*, an espionage thriller, in 1996 (though with his typical self-effacement, he refused to send it to publishers under his own name, and was accepted under a pseudonym). Acting remained their main pursuit, though, with Laurie already moving into straight acting in a central role in 1993's *All or Nothing at All*, while Fry made a return to historical comedy alongside Geoffrey Palmer and Nicholas Lyndhurst in *Stalag Luft*, both for ITV. In the latter, David Nobbs took the old POW camp chestnuts – desperate escape plans, and Nazi guards who are as keen to get away as the prisoners – and folded them into one feature-length comedy drama, allowing Fry to portray both a pipe-smoking upper-class wing commander and a heartless Nazi commandant.

---

* who was given the role of Verges in *Much Ado About Nothing* with the single instruction, 'Don't act.'

347

It was while the colleagues were putting together the second series of their BBC sketch show that they were invited to follow Rowan to commercial TV for the biggest challenge of their joint careers – taking on the mantle of perhaps the greatest double act in the history of English literature. Granada TV had recently launched a pitch-perfect adaptation of Agatha Christie's Poirot stories starring David Suchet, and the winning team of producer Brian Eastman and writer Clive Exton decided that their next bold move would be to return the most beloved creations of the most beloved comic author to the screen. In the fifteen years since Wodehouse had written his last, his celebrated master and servant had sunk so low from their earlier popularity on BBC TV in the guise of Ian Carmichael and Dennis Price that many people knew Jeeves and Bertie only as a grotesque pairing appearing in sherry adverts. Not least thanks to Hugh's performance in *Blackadder*, Eastman felt sure that nobody could embody the silly ass Bertram Wilberforce Wooster and his cerebrally blessed gentleman's personal gentleman Reginald Jeeves quite as well as Fry & Laurie. The duo's proximity in age may have seemed jarring at first to those who saw the valet as a venerable elder, but Fry's already infamous reputation as a brainbox was sure to make the relationship believable.

Wodehouse was a major inspiration for *Blackadder* – he was after all the original Master of the hilarious simile. But despite being lifelong devotees of Plum's work, like Elton, Curtis and most of the *Blackadder* crew,* Fry & Laurie were not quick to accept Granada's invitation. Taking the effervescent words from the page and translating them into flesh, with poor Stephen trying to personify a man who did not walk, but 'hovered' or 'trickled', and whose eyebrow was never permitted to rise more than a quarter of an inch at the greatest provocation, seemed a futile weight to heave onto their shoulders. But it only took a disappointed reply from the production team to the effect that they

---

* Stephen even had a letter and signed photograph from the great man.

would look elsewhere for Stephen and Hugh to bridle, and bite – if anybody was going to mess it up, they decided, it may as well be themselves. Duly, before series two of *ABOF&L* even began filming, Laurie had picked up his whangee and pulled on his spats, while Stephen perfected the art of trickling, and *Jeeves & Wooster* debuted in April 1990.

In the series, Exton tended to pick and choose from Wodehouse's short stories and novels, reshaping Bertie's escapades as the format required, but in doing so he helped to bring whole new generations of readers back to the original prose, albeit with Fry & Laurie in the mind's eye. The friends made one lushly designed and directed series per year for four years running, to great acclaim – Anne Dudley's BAFTA-winning music even led to an LP, *The World of Jeeves & Wooster*, which provided Laurie's real debut as a recording artist. It's true that by series four the scripts had taken jarring strides from the source material,* with bizarrely superfluous kangaroos and a climactic chase sequence straight out of *Benny Hill*, but it is unlikely that any actors will displace Fry & Laurie from the iconic roles in the public imagination for generations to come.

A Bit of Fry & Laurie came to a close a year or two later, but in even odder circumstances. It had become a quiet success on BBC2, with cherished script books accompanying every series. The duo's predilection for dressing up in period costume remained undimmed, be they warring Victorian lovers, or duellists, with Geoff McGivern playing referee:

Hugh and Stephen in period dress on a misty heath, about to duel . . .
REFEREE: Gentlemen, I believe you both know the
                    purpose of this meeting.

---

* Laurie's subsequent claim that they had 'filleted the oeuvre' of Wodehouse's books was not quite the case – besides a few short stories, the entire last novel *Aunts Aren't Gentlemen* remained untouched.

STEPHEN: Thank you, Mr Tollerby, but we have no need of explanation. The circumstances are well known to us.

HUGH: Quite right. Let us be about the business.

STEPHEN: *The business?* Let us be about it . . .

REFEREE: Very well, gentlemen. Sir David, I understand the choice is yours – sword or pistol?

HUGH: Sword . . . The only weapon for a gentleman.

REFEREE: Quite so. That means, Mr Van Hoyle, that you have the pistol . . .

Fatally, for the fourth series, the pair were plucked from Auntie's second channel and upgraded to prime-time BBC1 – two sparkling Footlighters guaranteed to bring a chuckle to the nation on Sunday nights. This was despite the controversial seasonal experiment, *Christmas Night with the Stars*, a year earlier, in which Stephen and Hugh were given the task of fronting an attempt to revive the festive TV entertainment, over twenty years after its cancellation. With Geoff Posner directing, the programme was lined up to be as spectacular as ever, but the hosts' tongues were poked right through both cheeks as they introduced not just vintage favourites Sandie Shaw and Ronnie Corbett but new comedy stars Reeves & Mortimer, Alan Partridge and their ex-decorators Paul Whitehouse and Charlie Higson, in their *Fast Show* guises. Middle England families who sat down expecting a straightforward tribute to light entertainment of yore were banjaxed by Fry & Laurie's gleefully unctuous insincerity and free use of the word 'cock', and so many letters of complaint flooded in that Hugh was compelled to respond, 'I quite understand people feeling excluded from something because they think it's trying to offend them. I don't think either of us would set out to do that.'

But this was Fry & Laurie's curse – with their dinner-jacketed cocktail-shaking antics around the grand piano, they bore all the hallmarks of being respectable – or even 'safe', which is far worse – but in practice they were anything but, and their whimsy was always tempered with bouts of satirical anger, and unapologetic sickness. The final series of *ABOF&L*, despite its new, cosy format and scheduling, was steeped in an unprecedented darkness and weariness, from a tear-sodden climactic 'Soupy Twist' right back to the very first misanthropic moment:

HUGH: I've got this feeling that my life is grey and hopeless.

STEPHEN: Grey and hopeless? Oh now, come on. What are you talking about?

HUGH: . . . Films and music are crap. Books are crap. The streets are so full you can't walk in a town without being pushed off the pavement, the roads are unusable, the trains are a joke, the politicians are so feeble-minded and gutless you can't even hate them . . . You smile at someone in the street, you're either knifed in the kidneys or in court for rape.

STEPHEN: It's frigging useless, isn't it?

HUGH: We're done for. . .

Pause: an incredibly long one. Turn to the camera.

STEPHEN: Well, first of all, m'colleague and I would like to welcome you to this brand-new spanking series of the show that tries to bring a little jolliness into the darker corners of modern Britain, but doesn't.

To make matters worse, whatever mitigating twinkle there may have been in th'colleagues' delivery was dimmed when, one week after the series began, Fry's face was all over the news-stands, the headlines screaming: 'FEARS AS FRY GOES MISSING'.

The cold coals of Fry's 'Bruges episode' have been raked over enough times already – Simon Gray even wrote a memoir, *Fat Chance*, about the debacle – and in retrospect Stephen's diagnosis as a cyclothymic manic-depressive puts the affair so neatly in context that the extent of the dismay at the time has been largely forgotten. Gray's new Cold War play, *Cell Mates*, reuniting his favoured young actors Fry and Mayall, had played to great success on its pre-London run, but within three days of the West End opening on 17 February 1995, Fry had taken his critical notices to heart, and fled the production, leaving only a single note of contrition. As the final episodes of *ABOF&L* were broadcast, their star was wrestling with a suicidal compulsion – not for the first time – which only the thought of his family's reaction helped him to vanquish, choosing instead to secretly abscond across the Channel and disappear. In his absence, the tabloids had a free-for-all on Fry's life, running exposés on his addiction to cocaine (which he insisted was taken as a relaxative from his hectic schedule) alongside the unfolding drama of his self-imposed exile.

Despite the best efforts of the remaining cast and crew, *Cell Mates* was doomed, and the effect of the play's demise was felt keenly not just by the playwright but by Rik, whose highly praised performance had been overshadowed by the media circus surrounding Stephen. A week before the last night he was arrested in the small hours for wandering around Covent Garden brandishing what was obviously a prop revolver at a pair of American tourists, yelling, '*You want some, you mothers?*' and had to make a public apology after a few hours in the cells.* Far worse was to come – the next time Mayall hit the headlines he was in a coma after a horrific quad bike accident in April 1998, during which,

---

* Ten years later, Mayall was to claim in his near-memoir *Bigger Than Hitler, Better Than Christ* that he was upset at the time due to Fry fleeing abroad, pregnant with his child.

he claims, 'I was technically dead for five days. That's why I'm better than Christ. He was dead on Good Friday, but came to life on Easter Sunday. Whereas, on what's called Crap Thursday in my household, I had my accident. Assassinated by the Tony Blair administration. I was technically dead until the following Bank Holiday Monday, five days later. So I beat Jesus Christ five–three.'

Returning to Blighty (and sitcom) to play Blaster-Sump was one of Fry's primary steps back into the fray, as he began to reorder his priorities, at least in his personal life – given the fillip of his triumphant central performance in 1997's *Wilde*, his professional life rapidly returned to breakneck speed. The real tragedy of this life-changing experience, however, is that Fry & Laurie's professional partnership has never recovered. 'I don't remember why we stopped,' Hugh pondered. 'Did they have enough of us or did we have enough of them? Not absolutely sure, maybe I'm so traumatised by the circumstances that I've actually blanked it out, I've got some false memory syndrome. And I'm going to imagine that they sent us a big cake, you know, "Any time you want to come back!" . . . That probably didn't happen though. I think they just had enough of us.' Despite the odd fleeting reunion*, the double act has not collaborated on any of their own comedy together since a positively final performance of 'The Hedge Sketch' from the one-off *Hysteria* successor *Live from the Lighthouse* in 1998. That is, of course, unless you count *Blackadder Back and Forth*.

Time for Blackadder

From the moment Blackadder went over the top, there had been incessant rumours about where the family's filthy genes would show up next, but what was unexpected was that the eventual impetus for his return would come not from within the group, but from the government.

---

* With both colleagues hinting at some kind of new project in 2012

Or, at least, from the New Millennium Experience Company who were trying, to the great mirth of the nation's satirists, to find something to draw the crowds to an enormous dome in Greenwich, which had been proposed by John Major's government, and adopted by New Labour at great public expense. One confirmed attraction was the Sky-funded Skyscape cinema, but finding something to be actually shown on this mega-screen several times a day for the whole of 2000 was no easy task – initially, a special *Only Fools and Horses* was mooted, but at such an epochal time, nothing could fit the bill better than *Blackadder*. What a coup it would be for the beleaguered Millennium Dome to reunite the team after a decade apart – and as Fry insisted at the time, 'I'm extremely loath to join the usual, sneering, British, "it's-all-so-crap-before-it's-even-happened" lot. There would be nothing clever in doing *nothing* about the Millennium.'

The dream booking, however, came up against the inevitable complication of the team's irreconcilable schedules. Richard was immersed in the production of the second Hugh Grant vehicle *Notting Hill*, with Tim prominent in the cast. Ben, meanwhile, having followed *The Man from Auntie* with the more variety-filled *Ben Elton Show* on BBC1, was preparing his own move into films and pre-empting Curtis by directing, as well as writing, his debut. His 1999 novel *Inconceivable* was openly inspired by the Eltons' own experiences of fertility treatment – treatment which was ultimately more than successful, resulting in the arrival of twins halfway through the filming of the screen version, *Maybe Baby*. With Hugh developing his burgeoning career as a matinee idol by starring as the sexually beleaguered BBC executive Sam Bell and Rowan cropping up as tactless gynaecologist Mr James, a full *Blackadder* reunion was not on the cards.

Nobody, however, told Lloyd that the Millennium deal was out, he having also been enticed back to comedy production in the country's hour of need, after a decade of family life, funded by directing commercials including Leslie Nielsen's *Police Squad*-aping cider ads, (which led to John turning down a lucrative offer to direct a *Naked Gun* sequel), and the highly successful Barclaycard series which was at first supposed to star Michael Palin, but evolved into a spy spoof featuring Atkinson as the inept operative Richard Latham. Of his change of career, Lloyd acknowledges, 'It's completely, utterly amoral and without justification apart from the fact that I've put in my time as a public servant on very small wages for very long hours, and this is a way for me to see my children, which is more important to me than certainly any sort of career I might have had . . . this is the way of the world: the more worthless your profession – PR people, advertising and marketing, bankers, for God's sake! – the more you're paid. It's an inverse law of worth. It's rotten to the core, really.'

Faced with the task of entertaining Dome visitors, John recalls, 'Ben wasn't free, and he and Richard didn't want to do it, so I got the job. Because they didn't want to write it, we were going to do a sort of historical sketch show,* linked by Blackadder and Baldrick. Years ago I said to the BBC that they should invest in doing the history of Britain from a Blackadder perspective. So, slightly like what they've done with that rather wonderful adaptation of Terry Deary's books, *Horrible Histories*, you can actually do teachable school history, say the Battle of Hastings, and have Tony and Rowan drop in for comments, you know, "Well, Baldrick, what did you think of William the Conqueror?" "Oh, I didn't like him sir, I thought he was a big fat bastard . . ." And you'd have proper actors doing sketches and so on. I thought that would be worth spending five years of your life on.' With Atkinson and Robinson confirmed for this journey through British History, young comic writers including *Black Books* and late-period *Spitting Image* scribes Kevin Cecil

---

* This idea was adopted by the BBC for Jon Plowman's *The Nearly Complete and Utter History of Everything*, an epic special aired in the first days of the new millennium, and featuring a truly incredible roll-call of comedy stars appearing in epochal scenarios, including Brian Blessed's debut as a very loud Henry VIII and Stephen and Hugh joining Patrick Barlow, James Dreyfus and Robert Bathurst for an investigation into how the crowned heads of Europe divided the Continent with the Treaty of Westphalia in 1648.

and Andy Riley were already planning out suitable sketches and links. 'Then when Ben heard it was going to be done under the *Blackadder* name without him, he came back with Richard. The other writers who'd been commissioned were let go, and I didn't hear any more. By the time they'd got it going I wasn't free, but I wasn't wanted much anyway. It was very much "let's get rid of John – he's annoying". I was dreadfully hurt and cross, but I bit my tongue and didn't do anything about it.'

By the time the £3 million Dome project, then entitled *Time for Blackadder*, was unveiled at the Montreux TV Festival in April 1999, Curtis & Elton had put their heads together to bash out a short but cinematic trawl through Anno Domini, and all the cast had been squeezed into a tight schedule of recording on location and at Shepperton Studios in May and June. Richard joked, 'I think we're the only thing they've got for the Dome, frankly – and all for £57 per family. It's an irreverent trek through British history – a time-travel adventure story consisting entirely of people who are either rude or stupid.' At the same time, Rowan insisted, 'Bringing *Blackadder* to the big screen has always been an ambition. I am delighted to be realising it to celebrate the arrival of the twenty-first century. But I'm a bit worried at the prospect of travelling through time with Baldrick . . .'

Nobody had a tougher schedule than Tony, who was well established in his third or fourth career by the turn of the millennium. *Maid Marian* had flourished – though not matured – over four series, a range of comic-book spin-offs and a pantomime-esque live show before CBBC called it a day in 1994. A new series relocating the cast to Roman Britain with Kate Lonergan as a feisty Boudicca never saw the light of day, but in a pleasing echo of Curtis's sponsorship of Robinson, the actors who portrayed the Sheriff's two right-hand goofs Gary and Graeme, David Lloyd and Mark Billingham, began their own successful writing careers with another historical kids' sitcom, *Knight School*, thanks to Tony's patronage. Although he continued to write and perform, in the same year that he took off the Sheriff's goatee for the final time,

Robinson made his debut as presenter of Channel 4's *Time Team*. The revolutionary archaeological series was created by Tim Taylor, who had attempted programmes featuring live historical digs in the past, but it wasn't until rainbow-jumpered archaeologist Professor Mick Aston met Tony on holiday in Greece and discovered that the Baldrick actor had a genuine obsession with history that the winning formula was devised, and by 2000, Tony had racked up not just seven series of digs all over the country, but had branched out into presenting series on an array of topics, as the fourth channel's most ubiquitous documentarian, and authored a whole avalanche of tie-in non-fiction books. When the call to get back into the stinking breeches came, he heeded it, but admits, 'All of us were off doing wildly different things, the production was rather tortuous. There were a couple of scenes where I just disappeared. Rowan was walking down a corridor with me and then in the next shot I just wasn't there, because I had to go off and do a couple of episodes of *Time Team*. I was filming on a pretend Hadrian's Wall just outside Guildford for *Blackadder*, and at the end of that day's filming, I was driven up to the *real* Hadrian's Wall to start excavating!'

Although John was not on the team, there was a strong crew committed to bringing *Blackadder* to the big screen, with Geoffrey Perkins and Peter Bennett-Jones keeping an eye on things for Tiger Aspect (producer Sophie Clarke-Jervoise was eight months pregnant at the time), and Paul Weiland in the director's chair. 'The strength of *Blackadder* had always been that it was just dialogue in one room, very witty dialogue,' Weiland acknowledges, 'so what we had to do was give it a sense that this was going to be a bigger treat than usual. You get all the qualities of the old *Blackadder*, but on a scale that is like a huge American movie.' 'Paul was rather sweet about it,' John says. 'He said, "This is ridiculous, you should be doing this job." Of course, I had directed an awful lot of stuff in the meantime.' In John's absence, Richard was mindful to say, 'We've always made a lot of changes in rehearsal, because the standard set by John was that we should try and make every single line as funny as we could.' Tony admits that this occurred 'Much, much less – John always egged us on, because I think he just wanted to see as many comic alternatives as possible, whereas with Richard in the room for the vast majority of the time, he would allow us to play with his ideas, but keep within much tighter parameters. And I think everybody respected that, nobody worried about it, it was just a different way of working.'

Nonetheless, when the central cast were assembled, some habits were impossible to kill off, as Curtis was happy to admit when interviewed for the *Sunday Times* during the filming: 'Today we've got Hugh saying a line about how excited he is. Well, that started life as, "I'm as excited as a person who's just bought a jam doughnut only to discover that he's got a double portion of jam." With all the actors chipping in their ideas, it has developed into, "Gosh, this is as exciting as discovering that, due to an administrative error, the new boy in dorm is in fact a girl with a large chest, a spirit of adventure and no pants." In fact it had gone further, and at one point the girl had "big breasts, two friends and a packet of condoms", but we got worried about the kids in the Baby Dome audience, so that got cut out.' 'I actually went to the first day of the readthrough,' Lloyd says, 'and it was fairly obvious that the actors weren't happy. Because however difficult *Blackadder* was – and we did get cross with each other, heated arguments and pain on all sides – the point was: it worked. And I think Richard and Ben decided they could do it better on their own, which proved not to be the case. Because although it's a very professionally produced piece of work – there are funny moments and it looks great – it doesn't have the *Blackadder* spirit.' 'We missed him without any doubt,' Robinson adds, 'but having said that, the working relationship between Richard and Ben on one hand and John on the other had broken down to such a degree that it wasn't possible, so I think I was fatalistic about that. I know that John was very hurt not to have been asked to direct it.' 'I understand that the group rewriting process had been very painful, especially for Richard,'

The final historical meeting of Ade Edmondson and Rik Mayall made for one of *Blackadder*'s most explosive half-hours. The real Manfred von Richthofen was only twenty-five years old when he was shot down in 1918, and had little interest in lavatorial humour.

'One more, Bob?'

Masters and servants: The meeting of the top brass and the ignoble Tommies provided the precise rigidity of hierarchy that *Blackadder* required to thrive. Atkinson: 'He's got a ladder to climb, but he's so cynical about climbing it. And he's also cynical about those who are climbing up towards him. He's just a fantastically cynical man.'

'Just because I can give multiple orgasms to the furniture just by *sitting* on it, doesn't mean that I'm not sick of this damn war: the blood, the noise, the *endless poetry*…' The Lord Flashheart was allegedly at least partly based on the dashing Piers Fletcher – old friend of Lloyd, Oxford contemporary of Curtis, former soldier, and current producer of *QI*. He modestly refuses to accept the honour – but if called, he does still answer to the name of 'Flash'.

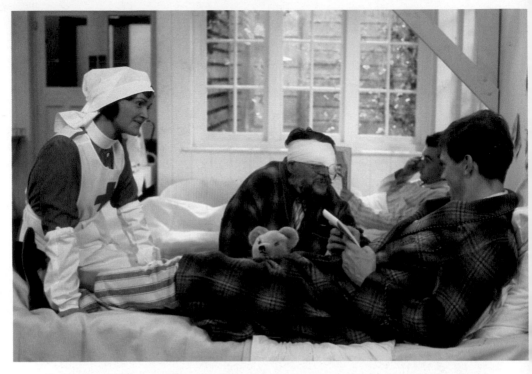

The descendents of Elizabeth, Ploppy and Ludwig having a whizzy-jolly time
while millions die all around them.

Colthurst St Barleigh of the Bailey has Darling on the ropes:
'Captain, leaving aside the incident in question, would you think of
Captain Blackadder as the sort of man that would *usually* ignore orders?'

Cluck cluck, gibber gibber, my old man's a mushroom, et cetera –
not to say, 'Wibble' and similar gobbledegook.

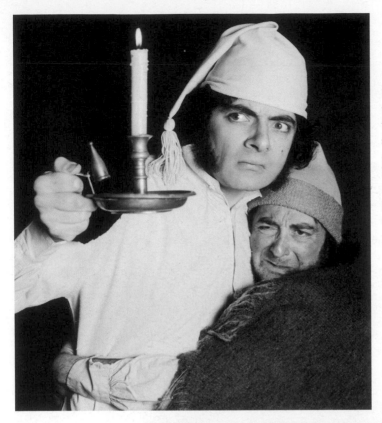

'To edge his way along the crowded paths of life, warning all human sympathy to keep its distance, was what the knowing ones call "nuts" to Scrooge' – and it suited most of the Blackadder family equally well.

The *fin de siècle* fraternity posing on-set in the summer of 1999. Rowan Atkinson's goatee beard would go on to establish a cult all of its own.

John Lloyd recalls the creation of one of the greatest TV moments of the twentieth Century: 'You watch it and it's like being in church. There's the sudden sense that you've touched something that isn't usually touched. A kind of epiphany, I suppose.'

At the going down of the sun and in the morning, we will remember them…

BLACKADDER
© BBC tv MCMLXXXIX

Lloyd concludes, 'so I quite understand he didn't want to go through that again. But without it, it didn't really work. Anyway, thankfully, we've long since made up.'

In time, the show's star would echo John's misgivings. 'It was very difficult, and in my opinion not wholly successful. I don't much enjoy *Back and Forth*. I mean, I think it has its own particular qualities, but it was one of those classic things, really – it was made to a commercial brief. It was the Millennium Dome Authority wanting something to raise the profile – and I suspect attempting to glean a lot more respect from the population for their enterprise. I thought it was misjudged, really, the whole thing . . . I do remember John being in rehearsals, although his role was definitely more peripheral than previously. Whether his lesser input was responsible for what was, in my personal view, the least successful half-hour of *Blackadder* we ever made, is not for me to say – and that half-hour was, ironically, also by far the most expensive that we ever made!' Elton has also confessed in hindsight, 'We had to do the whole two thousand years in twenty-eight minutes, it was pure frustration, in that it was all we could do,' but even at the time, during the height of promotion, he was characteristically sincere in admitting, 'Look, I don't know if what we've done is ideal, to be honest. We did resist it but it turned into a bit of a "Your country needs you" thing. You don't normally start projects with a venue and say, "Well, let's fill it." But we did get very excited about it. It's a convivial family entertainment with familiar friends, faces, and Stephen Fry in the shortest skirt in history, and that will be an extremely pleasant way to spend twenty-five minutes. But it's not the next place for *Blackadder*.'

The Greatest Genius Who Ever Lived

It's difficult to gauge the success of a millennial comedy special, if only because they don't come round very often. Reneging on the lessons learned from *The Black Adder* by taking Edmund out of the three-camera set-up and dismissing the audience was always going to be a gamble comedically, but as fan service, *Blackadder Back and Forth* was undeniably cunning, managing to introduce at least two new incarnations of the Adder (with allusions to several more, male and female, as the sumptuous opening credits pan over Blackadders through history, from the Bayeux Tapestry to Thatcher's Cabinet) and giving an ultimate conclusion to the Chronicles, in just two minutes short of a half-hour.

The time restrictions did require a certain amount of backstory-skipping – there's no real explanation as to who this Lord Blackadder is,* and why his closest friends just happen to be Lady Elizabeth, Bishop Flavius Melchett, Archdeacon Darling and some military type called the Viscount George Tufton-Bufton. Nonetheless, it is New Year's Eve 1999 at Blackadder Hall (a portrait of the brave Captain B adorns the dining-room wall), and this Blackadder has a ridiculous bet to win, abetted by 'the man who empties the septic tank', temp chef Baldrick. One irksome truism about bringing Blackadder into the present day is that where once Rowan's character was a modern voice surrounded by antiquated idiocy, his sneering at contemporary values tends to make the character more of a right-wing throwback, an establishment-supporting bounder which it's harder to like. This Blackadder is interested in nothing but cash and sex, but gets more than he bargained for when his plan to hoodwink his friends by pretending to travel through time, collecting their chosen ancient artefacts, is spiked by Baldrick's unwitting savantism in building an actual working machine, to the design of Leonardo da Vinci (not, sadly, Acropolis):

EDMUND: Well, Balders, this is a turn-up for the books
           – you have built a working time machine and

---

* Although it's easy to imagine the Edmund who was converted to charitable causes in the 1991 comic capitalising on his donations to bag a peerage from New Labour.

are therefore, rather surprisingly, the greatest
genius who ever lived.

BALDRICK: Thank you very much, my Lord.

EDMUND: Right, let's get out of here, shall we? Can you
set the date so we can get home?

Baldrick reaches up to turn switches and pull levers.

BALDRICK: Yeah, I just turn that there, pull that there,
reset that there, pull this lever like that and
the date should come up . . . But unfortunately
it doesn't, cos I was gonna write the numbers
on in felt pen, but I never got round to it.

The counter spins – it's actually a fruit machine.

EDMUND: Right. So the date we're heading for is actually
two watermelons and a bunch of cherries?

BALDRICK: That's right, my Lord.

EDMUND: In other words – we can't get home.

BALDRICK: Not as such.

EDMUND: Excellent . . . Rather a spectacular return to
form after the genius moment, Baldrick.

This device was obviously ideal for shoehorning in as much British
history as possible – and for ramping up the cinematic dimension by
bringing our heroes face to face with budget-slaking dangers, from
an outraged T-rex (Baldrick's trousers causing the extinction of the
dinosaurs) to a *Star Wars*-referencing battle out in the distant realms of
future space. Time travel had long been a particular interest of Curtis's,
and at one point there were even thoughts about making a *Doctor Who*-
spoofing *Blackadder* special with Edmund and Baldrick in the Tardis,
called *Doctor Whom*. This transmuted into the Comic Relief special
The Curse of Fatal Death, a non-canonical spoof filmed at the start of

the year and starring Atkinson as the 'Ninth Doctor', facing off against Jonathan Pryce's Master and the Daleks – though, luckily for him, with Julia Sawalha as his companion rather than Baldrick. As this Doctor regenerates several times in the story, the fact that both Jim Broadbent and Hugh Grant get their fleeting moments in the Time Lord's costume may have led viewers to believe that this was a Curtis script, but the Comic Relief supremo had called in sitcom scribe Steven Moffat to write the most fanboyish lampoon imaginable, exactly a decade before Moffat took over the reins of the revamped franchise itself. The tables were turned in his first series as script editor of the show, for which Curtis provided his first completely straight time-travel tale, *Vincent and the Doctor*, an emotionally charged series highlight in which the Doctor helps Van Gogh to conquer his demons, and finally realise the magnitude of his artistic legacy. With this success under his belt, in 2012 Curtis began a further time-travelling tale for his next romcom project – *About Time* – still drawing inspiration from his original teenage heartbreak.

Moffat's 'timey-wimey' shenanigans would be good practice for Blackadder's own journey through time and space, in Baldrick's carriage-clock-shaped time-shed. Robinson returned to Sherwood Forest as the pair bumped into Robin Hood – a Flashheart progenitor with a band of 'woofing' Merry Men and gay jokes straight out of *Up the Chastity Belt*. Mayall was on fine form after his difficult recovery, buoyed by the addition of a new on-screen paramour – as Curtis announced, 'For Maid Marian we needed someone new, so we thought we'd pick the best-looking woman in Britain, nay the world,' and model Kate Moss didn't need to be asked twice to have the honour of joining the by now immortal *Blackadder* team.

Then came the briefest glimpse of the first-millennium equivalent of Captain Blackadder's squalid bit of line on the Somme, as the time machine homed in on Blackaddercus, a centurion fated to die on Rome's Northern Front:

BLACK'US:	Brilliant. Just brilliant.
BALDRICKUS:	What, O Centurion?
BLACK'US:	We're facing a horde of ginger maniacs with wild goats nesting in their huge orange beards, or, to put it another way – the Scots. And how does our inspired leader Hadrian intend to keep out this vast army of lunatics? By building a three-foot-high wall – a terrifying obstacle, about as frightening as a little rabbit with the word 'boo' painted on its nose.
GEORGIUS:	Oh come now, Centurion, I won't have that. This wall is a terrific defence mechanism. Why, surely you're not suggesting that a rabble of Scots could get the better of Roman soldiers? Great spirit of Jupiter, our culture is centuries ahead of theirs! Why, we have toilets! And wipe our bottoms with vinegar-soaked sponges!
BLACK'US:	Yes. And they wipe their bottoms with Roman soldiers.

Whether by design or not, the Roman Blackadder just happened to be placed precisely contemporary to *Chelmsford 123*, and, for Fry's General Melchecus, even used the same trick of having his dialogue spoken in Latin – agonisingly delivered from a series of cue cards (dubbed 'Intelligent Person Boards' by Stephen). It can only be presumed that if the Emperor Hadrian had shown up, he would still have been played by Bill Wallis.

The show's first return to an established epoch exemplified the writers' celebrated disdain for conventional history, as the modern Edmund came face to face with Queenie, Nursie and Melchie. Despite the loss of the cosiness of the studio set, the Tudor trio didn't look a day older on film, but (besides the unsavoury element of product placement for Dome sponsors Tesco's, even if that was just to make a mockery of the concept of supermarket loyalty cards) the Elizabethan stop-off was one which it wasn't wise to think about too intently. Chief among the brain-busting anachronisms was the presence of Shakespeare, clutching the script for *Macbeth*, but you can't blame Curtis for taking his chance finally to directly attack the man who had made his schooldays so miserable, sixteen years after he provided 'additional material' for *The Black Adder*. The playwright's appearance may have been a touch of 'stunt casting', but Curtis explained: 'Colin Firth has actually refused to do all sorts of things for me throughout his career, so we thought we'd pay him back by having the shit kicked out of him by Rowan.' While they were at it, they also got the boot in on the director who had cast Brian Blessed, Fry & Laurie and Elton in his films:

Blackadder knocks Shakespeare down with one clean punch.

EDMUND: That is for every schoolboy and schoolgirl for the next four hundred years. Have you any idea how much suffering you are going to cause? Hours spent at school desks trying to find one joke in *A Midsummer Night's Dream*? Years wearing stupid tights in school plays and saying things like, 'What ho, my lord' and 'Oh look, here comes Othello, talking total crap as usual'? Oh, and . . . (*a further kick*) That is for Ken Branagh's endless uncut four-hour version of *Hamlet*.

SHAKESPEARE: Who's Ken Branagh?

EDMUND: I'll tell him you said that. And I think he'll be very hurt.

The final stop-off on this patriotic odyssey revisited another familiar period, but far away from the goings-on in Prince George's household – indeed, as the Battle of Waterloo is in full flow, presumably after the real Prince's death. Reprising the role of Wellington was an especially strange experience for Fry, as in the same year he also played the Duke in a Spanish–French–British co-funded farce, *Sabotage!* – essentially a screwball romantic comedy with David Suchet's Napoleon as the hero. The casting of his counterpart in *Back and Forth*, on the other hand, allowed Fry to share a comedy cast list with his Cambridge contemporary Simon Russell Beale, twenty years after failing to lure him into Footlights. McInnerny was also called upon to originate two new members of the extended Darling family to play the aide-de-camp of both leaders, in addition to his Archdeacon.

The crushing of Wellington, like the murder of Robin Hood and the introduction of Shakespeare to the ball-point pen, requires Blackadder to return to all the scenes of his time-meddling – the reason for the second time round being, of course, flagrant Francophobia. With thousands of years of British History to celebrate, *Back and Forth*'s ultimate declaration of national pride revolves solely around the fact that we are not French – which is to say, we are not garlicky and effete. As ever, the anti-French sentiment was taken to a cartoonish degree, with Edmund's alternative universe guests singing 'La Marseillaise' and eating an enormous garlic cake, but that only a xenophobic fear of poofiness compelled Blackadder to undo his historical sabotage was not exactly the kind of thing to inspire the swell of British pride which the average Dome visitor was expecting.

This would not be the end of the meddling from the last of the Blackadders though, as an innocent exchange with Baldrick inspired a final cunning plan which, echoing Baldrick's unspoken scheme on the Somme, is 'as cunning as a fox what used to be Professor of Cunning at Oxford University, but has moved on and is now working for the UN at the High Commission of International Cunning Planning':

BALDRICK: As we approach the end, my Lord, what do
you think we've learned on our great journey?

EDMUND: Good question, Baldrick. I suppose I've
learned that I must buy you a much stronger
mouthwash for Christmas this year. How
about you?

BALDRICK: Oh I don't know. I suppose I've learned that
human beings have always been the same
– some nice, some nasty, some clever, some
stupid. There's always a Blackadder and
there's always a Baldrick.

EDMUND: Yes, very profound, Baldrick.

BALDRICK: Also, it occurs to me –

EDMUND: Oh God, there's not more, is there?

BALDRICK – if you're in the right place at the right time,
then every person has the power to go out
and change the world for the better . . .

Of course this sentimental claptrap does not wash with a cynic like
Edmund, who argues that change can only come from 'huge socio-
economic things that individuals have no effect on' – unless, of course,
they are world leaders . . . like a king. How the Lord's meddling with
time finally allowed him to achieve what his DNA had been reaching
out for since time immemorial – a safe seat on the British throne – we
shall probably never know, but if you want to make a final sign-off from
a sitcom character, there is no surer way of doing it than giving them
what they have always wanted – the Trotters became millionaires, and
Blackadder became King Edmund III (his ancestor's thirty seconds
as monarch presumably not really counting). With his consort Maid
Marian on one side, and the scruffy Prime Minister Baldrick on the
other, at last Blackadder takes it all, becoming that least likely thing
in any British sitcom: a winner. The new monarch and his powerless

sidekick even granted special interviews to the *Sunday People*, explaining how this new style of democratic fascism worked, to the benefit of Britons everywhere:

Q: Sir, given your sometimes robust comments on modern architecture, can you share your thoughts on the Millennium Dome with us?

KING E: Certainly, it's the most beautiful and exceptional piece of architecture since the Parthenon, and I will be spending the money that the Prime Minister paid me to answer that on a very fast new car . . .

Q: Prime Minister, do you feel that your socialist plans to make the monarchy more relevant in the twenty-first century have been in any way changed by the deep and abiding debt of gratitude you owe your close friend King Edmund?

BALDRICK: I am certainly happy to concede that the King had a strong influence on my decision to make the monarchy more relevant in the twenty-first century by giving the King total power over everything except the price of a dog licence.

This epic final twist allowed for a jubilant close to the mini-movie, thanks to the rousing new orchestration of the theme by Howard Goodall. For all the comedic imponderables in *Back and Forth*, it unquestionably looked, and sounded, wonderful, and Goodall's cinematic soundtrack was a large part of that. 'It was great actually,' he recalls. 'The whole nature of it required there to be a bigger scale, and it was nice to do the score and the song at the end with those bigger resources, and a great recording. I knew by then that the BBC had lost all the original recordings we'd made, so it was nice to have a higher-quality version of it. From time to time I've thought of going back to the King's Singers people who sang on the originals, Simon Carrington, and then Jeremy Jackman who sang series two, and re-recording them from scratch.'

Another problem with *Back and Forth* is that, since its final airing in the Skyscape cinema, it has only been seen out of context. Dome visitors approached the cinema past enormous cut-outs of the *Blackadder* team, posed for photographs with Baldrick's time machine, and then queued up to watch the then exclusive film on a huge screen, with a laughing audience all around them. The special was eventually broadcast, after much corporate back-stabbing, on both Sky and BBC1, and though the latter broadcast did include an audience recording, the commercially available version lacks any of that atmosphere (even if it did come bundled with *Baldrick's Video Diary*, a behind-the-scenes featurette in which everyone is interviewed, bar Baldrick himself). Visitors to the Dome could also buy a special programme with proceeds going to Comic Relief, which featured the whole script of *Back and Forth*, as well as new material put together by the retained stand-in scribes Cecil & Riley, including a Blackadder Insult Generator, an interview with Rowan's false goatee beard and a guide to Baldrick's Dome (which boasted the world's biggest turnip, the Belly Button Fluff Zone, and of course the movie *Baldrick Back and Forth*). Without this programme, the viewer also loses the King's highly suspicious disclaimer:

> '*As you know, generation after generation, my family have only ever wanted one thing: to bring pleasure to all mankind. (Except Baldrick.) May God bless you all in the new millennium.*'

> EDMUND BLACKADDER REX

Blackadder, by Royal Appointment

Whatever perceived offence may have been caused by Blackadder dethroning the reigning Windsor family, it is the notable affection shown for the character by HRH Prince Charles and his family which has kept the *Blackadder* name ticking over, such as it has, in the twenty-first century. Indeed, *Back and Forth* was not even the character's comeback, Atkinson and Fry having revived a long-dead Blackadder live onstage two years earlier, especially for the Prince of Wales's fiftieth birthday.

The traditional image of king and jester was never quite reflective of real court life, but there's still a long history of Humour by Royal Appointment in Britain – Henry II was a big fan of Roland the Farter's annual Christmas show, Henry VIII doted on his court jester Will Sommers, and most *Blackadder*-esque of all would be Edward II's commissioning in June 1313 of a special nude dance, to be performed by none other than Bernard the Fool. But no royal figure has done more to revive the link between monarchy and mirth than Prince Charles. Since his days as a young *Goon Show* fan, impressing Milligan and Sellers with his Bluebottle impressions behind closed doors, the heir to the throne has proven himself to be a devoted comedy aficionado, from generation to generation, and time and again the country's best comics have reciprocated this affection, with each Royal Variety Performance still a dream booking for many comics today. And just as the sitcom's military theme made it popular with the armed services, few comedies have wibbled the royal frusset pouch as pleasantly as *Blackadder*.

Like any good Licensed Fool, Blackadder's appearances before royalty have tended to stress the 'comedy roast' element of the role, pricking a royal family who have always been keen to be seen laughing at their own expense – within reason. But as a self-proclaimed supporter of the establishment, in a real-life echoing of Edmund's own deference, there aren't many comedians who have received royal patronage as readily as Atkinson, as his own roasting in *The Tall Guy* hinted. He and Curtis sent a telegram from their West End show for the Prince of Wales's first wedding in 1981: 'All love, fun and laughter from the cast and company of the Rowan Atkinson Revue', and received the reply, 'Enormous thanks for your wonderful message which is heartily reciprocated.' Six years later, having received invitations to a private audience with the Prince (the two of them bonding over a love for Aston Martins), Rowan was very nearly reprising the role of Lord Blackadder for *The Grand Knockout Tournament*, Prince Edward's infamous historical pageant and charity extravaganza in which Atkinson's Lord Knock – master of Alton Towers and husband to Barbara Windsor's Lady Knock, but Blackadder in all but name – opened the proceedings with a deadpan speech presaging a host of celebrities (including John Cleese and the rest of the *Not* team) participating in gunge-filled festivities.

He was also no stranger to the Royal Variety Performance, performing numerous monologues over the years, but Blackadder's royal debut was created for a separate birthday entertainment, staged in October 1998, and broadcast on ITV a month later. We discover the Cavalier Sir Edmund in the same quandary as the Black Adder in the original pilot – arranging a royal entertainment against his will:

SIR EDMUND: To my Lords of the King's Own Council. I received this morning your kind invitation to organise a gala performance, to celebrate his gracious majesty, King Charles, surviving another year with head and shoulders still attached. I am replying by return to thank you. And when I say 'to thank you', I mean of course, to tell you to sod off. I would rather go to Cornwall, marry a pig, have thirteen children by her and see them all become

Members of Parliament . . . My reasons, my lords, are twofold. In the first part, it is a well- and long-established fact, that royal galas are very, very, very dull. So dull that strong men have been known to stab their own testicles in an effort to stay awake through the all-singing, all-dancing, no-talent tedium that represents British Variety at its best. There are more genuine laughs to be had conducting an autopsy. There is more musical talent on display every time my servant Baldrick breaks wind. If the King has even half a brain – which I believe is exactly what he does have – he will spend his birthday in pious prayer, naked, in a bramble patch, with mousetraps attached to his orbs and sceptre. I hope I make myself clear. I am yours, as ever, Lord Blackadder, Privy Counsellor. Shortly to be Privy Attendant, if Cromwell has his way with the aristocracy . . . (*Fanfare. Enter Charles I.*)

CHARLES I: Behhh, Slackbladder! Fol-de-rol and hi-de-hi. Behhh! It's my birthday and I'll 'behhh' if I want to! I just popped in to see if you were going to organise my royal gala?

SIR EDMUND: Well, Your Majesty, it's interesting that you should mention it . . .

CHARLES I: I was talking about it the other day to Lord Rumsey, and the cringing cur dared to suggest that we tone things down a bit to pander to the popular mood. I want you to kick his arse and give him a good clout about the head.

SIR EDMUND: Well, certainly, sir, but –

CHARLES I:	You'll find his arse in a ditch in Tyburn and his head on a spike at Traitor's Gate . . . Show me what you can do. Improvise, let's have a look.
SIR EDMUND:	Um . . . well . . . Your Majesty, your Royal Highnesses, my lords, ladies and gentlemen. I stand here tonight as excited as a masochist who has just been arrested by the Spanish Inquisition. What you are about to witness will be the most exciting piece of entertainment since Bernard the Bear Baiter stopped using a big brown cushion and actually got himself a bear . . .

The most extraordinary thing about this surprise return to the Stuart period, as any *Blackadder* fan could see, was Fry's depiction of Charles. Where his Comic Relief persona had been dithery and eccentric in an undeniably familiar way, before HRH himself Fry's performance was pure Melchett bombast (although perhaps one could suggest that by the time of his arrest in *The Cavalier Years*, a few nights in a blackcurrant bush had extinguished Charles's 'behhh'). Fry adds, 'I think it's well known, a) that I'm friendly with the Prince of Wales, and b) that he has a great sense of humour. Well, everyone does, but he *really* does. He idolised Spike of course and Barry Humphries and many others. I do dozens of charity performances and if I can't do one for a man I admire and more importantly *like*, whatever the world might think about him, then it would be weird indeed. Especially given the astounding achievements of the Prince's Trust. In America comedians perform in front of an elected president, which means at least half the country hate them for it. The beauty of a constitutional monarchy heading the state is that they have no politics, so you don't get the stupid nonsense of Kenny Everett doing Tory Party conferences and *bien-pensant* Labour comedians doing the same for Labour.'

Ben Elton's relations with the Windsors have had their ups and downs, as has his estimation of the Labour Party, in the light of New Labour and the Blair administration.* But as a history-loving patriot from another German immigrant family, and an ambassador for the Prince's Trust, Elton was proud to get the gig of presenting sections of the Royal Variety Performance and indeed the Queen's Golden Jubilee concert. Some of his subsequent stand-up material was used by the press to depict him as a yob, of course, and he used the *Daily Mail* of all papers to try and set the record straight. 'I wrote to Prince Charles to apologise for calling the Queen a "sad little old lady" and her husband "a mad old bigot" . . . I was doing a comedy routine and it was quoted out of context as if it was a diatribe. There's not much in comedy that can't be made to look cruel and ridiculous when taken out of context. I've been doing that routine about the Royals for years. The point is that in all its dysfunction her family is just like the rest of us . . . Although the whole principle of monarchy is nutty, I personally believe if you must have a head of state, I would rather have someone who has to do the job than who wants to do the job. Intellectually there is no argument for the monarchy, but as I always say, if you have to go to a disco with the world's heads of state, who would you trust with your keys and your handbag? It would be Yer Majesty.' However, he reasons, 'The monarchy is absurd and illogical. There's no moral justification for a single family always providing the head of state. Nevertheless, it has delivered a great deal of stability. We're fortunate that our Royal Family appears to be made up of decent, caring, flawed but honest individuals. So, while the system is ridiculous, it seems to work.'

It was Elton who wrote and introduced Blackadder's final live appearance to date, presenting a tangential military member of the

---

* He opened sets with 'Everybody's been asking me if I'll still be doing all the lefty politics now that Labour are in. Well, no I'm not. They don't bother any more, why should I?'

family on to the stage at the Dominion Theatre, while *Back and Forth* was still airing at the Dome:

ELTON: Tonight we are celebrating a great British tradition and tradition is something we do very well in Britain. Some of our noblest families go back many, many centuries . . . and some popped over from Germany a lot more recently. Perhaps our oldest and most celebrated family of all is the Blackadder dynasty and now, representing the current generation of malcontents please welcome from Her Royal Highness's Regiment of Shirkers: Captain, the Lord, Edmund Blackadder.

EDMUND: All right, settle down, settle down. Your Royal Highness, ladies and gentlemen. The world is changing and Her Majesty's armed forces must change with it. Consider Britain and its position in the world today. At the beginning of the last century just two hundred years ago, Britain kept the peace in a quarter of the entire globe. The sun, they say, never set on the British Empire. Now what have we got? The Channel Islands . . . The Germans have bought Rolls-Royce. All the newsreaders are Welsh – although that may not be relevant. And most foreigners think that the Union Jack is based on an old dress design for one of the Spice Girls. So what is to be done? Well, the answer, to my mind, is very simple. If we are to re-establish our position in the world, the army must return to its traditional role, the very reason for which it existed in the first place – we must invade France. No no, no no, I'm serious. Our advanced guard of mad cows has already done a superb job. And the French are in disarray. Now is the time for actual occupation. Now you may say, 'Why France?' Well that's a very good question. But I can think of three reasons. Firstly, whenever we try to speak their language they sneer at us and talk back to us in English . . . God, they are *so irritating*! Secondly, they deliberately won the World Cup by maliciously playing better football than us. And thirdly, simple political strategy. Look at the history books – whenever Britain fought the French, we were top dog. For five hundred years from Agincourt to the Battle of Waterloo, Britain went from strength to strength and gained the greatest empire the world has ever known. The minute we start getting chummy with the garlic chewers, within three short decades we're buggered. *Hello?* Obvious connection alert!

And thus the live *Blackadder* legacy ended, just as the Dome movie itself – by sticking it to the French. Excepting, maybe, the truly last relative to surface – Sir Osmund Darling-Blackadder, Keeper of the Royal Sprinklers, who popped up in a TV spot during the Jubilee preparations in 2002 to remind the monarch that she was 'not Fatboy Slim', and that holding a rock concert at Buckingham Palace was out of the question.

For all these royally commissioned swansongs delivered by Ben, Rowan and Stephen, the only members of the *Blackadder* team to have accepted honours to date are Howard Goodall, Richard Curtis and John Lloyd, who all have CBEs, and Hugh Laurie, OBE. Tony Robinson, however, is not holding his breath for his date at Buckingham Palace.

He too has revived Baldrick for live performances in the past, but only for charity (the Tudor incarnation of the little peasant presented *Comic Relief's Debt Wish Show* at the Brixton Academy in June 1999), and as a staunch anti-monarchist and Labour activist, it's unlikely that he will be answering any royal edicts in the future. Belying Baldrick's totally inept brand of socialism, Robinson's radical background led to his not just becoming vice president of the acting union Equity, but also being elected to serve on the Labour Party's National Executive Committee for four years, a calling of which he was proud, despite his outspoken disapproval of the Iraq War, and Blairite politics in general. On the subject of his colleagues' noble connections, he is more politic, only diplomatically admitting, 'When I see then turn up at those dos, I just smile to myself . . .'

And Then I Want to Be Middle-Aged and Rich . . .

There was a clear warning at the outset of this narrative that it would be festooned with very talented young performers basking in their flowering of comic brilliance, and deservedly so – but British comedy and television have mutated so dramatically since the turn of the millennium that this generation of comedians can often seem like a lost one, with many members too anarchic to comfortably accept their place as comedy's elder statesmen, and too far removed from the demographics chased by today's breed of TV executives to hold on to their former ubiquity. But then, history has shown that the number of comedians – especially graduate comedians – who have managed to retain their thirst for creating comedy from debut right through to death can be counted on a leper's fingers. Despite never losing one iota of his wit, Peter Cook's youthful industry gave way to the chat-show circuit, while Michael Palin set a trend when he abandoned silliness to travel around the world, and the eighties generation have similarly moved beyond sketches and sitcom into straight acting, presenting, and making documentaries on any subject to which the next middle-aged comic has neglected to stake a claim. Like Tony and Rory McGrath, even Rik Mayall presented his own history show, *Violent Nation*.

In some ways, the comedy industry has changed so much around the Alternative veterans that they cannot be blamed for moving on in their careers – Ben Elton is one of the few to persevere as a TV comedian in the new millennium, and has experienced the difficulty of moving with the comedic times as a result. The studio-bound sitcom has weathered an incredibly hostile decade, in the wake of *The Office* – despite Gervais & Merchant's hit being a mockumentary in much the same vein as previous series like *Operation Good Guys* and *People Like Us*, its sudden runaway success meant that the idea of a live audience laughing at a live performance became outdated to TV bosses, if not taboo. 'Comedy does have fashions that come and go,' Elton concedes. 'I gave it the term "the new minimalism" (I don't know if anyone else picked up on it!), but it didn't start with Ricky, but *The Royle Family*, in my view. When Victoria Wood and I were doing *Dinnerladies* and *TTBL* in the mid-nineties, we did suddenly look quite old-fashioned. I was working in a very specific tradition of comedy, the big, broad studio-based sitcom, and just around that time *The Royle Family* was storming the barricades, and a brilliant show it was indeed, and shortly thereafter came shows like *The Office*, and a minimalist, closely observed approach to non-gag-based comedy came to the fore. Big, ballsy gag-based silliness was out, and commissioners have to go where they will go. Really it just comes down to whether the show is any good – take a piece of work like *Outnumbered*, which is brilliant. I like an audience, but I don't think you should be too concerned about pitting genre against genre – artists find the format to fit the work. Two of the greatest sitcoms ever made, *Seinfeld* and *Curb Your Enthusiasm* – one was studio and one was not, both brilliant pieces of work made by the same team.'

Ben did work within the 'new minimalist' environment by writing and directing 2005's *Blessed* but, continuing his parenting theme from *Maybe Baby*, the rant-filled tribulations of struggling new parents Ardal O'Hanlon and Mel Giedroyc weren't a hit with critics or viewers, and further experimentations with TV comedy *Get a Grip* and Australian series *Live from Planet Earth* also drew more flak than acclaim[*]. It would be fruitless to deny that Elton remains one of our most pilloried comedians, barracked from the right and the left, nominated for purgatory on the Hat Trick TV series *Room 101* and unable to get through any interview without having to deal with charges of 'selling out'. Admittedly, there was never a time when the comic enjoyed complete public approval, and perhaps he has been hoisted by his own petard at times, trying to reconcile two awkward bedfellows, mainstream popular entertainment and passionate social commentary. But if by a man's friends shall ye know him, Elton's bad rap remains an injustice – as Douglas Adams once protested: 'The trouble with the stand-up stuff – although it was brilliant – is that it was only presenting a very small aspect of a very complex, rather thoughtful and warm-hearted man. People just got the wrong idea.'

The term 'sell-out' has to be one of the least useful in our language, carrying as it always does an inherent need for the user's personal definition, and judgemental connotation, before its meaning can even begin to be understood. Like the word 'smug', the bandying about of the insult often says more about the user than their target, and besides, you cannot truly 'sell out' unless you first publish a specific manifesto, something which so few entertainers get round to. By some critics' reckoning, perhaps every bright young thing depicted in this history has 'sold out' some inferred principle, be it via advertising, acquisition of wealth, mainstream popularity or even specific political

---

[*] A return to mainstream studio-based sitcom is in the air for Elton – a new series starring David Haig as a beleaguered Health & Safety Officer, *Slings and Arrows*, was piloted for BBC1 in the summer of 2012.

statement, since they set out on their lives in comedy. But in many ways, Elton has remained more true to himself than any of his peers, always powered by an intense desire to entertain, coupled with a social conscience which he cannot keep bottled up – and of course, bar one unpaid ad for Fairtrade chocolate, he has also eschewed advertising where others have embraced it.*

By returning to his earliest love, musical theatre, Elton found his greatest international success, but once again earned the opprobrium of talking heads, not least for working with the Tory peer Andrew Lloyd Webber, on the Irish troubles musical *The Beautiful Game* (a song from which was used for George W. Bush's inauguration, without Elton's approval) and the *Phantom of the Opera* sequel, *Love Never Dies*. His biggest hit, however, has been the Queen jukebox musical *We Will Rock You*, which he has helped to steer to success around the globe (as well as penning a sequel, and another jukebox musical for Rod Stewart, *Tonight's the Night*). His futuristic book for *WWRY* may only provide the lightest thread to link the Queen hits, but comprises the by now familiar Elton themes of homogenised dystopia, shallow glamour and corporate greed. These also remain regular themes in his novels, with perhaps one notable exception – the World War I murder mystery *The First Casualty*. Returning to World War I was a brave move for Elton, particularly as any *Blackadder* fan would find it difficult not to make comparisons with *Goes Forth*. The hero, policeman Douglas Kingsley, may have little of the Captain B in him, but his dispatch to uncover a wrongdoer on the Ypres front in 1917, involving romance with a modern-minded nurse at the field hospital, and a feud with an oversexed handsome celebrity, certainly resonates with echoes of the series. A Second World War novel based on his father's experiences, *Two Brothers*, was published in 2012.

---

* Rik Mayall has even channelled Flashheart, albeit nineteenth-century style, to play 'The Bombardier', an unctuous advocate of ale.

Curtis also revisited the Great War in his work on *War Horse*, undertaken as the UK's top screenplay troubleshooter – he also helped Helen Fielding to guide her best-seller *Bridget Jones's Diary* to huge cinema success. Like any artist of his generation of course, Curtis's Midas touch has not been unwavering, with the epic goodwill of *Love Actually*, despite its huge popularity worldwide, proving too saccharine for some moviegoers' tastes* and his return to period comedy in his love letter to sixties rock and roll, *The Boat That Rocked*, or *Pirate Radio*, similarly split British audiences on release. It is as grand supremo of Comic Relief that he remains untouchable, and the biennial Red Nose Day evenings have remained a haven for every generation of comedian – often the one night in the calendar on which celebrity documentary-makers remember that they started out as jokers. It's rare that Curtis comments on this side of his career, but does admit, 'It doesn't allow you to think that the viewing figures that your situation comedy gets are an important thing. Which they ain't.' Despite his big-screen success, Richard still believes he has one more TV programme in him. 'There is a specific rhythm about that half-hour which you learn. There's a lovely thing about planting the information, then taking time off in the middle to be as stupid as you like and then winding it up and reminding people of something that happened. There seems to be a rhythm which is a joy.'

Although Blackadder himself has remained in the shadows for Comic Relief, 2005's spoof *Spider-Plant Man* relied heavily on love for the show, when Atkinson's turn as an inept teenage superhero in tight spandex results in a clash with Batman and Robin – or rather, Jim Broadbent and Tony Robinson, in ill-fitting fancy-dress costumes being mistaken for Fathers 4 Justice protesters. Rowan once mulled over the idea of doing a comic-book spoof called *BatAdder* – this is the closest he got:

---

* Perhaps if the mysterious shop assistant Rufus (the last movie role written by Curtis for Atkinson) had been revealed to be an angel as was the original intention, the number would have been higher.

Spider-Plant Man has Batman in a headlock, and is kicking his arse.

ROBIN: Holy plot-twists, Batman, it's meee!

BATMAN: Robin! Help me!

ROBIN: First, let's renegotiate. How about 20 per cent
                of the Bat merchandise this time?

S-P MAN: . . . No, Robin, come and work for me! I'll
                give you 25 per cent on all franchised pyjamas
                and a breakfast cereal named after you with
                real marshmallowy bits in it . . .

Robin punches Batman into oblivion.

BATMAN: Nooooo!

S-P MAN: Well, am I glad you did that! In fact, I'm as
                glad as Bernard Gladboy McGlad, on the
                gladdest day of his life when he'd just won
                the Gladdest Man in North Gladmanshire
                competition, beating into second place Gladys
                the Glad!

ROBIN: All right, all right, I know, you're glad . . .

Since 2003, there has also traditionally been a corner of the Red Nose Day proceedings reserved for John Lloyd's creation, *Quite Interesting*, or, rather, *QI* – the result of a decade's self-imposed re-education, in the wake of his Scrooge-like experience that Christmas Eve. As he explained at the time of the series' launch, 'The core idea of *QI* is that we're taught the wrong way up. We're taught all the "important" things, all the boring things, all the lists, all the things that are hard to remember, such as times tables and irregular verbs and vocabulary. Meaningless stuff. And then if you get through all those and you get to do a PhD, eventually they start telling you how things really work.' Translating this 'Quite Interesting' philosophy into a TV panel game with the partnership of publisher John Mitchinson, Lloyd found that even with over a decade away from TV production, he still had the ability to create award-winning, popular television. Halfway through its planned twenty-six alphabetical series, it would not be an exaggeration to call *QI* a British institution, with a philosophy all of its own, spawning successful books, DVDs, Twitter apps and the spin-off Radio 4 show, *The Museum of Curiosity*, presented by Lloyd himself. The show has also featured numerous Adder veterans, including Laurie, Atkinson-Wood and Goodall, while Atkinson is a regular feature of the *QI* annuals. Forty years after stumbling out of the footlights and plunging into BBC Radio, Commander Lloyd's triumph in popularising his philosophy of fascination has placed him more in the limelight than he may have intended, but this fresh success perfectly complements the deep respect and affection in which he was already held by comedy fans, as one of the nation's most influential living comedy creators.

Stephen Fry may happily double for Lloyd as the figurehead for *QI* but he was not the first choice for presenter, the original candidate being Michael Palin, as with Lloyd's Barclaycard ads. Having stepped into the breach, however, Fry's schoolmasterly role on the show has become one more avenue for his public veneration as an actor, presenter, writer and all the other dizzyingly myriad occupations that make up his chat-show introductions. That Fry has become such a National Teddy Bear, a kind of millennial Betjeman, for the whole population to hug (or indeed kick) at any opportunity, from an arguable starting point of being a closeted qualification-free convicted felon at the age of seventeen, may be the infamous polymath's one holistic achievement. It's sadly forgotten that he has also remained loyal to sitcom, and got to play a comedy bastard worthy to stand alongside Blackadder, in the despicable PR guru Charles Prentiss. Originally created as a snobbish BBC Radio controller by writer Mark Tavener for his comedy murder-mystery novel *In the Red*, Prentiss went on to feature alongside John Bird's more sanguine Martin McCabe in the Radio 4 and BBC2 adaptations, plus a number of radio sequels (one featuring Laurie as an obvious Blair cipher), before the pair were reborn as spin doctors in their own radio sitcom *Absolute Power* – with Helen Atkinson-Wood once guesting as Martin's ex-wife. Rather than cunning plans, Charles was fond of pulling off the odd colossal 'wheeze', as a moral vacuum meddling with the processes of government. It's tragic that the TV version of *Absolute Power* was compromised by the fatal illness of Tavener, and the glossy result, despite lasting for two series on BBC2 in 2003 and 2005, was fated to be overshadowed by *The Thick of It*, with Peter Capaldi's Malcolm Tucker becoming the iconic sitcom spin doctor of the decade.

Fry remains a successful actor by any means, but, he would be the first to acknowledge, not one to compete with his erstwhile colleague's transformation into the most highly paid TV actor of all time, and the sexual fantasy of millions of fans of the medical drama *House* all over the world. Perhaps it was not easy for someone with Laurie's crippling sense of humility to have finally lived up to the predictions of his *Blackadder* friends and graduated from supporting roles in Hollywood movies to portraying the generation's most infamous TV doctor Gregory House (especially as his own father earned considerably less as a real doctor), but the magnitude of Hugh's success has palpably led to the long-time self-flagellator gaining a greater sense of his own ability, and a new comfort within his own skin which has empowered him to realise his greatest ambition: becoming a blues musician – his first solo release *Let Them Talk* was one of the best-selling hit albums of 2011.

The rest of the actors who make up the extended *Blackadder* brethren could not be said to have done at all badly either, with Oliviers, Golden Globes, BAFTAs, the odd Oscar and high-profile roles abounding on their CVs, comprising an opulent bounty of characters. Tim McInnerny's wish to avoid typecasting has certainly been granted, having taken on roles as diverse as Dr Frank-N-Furter and Cruella de Vil's sidekick Alonzo in *101 Dalmatians* (where he co-starred with Laurie), while the wealth of historical characters he has portrayed in TV dramas such as

The Devil's Whore and movies like *Black Death** have never brought to mind the foppery of Percy or slipperiness of Darling. Comedy remains crucial to his career, however, and he even became an honorary member of the Comic Strip, alongside Miranda Richardson, who co-starred with him in the surreal *Les Dogs* as well as making her own return to sitcom with regular roles in the Jennifer Saunders comedies *Absolutely Fabulous* and *The Life and Times of Vivienne Vyle*. Like McInnerny, Richardson has also been no stranger to the whalebone corset, with a number of historical movies on her CV and central roles in films like *Sleepy Hollow* and *Made in Dagenham*, and the *Harry Potter* series, reuniting her with many of the *Blackadder* alumni – Margolyes, Broadbent and of course Coltrane as Hagrid (though Mayall's turn as the Hogwarts poltergeist Peeves was criminally cut out).†

But what of the Adder himself? Leaving aside the many doings of Mr Bean, much of the new century has seen Atkinson cropping up in the press for uncomedic reasons – taking the controls of a doomed plane in 2001, and occasionally worrying his fans by crashing expensive cars at high speed. Tony says, 'He's one of the few mega performers who genuinely has a full and fulfilling life away from show business. In my experience, I can't tell you how rare that is. He has a beautiful wife and family and good on him. Yet he remains for me the consummate comedy performer of his generation.' Besides his headline-grabbing Mr Toad impressions, however, comedy has remained Rowan's most serious occupation, and he also hit the headlines in 2005 as an outspoken opponent of an Incitement to Religious Hatred Bill which was being steered through the House of Lords, and which could have effectively left any comedian or artist open to criminal prosecution on the grounds of blasphemy. At the time,

---

* As well as returning to the plot of *The Black Adder* by playing Catesby in Richard Loncraine's *Richard III*, one of many Shakespearean performances, which include stealing the show as Iago at the Globe Theatre.

† Although absent from the films, Fry indoctrinated a whole new generation into a love for his sumptuous tones, as narrator of the *Potter* audiobooks.

Fry commented, 'Religion, surely, if it is worth anything, doesn't need protection against anything I can say,' and in his speech to the House, Atkinson concluded, 'The freedom to criticise ideas – any ideas, even if they are sincerely held beliefs – is one of the fundamental freedoms of society and any law which attempts to say that you can ridicule ideas, as long as they're not religious ideas, is a very peculiar law indeed.'

It's a long time since Atkinson had a TV vehicle or staged a live show (although the incessant links between *Blackadder* and *Oliver!* continued when he appeared as Fagin in the West End in 2009 and in 2013 he took the title role in a revival of Simon Gray's *Quartermaine's Terms*), as cinema has remained his chief playground for over a decade, despite his admitting in the past, 'I see the film world as a big bag of worry, a slightly bleak minefield which you might make it across. The only reason for doing film is to stretch yourself . . . I don't want to take so many risks. It is better to make no films than bad films.' Supplemental to Mr Bean's movie success, Rowan bagged the starring role in *Keeping Mum* (in which he played, of course, a vicar), and his main comedic preoccupation in recent years has been Johnny English, the big-screen incarnation of Lloyd's BAFTA-winning Barclaycard adverts.* Despite being another manifestation of the star's strong sense of patriotism, trouncing the French and protecting Queen and country with pratfalls, the first instalment did better business in the Mr Bean-loving quarters of the globe than in the UK, and left the perfectionist Atkinson keen to give the inept but deluded secret agent a second go, resulting in the more critically acclaimed and highly silly sequel *Johnny English Reborn* in 2011 – in which he was aided in no small manner by the debut of McInnerny as English's 'Q' figure, Patch Quartermain.

Having achieved so much, becoming an undeniable comic icon all around the world and now in his fifth decade as a professional comedian,

---

* Lloyd was on board at the birth of the movie franchise but, as he likes to lament about so many projects in his life, he was swiftly sacked by the money men on both instalments.

it would be fair for Rowan to devote the rest of his life to racing cars and his other hobbies. As Stephen has observed, 'Rowan has not an ounce of showbiz in him. It is as if God had an extra jar of comic talent and for a joke gave it to a nerdy, anoraked northern chemist.' And he himself is happy to admit, 'I sometimes speculate about where I'd be now if I hadn't decided to take that plunge and write to those agents and take it seriously. And whether I'd be, you know, in some small research laboratory near Swindon, doing amateur dramatics every three months. And I'm sure I'd be enjoying it greatly!' But the devotion to making people laugh which possessed Atkinson as a student has not gone away, as his activism in the blasphemy case suggests, and the press junkets for *Johnny English Reborn* showed that he was still looking for a new direction for his comedy – or, indeed, that he could countenance a return to the character for which his compatriots love him the most . . .

The Slither of Tiny Adders

For the entirety of the 1970s, the crushing inevitability of the question 'Are you planning a reunion?' became such an unsavoury running joke among the four Beatles that they often answered it, unheeded, before a single question was asked – and no subsequent artists can have such a deep understanding of how they felt, as the *Blackadder* team. With every member still with us, still compos mentis and still friends despite previous hiccups and their vastly disparate career paths, not a year goes by without some rumour bubbling up, usually in the tabloids, either blowing an offhand comment about the show out of all proportion, or completely inventing a story from scratch.

London 2012 Olympics aside, we live in a time when admitting to even the slightest twinge of patriotic feeling can be misconstrued as tantamount to a confession to voting for the BNP, but the comically jingoistic *Blackadder*'s popularity remains undimmed among the British people. Rowan was delighted to play a central role in Danny

Boyle's opening ceremony – as directed for TV by Geoff Posner – and Prince Edmund himself joined the carnival of British pride, flickering across the Olympic Park's titanic screens, limply squeaking 'Hooray!' Perhaps some element of the show's power to unite Britons comes from *Blackadder*'s essential sarcasm, which never allows flag-waving to go unmocked, but there is also the fact that the comedy was written by two first-generation immigrants from central Europe. Curtis concedes, 'Ben's much more passionate about the history than I am, but there probably is a point to make about people who are first-generation British. You know, Tom Stoppard is the definitive English writer and his family is Czech, and Anthony Minghella's was Italian. George Bernard Shaw and Oscar Wilde were both Irish. There is something about people who come from another country, and can look at Britain and write about it in a different way.' Elton says, 'I think the term "pride in being British" is a very misleading one, because it does have all sorts of connotations. I think a *joy* in being British. I take enormous delight in British History, and without Britain I wouldn't be here, so I'm extremely conscious of my admiration and affection for British institutions and that very broad church which may be called British culture. I consider myself to be British, even though I now have dual nationality. But if "patriotism" means thinking that you're *better* than other people then I don't consider myself remotely patriotic. On the other hand, I have been shaped by the country in which I grew up, and I'm definitely a creature of its history and culture.'

Nevertheless, fans are not confined to the UK – in 2010, Lord Blackadder's codpiece drew bids from all over the world when it formed the centre of a TV auction, and the show's popularity in an array of dubbed languages on YouTube,* copious international repeats and subsequent commercial releases have only increased the despicable family's reach

---

* And indeed Facebook, where the unofficial fanpage never fails to gather *thousands* of comments and 'Like's within minutes of posting any random quote.

around the globe. As a 'property' now co-owned by Atkinson, Curtis, Lloyd and Elton, there has only been the minimum of merchandising designed to capitalise on this popularity since the TV series' conclusion, with a number of DVD and audio releases. Transcripts of the four series, supplemented with diversions such as Mrs Miggins' Coffee House Menu and Private Baldrick's school report, were finally published as *The Whole Damn Dynasty* in 1998, accompanied by a press release claiming that the documents within had been discovered in a treasure chest by construction workers on the Millennium Dome site – plus a disgusted disclaimer from the family that all proceeds would be going to Comic Relief. The book was of course a mammoth hit, even though most buyers were likely to know the scripts off by heart already, few shows lending themselves to enthusiastic quotation* quite like *Blackadder*.

Despite *Blackadder* never having a strong official web presence, the BBC's early online experiments did give us a collection of strange promotional video games, which were collected for a CD-ROM in 2000. Besides sound bites and picture galleries, the disc gave PC owners the chance to duel against the Red Baron in the sky or the Duke of Wellington with cannons, or to play a maze game where you guide Lord Blackadder to riches without getting caught by the Queen or the Bishop of Bath and Wells. 'There was a craze for CD-ROMs, but we were all too busy to do it,' John admits. 'I gave it to my son who was then about thirteen, and he said, "Dad, it's complete rubbish!"' Otherwise, the four guardians of the Adder have been stringent about not cashing in. Rowan says, 'The only merchandising idea that I can recall was "Blackadder Magic", based on the well-known confectionery: a two-tier box of dark chocolates, consisting of an extremely smart upper tier (the Blackadder tier) and a hideous lower tier (mangled, half-eaten abominations – the Baldrick tier). My recollection was that Richard

---

* Or indeed, loud misquotation, to the disgust of the true devotee – a trait highlighted by Harry Enfield via his character Kevin the Little Brother's regular irritating expostulation, 'Bloody hell, Baldrick!'

led disapproval of the notion, because Black Magic is/was owned by Nestlé, a company around which there was controversy because of its sale of powdered baby milk to the Third World. "Blackadder Magic" never happened!' 'I sometimes think that the problem is that we did all move on pretty quickly,' Curtis says. 'Last year I was contacted about doing some *Blackadder* posters, just for people who like it, but the truth of the matter is that no one's ever needed the money, and we do all find it quite easy to disagree on things.'

John has tended to be the man to bring the team back together for special occasions, helming a radio documentary, *I Have a Cunning Plan*, for the twentieth anniversary, and a feature-length TV special, *Blackadder Rides Again*, for the twenty-fifth, which perfectly encapsulated the difficulty of any kind of reunion by showing the producer travelling from chilly Alnwick all the way to the Californian lot of *House* in order to accommodate everyone. '*Rides Again* had an honesty about it,' Lloyd says, 'but it was about closure. I think the subtext was that *Blackadder* was worth doing, because it was such a good thing, but I tried to get across the idea that *nothing "great" is easy*. Not ever.' The twenty-fifth anniversary also brought some of the team back together for UKTV Gold's celebration *The Whole Rotten Saga*, which united the nation's Blackadders and allowed viewers to choose their own *Most Cunning Moments*. Like the episodes themselves, these celebrations and clip shows are often repeated, particularly at Christmas time, for the simple reason that *Blackadder* still gets good ratings, thirty years after its inception.

Also testament to *Blackadder*'s influence is the fate of historical sitcom in the last twenty years. Where TV commissioners once sneered at period comedy because 'it didn't work', the fact that flop after flop has been dismissed as 'no *Blackadder*' has subsequently plagued the genre. Not that this has prevented anyone from trying to transcend comparison, with series like the French & Saunders French Revolution sitcom *Let Them Eat Cake* and Rob Grant's millennial ITV show *Dark Ages* littered among the reject pile, alongside the likes of Craig Charles's pirate comedy *Captain Blood*, which was weaker than Atkinson-Wood's CITV equivalent *Tales From The Poopdeck*. Even the one top-grade period sitcom of the 1990s, Arthur Mathews's *Hippies*, was badly received and only lasted for one series. Radio 4 has, however, played host to many more successful historical comedies, with Kim Fuller's anachronism-packed *The Castle* and especially Andy Hamilton and Jay Tarses's sublime *Revolting People* (produced of course by Paul Mayhew-Archer, and a far funnier exploration of life in revolutionary America than *1775*) chief among the station's successes.

It wasn't until the CBBC sketch show *Horrible Histories* began to get wider acclaim that historical comedy on TV began to thaw out – and although that series was good enough in its own right, when it was repackaged for a wider audience, there was something fitting about Stephen Fry being chosen to provide scholarly historical links. Fry has dipped his toe back into Adder-ish waters more than anyone else on the team, and often in a villainous role. Lionshead Studios' role-playing series *Fable* has referenced *Blackadder* numerous times through each epoch of its throne-grabbing narrative – even teasing the Xbox 360 instalment *Fable III* with artwork featuring a male prostitute holding a 'Get It Here!' sign – but the closest link is Fry's recurring role as the villainous industrialist Reaper, a snarling combination of Flashheart and Blackadder there to tempt the player over to the dark side. His other villainous return to the past has been as the cartoonish bastard Malifax Skulkingworm in *The Bleak Old Shop of Stuff*, the TV incarnation of Radio 4 series *Bleak Expectations*, written by Mark Evans and produced by Mitchell & Webb collaborator Gareth Edwards. Despite Ben Elton's years of hankering after a whole series on Dickens, the *Bleak* team got there first – although the show's outlandish absurdism is of a very different comedic vein to *Blackadder*, and once again, it lacked a live audience. It did, however, provide the first chance in a generation for Stephen to overact in period clothing – as well as being succeeded by the equally despicable Harmswell Grimstone, played by a manic McInnerny. 'I think *Blackadder* held back things like

Horrible Histories and the wonderful *Bleak Shop* series,' Stephen muses. 'Shows like *Blackadder* can cast a long shadow.'

Live audience sitcom remains on the critical list in the second decade of the twenty-first century, not helped by a number of high-profile flops, sadly including Tony Robinson's foray back into sitcom as the deadpan shyster Erasmus in the circus comedy *Big Top*, which was awkwardly broadcast on BBC1 after a difficult production, with the death of original director John Stroud requiring a last-minute replacement by Geoff Posner. Robinson says, 'Geoff was great, he just came in and pulled the whole thing together. But it's rather sad that when a series doesn't take off, the hard creative work that individuals have done on it is never noticed . . . We all knew what was wrong with *Big Top*, really from day one, but by that time the scripts were written, the roles were cast, the sets were built . . . If it had been made in the eighties I think it would have got a second series.'

Numerous homages and the resurgence of historical sitcom in recent years, however, do not silence the clamouring for a new *Blackadder*. There have been many false alarms, close calls and d'you-mind-if-I-don't's since 1989, and recently Tony admitted to the press, 'I'd love to do one again. I love those people even if they are toffs. We had this idea that we would do a phone-round in 2010 and see how we felt. There is the argument that it's best left alone – that way it will stay in people's memories. There's also the argument, wouldn't it be good to get together for one last time? I think it is down to Richard and Ben. If the recession hits Ben's book sales and no one will give Richard money to make any more movies then maybe it will happen. There may be a silver lining to the Credit Crunch after all!' However, he subsequently said that if there was a 2010 meeting, '*I* didn't go. I sometimes have this paranoid fantasy that everyone else met up and they didn't invite me, but assuming that wasn't the case . . . I don't think so. I know that Tim, for instance, just thinks the moment's gone, that time is passed, and it would be undignified and imprudent to revisit it. And I think that unless Richard or Ben or Rowan had some really driving desire to bring it back in some form or other and a very strong idea, it wouldn't happen. People are too bound up with their lives now to want to recapture the triumphs of yesteryear.'

There's been no shortage of ideas coming not just from the writers, but all members of the fraternity, as they dangled reunion-hungry journalists on their hook. So many *Blackadder* instalments have been mooted indeed, that it would be simplest to list definitively what might have been . . .

Prehistoric Blackadder

J. H. W. Lloyd's history of the family began in pagan times, but there has always been the temptation to go back further, outlining a time when the first Baldrick would have been King of the Monkeys, until the arrival of Homo Blackadder, a presumably far less verbally gymnastic progenitor. 'But then,' Elton said, 'how many times can you do jokes along the lines of: "We are dragging this cart along the ground, what we need is some kind of tool to make it travel more easily . . ."?'

The Six Wives of Blackadder

A brilliant title – and little else. Whether it could have aped *The Six Wives of Henry VIII* by centring on Cardinal Blackadder, we shall never know.

The Magnificent Seven Blackadders

Only mentioned in passing, Lloyd suggested that a Wild West *Blackadder* loosely based on *Bonanza* could feature all of the regulars as highly unlikely brothers running a ranch in the Old West, and getting into gunslinging scrapes as they feud with each other – to which Miranda happily responded, 'I'd do that, definitely! Would I get to be a sort of Calamity Jane or something? Fantastic!'

RedAdder

This idea for a movie, dreamt up by Rowan and John and then sketched out by Ben, would have done away with one of the series' central themes – British History. Nonetheless, Atkinson was intrigued, ruefully admitting, 'I think it was one of those things when it became a victim of people being not sure that they wanted to do that kind of thing. It was set in the Russian Revolution. Blackadder and Baldrick are members of the secret police for the Tsar in 1916 – and then the Russian Revolution happens in 1917, and at the end of it, they're in exactly the same office with the same typewriter, but now they've got red bands around their caps instead of blue. *Plus ça change*, as it were.' Featuring Soviet relatives who coexist with Captain Blackadder and co. on the Somme was a sizeable imponderable, but it did inspire some curious set pieces, such as a 'bore hunt', in which dissidents Tolstoy and Dostoevsky were released and tracked down for sport. 'It was rather a fun idea, actually. It was a nice context. I mean, *Blackadder* always worked well when there was a hierarchy – the Elizabethan Court or the army. Places like that are great for the Black Adder, because he's so cynical of people who are above him, and he's so rude to those who are below him, and it's nice if you've got that hierarchy for him to play in.'

Blackadder in Colditz

The generally approved set-up in recent years has centred on that most exhausted of chestnuts – the World War II escape plot. Atkinson was keen. 'I always felt if we ever did a fifth series, I would love to have done a Colditz escapee sort of one. Because I think a POW camp has got that sort of claustrophobia, and the sense of hierarchy.' For all the tiredness of the concept, Lloyd enlarged on the idea in such a way that it not only made more sense, bearing in mind the average age of the team, but also had a uniquely epic scope. 'We got quite far talking about one set in World War II, with a platoon of Dad's Army soldiers in a seaside resort. One day a German submarine appears, lands on the pier, captures them and takes them to Colditz, where they have to escape. I thought that was quite funny . . .'

The Blackadder 5

The most widely reported return for Edmund was first let out of the bag by Mayall soon after the end of the fourth series, and was to make full use of Elton & Curtis's pop-music obsession by featuring Blackadder as a swinging entrepreneur and rock-band manager – part Brian Epstein, part Austin Powers. Few details of this idea have ever escaped, besides Rik's suggestion that the shiny-headed drummer in Blackadder's answer to The Beatles would have been called 'Bald Rick', and Curtis's musing that the drummer could turn out to be the man who really shot Kennedy in Dallas in 1963. 'That would be great!' Elton said. 'You could see a naturally conservative man like Blackadder up against all the excesses of the sixties, with Baldrick as a naturally bedraggled hippy . . .'

Blackadder: The Thatcher Years

Perhaps the most inventive concept was outlined by Curtis, and has been made canonical by the opening titles for *Back and Forth*, which has a Blackadder showing scant respect for Thatcher in her premier pomp. Although the existence of Alan B'Stard makes a Tory Blackadder almost redundant, the writer explained, 'We did have this idea that if we ever did it again, when we *should* set it is actually when we started it. That Blackadder should be working for Margaret Thatcher. It would be a funny idea to be satirical about the time when we were actually making the series – that they'd be watching! And Blackadder would be very annoyed about the fact that there's a series called *Blackadder* on the television . . .'

Set in a similar time, Robinson mused on a concept guaranteed to embarrass his royalist colleagues, but which would be difficult to pull off. 'My favourite suggestion for a new series is Blackadder as the current Queen Elizabeth's bastard son who is always lurking around Buckingham Palace. And they have to make all these rumours about there being intruders in the Palace when there aren't any at all – it's this bastard son who isn't recognised. And as for Baldrick – he'd be the real royal intruder!'

In 1988, long before he had ever played a contemporary Blackadder, Atkinson said, 'A present-day Blackadder is probably what John is most keen to exploit.' With no small note of self-awareness, he suggested that this modern Edmund would be 'some kind of media hack, who drives around in an Aston Martin and has his mechanic, who would probably be Mr Baldrick, in greasy overalls, who would service his motor cars. And he would undoubtedly be something and somewhere around the royal family, probably some minor aristocrat, and then you can get all the contemporary problems of being in the royal family in the present day and age, and what an anachronism it is, and the press and television, and you know, the Archbishop of Canterbury, and all the characters you can have from the present day. And I think it would be an interesting series to do, but quite different from virtually anything else that we've done on *Blackadder*, so we'd have to change gear.'

Blackadder at Oxford

Curtis's final gambit harks back to his alma mater, outlined as part of his round-up of contemporary Blackadders (including the 'Blackadder 5' manager) in the *Radio Times*: 'We don't know the full story, but one of his descendants now holds quite a powerful position at Buckingham Palace and was responsible for trying to block the Jubilee pop concert. Another is a professor at Oxford, where a Mr S. Baldrick has been his scout for forty-seven years. The final descendant of note is a retired pop svengali and heroin addict, now living in Switzerland with his sixteen-year-old wife.' He expanded elsewhere, 'We like the idea that when we wrote the first *Blackadder* we were young and scornful, so we love the idea of being old and scornful, of being old men who use the sarcasm of *Blackadder* to attack what's happened to the world since we were young. One idea we had was that Blackadder should be a very fed-up and corrupt university don and Baldrick would have been his scout for the last forty years, so they would in effect have been married for forty years . . .' This final idea would at least make allowances for the passing of time. 'We might do one when we're old, but Tony is so old, I mean, he's in his early eighties now, that I'm not sure he'll be alive when we want to go back to work . . .'

Staradder

Always high on the list even before the glimpse of what the future could hold in *Christmas Carol*, the sci-fi antics of the Blackadder family have never really been looked into, not least because, as Richard joked, 'We did think about a science-fiction series, but then we remembered that John was a bit of an expert on space. The interference would have been awful.' Elton has suggested that such an idea would have been more *Star Trek*-inspired than the vision of Christmas Yet to Come – but then *Red Dwarf* has already provided the ultimate piss-take of Gene Roddenberry's creation.

Farewell, You Horrid Man

'Success has never surprised me. I didn't *assume* it would happen, but when it came it just seemed logical in relation to applied effort,' Rowan acknowledged as early as 1990, going on to make it clear that even then, as far as *Blackadder* was concerned, 'success spoils you. You don't have to work as hard as you did because you get paid more money for what you do. Suddenly it is not the challenge or the fun that it used to be . . . What we are really talking about is ego, and the simple fact that everyone is scared of failure. The more people keep referring to *Blackadder* as a classic, the more afraid everyone is of carrying on. The last thing we want is to make another one and see it dismissed as not as good as the ones that went before.'

At least one team member has found some way to quash each of the above ideas as they have been thrown up over the years, and it's widely felt that the repertory company established by *Goes Forth* is essential, even though that group only came together for that one series. Empirically, as this History shows, for something to be canonical *Blackadder*, all that's required is Atkinson as a member of the Blackadder family, with Robinson's Baldrick by his side, speaking dialogue at least partly written by Curtis – *Blackadder* has existed without any input from Elton and Lloyd in the past, while the other core actors all flitted in and out of the series. This is irrelevant to the star of the show, however, who ultimately argues, 'It was representative of a moment in all our lives, that's why I think it's futile really to talk about reunions or a fifth series or anything like that because I think it represented a comedy consensus between a group of individuals at a certain time, and as soon as you try and recreate that chemistry five or ten or thirty years later, it's very difficult . . . when everyone has moved on into so many different areas, and probably become more choosy about what they do, and less flexible, let's say, at accommodating other people's whims and wishes.' And his irreplaceable sidekick backs him up. 'I think in the end it's all about taste. That's why the series was so successful, you've got a bunch of highly intelligent and culturally sophisticated people who for a brief moment of time shared the same taste about a particular piece of work, and all of them were informing that work with that sense of taste . . . We're on a hiding to nothing. Everybody will say it wasn't as good as the last series. The only people who have managed to do that brilliantly were *The Likely Lads. Whatever Happened to the Likely Lads?* was, for me, a better series than the original. But, by and large, when things do come back they look like a thin version of the original.' Despite all this, he adds, 'I would love to do another series. I've always been very hawkish but it's not my call.'

This back and forth is a familiar quandary for any veteran entertainers keen to have a celebratory lap of honour, whether it's the Beatles' *Anthology*, the thirtieth-anniversary *Monty Python Night*, or indeed a musical based on Queen – and the question burns even among the most devoted *Blackadder* fans, with an ever-fluctuating divide between the purists (who predict disaster for any reunion and believe that the character should remain in his grave) and the optimists (for whom the slightest glimmer of a new reincarnation would be like a lifetime of Christmases coming at once). The argument that the show should remain pristine, post-'Goodbyeee' is already dented by *Back and Forth*, but even then, the idea that any subsequent reunion could tarnish the existing shows is nonsense, *Blackadder* remains secure for generations to come, no matter what happens. Brian Blessed, who loudly confesses that he 'would come running' if asked to be in any reunion, goes so far as to say, 'From the way each generation has embraced it, I think *Blackadder* will go on for thousands of years; there is a universality about it, and I think that it has very long legs . . . In the end, more than Mr Bean, more than whatever, Rowan's Blackadder is the finest comic performance in television history.' Atkinson shares the purists' misgivings, however, admitting in recent years, '*Back and Forth* wasn't a very good omen, I didn't think. We'd have to have a much more professional and rigorous and sort of genuine approach to it. We couldn't have the instigation coming from outside commercial sources. It's got to be those who are involved in it saying, "You know what would be good?" There's got to be a genuine creative impetus.'

For a film, he continues, 'You have to explore more facets of the character. You can't just have a single attitude. The great thing about sitcoms is that you can get away with a character with, really, one attitude. Like, Blackadder is just a relentlessly cynical man. And that's the joke. He's cynical and negative in a very witty way. If we tried to make a *Blackadder* movie, if you just had a relentlessly cynical man who never acknowledged the ramifications of his own actions, etc., then I think it would be a very odd movie . . . I like variety. I like to move on, but I don't – in any sense – ignore the old. I mean, I'm someone who tends to return to characters quite a lot. I could easily have left *Mr Bean* as a TV series, but when the notion of making a movie was put forward, it kind of interested me. Because I thought, "I suppose that could be fun . . ." I would return to the Blackadder character if the opportunity came up. I have no qualms about that at all.'

Indeed, though history has shown that making any great prophecy about a new *Blackadder* is a mug's game, there's never been a better time for his return than the second decade of the third millennium, with Atkinson freely rhapsodising about the idea on the *Johnny English Reborn* press junket, and even Hugh's punishing schedule on *House* reaching a climax. Laurie himself openly admits that we have not totally lost him to the world of drama and music when he says, 'The possibilities for Blackadder going further back into the past, or into the future or to other continents . . . there are always possibilities, because Richard and Ben are immensely talented writers, and they could make an awful lot of different kinds of things work . . . We're eternally bound together, you know, by that experience. Every year we meet under the clock at Paddington Station, ten to four, all wearing the tie – we've got a tie made, you know, nice.' 'We will take the piss out of him non-stop and tell him what an appalling American accent he has,' Tony laughs, 'but we are all deeply proud of him.'

Blackadder's extended thespian family all agree that they would be proud to receive any call from Lloyd for a new incarnation, and Miriam

Margolyes for one says, 'It was a very, very happy programme to work on; I feel it was an honour to have been even a tiny part of it. It's something I cherish in my career that I was part of something that still, after twenty-five years, is so fresh, clever, inventive and extremely funny. It's one of the classic pieces of television comedy, like *Dad's Army* or *Fawlty Towers*, there are just a few series that are outstanding, and I think that that was one of them.' Fry concludes, 'We made some people very happy and had a damned good time (well, some of it was good) making it. I'm terribly pleased to have been involved. Laughter is an astounding gift to be able to give people, especially laughter that isn't cool, look-at-me, wearing sunglasses and being hip.'

Tony is equally positive about the show, no matter what happens. 'I am so proud to have been in *Blackadder*. I don't feel like some actors would – "Oh, I don't want to mention that character, I'm in fear of being typecast!" I don't feel like that at all . . . There are lots of other shows that I've done that have taken more time to do, that have taken more toll on me,* or where I've actually made more money! But the fact that I'll go to my grave as Baldrick isn't something I shy away from . . . I feel like the curator of Museum Baldrick. Every few years a new generation want to bring him out and dust him off. It's not that he is me, but I feel I have a very warm and close relationship with him.' With typical self-criticism, the man forever to be seen as Baldrick's master divulges, 'I was travelling on a plane several years ago, and an episode came up on the entertainment channel, and it was the Nurse episode from the fourth series, with Miranda. And as far as I'm aware it was an episode that I had never, ever seen . . . I'm not a great laugher, sadly, but I might have sniggered at it. Which was my way of saying that it was very funny . . . I think one of the most striking things about it is how it's lasted, actually. It doesn't seem to date. I suppose it helps that we

---

* In exploring the most Baldrick-worthy occupations mankind has put up with for his series *The Worst Jobs In History*, Tony gutted pigs, trod stale urine and was thrown off cliffs.

set the sitcom in different periods of British History, and therefore it's not like watching those seventies sitcoms, where people seem to have embarrassingly long sideboards and things, which immediately dates it, and distances you from the comedy. Whereas because we tended to do it in quite a serious way, most of the programmes look as though they could have been made yesterday.'

Everyone agrees that if anyone has the power to bring another Edmund Blackadder back from the dead, it is the writers, and in 2011 Elton did admit that he and Curtis were working together on a new script for the first time since the millennium – and, as Atkinson outlined, they are doing so in their own time, and not to a commercial brief. This is not *Blackadder*, however, but a Curtis movie idea with Elton input (Ben nearly collaborated on *The Boat That Rocked*, but schedules clashed).

Nevertheless, the show's thirtieth anniversary does make a resurgence for the country's most jingoistic comedy character seem more likely than it has been in years. Whether buoyed by the 2012 Olympics and Queen Elizabeth II's Diamond Jubilee or not, for the majority of the British public, monarchist or republican, *Blackadder*, with its searing sarcasm, poetic wit, ironic jingoism and cheering regular doses of lavatorial filth, remains a genuinely unifying national touchstone. The texts constructed by Curtis & Elton and plumpened by everyone else are already in many ways as embedded in the British consciousness as Shakespeare – or at least, for years now, amateur dramatic companies have performed episodes with comparable regularity (with all proceeds usually going to Comic Relief).

It would be glib to portray the four protectors of the *Blackadder* name as the victorious elder statesmen of British comedy – Rowan, the King in exile, keeping his next comic gambit shrouded in secrecy, Richard the venerable Archbishop of Love and Charity, Ben the international impresario and Pope John Lloyd, commander of curiosity. But none of them has lost the hunger to amuse which propelled them to their lofty positions, and none of their successes, particularly with regard to *Blackadder*, were achieved without collecting scars, both professionally and emotionally. Where the surviving Pythons are happy to laughingly rake each other through the dirt until they die, the *Blackadder* team in many ways have a deeper affection for each other, and thus a greater fragility when rancour has arisen in the past, no matter how much water has gone under the bridge. Theirs was an explosive chemistry which has been carefully kept separate for many years, and yet, as witnessed at first hand, the depth of personal affection between each of the creators of *Blackadder*, and the strength of the protective code which still binds them three decades on, is tangible. The combustible collaborative spirit which united them in the 1980s has been sacrificed for the benefit of their close friendships, so perhaps for that reason alone *Blackadder* is a blueprint best left in a locked drawer.

The last lines of *Blackadder* dialogue written prior to the latest rumours was a short scrap of Tudor apocrypha written by Curtis for a charity auction in 2006, where famous writers had to offer something on the theme of 'Between the Lines':

EDMUND: What are you doing?

BALDRICK: I'm reading, sir . . .

EDMUND: You might find it easier if you had it the right way
            round.

BALDRICK: Thank you, sir.

EDMUND: And if it was in English, not ancient Greek.

BALDRICK: I thought it looked a bit funny.

EDMUND: It is the *Iliad* by Homer – so it is not the slightest
            bit funny. But am I to surmise, reading between the
            lines, Baldrick, that you do not actually know how
            to read?

BALDRICK: No, sir, not a word.

EDMUND: So why were you sitting with a book in your lap

when I entered the room?

BALDRICK: I was hoping to impress you, sir . . .

EDMUND: If I came into the room and William Shakespeare was on his knees begging you to help him finish his next play, and Queen Elizabeth was on her knees giving you a blow job, I would still not be impressed.

BALDRICK: Why not, sir?

EDMUND: Because I know you to be the lowest creature ever created by God and every time he looks down and sees you, he hits his forehead with his fist and shouts – 'Stupid! Stupid! Stupid! I totally and utterly fucked up that time.'

BALDRICK: In which case, I will never try to impress you again.

EDMUND: Good decision. Now . . . I want you to take this scroll to Ben Elton and ask him to do a rewrite on this scene – Richard Curtis can't think of a punchline . . .

Whether any new collaboration from Ben and Richard sees the light of day or not, Curtis says, 'My general feeling about *Blackadder* is that I feel *massively* lucky about how it turned out. While we were doing it, I remember saying to Ben, "It's good, but it'll never be great." And so it's a surprise, these years later, that it lasted so well. To be honest, I write films most of the time now, and I believe in television more. When you write something of which there are a lot of episodes, they can be a bigger part of people's lives. I think sitcoms have a way of being a part of the texture of the life that you lead. *Python* isn't a sitcom, but *Python* and *Fawlty Towers* were that for me. And it's a fantastic thought, a big achievement, if *Blackadder* is that for other people . . . The charms about *Blackadder* are, one, it's quite lovely to look at because it's so lusciously designed and dressed, and, two, it's very dense, there are more words in it than one would expect and sometimes those give me pleasure. I have to say that it was exceptionally hard work, so if it turned out well, that would be why.' Elton, traditionally jaded about his past work, and eager to promote his next, has admitted, 'I've recently watched *Blackadder* again for the first time in nearly twenty years and I've taken enormous joy in the fact that my kids love it. That's something I never thought about when it was happening, that twenty years later I'd be watching it with my children . . . I'm flattered about how fond people are of *Blackadder*. I'm not running it down here. *Blackadder* is not finished. We'll never give up on it. It could be a middle-aged show. We'll never officially close it down. Ever.'

This True History, therefore, can have no ending. While the cream of the eighties generation who bonded together to make *Blackadder* are still around, there will always be the promise of more. And for long after they *aren't*, the Blackadder legacy will prove as immortal as the Adder himself, still making Britons as yet unborn laugh, and look at the existing history of the nation in a completely different way. 'Maybe what we are doing is providing the background buzz of inaccurate history. It's quite interesting that history education has moved in a *Blackadder* direction. It's trying to take the juiciness, violence, stupidity and oddness of old eras and look at it through a young kid's eyes,' Curtis concludes. 'It does make you slightly wonder whether we didn't take our responsibilities seriously, and whether we could have actually said some more interesting things about history all the way through. Perhaps we should go back and do the series in a more responsible manner next time.'

ACKNOWLEDGEMENTS

Bravo — at an annoyingly loud volume . . .

I originally tumbled into comedy chronicling after articles I'd written celebrating the *I'm Sorry* legacy led to a chat with Barry Cryer, in which a full history of *I'm Sorry I'll Read That Again* and *I'm Sorry I Haven't a Clue* was mooted. The resultant *Clue Bible* proved to be a titanic undertaking, covering half a century of comedy, and sadly contending with numerous tragedies during composition. After such a blazing trial by fire, Preface Books' invitation to suggest a follow-up required much thought. Having tackled such an enormous topic, I couldn't turn back and plump for the simple life; my next subject had to be as huge, as terrifying and as difficult as *Clue*.

It just so happened that *Blackadder*, by far the most important, influential and beloved comedy in my own life, presented the perfect challenge. The sitcom's status *demanded* a print celebration, and I felt that if the job was worth doing (and as one of the few great sitcoms not to have been properly documented in print, it certainly was), then it was worth obsessing about for years, leaving no avenue unexplored to tell the *Blackadder* story in the greatest detail. From the start, I knew that the team behind the show would be near impossible to pin down – John Lloyd's own journeys to bring everyone together for *Blackadder Rides Again* proved that anyone wishing to write about this gang was liable to be facing more snakes than ladders. Luckily I had a head start, having been researching the topic passionately since the age of nine, and so my first thanks should go to my brothers, Nick and Tim, who were there when the *Blackadder* fascination took hold, and were witness to the original creation of the juvenile scrapbooks which formed the basis of the years of intense research which went into the making of this book. Another head start came from the fact that Lloyd and Stephen Fry (and his eternally wonderful sister Jo Crocker) had been extremely encouraging to me with my first book, and if they hadn't agreed that *The True History of the Black Adder* was a worthwhile project from the off, it would never have happened.

My very first interviewee, however, was Terry Jones, who helped me ease back into author mode with a few pints and a long chat about medieval propaganda. With Tony Robinson and Howard Goodall next to come on board, I was filled with the confidence to use every cunning ploy I could to talk to as many of the Adder family as possible, and thus followed chats with Miriam Margolyes, who led me to Patsy Byrne, then Gabrielle Glaister, Robert East, Helen Atkinson-Wood, Warren Clarke, Humphrey Barclay, Geoff Posner, Mandie Fletcher, Charles Armitage, Jeremy Hardy, Lee Cornes, Peter Bennett-Jones, even young Natasha King . . . all of them as kind and helpful as the last – and yet the greatest fillip of all had to be the vigorous pep talk from Brian Blessed, who urged me, 'Do see Rowan, just *go and fucking see him*! Say, "Please, I beg of you! Brian says do *him* a favour, Brian loves and trusts me!" What you're doing is so worthwhile. *Keep at it!*'

With that kind of wind in my sails it was hard to feel too despondent, and Commander Lloyd – having already recommended the celebrated historian Justin Pollard (who did *not* die) to be our historical expert – brought further cheer by personally contacting the remaining members of the *Blackadder* team, resulting in the input of the Adder himself. Having always known how passionately Atkinson protects his private life and his work, this was an unhoped-for honour and the book's crowning glory. Subsequently realising the ambition of a lifetime by meeting both Richard Curtis and Ben Elton was the cherry, icing and smarties on the cake.

The achievement of so much of the above of course relied on the goodwill and help of many agents and PAs, and I'd like to thank Stephen Gittins, Lucy Fairney, Giacomo Palazzo, Sarah Dalkin, Alison Lindsay, Arthur Carrington, Paul Carney, Sarah Douglas, Adele Fowler, Louise Bedford, Sarah McDougall, Aude Powell and Pru Bouverie. Archival help came from a number of shadowy sources, but special mention should go to Reinier Wels, and Jeff Walden at the BBC Archives in Reading. My own scrapbooks were consistently supplemented by the wonderful archive shared by the SOTCAA team, and the excellent T. J. Worthington was also disarmingly complimentary when he agreed to be the very first person to read the fruits of my labour. Further outpourings of gratitude are due to the numerous journalists, periodicals and website editors who have shared some of their interviews for this chronicle (*see* fig. 1).

The unceasing support of Trevor Dolby and his team at Preface, including Katherine Murphy, Phil Brown, Nicola Taplin and others, of course was also crucial in making this book the celebration which *Blackadder* deserved. But above all, John Lloyd has been the patron saint of this chronicle, an alpha and omega, and it's down to his own kindness, sincerity and bulldog spirit that this True History exists at all.

As for anyone else, may the Yuletide log slip from your fire, and burn your house down.

Jem Roberts, Autumn AD MMXII

APPENDIXES

Fig.1 BLACKADDER BUYER'S GUIDE

BLACKADDER REMASTERED – THE ULTIMATE EDITION (BBC DVD 2009)

DVD box set containing all four series, two specials and *Back and Forth*, plus *Blackadder Rides Again*, *Baldrick's Video Diary*, extended interviews and commentaries from Lloyd, Curtis & Elton, Lloyd and Atkinson, McInnerny and Robinson, and Fry.

BLACKADDER: THE COMPLETE COLLECTED SERIES (BBC AUDIO 2009)

Anniversary collection of all four series and two specials on CD, plus *Back and Forth*, *I Have a Cunning Plan*, *Woman's Hour Invasion*, *Shakespeare Sketch*, *Army Years*, and *Britain's Best Sitcom*.

BLACKADDER: THE WHOLE DAMN DYNASTY (MICHAEL JOSEPH 1998, PENGUIN BOOKS 1999)

Transcripts of all four series, plus further historical research and oddities.

BLACKADDER BACK AND FORTH (PENGUIN BOOKS)

Transcript of the film, with supporting material, exclusively available at the Millennium Dome.

THE BLACKADDERS CD-ROM (BBC WORLDWIDE, 2000)

Games, PC themes, galleries and other defunct features.

BOOKS BY THE BLACKADDER TEAM

ATKINSON, ROWAN
  (with Robin Driscoll) *Mr Bean's Diary*, Boxtree 1993

CURTIS, RICHARD
  Six Weddings and Two Funerals: Three Screenplays, Michael Joseph
    2006
  (with Tony Robinson) *Odysseus: The Greatest Hero of Them All*,
    Knight Books 1986; *Odysseus II: The Journey Through Hell*,
    Knight Books 1987; *Theseus: The King Who Killed the Minotaur*,
    Knight Books 1988
  (with Simon Bell and Helen Fielding) *Who's Had Who*, Warner
    Books 1990
  (with Paul Mayhew-Archer) *The Vicar of Dibley: The Complete
    Companion to Dibley*, Michael Joseph 2001

ELTON, BEN
  Stark, Sphere 1989; *Gridlocked*, Sphere 1991; *This Other Eden*,
    Sphere 1993; *Popcorn*, Simon & Schuster 1996; *Blast from the
    Past*, Bantam 1998; *Plays: 1*, Methuen 1998; *Inconceivable*,
    Sphere 1999; *Dead Famous*, Bantam 2001; *High Society*, Bantam
    2002; *Past Mortem*, Bantam 2004; *The First Casualty*, Bantam
    2005; *Chart Throb*, Bantam 2006; *Blind Faith*, Bantam 2007;
    Meltdown, Bantam 2009
  (with Rik Mayall & Lise Mayer) *Bachelor Boys: The Young Ones
    Book*, Sphere 1984

FRY, STEPHEN
  The Liar, Heinemann 1991; *Paperweight*, Heinemann, 1992; *The
    Hippopotamus*, Random House 1994; *Making History*, Random

House 1996; *Moab is my Washpot*, Random House 1997; *The Stars' Tennis Balls*, Hutchinson 2000; *Stephen Fry's Incomplete and Utter History of Classical Music*, Boxtree, 2004; *The Ode Less Travelled*, Hutchinson, 2005; *Stephen Fry in America*, HarperCollins 2008; *The Fry Chronicles*, Michael Joseph 2010
(with Hugh Laurie) *3 Bits of Fry & Laurie*, Heinemann 1992; *Fry & Laurie Bit No. 4*, Mandarin 1995

GOODALL, HOWARD

Big Bangs: Five Musical Revolutions, Vintage 2001; *The Story of Music*, Chatto & Windus 2012

LAURIE, HUGH

The Gun Seller, Heinemann 1996

LLOYD, JOHN

(with Douglas Adams) *The Meaning of Liff*, Pan 1983; *The Deeper Meaning of Liff*, Pan 1992
(with Sean Hardie, Editors) *Not! the Nine O'Clock News*, BBC Books 1980; *Not the Royal Wedding*, Pavilion 1981; *Not the General Election*, Sphere 1983
(with John Mitchinson – selected) *QI: The Book of General Ignorance*, Faber & Faber 2006; *QI: The Book of Animal Ignorance*, Faber & Faber 2007; *If Ignorance Is Bliss, Why Aren't There More Happy People? Smart Quotes for Dumb Times*, Harmony 2009; *QI: The Book of the Dead*, Faber & Faber 2010; *The EFG Bumper Book of QI Annuals*, Faber & Faber 2010

MAYALL, RIK

Bigger Than Hitler, Better Than Christ, HarperCollins 2006
(with Adrian Edmondson) *Bottom: The Scripts*, Penguin 1995

ROBINSON, TONY (selected)

Boudicca series, Blackie & Son Ltd 1989; Maid Marian series, BBC Books 1989–1992; Maid Marian and Her Merry Men: Script Book, BBC/Longman 1996; The Hutchinson Book of Kings and Queens, Hutchinson 1999; In Search of British Heroes, Channel 4 Books 2003; The Worst Jobs in History, Boxtree 2004; The Worst Children's Jobs in History, Macmillan 2005; My Life: In Words & Pictures, Honest Programmes, 2007

(with Mick Aston) Archaeology Is Rubbish: A Beginner's Guide, Channel 4 Books 2002

(with Debbie Gates) Tales from Fat Tulip's Garden, Hippo 1985

BIBLIOGRAPHY: GENERAL

Adams, Douglas (ed.): The Utterly Utterly Merry Comic Relief Christmas Book, Fontana 1986; Bradbury, David & Joe McGrath: Now That's Funny!, Methuen 1998; Cross, John Keir: Blackadder: A Tale of the Days of Nelson, Frederick Muller 1950; Dale, Michael: Sore Throats and Overdrafts: An Illustrated History of the Edinburgh Fringe, Precedent Publications 1988; Dessau, Bruce: Bean There Done That, Orion 1997; Rowan Atkinson, Orion 1999; Fielding, Helen: Cause Celeb, Picador, 1994; Gaiman, Neil: Don't Panic, Titan 2002; Gray, Simon: Fat Chance, Granta 2005; Hamilton, Paul, Peter Gordon, Dan Kieran: How Very Interesting: Peter Cook, His Universe and All That Surrounds It, Snowbooks 2006; Hewison, Robert: Footlights!, Methuen Publishing 1984; Hind, John: The Comic Inquisition, Virgin Books 1991; Howarth, Chris & Steve Lyons, Cunning, Virgin Books 2000; Lewis, Martin & Peter Walker (eds): The Secret Policeman's Other Ball, Methuen 1981; Marks, Laurence & Maurice Gran: The B'Stard Files, David & Charles 1988; Mayer, Lise and Rachell Swann (eds): Amassed Hysteria, Penguin 1991; Rhys Jones, Griff: Semi-Detached, Penguin 2007; Tavener, Mark: In the Red, BBC Books

1989; Thompson, Harry: *Peter Cook*, Sceptre 1997; Various: *The Utterly, Utterly Amusing and Pretty Damn Definitive Comic Relief Revue Book*, Penguin 1989; *Comic Relief Comic*, Fleetway 1991; *Peter Cook Remembered*, Mandarin 1997; Webb, Nick: *Wish You Were Here: The Official Biography of Douglas Adams*, Headline 2003; Wilmut, Roger & Peter Rosengard: *Didn't You Kill My Mother-In-Law?*, Methuen 1989

BIBLIOGRAPHY: HISTORICAL

Ambrose, Tom: *Prinny and His Pals*, Peter Owen 2009; Baldwin, David: *The Lost Prince*, Sutton 2007; Carson, Annette: *Richard III: The Maligned King*, History Press 2008; Elton, G. E.: *England Under the Tudors*, Methuen 1955; Jones, Philippa: *Elizabeth: Virgin Queen?*, New Holland 2010; Jones, Terry: *Who Murdered Chaucer?*, Methuen 2003; Mortimer, Ian: *The Time Traveller's Guide to Medieval England*, Vintage 2009; Niles, William Ogden, *Niles' Weekly* Register, 1819; Parissien, Steven: *George IV: The Grand Entertainment*, John Murray 2001; Peach, L. Du Garde: *Kings and Queens of England*, Ladybird 1968; Schama, Simon: *A History of Britain*, Bodley Head 2000; Sellar, W. C. & R. J. Yeatman, *1066 and All That*, Methuen 1998; Sheffield, Gary: *Forgotten Victory*, Headline 2001; Unstead, R. J.: *Looking at History*, A&C Black 1955

VIDEOGRAPHY (selected)

1775, CBS 1992; *A Bit of Fry & Laurie – The Complete Collection*, 2 Entertain 2006; *A Kick Up the 80s*, BBC2 1981–84; *Alfresco – The Complete Series*, Network DVD 2009; *BAFTAs*, BBC1 1990; *Behind the Britcoms – From Script to Screen*, PBS 2010; *Behind the Scenes: Blackadder*, A&E TV 1988; *Behind the Screen*, BBC1 1989; *Ben Elton: Laughing at the 80s*, Channel 4 2011; *Ben Elton: The Definitive Live Collection*, Spirit Entertainment 2007; *Bernard & the Genie*, BBC1 1991; *Best of British: Ben Elton*, BBC1 1999; *Beyond the Fringe*, Acorn Media 2005; *Black Death*, Sony Pictures 2010; *Big Top*, BBC1 2009;

Blackadder: The Whole Rotten Dynasty/Most Cunning Moments, Gold 2008; *Bleak Old Shop of Stuff*, BBC2 2011; *Blessed*, BBC1 2005; *The Boat That Rocked*, Universal Pictures DVD 2009; *Britain's Best Sitcom: Blackadder*, BBC2 2004; *Buster Keaton Collection*, 2 Entertain 2006; *Carpool*, Llewtube.com – Paul Jackson 2009, John Lloyd 2010; *Carry On – The Ultimate Collection*, ITV Home Studios DVD 2008; *Cellar Tapes*, BBC2 1982; *Chelmsford 123*, Acorn Media 2011; *Children in Need*, BBC1 1988; *Christmas Night with the Stars*, BBC2 1994; *Comedy Connections*, BBC1 – A Bit of Fry & Laurie 2005, Not the Nine O'Clock News 2005; *Complete and Utter History of Britain*, LWT 1969; *Comedy Playhouse: No Peace on the Western Front*, BBC2 1972; *Comic Relief: The Fool's Guide*, BBC1 2009; *Common Pursuit*, BBC2 1992; *Dark Ages*, ITV 1999; *Court Jester*, Paramount Home Entertainment 2007; *Dance with a Stranger*, Channel 4 1985; *Dead on Time*, Michael White Productions 1983; *Fact or Fiction: Richard III*, Channel 4 2004; *Film 89*, BBC1 1989; *Filthy, Rich & Catflap*, BBC2 1986; *First on Four: Saturday Live*, Channel 4 1998; *Four Weddings and a Funeral*, Twentieth Century Fox DVD 2004; *Frankie Howerd Collection*, 2 Entertain 2006; *Frost on Satire*, BBC4 2010; *Fry & Laurie Reunited*, Dave 2010; *Get a Grip*, ITV 2007; *Girl in the Café*, 2 Entertain 2005; *Going Live*, BBC1 1993; *Grand Knockout Tournament*, BBC1 1987; *Happy Families*, BBC1 1987; *Heroes & Villains: Full Throttle*, BBC1 1995; *Hippies*, Fremantle Media DVD 2008; *History of Alternative Comedy*, BBC2 1999; *Hysteria 1–3*, Palace Video/Laughing Stock 1987–91; *Horrible Histories*, CBBC 2009; *House*, Fox TV 2004–12; *Jeeves & Wooster: Complete Collection*, ITV Studios DVD 2011; *John Howard Davies – A Life in Comedy*, BBC2 2011; *Johnny English*, Universal Pictures DVD 2003; *Johnny English Reborn*, Universal Pictures DVD 2012; *Keeping Mum*, Entertainment in Video 2006; *Laughing Matters*, BBC2 1992; *Laughter in the House*, BBC2 1998; *Let Them Eat Cake*, Playback DVD 2007; *Lion King* Disney 1994; *Live From Planet Earth*, Nine Network 2011; *London Tonight*, ITV 2005;

Love Actually, Universal Pictures DVD 2004; *Madness: Gogglebox, Lucky Seven* 2011; *Maid Marian and Her Merry Men*, Eureka Video 2008; *Maybe Baby*, Lions Gate DVD 2000; *Mr Bean: The Complete Collection*, Universal Pictures DVD 2010; *Monty Python and the Holy Grail*, Sony Pictures DVD; *Nearly Complete and Utter History of Everything*, BBC1 1999; *New Statesman: Complete Series*, Network DVD 2006; *Noel's Saturday Roadshow*, BBC1 1988; *Not Again*, BBC1 2009; *Not the Nine O'Clock News*, BBC2 1979–82; *Notting Hill*, Universal Pictures DVD 1999; *Old Flames*, BBC2 1990; *Omnibus – What a Relief!* BBC1 1996; *Parkinson*, BBC1 2006; *Peter's Friends*, Eiv DVD 2001; *Princes in the Tower*, Channel 4 2004; *Remember the Secret Policeman's Ball*, BBC2 2004; *Richard III*, Pathé 2000, *Richard III: BBC Shakespeare*, BBC1 1983; *Rowan Atkinson Presents: Canned Laughter*, LWT 1979; *Rude for a Reason*, BBC Video 1999; *Sabotage!*, Divisa DVD 2005; *Saturday Live, Friday Night Live*, Channel 4 1985–88; *Scooby Doo: The Movie*, Warner Home Video 2002; *The Secret Diary of Desmond Pfeiffer* UPN 1998; *South Bank Show: Footlights* ITV 2009; *Spitting Image*, ITV 1984–96; *Stalag Luft*, ITV 1993; *Story of Bean*, Tiger Aspect 1997; *Tall Guy*, MGM DVD 2003; *Terry Jones' Medieval Lives*, BBC2 2004; *The Thin Blue Line*, Vision Video Ltd 2001; *This Is David Lander*, Channel 4 1988; *Time Team*, Channel 4 1994–2012; *Tony Robinson's Cunning Night Out*, Acorn Media DVD 2007; *Vicar of Dibley – The Ultimate Collection*, Universal Pictures DVD 2007; *Who Dares Wins*, Channel 4 1983–88; *Wogan*, BBC 1 1988; *The Worst Jobs in History*, Channel 4 2004–7; *The Young Ones*, BBC Video 2007

AUDIOGRAPHY (selected)

Atkinson People, BBC Radio 3 1978; *Bleak Expectations*, BBC Audio 2011; *A Brief History of Cunning*, BBC Radio 3 2008; *The Castle*, BBC Radio 4 2007–10; *Chain Reaction*: Clive Anderson/John Lloyd, BBC Radio 4 2007; *Comedy Zone: Ben Elton*, BBC Radio Scotland

2001; *Delve Special*, BBC Radio 4 1984–87; *Desert Island Discs*, BBC Radio 4: Rowan Atkinson 1988, Stephen Fry 1988, Ben Elton 1996, Hugh Laurie 1996, Richard Curtis 1999, Howard Goodall 2008, Tony Robinson 2011; *Dickens' Women*, BBC Audio 1993; *The Funny Side Of . . . Paul Jackson in Conversation With*, BBC Radio 4: Ben Elton 1999, Richard Curtis 2000; *Hitchhiker's Guide to the Galaxy: Complete Box Set*, BBC Audio 2005; *Hordes of the Things*, BBC Audio 2011; *I Have a Cunning Plan*, BBC Radio 4 2003; *Not Just a Pretty Face*, Polydor 1987; *Not the Nine O'Clock News: The Album*, BBC Records 1980; *Not the Nine O'Clock News: Hedgehog Sandwich*, BBC Records 1981; *Not the Nine O'Clock News: The Memory Kinda Lingers*, BBC Records 1982; *Radio Active*, BBC Radio 4 1980–87; *Reunion: Not the Nine O'Clock News*, BBC Radio 4 2005; *Revolting People*, BBC Radio 4 2000–6; *Rowan Atkinson Live in Belfast*, Arista Records 1980; *Very Nearly an Armful: The Galton & Simpson Story*, BBC Radio 2 2009

ARTICLES (selected)

Daily Express, 24 October 1999; *Daily Mail*: 1 October 2008, 7 March 2009, 12 December 2009; *Daily Mirror*, 22 January 1990; *East Anglian Daily Times*, 7 October 2008; *GQ Magazine* (Hugh Laurie), December 1993; *Guardian*: 1 September 2003, 29 January 2006, 2 April 2008, 11 April 2009; *Idler* (John Lloyd), May 2008; *Independent*: 4 August 1996, 26 May 2006, 26 November 2007, 15 June 2009; *Intelligent Life*, November 2011; *Loaded* (Stephen Fry), October 1997; *Mustard Magazine*, Issue 6, Summer 2011; *New Humanist*, July 2007; *The New York Times*, 15 October 1986; *Number One*, November 1989; *Observer*: 30 March 2003, 16 November 2003, 28 December 2008; *Radio Times*: 26 September 1987, 23 September 1989, 23 October 1993, 4 December 1993, 5 November 1994, 19 November 1994, 13 September 2003, 25 October 2003, 11 September 2010; Reuters, November 2011; *Skyview*, June 1999; *Smash Hits* (Comic Relief), April 1986; *Sun*, December 1989; *Sunday People*, June 1999; Daily

Telegraph and *Sunday Telegraph*: 21 October 1989, 1 November 2003, 2 April 2005, 17 November 2009; *The Times* and *Sunday Times*: 3 May 1996, 29 September 1997, 5 October 1997, 21 October 1997, 31 October 1999, 6 September 2003, 29 March 2008, 23 September 2008, 1 December 2008, 7 October 2010; *Today*, February 1995

LINKS

The Arts Desk: theartsdesk.com; BFI Database: bfi.org.uk; Blackadder @ BBC: bbc.co.uk/comedy/blackadder; Blackadder Hall (Unofficial): blackadderhall.com; Book Aid International: bookaid.org; Comic Relief: comicrelief.com; Footlights: footlights. org; Howard Goodall Official: howardgoodall.co.uk; Idler: idler. co.uk; Ken Plume Interviews: asitecalledfred.com; More Intelligent Life: moreintelligentlife.com; Movieweb: movieweb.com; Mustard Magazine: mustardweb.org; New Humanist: newhumanist.org.uk; Oxford Revue: oxfordrevue.com; Oxford Student News: Cherwell. org; PBJ Management: pbjmgt.co.uk; Phil McIntyre Management: mcintyre-ents.com; QI Official: qi.com; Queenie's Cunning Page: lunaestas.com/blackadder; SOTCAA: sotcaa.net; Tibby's Bowl Online Entertainment: tibbybowl.com; Tiger Aspect: tigeraspect. co.uk; Tim McInnerny fansite: tim-mcinnerny.webs.com; Tony Robinson fansite: unofficialtonyrobinsonwebsite.co.uk; TV Time Warp: tv-timewarp.co.uk

Fig. 2 BLACKADDER EPISODE GUIDE

THE BLACK ADDER (UNTRANSMITTED PILOT)

Recorded 20 June 1982

Prince Edmund	ROWAN ATKINSON
The King	JOHN SAVIDENT
The Queen	ELSPET GRAY
Prince Henry	ROBERT BATHURST
Percy	TIM McINNERNY
Baldrick	PHILIP FOX
McAngus	ALEX NORTON
Rudkin	SIMON GIPPS-KENT
Jesuit	OENGUS MACNAMARA
Written by	RICHARD CURTIS & ROWAN ATKINSON
Music by	HOWARD GOODALL
Director	GEOFF POSNER
Executive Producer	JOHN HOWARD DAVIES

THE BLACK ADDER

Recorded February (EXT), 10 April–15 May 1983

1) THE FORETELLING – TX 15/06/83 BBC1

Cast in Order of Precedence

Richard III	PETER COOK
Richard IV	BRIAN BLESSED
Henry VII	PETER BENSON
Harry, Prince of Wales	ROBERT EAST
Edmund, Duke of Edinburgh	ROWAN ATKINSON
Percy, Duke of Northumberland	TIM McINNERNY
The Queen	ELSPET GRAY
Painter	PHILIP KENDALL
Goneril	KATHLEEN ST JOHN
Regan	BARBARA MILLER
Cordelia	GRETCHEN FRANKLIN
Baldrick	TONY ROBINSON

2) BORN TO BE KING – TX 06/07/83

Cast in Geographical Order

The Laird of Roxburgh, Selkirk & Peebles	ROWAN ATKINSON
Richard XII of Scotland	BRIAN BLESSED
McAngus, Duke of Argyll	ALEX NORTON
Percy, Duke of Northumberland	TIM McINNERNY
Gertrude, Queen of Flanders	ELSPET GRAY
Harry, Prince of Wales	ROBERT EAST
Baldrick, Bachelor of the Parish of Chigwell	TONY ROBINSON
Jumping Jew of Jerusalem	ANGUS DEAYTON
Celia, Countess of Cheltenham	JOOLIA CAPPLEMAN
Sir Dominick Prique of Stratford	MARTIN CLARKE
2nd Wooferoonie	MARTIN SOAN
3rd Wooferoonie	MALCOLM HARDEE
Messenger	DAVID NUNN

3) THE ARCHBISHOP – TX 29/06/83

Cast in Order of Reverence

Herbert, Archbishop of Canterbury	PAUL McDOWELL
Godfrey, Archbishop of Canterbury	ARTHUR HEWLETT
Percy, Bishop of Ramsgate	TIM McINNERNY
William, Bishop of London	ARTHUR HEWLETT
Mother Superior	JOYCE GRANT
Sister Sara	CAROLYN COLQUOHOUN
Harry, Prince of Wales	ROBERT EAST
The Queen	ELSPET GRAY
The Duke of Winchester	RUSSELL ENOCH
Cain, A Peasant	BERT PARNABY
Abel, A Peasant	ROY EVANS
Messenger	DAVID NUNN
Sir Justin de Boinod	BILL WALLIS
Sir George de Boeuf	DAVID DELVE
Lord Graveney	LESLIE SANDS
Brother Baldrick	TONY ROBINSON
King Richard IV	BRIAN BLESSED

Edmund, Archbishop of Canterbury   ROWAN ATKINSON

4) THE QUEEN OF SPAIN'S BEARD – TX 22/06/83

Cast in Affable Order

Edmund, Duke of Edinburgh	ROWAN ATKINSON
King Richard IV	BRIAN BLESSED
The Queen	ELSPET GRAY
Harry, Prince of Wales	ROBERT EAST
Percy	TIM McINNERNY
Baldrick	TONY ROBINSON
Infanta Maria Escalosa of Spain	MIRIAM MARGOLYES
Don Speekingleesh, An Interpreter	JIM BROADBENT
Mrs Applebottom	JANE FREEMAN
Rev. Lloyd	JOHN RAPLEY
Mr Applebottom	HOWARD LEW LEWIS
Lord Chiswick	STEPHEN TATE
1st Messenger	KENN WELLS
2nd Messenger	RICHARD MITCHLEY
3rd & 4th Messengers	DAVID NUNN
Archbishop	WILLOUGHBY GODDARD
Princess Leia of Hungary	NATASHA KING
Lady on Ramparts	HARRIET KEEVIL

5) WITCHSMELLER PURSUIVANT – TX 13/07/83

Cast in Order of Witchiness

The Great Grumbledook	ROWAN ATKINSON
The Witchsmeller Pursuivant	FRANK FINLAY
The Witch Queen	ELSPET GRAY
Percy, A Witch	TIM McINNERNY
Baldrick, A Witch	TONY ROBINSON
Ross, A Lord	RICHARD MURDOCH
Angus, A Lord	VALENTINE DYALL
Fife, A Lord	PETER SCHOFIELD
Soft, A Guard	STEPHEN FROST
Anon, A Guard	MARK ARDEN
Daft Ned, A Peasant	PERRY BENSON

Dim Cain, A Peasant	BERT PARNABY
Dumb Abel, A Peasant	ROY EVANS
Dopey Jack, A Peasant	FORBES COLLINS
Officer, An Officer	PATRICK DUNCAN
Jane Firkettle	BARBARA MILLER
Princess Leia	NATASHA KING
Piers, A Yeoman	HOWARD LEW LEWIS
Mrs Field, A Goodwife	SARAH THOMAS
Mrs Tyler, A Goodwife	LOUISE GOLD
Richard IV, A King	BRIAN BLESSED
Stuntman	GARETH MILNE

6) THE BLACK SEAL – TX 20/07/83

Cast in Order of Disappearance

Murdered Lord	JOHN CARLISLE
Cain, A blind beggar	BERT PARNABY
Abel, A blind beggar	ROY EVANS
Trusting Father	FORBES COLLINS
Person of unrestricted growth	DES WEBB
Old Man	JOHN BARRARD
Mad Gerald	HIMSELF (RIK MAYALL)
Pigeon Vendor	PERRY BEVON
Friar Bellows	PAUL BROOKE
Jack Large	BIG MICK
Three-Fingered Pete	ROGER SLOMAN
Guy de Glastonbury	PATRICK MALAHIDE
Sir Wilfred Death	JOHN HALLAM
The Hawk	PATRICK ALLEN
Sean the Irish Bastard	RON COOK
Harry	ROBERT EAST
The Queen	ELSPET GRAY
Richard IV	BRIAN BLESSED
The Black Adder	ROWAN ATKINSON
Baldrick	TONY ROBINSON
Percy	TIM McINNERNY

SERIES CREDITS

Written by RICHARD CURTIS & ROWAN ATKINSON
With additional dialogue by WILLIAM SHAKESPEARE
Music by	HOWARD GOODALL
Graphic Designer	STEVE CONNELLY
Production Assistant	JAN HALLETT
Assistant Floor Manager	HILARY BEVAN-JONES
Costume Designer	ODILE DICKS-MIREAUX
Make-Up Designer	DEANNE TURNER
Technical Manager	TERRY BRETT
Lighting	BRIAN CLEMETT
Sound	RICHARD CHAMBERLAIN
Production Manager	MARCUS MORTIMER
Videotape Editor	MYKOLA PAWLUK
Vision Mixer	ANGELA WILSON
Designers	NIGEL CURZON, CHRIS HULL
Director	MARTIN SHARDLOW
Producer	JOHN LLOYD

A BBC TV Production in association with the Seven Network,
Australia. Made in glorious TELEVISION.

BLACKADDER II

Recorded 30 May (EXT), 9 June–7 July 1985

1) BELLS – TX 09/01/86 BBC1

Edmund Blackadder	ROWAN ATKINSON
Lord Percy	TIM McINNERNY
Baldrick	TONY ROBINSON
Queen Elizabeth I	MIRANDA RICHARDSON
Lord Melchett	STEPHEN FRY
Nursie	PATSY BYRNE
AND	
Kate	GABRIELLE GLAISTER
Flashheart	RIK MAYALL
Dr Leech	JOHN GRILLO
Kate's Father	EDWARD JEWESBURY

Wisewoman	BARBARA MILLER
Young Crone	SADIE SHIMMIN

2) HEAD – TX 16/01/86

Lady Farrow	HOLLY DE JONG
Gaoler Ploppy	BILL WALLIS
Mrs Ploppy	LINDA POLAN
Earl Farrow	PATRICK DUNCAN

3) POTATO – TX 23/01/86

Captain Rum	TOM BAKER
Sir Walter Raleigh	SIMON JONES

4) MONEY – TX 06/02/86

Bishop of Bath and Wells	RONALD LACEY
Molly	CASSIE STUART
Mrs Pants	LESLEY NICOL
Mr Pants	BARRY CRAINE
Arthur the Sailor	JOHN PIERCE JONES
Mad Beggar/Minstrel	TONY AITKEN
Leonardo Acropolis	PHILIP POPE
Messenger	PIERS IBBOTSON

5) BEER – TX 13/02/86

Lady Whiteadder	MIRIAM MARGOLYES
Lord Whiteadder	DANIEL THORNDIKE
Simon Partridge	HUGH LAURIE
Geoffrey Piddle	ROGER BLAKE
Monk	WILLIAM HOOTKINS

6) CHAINS – TX 20/02/86

Prince Ludwig	HUGH LAURIE
Torturer	MAX HARVEY
1st Guard	MARK ARDEN
2nd Guard	LEE CORNES

SERIES CREDITS

Written by	RICHARD CURTIS & BEN ELTON
Music by	HOWARD GOODALL
Graphic Designer	GRAHAM KERN
Costume Designer	ANNIE HARDINGE
Make-Up Designer	VICKY POCOCK
Production Assistant	AMITA LOCHAB
Assistant Floor Manager	SARAH GOWERS
Videotape Editor	CHRIS WADSWORTH
Technical Co-Ordinator	RAY HIDER
Lighting	DON BABBAGE
Sound	NEIL SADWICK
Production Manager	PRUE SAENGER
Designer	ANTONY THORPE
Director	MANDIE FLETCHER
Producer	JOHN LLOYD

© BBC MCMLXXXV A.D.

BLACKADDER THE THIRD

Recorded 5 June–20 July 1987

For the BENEFIT of SEVERAL VIEWERS MR CURTIS & MR ELTON'S Much Admir'd Comedy . . . was performed with appropriate Scenery, Dresses etc. by . . .

1) DISH AND DISHONESTY – TX 17/09/87 9.30pm BBC1

Edmund Blackadder, butler to the Prince	MR ROWAN ATKINSON
Baldrick, a dogsbody	MR TONY ROBINSON
The Prince Regent, their master	MR HUGH LAURIE
Mrs Miggins, a coffee shoppekeeper	MISS HELEN ATKINSON-WOOD
Mr Vincent Hanna, his own great-great-great-grandfather	MR VINCENT HANNA
Sir Talbot Buxomly, a Member of Parliament	MR DENIS LILL

Pitt the Younger, the Prime Minister   MR SIMON OSBORNE
Ivor Biggun, a candidate   MR GEOFF McGIVERN
Pitt the Even Younger, a tiny Whig   MASTER DOMONIC MARTELLI

2) INK AND INCAPABILITY – TX 24/09/87

Dr Samuel Johnson, noted for
  his fat dictionary   MR ROBBIE COLTRANE
Shelley, romantic junkie poet   MR LEE CORNES
Byron, romantic junkie poet   MR STEVE STEEN
Coleridge, romantic junkie poet   MR JIM SWEENEY

3) NOB AND NOBILITY – TX 01/10/87

Lord Topper, fop   MR TIM McINNERNY
Lord Smedley, fop   MR NIGEL PLANER
Ambassador, a fearsome revolutionary   MR CHRIS BARRIE

4) SENSE AND SENILITY – TX 08/10/87

Keanrick, thespian   MR HUGH PADDICK
Mossop, thespian   MR KENNETH CONNOR
Anarchist   MR BEN ELTON

5) AMY AND AMIABILITY – TX 15/10/87

Amy Hardwood, the elusive Shadow   MISS MIRANDA
    RICHARDSON
Mr Hardwood, her father   MR WARREN CLARKE
Sally Cheapside, a young lady of
  doubtful virtue   MISS BARBARA HORNE
The Duke of Cheapside, her father   MR ROGER AVON

6) DUEL AND DUALITY – TX 22/10/87

The Duke of Wellington, a famous soldier   MR STEPHEN FRY
King George III, a mad Monarch   MR GERTAN KLAUBER

SERIES CREDITS

Music (never perform'd before)   MR HOWARD GOODALL

Designer of graphics	MR GRAHAM McCALLUM
Buyer of properties	MISS JUDY FARR
Designer of costumes	MISS ANNIE HARDINGE
Designer of make-up	MISS VICKY POCOCK
Mixer of vision	MISS SUE COLLINS
Designer of visual effects	MR STUART MURDOCH
Editor of videotape	MR CHRIS WADSWORTH
Assistant to production	MISS NICKY COCKCROFT
Assistant manager of floors	MR DUNCAN COOPER
Manager of production	MISS OLIVIA HILL
Designer	MR ANTONY THORPE
Director	MISS MANDIE FLETCHER
Producer	MR JOHN LLOYD

To conclude with Rule Britannia in full chorus.

NO MONEY RETURN'D

BLACKADDER: THE CAVALIER YEARS

Recorded 10 January 1988, TX 05/02/88 BBC1

Sir Edmund Blackadder	ROWAN ATKINSON
Baldrick	TONY ROBINSON
King Charles I	STEPHEN FRY
Oliver Cromwell	WARREN CLARKE
Narrator	HARRY ENFIELD

Written by	RICHARD CURTIS & BEN ELTON
Music by	HOWARD GOODALL
Director	MANDIE FLETCHER
Producer	JOHN LLOYD

BLACKADDER: THE WOMAN'S HOUR INVASION

TX 18/11/88, BBC Radio 4

Blackadder	ROWAN ATKINSON
Baldrick	TONY ROBINSON
Also Featuring	JENNI MILLS, JOHN SESSIONS

Written by	RICHARD CURTIS & ROWAN ATKINSON
Production Assistant	BEE DAVIES
Producer	JOHN LLOYD

BLACKADDER'S CHRISTMAS CAROL
Recorded 4–11, 18 December 1988; TX 23/12/88 BBC1

Blackadders	ROWAN ATKINSON
Baldricks	TONY ROBINSON
Queens Elizabeth I/Asphyxia XIX	MIRANDA RICHARDSON
Lords Melchett/Frondo	STEPHEN FRY
Princes Regent/Pigmot	HUGH LAURIE
Spirit of Christmas	ROBBIE COLTRANE
Queen Victoria	MIRIAM MARGOLYES
Prince Albert	JIM BROADBENT
Nursie/Bernard	PATSY BYRNE
Beadle	DENIS LILL
Mrs Scratchit	PAULINE MELVILLE
Lord Nelson	PHILIP POPE
Millicent	NICOLA BRYANT
Ralph	RAMSAY GILDERDALE
Enormous Orphans	DAVID BARBER, ERKAN MUSTAFA, DAVID NUNN

Written by	BEN & ~~CHARLES~~ DICKENS
Music by	HOWARD GOODALL
Graphic Designer	TOM BROOKS
Properties Buyer	JOHN WATTS
Visual Effects Designer	STEVE LUCAS
Vision Mixer	ANGELA BEVERIDGE
Videotape Editor	CHRIS WADSWORTH
Lighting Director	HENRY BARBER
Costume Designer	RICHARD CROFT
Make-Up Designer	VICKY POCOCK
Production Assistant	JANE SPOONER
Production Secretary	HILARY CHARLES
Production Manager	SARAH COWERS

Assistant Floor Manager	LINDSAY TRENHOLME
Designer	ANTONY THORPE
Director	RICHARD BODEN
Producer	JOHN LLOYD

A merry messy Kweznuz.

BLACKADDER GOES FORTH
Recorded 20 August–24 September 1989

1) CAPTAIN COOK – TX 28/09/89 BBC1

Captain Edmund Blackadder	ROWAN ATKINSON
Private S. Baldrick	TONY ROBINSON
General Sir Anthony Cecil Hogmanay Melchett	STEPHEN FRY
Lt the Hon. George Colthurst St Barleigh	HUGH LAURIE
Captain Kevin Darling	TIM McINNERNY

2) CORPORAL PUNISHMENT – TX 05/10/89

Corporal Perkins	JEREMY HARDY
Corporal Jones	STEVEN FROST
Private Fraser	LEE CORNES
Private Robinson	PAUL MARK ELLIOTT
Private Tipplewick	JEREMY GITTINS

3) MAJOR STAR – TX 12/10/89

Driver Parkhurst	GABRIELLE GLAISTER

4) PRIVATE PLANE – TX 19/10/89

Squadron Commander Lord Flashheart	RIK MAYALL
Baron von Richthoven	ADRIAN EDMONDSON
Lieutenant von Gerhardt	HUGO BLICK

5) GENERAL HOSPITAL – TX 26/10/89

Nurse Mary Fletcher-Brown	MIRANDA RICHARDSON
Brigadier Smith	BILL WALLIS

6) GOODBYEEE – TX 02/11/89

Field Marshall Haig   GEOFFREY PALMER

SERIES CREDITS

Written by	RICHARD CURTIS & BEN ELTON
Title Music Composed and Arranged by	HOWARD GOODALL
Bandmaster, the Band of the 3rd Battalion the Royal Anglian Regiment (the Pompadours)	WOI TIM PARKINSON
Production Design	CHRIS HULL
Graphic Designer	GRAHAM McCALLUM
Properties Buyer	JAYNE LIBOTT
Costume Designer	ANNIE HARDINGE
Make-Up Designer	CAROLINE NOBLE
Production Assistant	VANESSA SHARPLES
Production Manager	DUNCAN COOPER
Assistant Floor Manager	J. KENNEDY
Vision Mixer	CAROL ABBOTT
Visual Effects	ROGER TURNER
Technical Coordinator	MIKE CHISLETT
Videotape Editor	CHRIS WADSWORTH
Lighting	HENRY BARBER
Sound	MARTIN DEANE
Director	RICHARD BODEN
Producer	597602 LLOYD, J.

BLACKADDER: THE KING'S BIRTHDAY

Recorded at the Lyceum Theatre, 13 January 1998; TX 14/11/98, ITV

Sir Edmund Blackadder	ROWAN ATKINSON
King Charles I	STEPHEN FRY
Written by	RICHARD CURTIS & BEN ELTON

BLACKADDER BACK AND FORTH

Filmed June–July 1999, debuted 06/12/99, SkyScape Cinema, Millennium Dome; TX 01/10/00, Sky One; Terrestrial TX 21/04/02, BBC1

All Blackadders	ROWAN ATKINSON
All Baldricks	TONY ROBINSON
All Melchetts	STEPHEN FRY
All Georges	HUGH LAURIE
All Darlings	TIM McINNERNY
All Elizabeths	MIRANDA RICHARDSON
Dinosaur	TYRANNOSAURUS REX
Nursie	PATSY BYRNE
William Shakespeare	COLIN FIRTH
Robin Hood	RIK MAYALL
Maid Marian	KATE MOSS
Friar Tuck	CRISPIN HARRIS
Napoleon	SIMON RUSSELL BEALE
Wellington	STEPHEN FRY
Scottish Hordes	HORDES OF SCOTS
Royal Reporter	JENNY BOND
Written by	RICHARD CURTIS & BEN ELTON
Make-up Designer	JAN SEWELL
Costume Designer	HAZEL PETHIG
Production Designer	ANDREW HOWE-DAVIS
Director of Photography	TONY PIERCE-ROBERTS, BSC
Music Composed by	HOWARD GOODALL
Editor	GUY BENSLEY
Executive Producers	PETER BENNETT-JONES, GEOFFREY PERKINS
Director	PAUL WEILAND
Producer	SOPHIE CLARKE-JERVOISE

Produced for the New Millennium Experience Company, in association with Sky TV, with grateful thanks to the BBC. A Tiger Aspect Production.

BLACKADDER: THE ARMY YEARS
Royal Variety Performance recorded at the Dominion Theatre on
5 December 2000; TX 17/12/00, BBC1

| Compère/Writer | BEN ELTON |
| Captain, The Lord Blackadder | ROWAN ATKINSON |

THE ROYAL GARDENER
'Party at the Palace' trailers TX May–June 2002, BBC1

| Sir Osmund Darling-Blackadder | ROWAN ATKINSON |
| Directed by | JOHN LLOYD |

Fig. 3 CONCISE GUIDE TO HISTORICAL ANOMALIES

- There is no such species as a 'black adder', and no black snakes have ever been native to the British Isles.

- The Emperor Hadrian never poisoned his mother, nor married his horse, according to existing records.

- There were no 'Jumping Jews' in England in the fifteenth century, Edward I having expelled the race, who were not legally readmitted until 1653. Remaining Judaists were compelled to keep their faith secret, and were not known for notable skill at jumping.

- There was never a holy festival known as 'Garethstide', nor 'Norristide'.

- Prince Edmund's temptation with 'ten thousand sovereigns' could not have worked, as sovereigns were not minted until Henry VII's reign, in 1489.

- The title of 'Duke of Edinburgh' was not instituted until the union with Scotland in 1707.

- The greeting 'hello' was not in use until several centuries after the instances given in the Chronicles.

- There was only one Pope at any one time during the fifteenth century, never three at once.

- There was no Earl of Doncaster, homosexual or otherwise, until the seventeenth century.

- Geoffrey Chaucer died almost a century before the events of 'Witchsmeller Pursuivant', so his appearance would have been a bad omen, whether mooing like a cow or not.

- The execution of the Earl of Essex is referred to forty years too early.

- Queen Elizabeth's Nurse suggests that Sir Thomas More was present at the monarch's birth, but official records show that he was imprisoned before September 1533. Also, he was beheaded, not burned at the stake.

- Rhinoceroses do not rut.

- Neither Sir Francis Drake nor Lord Effingham were ever under sentence of death – they were victors against the Spanish Armada, and rewarded accordingly.

- Queen Mary I was never beheaded – although, as this claim was made by Elizabeth's Nurse, her every pronouncement can safely be dismissed as insanity.

- Elephants are not orange.

- There is no record of boomerangs appearing in Britain until after the first recorded discovery of Australia by Captain Cook in the eighteenth century.

- The song 'Happy Birthday to You' was written at the turn of the twentieth century.

- If a horse was ever made Pope, the Vatican did not record it, nor allow anyone in Christendom to know about it.

- Sir Thomas Herriott actually introduced the potato to Britain from Colombia in 1586.

- Sir Walter Raleigh was not born until two years after the expedition he claims to have embarked on in 1552.

- The Cape of Good Hope had already been navigated by 1488, by Portuguese explorer Dias.

- Blackadder could not have called the police, two and a half centuries before their creation.

- Lord Percy's suggestion of inviting Cardinal Wolsey to a party is peculiar, given Wolsey's death thirty years earlier – although Percy perhaps wasn't to have known that.

- Prince Ludwig's demand for Swedish kronor comes three hundred years before the currency's invention.

- Charles I was captured two years before 1648, the beginning of Sir Edmund's Chronicle. Oliver Cromwell was also not known as 'Lord Protector' until after Charles's execution. In addition, King Charles never lived to have a fiftieth birthday.

- Pitt the Younger's insistence on war with Napoleon could not have been mentioned in his maiden speech as Prime Minister, as Napoleon did not rise to power until a decade later – the French Revolution preceded Napoleon's threat.

- William Pitt's younger brother died before he took office. Also, Pitt could not have been bullied at school, as he was tutored at home.

- The first edition of *Who's Who* was not published until the nineteenth century.

- Samuel Johnson completed his dictionary before the birth of George IV, and did not receive his doctorate until ten years after that.

- The Earl of Sandwich of bread-based-snack fame was christened John, not Gerald.

- Nelson was not made a Lord until 1798.

- Wellesley and Nelson only met on one occasion, just prior to the latter's death at Trafalgar. The former was not made Duke of Wellington until a decade later.

- Mark Twain wrote *The Prince and the Pauper* in 1881.

- George III, even in his worst bouts of porphyric insanity, never ended sentences with the word 'penguin', preferring instead the expostulation 'peacock!'

- If Captain Blackadder had been in the British Army for fifteen years by 1914, he would have received promotion to Major in 1915.

- Captain B imitates the Shipping Forecast, which was not first broadcast until six years after the end of World War I.

- There was no such position as Air Chief Marshal for the Royal Flying Corps, it being a subsequent RAF invention.

- The US Army entered WWI in April 1917, more than six months before the Russian Revolution.

- The University of Hull did not officially exist until 1954, having been founded as a college in 1927. That may, however, have been Captain B's point.

- When Dr Johnson uses the simile 'as pointless as fitting wheels to a tomato', he should of course have said 'as pointless as listing historical inconsistencies in a sitcom'.

BLACKADDER IN BETHLEHEM

A Fragment

Richard Curtis

This previously unpublished rough script for a 1988 Christmas special
was thrillingly offered up for this True History by Richard Curtis,
unbidden. His kindness knows no bounds, so nor should our gratitude.
What follows is a selection of scenes from an incomplete first draft,
and canon-wise, can only be labelled 'apocryphal'.

'BLACKADDER IN BETHLEHEM' (EXTRACT)

ROLLER & VOICE-OVER (WITH CHORAL
ACCOMPANIMENT, ANGELS, ETC.)

> 'And it came to pass, in those days when a decree went out
> from Caesar Augustus that all the world should be enrolled.
> This was the first enrolment, when Quirinius was Governor
> of Syria. And all went to be enrolled, each to his own city.
> And this did constitute an enormous business opportunity for
> Hoteliers all over the land of Judah, not least in the city of
> David, which is called Bethlehem.'

*Cut to the outside of the inn; the sign reads 'Blackadder Inn: Merry
Enrolment Day!' Caption: 24 December.*

SCENE 1. THE FOYER.
*It should be quite realistic, not a romanised reception desk. Enter
Blackadder. He has long Jewish locks – looks Arabic.*

BLACKADDER: Baldrick! (*Enter Baldrick. He looks awful, as
usual.*) Where the hell is that turkey?
BALDRICK: What turkey, master?
BLACKADDER: I told you to buy a turkey for tonight's special
supper. For Jehovah's sake this is the most
important night in the history of this hotel
– please our customers tonight and we'll get
them back every year – tonight could be the
beginning of something big, something which
will change the world.
BALDRICK: All right, I'll go out and get it . . .

SCENE 2. THE KITCHEN

Baldrick is arriving back. He takes a big turkey out of his sack, clears the table, and begins to pluck it. But as he pulls out the first feather . . .

TURKEY:	What the hell are you doing?
BALDRICK:	Who said that?
TURKEY:	Me.
BALDRICK:	O my God.
TURKEY:	What an incredible way to behave – bring me back here to your house, and then start tearing my bloody feathers out. You little bastard!
BALDRICK:	But I have to do it; you're the master's supper.
TURKEY:	(*utter outrage*) I beg your pardon?
BALDRICK:	You're the special dinner.
TURKEY:	Wait a second – you mean, not satisfied with tearing my feathers out, you're actually going to eat me as well?
BALDRICK:	That's right.
TURKEY:	But I'm a talking turkey – with me, you could buy a hundred ordinary turkeys.

Enter Blackadder slightly flappy.

BLACKADDER:	Baldrick – we need some entertainment for tonight.
BALDRICK:	We've already got it, lots of wine and our special feast. Although –
BLACKADDER:	No, come on, come on – entertainments – you know, snake tamers, lion charmers, that kind of thing. Can you think of anyone in that line?
BALDRICK:	Well, my cousin is a very good all-round family entertainer.

BLACKADDER: (*suspicious.*) Really?

BALDRICK: Well, he's not a bad magician.

BLACKADDER: Tell the truth, Baldrick. (*Hits him.*)

BALDRICK: My cousin's a crap magician, but he's got a collection of funny hats. (*Blackadder just hits him.*) My cousin's got one funny cap.

BLACKADDER: Then get him round here at once – and finish plucking that turkey.

BALDRICK: I can't.

BLACKADDER: Why not?

BALDRICK: Well, I'll let the turkey answer for itself.

BLACKADDER: I'm sorry?

BALDRICK: It's a talking turkey.

BLACKADDER: Of course it is. (*To the turkey.*) Tell me, we're undecided what vegetables to do with you. What do you think? Peas or parsnips? (*Pause.*) Sorry – didn't quite catch that. (*Pause.*) Mmm – Baldrick – do you remember what the punishment for lying and time wasting is under Roman law?

BALDRICK: Ahm . . .

BLACKADDER: It's something to do with a hand and a very sharp axe, isn't it?

BALDRICK: O yes.

BLACKADDER: Now, get that cousin, and round up any other entertainers, or we're in trouble. And get that turkey in . . . NOW!
(*Blackadder leaves.*)

BALDRICK: Why didn't you say anything while he was here?

TURKEY: I was shy.

BALDRICK: Well, I'm going to have to do it anyway.

TURKEY: You cruel bastard.

BALDRICK: But I'll go and talk to my cousin first.

TURKEY: Phew. At least it gives me time to make peace
               with God . . . O, and by the way . . . if it comes
               down to parsnips or peas, I prefer parsnips.

BALDRICK: Brilliant.

SCENE 3. FOYER.

A bunch of people are checking in. Blackadder is quite thrilled . . .

BLACKADDER: Excellent, excellent. (*He eventually has
               to write 'No' in front of 'Vacancies'.*) Brilliant.
               The place is full. Rachel – Baldrick – if anyone
               else comes – it is full. We haven't got room to
               squeeze in a mouse . . .

*He exits, as Rachel potters round the desk. There is a sound of angels
vaguely in the background – and Joseph enters, a nice man with a beard.*

JOSEPH: Good evening. Is there any room at the inn?

RACHEL: I'm afraid not.

JOSEPH: What – totally sold out?

RACHEL: Totally booked up.

JOSEPH: Fine. Fine. O god. (*He starts to cry.*)

RACHEL: What's the matter?

JOSEPH: O no, it's fine. It's just that my wife and I have
               been travelling for weeks now – and she's about
               to give birth, I mean literally it could be at any
               moment. And, well, I suppose she'll just have to
               have the baby in the street.

RACHEL: Well, maybe we could find somewhere. Go on,
               bring your wife in.

JOSEPH: O thank you very much. (*He goes to the door.*)
               Darling – there's a place!

It turns out that Blackadder is actually returning, and nose to nose with him. Blackadder is not happy.

BLACKADDER: I'm sorry?

JOSEPH: I was just telling my wife there was a room here.

BLACKADDER: Ah – and who told you that?

RACHEL: It was me.

BLACKADDER: And where is this extraordinary room going to magically spring from?

RACHEL: Well, I thought perhaps they might stay . . . (*Enter Baldrick.*) In Baldrick's room.

BLACKADDER: O well, yes, all right. How about I offer you this young man's room?

JOSEPH: That sounds excellent.

BLACKADDER: Yes. It's not that excellent – less of a room, more of a manger.

JOSEPH: As long as it's inside, it'll do us.

BLACKADDER: Ah.

JOSEPH: It's outside?

BALDRICK: Outsidish. Come on – you'll be all right.

BLACKADDER: Great, let's get on with the evening. And tell her, if she does have the kid, to keep the noise down. We don't want him crying during the entertainment. Which reminds me . . .

SCENE 4. THE MANGER.

Baldrick leads Joseph in. It is a total hole.

BALDRICK: Here we go. Had any thoughts about what you're going to call the baby?

JOSEPH: Not really. If it was a girl we thought maybe after its mother.

BALDRICK: What's her name?

JOSEPH: Mary. We're having a lot more trouble with
              the boy's name. Any ideas?

BALDRICK: Well, my name's Baldrick, but I doubt if you'd
              want that.

JOSEPH: Well, it's not bad. Baldrick. Yes, not bad . . .

Then perhaps on with the proper plot . . .

FOYER.

This might be the hotel where the returning officer is staying.

BLACKADDER: So tell me, if people don't enrol what
              happens to them?

OFFICER: They don't exist, officially.

BLACKADDER: I see.

OFFICER: So if for instance a man comes up and says,
              My house has been broken into – we say, I'm
              sorry, but it can't have been, you don't exist.

BLACKADDER: Very difficult job.

OFFICER: You're not bloody joking. This stuff with the
              names is absolute hell.

BLACKADDER: In what way?

OFFICER: Well, what's your name, for instance?

BLACKADDER: David, but I'm called Simon.

OFFICER: Exactly – EXACTLY, so what are you
              registered under?

BLACKADDER: Well, David.

OFFICER: Quite – so if I go out into the streets, and I
              ask for David, what are my chances of getting
              you?

BLACKADDER: Well, very small, you'll get Peter . . . who's
              called David. I see the problem – you'd be
              better off enrolling everyone under what
              they're called.

OFFICER: My point exactly. So you'd be called Simon. Now, I'm the tax collector, and I come to collect taxes – what do you say?

BLACKADDER: I'd say, I'd love to help, but my name's ACTUALLY David. It's a bugger.

OFFICER: It is a bugger . . .

PICTURE PERMISSIONS

Plate Section 1

Page 1 The Black Adder pilot frontispiece reproduced by kind permission of Geoff Posner

Page 2-4 The Black Adder series 1 images courtesy of John Lloyd

Page 5 Blackadder on a horse ©BBC Motion Gallery

Page 6 Brian Blessed as the King, Mr and Mrs Adder ©BBC

Page 7 Frank Finlay as the Witchsmeller Pursuivant ©BBC

Page 8 Peter Cook as King Richard III ©BBC

Plate Section 2

Page 1 Blackadder and Queenie ©BBC

Page 2 Pictures 1 & 2 ©BBC

Page 3 Young Bob and Blackadder ©BBC, Tom Baker as Captain Rum ©BBC Motion Gallery

Page 4 John Lloyd © Peter Brooker/Rex Features, Hugh Laurie © Johnny Boylan/Rex Features, Rowan Atkinson © Gemma Levine/ Getty Images, Ben Elton © Steve Pyke/Getty Images, Tony Robinson © Redferns/Getty Images

Page 5 Perrier Awards image ©Perrier/Penguin

Page 6-7 Baldrick, Blackadder and Percy ©BBC

Page 8 Baldrick and Arthur the Sailor ©BBC, Tony Robinson (Comic Relief) © Victor Watts / Rex Features

Plate Section 3

Page 1 Hugh Laurie as the Prince of Wales ©BBC

Page 2 Pitt the Younger, Blackadder, Baldrick and Vincent Hanna ©BBC Motion Gallery

Page 3 Baldrick ©BBC

Page 4 The Prince and Blackadder ©BBC, Stephen Fry as the Duke of Wellington ©BBC Motion Gallery

Page 5 Nigel Planer as Lord Smedly and Helen Atkinson Wood as
   Mrs Miggins ©BBC
Page 6 Robbie Coltrane as Dr Johnson with the Prince and McAdder
   ©BBC Motion Gallery
Page 7 The Actors and the Highway(wo)man ©BBC Motion Gallery
Page 8 Blackadder ©BBC

Plate Section 4

Page 1 Baldrick, Blackadder and Ade Edmonson as Manfred von
   Richtofen, Gabrielle Glaister as Bob and Hugh Laurie ©BBC
Page 2 Baldrick and Blackadder, and Tim McInnerney as Captain
   Darling and Stephen Fry as General Melchett ©BBC
Page 3 Rik Mayall as Flashheart ©BBC
Page 4 Miranda Richardson as Nurse Mary and Bill Wallis as
   Brigadier Smith, Tim McInnerney and George ©BBC
Page 5 George, Blackadder and Baldrick ©BBC
Page 6 *Blackadder's Christmas Carol* ©Tim Roney/Getty Images,
   The Cast of *Blackadder Back and Forth* ©Terry O'Neill/Getty Images
Page 7 The final Cunning Plan ©BBC Motion Gallery
Page 8 Over the top and closing credits ©BBC Motion Gallery

While every effort has been made to contact copyright holders, the
author and publisher would be grateful for information about any
material where they have been unable to trace the source, and would
be glad to make amendments in further editions.

INDEX